Right-Wing Critics of American Conservatism

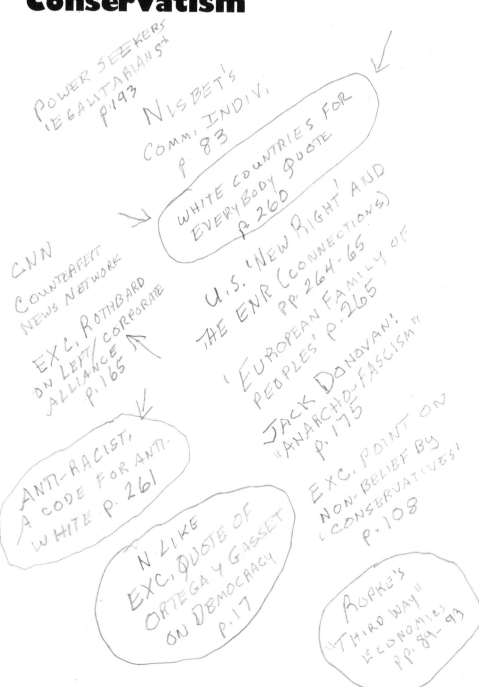

POWER SEEKERS 'EGALITARIANS' p.193

NISBET'S COMM, INDIV, p. 83

WHITE COUNTRIES FOR EVERYBODY QUOTE p. 260

CNN COUNTRAFEIT NEWS NETWORK

EXC, ROTHBARD ON LEFT/CORPORATE ALLIANCE p.165

U.S. 'NEW RIGHT' AND THE ENR (CONNECTIONS) PP. 264-65

'EUROPEAN FAMILY OF PEOPLES' P. 265

JACK DONOVAN: "ANARCHO-FASCISM" P. 175

ANTI-RACIST, A CODE FOR ANTI-WHITE P. 261

N LIKE EXC, QUOTE OF ORTEGA Y GASSET ON DEMOCRACY P.17

EXC, POINT ON NON-BELIEF BY 'CONSERVATIVES' P. 108

ROPKE'S "THIRD WAY" ECONOMICS PP. 89-93

Right-Wing Critics of American Conservatism

George Hawley

 UNIVERSITY PRESS OF KANSAS

© 2016 by the University Press of Kansas

Published by the University Press of Kansas (Lawrence, Kansas 66045), which was organized by the Kansas Board of Regents and is operated and funded by Emporia State University, Fort Hays State University, Kansas State University, Pittsburg State University, the University of Kansas, and Wichita State University

Library of Congress Cataloging-in-Publication Data

Hawley, George / Right-wing critics of American conservatism
Includes bibliographical references and index.
ISBN 978-0-7006-2193-4 (cloth)
ISBN 978-0-7006-2579-6 (pbk. : alk. paper)
ISBN 978-0-7006-2198-9 (ebook)
Conservatism—United States. | Right and left (Political science)—United States. |
Radicals—United States.
JC573.2.U6 H39 2015
DDC 320.520973—dc23
2015032191

British Library Cataloguing-in-Publication Data is available.

Printed in the United States of America

10 9 8 7 6 5 4 3

The paper used in this publication is recycled and contains 30 percent postconsumer waste. It is acid free and meets the minimum requirements of the American National Standard for Permanence of Paper for Printed Library Materials z39.48-1992.

For Wyatt

CONTENTS

ACKNOWLEDGMENTS

I am grateful to the many patient and generous people who helped make this project possible. As this book is a major deviation from my primary research agenda (my previous scholarly work was focused exclusively on public opinion, voter behavior, and demographics), I needed much assistance as I transformed a vague idea into a finished product.

I am grateful to those who read all or parts of this book and offered me valuable feedback. Charles Myers of the University Press of Kansas was an especially helpful, encouraging, and patient editor throughout this process. I also offer my thanks to the anonymous reviewers. They caught many important shortcomings in an earlier version of this book; their advice was invaluable. I hope they find that I have addressed their most important concerns.

I offer special thanks to Leonard Chan, who provided thorough critiques of a previous draft. Although he could not have known it at the time, Brickey LeQuire of Samford University also helped me substantially. By coincidence, Brickey sat next to me on a flight home from an academic conference. Over the course of our short conversation, he helped me clarify my thoughts on the nature of left and right. I am also grateful to Mike Taylor and all the great coaches at Headhunters Combatives; it turns out that MMA training is an excellent coda to a day otherwise spent in the library or in front of a computer screen.

I offer my thanks to the University of Alabama, which has generously kept me employed since 2013. I am especially grateful to Richard Fording, the chair of the Department of Political Science. Since arriving at UA, I have always felt free to follow my research interests wherever they take me, which is why I felt confident beginning this ambitious and time-consuming project. George Thompson, our publisher in residence, offered helpful advice throughout this project. I also thank the anonymous librarians who quickly processed my countless interlibrary loan requests.

I am most thankful to my wife, Kristen. For all of my books, she has served as a diligent editor and my greatest source of encouragement. A number of annoying habits plague my writing. Kristen patiently (and mercilessly) points out my weird sentence structures, repetitive word choices, misspellings, non sequiturs, and nonsensical phrases. If you find this book comprehensible, you have her to thank. I also thank my sons, Henry and Wyatt. Although my time with them eats into hours that could otherwise be spent writing and researching, they are also an indispensable source of motivation.

If this work is of any scholarly value, the credit must be shared with the preceding people. Any mistakes belong to me alone.

INTRODUCTION

The American conservative movement faces a crisis. Although the death of American conservatism has been heralded many times, the inescapable reality is that the mainstream conservative movement, and the Republican Party it endorses, will face an existential challenge in the decades ahead. An increasing percentage of the American electorate rejects many of the essential premises of the American right. The social milieu of twenty-first century America is fundamentally different than it was in the postwar years when the coherent ideology called conservatism was forged by journalists and public intellectuals like Russell Kirk, William F. Buckley, and Frank Meyer, along with politicians like Barry Goldwater and Ronald Reagan.

The United States is more racially diverse than ever before, which would not necessarily be problematic for conservatism were it not for the fact that American minorities are, on average, far more politically progressive than non-Hispanic whites. This trend shows no sign of abating. In the absence of major opinion change among African Americans, Asian Americans, and Latinos, the constituency for conservative politics will continue to shrink.

SAD

Americans are also increasingly secular. Although Christian faith is not a prerequisite for supporting conservative public policies, American conservatism has traditionally had a transparent religious quality, and devoted Christians have long been some of the most vocal supporters of American conservatism. If the trend toward secularization continues, the number of Americans who endorse an ideology that is at least implicitly religious will further decline.

CONS NEED TO GET NON OR ANTI-RELIGIOUS

World politics have changed profoundly since American conservatism as it is presently understood arrived on the political scene after World War II. It is impossible to overstate the importance of the cold war to American conservatism. The Soviet menace held the three disparate legs of the conservative stool together. Hostility to communism united Christian traditionalists, national security conservatives, and free-market capitalists—three groups that are not necessarily political allies. Since the end of the cold war, the conservative intellectual movement has been slow to adjust to the new global reality. When the Soviet Union collapsed, and the raison d'être of the American empire collapsed with it, few prominent conservatives endorsed scaling back American commitments overseas. The terrorist attacks of September 11, 2001, and the struggle against Islamic terrorism seemed to breathe new life into conservative arguments for America's role as defender of the free world. However, in the aftermath of a disastrous war in Iraq, the old national security conservatives appear increasingly anachronistic and out of touch with contemporary reality.

Prognosticators who speculate how conservatism can survive and even thrive in the twenty-first century tend to fall into two camps, depending on their own political persuasions. On one side are those making the case that conservatives must move to the political center and soften their harder edges. They do not necessarily say that the American conservative movement must abandon its fundamental premises, but it should relax its stance on issues like gay marriage and abortion and finally make a formal peace with the welfare state. In other words, they argue that conservatism should become Conservatism Lite.

On the opposing side, we have those who argue that conservatives, and Republicans in office, should double down and become even more aggressive as they pursue the same platform they have always endorsed. We see this line of thinking in the still powerful Tea Party movement. Those holding this position contend that conservatism never failed; it has never really been tried. According to this argument, by sticking to its principles and fighting for them even more forcefully, conservatism can win new converts and revive American greatness.

Such arguments demonstrate a lack of imagination on the part of contemporary political observers. Americans generally have a myopic view of the political right, assuming that the entire spectrum of right-wing thought exists between David Brooks and Rush Limbaugh. In truth, there is a strong tradition of antiprogressive thought in American history that stands completely outside the mainstream conservative movement.

This narrow view of the American right can be partially attributed to the energetic policing that occurs within the conservative movement. Almost from the beginning, the political and intellectual leaders of the conservative movement have been wary about offering seats at the conservative table and expelled those who strayed too far from established conservative dogma. This book tells the neglected history of purges within the conservative intellectual movement.

More importantly, this book will provide an overview of those intellectual movements on the right that were never fully incorporated into the American conservative movement and have been forced to live on the fringes of American intellectual life. These various intellectual movements differ both from mainstream conservatism and from each other when it comes to fundamental premises, such as the value of equality, the proper role of the state, the importance of free markets, the role of religion in politics, and attitudes toward race. This book will examine the localists who exhibit equal skepticism toward big business and big government, paleoconservatives who look to the distant past for guidance and wish to turn back the clock, radical libertarians who are not content to be junior partners in the conservative movement, and various strains of white supremacy and the radical right in America.

American conservatism has proven resilient. It would be premature to declare it on life support, but it faces unprecedented challenges. In the years ahead, organized conservatism may break down, and the conservative intellectual movement may lose its ability to determine the boundaries of acceptable right-wing thought. Furthermore, thanks to the Internet, dissident right-wing voices are now able to spread their message on a once-unthinkable scale. Whereas fringe ideologies were once reliant on pamphleteering and obscure print publications, anyone with an Internet connection is now able to spread a message across the world with relative ease. As a result of these developments, intellectual space may open up for one or more of these dissident right-wing ideologies. For this reason, a survey of marginalized right-wing intellectual movements is timely.

This book is not a comprehensive anthology of all groups and individuals who have criticized conservatism from the right—all such individuals and ideas could not be discussed within a single volume. I do wish to explain a few omissions, however. This volume does not discuss the Tea Party movement in any detail. I made this decision because I do not view the Tea Party as ideologically distinct from mainstream conservatism in America. The talking points of the prominent Tea Party leaders are expressed with great energy and force, but they are not fundamentally different from traditional Republican messages as advocated by Ronald Reagan and other major figures in the conservative pantheon. We might think of Tea Party supporters as ordinary conservative Republicans, only louder.

I also do not separately examine the major figures and institutions of the religious right, such as Focus on the Family and the Christian Coalition. In my estimation, the religious right is not distinct from the broader conservative movement. They still have a seat at the conservative table and the ears of Republican legislators. For the time being, the religious right remains an integral part of the conservative electoral coalition (in a way that radical libertarians, paleoconservatives, explicit racists, and other fringe groups are not). What is more, from my readings, most prominent members of the religious right consider themselves to be part of today's mainstream conservative movement, and they relish the influence they believe they have over the GOP. It is true that there are some elements of the religious right that have sought to create a genuine alternative to the conservative movement (Chuck Baldwin, a pastor and 2008 presidential candidate for the Constitution Party, comes to mind), but most appear content to remain in the broader conservative coalition.

I similarly do not discuss the arguments of moderate conservatives and Republicans (those politicians and pundits disparagingly called "Republicans in Name Only," or RINOs, by their critics on the right), as they similarly tend to share the same basic principles as mainstream conservatism but disagree predominantly on questions of rhetoric and the degree to which conservatives should be absolutists in pursuit of their goals. The groups and individuals I analyze in this volume disagree with American conservatism on more than just strategy and tactics. Although clearly on the right, they disagree with one or more of the basic premises of American conservatism, and these disagreements inform their critiques.

This book does not make the case for all or any of these ideologies, nor does it celebrate the potential demise of the established conservative intellectual movement. Although I find some of the arguments discussed in this book persuasive and consider others abhorrent, this book seeks to examine each of these ideologies dispassionately. In the pages that follow, I allow the varying ideologies to speak for themselves, offering little additional commentary.

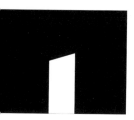

The Twilight of the Old Right and the Birth and Rise of the American Conservative Movement

Many observers take it for granted that the United States is politically a center-right nation. A quick check on the Lexis/Nexis Academic database indicates that the terms "United States" and "center-right nation" have appeared in 130 stories in the last ten years. In contrast, "United States" and "center-left nation" have appeared together only three times during this period. The notion that America is more conservative than other developed nations is rarely disputed. The United States has been described as "the Right Nation," largely defined by the political power of its exceptional, vigorous brand of conservatism.[1]

The validity of this classification depends on how one defines terms like right-wing and conservative. In the contemporary context, when we describe an American as politically conservative, we typically mean that this person favors limited government intervention in the economy, adheres to a traditional religious faith and believes these religious values should influence public policy, and generally favors a strong military presence abroad. Without knowing any context, there is no a priori reason one would infer that these three attributes are correlated with each other, or even that they are necessarily right wing. These policy preferences were not always associated with each other. The formation of the coherent conservative movement we know today can be traced no farther than the mid-twentieth century.

This chapter will provide a brief history of this political-intellectual movement, describing how disparate elements coalesced into a single unified ideology. It will also describe the political rise of the movement, explaining how this ideology ultimately became a dominant force in American politics in the latter decades of the twentieth century.

Problems of Definition

The lack of fixed, universally accepted definitions is a problem when using terms like conservative and right wing—just as it is a problem when discussing liberalism, progressivism, and the left. If we look at the origin of the terms left and right, we see that the original meaning of the words have only a superficial resemblance to their meaning today. The terms originated during the French Revolution based on the division of the National Assembly. Supporters of the king sat on the right, and supporters of the Revolution sat on the left.

Given these origins, it is unusual that more than two centuries later the United States is generally recognized as the most right-wing nation in the developed world. After all, the American Revolution was predicated on the rejection of kings and hereditary nobility. These values were enshrined in the American Constitution. Clearly the terms left and right have evolved considerably. The men who supported King Louis XVI during the French Revolution would have had no interest in wars to spread liberal democracy in the Middle East, a free-market capitalism that recognizes no social distinctions, or a populist form of evangelical Christianity. If he were transported to the present day, the famous reactionary Joseph de Maistre would surely not join the ranks of Rush Limbaugh's dittoheads.

Given their respective histories, it is perhaps inappropriate to speak of conservatism in the United States as though it is analogous to conservatism in Europe. In the United States, there never was a formal, hereditary aristocracy to conserve. Outside the South, there were few prominent, vigorous defenders of fixed social hierarchies. Although one could argue that the titans of industry who exerted tremendous political influence during the industrial revolution and beyond represented a new form of oligarchy, they were nonetheless qualitatively different from the hereditary nobles of Europe. They furthermore continued to speak in defense of meritocracy, even if levels of social mobility indicated that rags-to-riches stories were relatively uncommon.

The term liberalism is possibly even more problematic, especially in the United States. Many of today's American conservatives consider themselves the true heirs of the classical liberal tradition exemplified by such thinkers as David Hume, Adam Smith, and John Locke. To the extent that both classical liberals and contemporary conservatives defended property rights and markets, this is not an unfair claim. The fact that Edmund Burke—who is claimed by conservatives as one of the most important thinkers within their own intellectual tradition—is also often classified as a classical liberal further bolsters this argument.

Not all twentieth-century intellectuals who described themselves as classical liberals believed that they were interchangeable with conservatives. In *The Constitution of Liberty* (1960), the pro–free-market economist Friedrich Hayek—whose contemporary admirers are found predominantly on the political right—included a famous essay titled, "Why I Am Not a Conservative." Hayek did not use the adjective classical and described himself simply as a liberal—though Hayek recognized that this was becoming increasingly problematic. Hayek also sometimes used the term Old Whig to categorize himself politically. Hayek argued that before the dawn of socialism as a political force, liberalism (in the classical sense) was the primary opponent of conservatism. The birth of powerful socialist parties later forced conservatives and classical liberals to make common cause with each other. The fact that conservatives and classical liberals now have a common enemy in socialism does not indicate that the two are identical. In many respects, Hayek was just as hostile to conservatism as to socialism.[2]

In that same essay, Hayek expressed his desire to rescue the term liberalism—that is, that in common usage it would once again refer to people like himself. He expressed misgivings about the term libertarian, as he considered it a "manufactured term."[3] Libertarians never were able to successfully reclaim the term liberalism for themselves, and most Americans today view a liberal as someone who favors vigorous government intervention in the economy.

Nonetheless, the term liberalism seems to have fallen out of favor in recent years, as the term is now used almost as an insult in American discourse. With increasing frequency, those on the political left in the United States call themselves progressives. Although I do not endorse the reason for this development, I do welcome it. Given the strange evolution of the word liberalism, and the fact that the term can refer to both radical libertarians and enthusiastic supporters of the welfare state, it may be time for its retirement. Using conservatism and progressivism to signify opposite ends of the political spectrum furthermore seems more intuitive. This still does not help us precisely define the meaning of these terms, however.

Some have made the case that an individual's placement on the political spectrum can be determined by her fundamental views about the nature of reality. James Hunter argued that most people fit within one of two categories as a result of their worldviews. Those who believe that values and authority within a society stem from a transcendent source he labeled as orthodox, and those who believe values are created by human beings and are thus not necessarily permanent he described as progressive. Whereas the primary cultural fault lines were once between different, though similar, religious traditions, today the cultural conflict is between the religious and the secular:

> As we have seen, the cultural hostilities dominant over the better part of American history have taken place *within* the boundaries of a larger biblical culture—among numerous Protestant groups, and Catholics and Jews—over such issues as doctrine, ritual observance, and religious organization. . . . The older agreements have unraveled. The divisions of political consequence today are not theological and ecclesiastical in character but the result of differing worldviews. That is to say, they no longer revolve around specific doctrinal issues or styles of religious practice and organization but around our most fundamental and cherished assumptions about how to order our lives—our own lives and our lives together in society. Our most fundamental ideas about who we are as Americans are now at odds.[4]

Thomas Sowell, a conservative economist, developed a similar dichotomy. He argued that people can be classified based on whether they possess what he called a constrained or an unconstrained view of human nature. Those with a constrained view of mankind and society recognize limits on government's ability to improve human nature; they instead tend to respect tradition as a guide for a decent society. Sowell argued that many of America's founding fathers were perfect examples of men with a constrained vision.[5] We see this directly in the words of James Madison in Federalist 51: "If men were angels, no government would be necessary. If angels were to govern men, neither external nor internal controls on government would be necessary." Such an attitude holds that we must take human fallibility as a given and develop institutions that will channel our negative attributes (ambition, greed) in a less dangerous direction (electoral politics, capitalism).

According to Sowell, those with an unconstrained vision reject the idea that mankind cannot be improved—arguing that human beings can even be

THE LEFT - TOTALITARIANS

perfected—and they believe that the state can be a useful tool for shaping a new kind of person. Sowell credited Rousseau as an important founder of this kind of thinking, as he argued that poorly structured government was the primary cause of human problems. He similarly identified the political philosopher William Godwin as one of the most influential promoters of an unconstrained vision. In terms of public policy, Sowell argued that those with an unconstrained vision were more likely to trust government, under the leadership of specialists, to plan the economy and direct social interactions. Those with such a vision have little use for tradition or other ideas inherited from the past:

> Another recurring theme in the unconstrained vision is how profoundly different current issues are from those of the past, so that the historically evolved beliefs—the "conventional wisdom," in Galbraith's phrase—can no longer apply. Nor is this a new and recent conclusion. In the eighteenth century, Godwin declared that we cannot make today's decisions on the basis of a "timid reverence for the decisions of our ancestors." Such terms as "outmoded" and "irrelevant" are common dismissals of what, in the opposing vision, is called the wisdom of the ages.[6]

Sowell recognized limitations of his classification scheme. He noted, for example, that it did not perfectly track the usual left–right dichotomy. Marxism, for example, while clearly a left-wing framework, cannot be perfectly classified as an unconstrained vision. Although Marx envisioned a future utopia, he also believed mankind is constrained by inevitable social forces that place limitations on what can be accomplished during a particular epoch.[7]

Others have made the case that left and right refer to where one stands on the question of individualism and collectivism, or liberty and authoritarianism. This is more commonly heard from voices on the right, and it is a clever rhetorical move. Such a dichotomy allows all of the most loathed dictators of the twentieth century to fall into the left-wing category; if we embrace this definition, Hitler, Stalin, Pol Pot, and Mussolini were all leftists, and all politicians and ideologues on the left have important similarities with despised regimes. This argument was made most enthusiastically by the conservative author and columnist Jonah Goldberg, who suggested a strong ideological congruence between fascism and contemporary progressives like Hillary Rodham Clinton.[8]

Other scholars and journalists have attempted to precisely define the right. *The American Conservative* is a magazine that, as the title suggests, is on the right, but it is also generally skeptical of the Republican Party and the mainstream conservative movement. In 2006, this magazine printed a symposium on the definitions of conservatism and liberalism in which many notable scholars and journalists weighed in on two questions: "1. Are the designations 'liberal' and 'conservative' still useful? Why or why not?" and "2. Does a binary Left/Right political spectrum describe the full range of ideological options? Is it still applicable?"[9] The overwhelming majority of respondents expressed skepticism about the utility of this dichotomous distinction for people who wish to think deeply about politics, and they argued that now the terms are only useful for political partisans. Author and columnist Nicholas von Hoffman argued that "'liberal' and 'conservative' may be meaningless to anyone given to precise definition, but they remain useful for fisticuffs, serving as verbal mud pies in political disputes." Other contributors, such as political scientist Andrew Bacevich and columnist and former presidential candidate Patrick Buchanan, argued that conservatism is a worthwhile term, but they also argued that the Republican Party cannot be accurately described as conservative.

Many prominent conservatives have attempted to precisely define their political philosophy. These definitions are not always compatible. Russell Kirk, who is credited as one of the founders of contemporary conservatism, listed ten principles that are the hallmark of any conservatism. These included the belief in mankind's imperfectability, opposition to involuntary collectivism, and the principle of prudence.[10] Some of these attributes are unfortunately vague and perhaps not very helpful; if liberals are always the opposite of conservatives, does that mean that liberals always oppose prudence? Are all people on the left hopeless utopian dreamers?

According to Robert Nisbet, "the sole object of the conservative tradition . . . is the protection of the social order from the enveloping bureaucracy of the nation state."[11] This seems like a reasonable description, but it implies that conservatives view the government as the only possible threat to the social order; if this definition of conservatism is correct, then there is no substantive difference between conservatives and libertarians. Richard Weaver, another of the most influential conservatives in the mid-twentieth century, provided one of the more abstruse definitions. According to William F. Buckley, Weaver described conservatism as "a paradigm of essences toward which the phenomenology of the world is in continuing approximation,"[12] though Weaver himself provided less ambiguous definitions in his own writings.[13] Willmoore Kendall and George W. Carey noted that whether one acts as a conservative or a progressive is dependent upon the larger context:

> The progressive in a given society, organization, or activity . . . may achieve complete triumph and, as appears in Russia in the years following 1917, may impose an entirely new set of institutions, practices, beliefs, standards of judgment, etc. Then, the new system having been consolidated, the progressives may themselves begin to play a conservative role, resisting proposals looking to change and innovation that come simultaneously from new progressives and from the former conservatives. We thus arrive at the theoretical possibility of a conservative political movement dedicated to, for example, the preservation of communism.[14]

The only point that appears (more or less) agreed upon is that left and right represent opposing ends of the political spectrum, and that today in America, conservatism is associated with the right and contemporary liberalism (or progressivism) is associated with the left. Even if we make peace with the notion that left and right are fluid terms, however, we still require some characterizations of the words. For the purposes of this book, Paul Gottfried, a former professor at Elizabethtown College and prominent paleoconservative, provided one of the most useful definitions of the left and the right. In the symposium in *The American Conservative* mentioned above, Gottfried made the following assertion: "Defining the Right may be easier than defining the Left. The Right resists the Left with determination, however the Left may define itself at a given point in time." In a different short article, Gottfried provided a more concrete definition of the left: "In the case of the Left, there are many values that permeate its discourse, depending on the circumstances, scientific truth, secularism, freedom, etc. Leftists may in fact value all these ideals but do so in relation to their utility in advancing the Left's highest good, which is universal equality."[15] Throughout this book, the political left will be defined as containing all ideological movements that consider equality the highest political value.[16] THE LOWEST (DL)

One may be skeptical of my decision to use a thinker on the right to define what it means to be left wing. However, this definition is congruent with the ideals of the twentieth century's most influential liberal political philosopher, John Rawls. Rawls equated justice with equality; he argued that inequality can only be justified if it benefits the least advantaged. This definition is also congruent with the political taxonomy developed by Italian scholar and liberal socialist Norberto Bobbio. Bobbio argued that although the precise meanings of left and right are fluid and determined by context, the left–right distinction is legitimate over time and has real value. He argued that attitudes toward equality were the defining characteristics of the left and right: "There is an element which typifies the doctrines and movements which are called and universally recognized as left-wing, and that is the element of egalitarianism, by which we mean a tendency to praise that which makes people more equal rather than that which makes people less equal."[17]

Bobbio's argument that equality has been the predominant goal of all major left-wing ideological movements is correct. Different left-wing movements certainly disagree when it comes to methods, as well as the speed with which societies should move toward their ultimate goals, but they are in agreement that the objective should be a world with fewer economic and legal disparities, be they disparities between classes, races, nations, or entire regions of the world.

The left's opponents disagree with each other on more than just methods. They disagree with each other on the ends. The only unifying element of all nonleftist ideologies is the belief that some other value takes precedence over equality. Thus I do not entirely agree with Bobbio's classification scheme. His description of the ideological divide indicates that the right actually values inequality as a normative ideal. For some right-wing ideologues, this is certainly true, but it is not true of all groups and individuals on the right.

For this reason, contra Gottfried, I argue that the right is actually more difficult to define than the left—though, like pornography, most people can recognize the right when they see it. Although it is fair to say that throughout the world the left advocates universal equality, right-wing thought is more heterogeneous. In this volume, the right will be defined as encompassing all of those ideologies that, while not necessarily rejecting equality as a social good, do not rank it at the top of the hierarchy of values. The right furthermore fights the left in all cases where the push for equality threatens some other value held in higher esteem.

This expansive definition allows for a wide range of intellectual and political movements to fall into the category of right wing. A person may rank any number of social values above equality: individual liberty, job creation, traditional religion and morality, national security, strong communities, social harmony, honor and martial glory, or racial supremacy and purity. When relying on this definition, one is able to accurately describe such disparate writers as Wendell Berry, Murray Rothbard, Alain de Benoist, and Patrick Buchanan as thinkers and activists on the right.

I should note that many people who adhere to a nonleft political philosophy (as I have defined it) do not necessarily think of themselves as right wing or conservative. Further, although I believe all of the thinkers profiled in this volume can be accurately described as being on the right, this does not mean they have anything else in common. Although some of the writers discussed in the pages ahead are openly racist or reject fundamental democratic values, most do not, and I am not implying any kind of guilt by association.

Although I embrace a broad definition of right wing, commentators who speak of mainstream American conservatives typically have something very specific in mind. From the major figures of the conservative movement, we consistently hear the same values advanced: limited government, strong traditional families, and strong national defense. They pay homage to equality as a political value as well, and they often argue that their preferred policies will lead to more equal outcomes in the long run, but equality is not the highest-ranking value to American conservatives.

It must be explained, however, how these three principles came to define the American right. This intellectual and political development is itself an interesting story. For the best treatment of this subject, I recommend George H. Nash's text, *The Conservative Intellectual Movement in America Since 1945* (1976).[18] Although Nash is clearly sympathetic to the subject he studies, this does not diminish its scholarly value. For those unfamiliar with this narrative, a brief summary will be helpful. We will begin with the state of the American right in the years preceding World War II.

The Old Right and the "Superfluous Men"

Although the contemporary meaning of conservatism was not well established until the 1950s at the earliest, there was clearly a left–right divide in American politics before that point. However, the most prominent American critics of the American left in the early twentieth century had scant resemblance to American conservatives today. Furthermore, while in the United States today we tend to think certain policy preferences are naturally correlated, this was not always the case.

Many preeminent conservative leaders argue that they possess a rich intellectual heritage, and they insist with some regularity that ideas have consequences. The Leadership Institute, headed by Morton Blackwell, trains thousands of conservative activists and is well known within the conservative movement. This organization publishes a list of twenty-six books, many of them long and difficult texts, that "every conservative should read (and re-read)."[19] Although one may be skeptical that your average Republican political operative is familiar with all or even most of these works, the conservative movement in America clearly prides itself on the degree to which it takes ideas seriously.

Although it is now largely taken for granted that conservative intellectuals have a prominent place in American public life, this was not always so. As Lionel Trilling famously argued in 1950,

> In the United States at this time liberalism is not only the dominant but even the sole intellectual tradition. For it is the plain fact that nowadays there are no conservative or reactionary ideas in general circulation. This does not mean, of course, that there is no impulse to conservatism or to reaction. Such impulses are certainly very strong, perhaps even stronger than most of us know. But the conservative impulse and the reactionary impulse do not, with some isolated and some ecclesiastical exceptions, express themselves in ideas but only in action or in irritable mental gestures which seek to resemble ideas.[20]

Since that time, American conservatives have labored to defy this description.

Trilling and other writers of that period were not off base when attacking American conservatives for their lack of a coherent intellectual framework. In his anthology of conservative thought in America between 1900 and 1945, Robert Crunden described the disorganized collection of conservative thinkers of this period as "superfluous men"—a phrase he took directly from the title of Albert Jay Nock's memoirs.[21] These were writers who were largely ignored in mainstream public debate, and most of American society had no interest in what they had to say. The libertarian economist Murray Rothbard dubbed this loose coalition of intellectuals the old right. Throughout the first half of the twentieth century, there were no well-financed institutions or publications advocating an ideology called conservatism, and there was no collection of political principles universally recognized as conservative.

Before moving forward, I should note that the old right should be disaggregated from the anti-Semitic, fascistic right that also had a number of adherents in the United States during the interwar years. Radical anti-Semites like Charles Coughlin and William Pelley can be distinguished from the elitist, right-wing journalists and intellectuals who are generally labeled as old right.[22] This is not to say that the figures associated with the old right, such as H. L. Mencken, did not exhibit anti-Semitism. However, for lack of a better term, the figures I discuss below seemed to exhibit a rather casual anti-Semitism or said very little about Jews at all. That is, their anti-Semitism was not integral to their political philosophy. I do not discuss the prewar, pro-Nazi right in America in any detail in this chapter because it did not appear to have much influence on the later conservative movement.

Returning to our main subject, there is an interesting aspect of the conservative intellectual movement in America: very few of the intellectual antecedents of today's conservatives could be properly described as conservative as we now define the term. Many of the influential thinkers on the right who influenced the nascent conservative movement in America would today be properly classified as libertarians. On the subject of economics, many midcentury opponents of economic collectivism and redistribution took inspiration from Austrian School economics, which emerged in the nineteenth century with Carl Menger. Later economists from the Austrian tradition, such as Hayek and Ludwig von Mises, provided some of the most influential critiques of the welfare state and Keynesian economics, and many of their ideas were eventually appropriated by conservatives. As noted previously, Hayek did not consider himself a conservative, nor did Mises. The ideas of Hayek, Mises, and their disciples will be examined in greater detail in chapters 5 and 6, which discuss libertarianism in America.

Albert Jay Nock was another writer on the right in the years before World War II who eventually exerted great influence on the conservative movement; he was a friend of the Buckley family and influenced a young William F. Buckley Jr. Nock (who died in 1945) might be more accurately described as a libertarian, or even an anarchist, than a conservative—in fact, he was amused when someone described him as conservative.[23] One of his most influential books was titled *Our Enemy, the State* (1950).[24] As the title of his book suggests, Nock was a fervent antistatist and individualist. Nonetheless, his work was widely admired by influential conservatives such as Buckley, Russell Kirk, and Robert Nisbet.[25] In contrast to the populist conservative movement that exists today, however, Nock was an open elitist who disdained the masses. In his famous essay, "Isaiah's Job," Nock argued that a wise prophet who preaches to the public will enjoy little success; the overwhelming majority of people will not even listen to him.[26] Instead, the prophet's focus should be on a tiny, disorganized "Remnant" who will hear and understand the message. These are the only people a prophet can hope to influence, and a prophet can trust that the Remnant will always find him:

You do not know and will never know who the Remnant are, or where
they are, or how many of them there are, or what they are doing or will
do. Two things you know, and no more: first, that they exist; second,
that they will find you. Except for these two certainties, working for
the Remnant means working in impenetrable darkness; and this, I
should say, is just the condition calculated most effectively to pique the
interest of any prophet who is properly gifted with the imagination,
insight, and intellectual curiosity necessary to a successful pursuit of
this trade.[27]

Although Nock was certainly an original and interesting thinker, it seems
strange that he exerted such an influence on conservatives interested in
building a mass-based political movement that would challenge the dominant liberalism. Other writers on the right from this period were similarly
distrustful of the masses, which translated into a distrust of mass democracy.
H. L. Mencken, one of the most blistering critics of Franklin Roosevelt and
the New Deal, once famously remarked, "As democracy is perfected, the
office of president represents, more and more closely, the inner soul of the
people. On some great and glorious day the plain folks of the land will reach
their heart's desire at last and the White House will be adorned by a down-
right moron."[28] At another point, Mencken remarked, "All government, in
its essence, is a conspiracy against the superior man: its one permanent object is to oppress him and cripple him."[29]

The renowned architect Ralph Adams Cram perhaps took this elitism
even further. Cram rejected all doctrines of progress, particularly the idea
that things that occurred more recently in time were necessarily better than
events and institutions of the more distant past. He also considered mankind's unbroken history of monstrous behavior and attempted to explain
"why we do not behave like human beings."[30] His answer is that most people
cannot even be properly defined as human beings, and this has always been
the case. On occasion, great men may emerge, but the masses beneath maintain the barbaric characteristics of Neolithic man. Cram was clear that his
vision of humanity, if correct, implied that democracy, popular sovereignty,
and the Protestant religion would leave us "lapped in confusion and numb
with disappointment and chagrin."[31]

The disdain for the masses and crowd culture—and a corresponding distrust of democracy—was a common theme of American thinkers on the
right during this period. A simplistic examination of the left and right might
suggest that right-wing thinking necessarily leads to authoritarianism and

even totalitarianism. However, in many ways, right-wing intellectuals in the interwar years based their elitism and hostility toward the masses on their revulsion toward totalitarianism; they thought that totalitarianism was the logical conclusion of populism and the celebration of the common man. Spanish author Ortega y Gasset suggested that totalitarianism might be more properly labeled what he called hyperdemocracy in *The Revolt of the Masses* in 1929:

> The mass crushes beneath it everything that is different, everything that is excellent, individual, qualified and select. Anybody who is not like everybody, who does not think like everybody, runs the risk of being eliminated. And it is clear, of course, that this "everybody" is not "everybody." "Everybody" was normally the complex unity of the mass and the divergent, specialized minorities. Nowadays, "everybody" is the mass alone. Here we have the formidable fact of our times, described without any concealment of the brutality of its features.[32]

Richard Weaver, whose ideas will be discussed in detail in the pages ahead, blamed the horrors of twentieth-century warfare on the increasing democratization of society. Indeed, the egalitarian impulse of the modern world led to a weakening of chivalric distinctions between soldiers and civilians: "The terrible brutalities of democratic war have demonstrated how little the mass mind is capable of seeing the virtue of selection and restraint. The refusal to see distinction between babe and adult, between the sexes, between combatant and noncombatant—distinctions which lay at the core of chivalry— the determination to weld all into a formless unit of mass and weight—this is the destruction of society through brutality."[33] According to Weaver, it was the rejection of hierarchy and distinction that led to the birth of total war.

Many of the writers who influenced the later conservative movement were also secular, sometimes aggressively so. Mencken was a famous religious skeptic; he is perhaps best known for his scathing reports of the Scopes "monkey" trial, which considered the teaching of the theory of evolution in Tennessee schools. Mises was ethnically Jewish but not personally religious, as was the libertarian Frank Chodorov. Nock was once an Episcopal priest, but he lost his faith before beginning his career as a journalist. George Santayana, though an admirer of religion who recognized its value, had no religious faith. The same could be said of Irving Babbitt.

This is not to say that right-wing cultural critics in the early twentieth century were uniformly atheist or agnostic. There were many deeply religious thinkers on the right during this period, such as T. S. Eliot. I only note the many secular right-wing intellectuals who wrote during this period in order to emphasize that within relatively recent memory, the correlation between religious conviction and placement on the political spectrum was weaker than it is today.

Hostility to militarism was another hallmark of many prominent thinkers on the right before the creation of contemporary American conservatism. This may seem particularly odd given the degree to which a strong national defense has been one of the most consistent elements of the American conservative movement for many decades. It is less frequently remembered that Roosevelt's right-wing opponents in the 1930s and 1940s were condemned for their isolationism. Nock, for example, damned attempts to generate hysteria about foreign threats to the United States: "No alien State policy will ever disturb us unless our Government puts us in the way of it."[34] The journalist John T. Flynn was an early critic of what would later be dubbed the military-industrial complex: "The great and glamorous industry is here—the industry of militarism. And when the war is ended the country is going to be asked if it seriously wishes to demobilize an industry that can employ so many men, create so much national income when the nation is faced with the probability of vast unemployment in industry."[35]

Other figures that would be later associated with the nascent conservative movement in the postwar years expressed similar skepticism of American military intervention abroad. Robert Nisbet was unhesitant in his condemnation of war, even after the mainstream conservative movement had taken a decisively militant turn:

> War and the military are, without question, among the very worst of the earth's afflictions, responsible for the majority of the torments, oppressions, tyrannies, and suffocations of thought the West has for long been exposed to. In military or war society anything resembling true freedom of thought, true individual initiative in the intellectual and cultural and economic areas, is made impossible. . . . Nothing has proved more destructive of kinship, religion, and local patriotisms than has war and the accompanying military mind.[36]

Russell Kirk, who was conscripted during World War II, mocked the notion that military life improved the character of young men,[37] and he further expressed his concern about the tendency of many prominent Americans to dehumanize Germans during and after the war.[38]

From this milieu of thinkers that often had little resemblance to contemporary American conservatives, how did the American right as we now know it come to be? This new ideology, which eventually came to dominate American politics for decades, was largely the result of the cooperative efforts of a small number of journalists and academics.

The Origins of American Conservatism

A complete discussion of every text that helped shape postwar American conservatism is beyond the scope of this work; many important figures and texts are neglected here in the interest of space. However, a relatively small number of authors, and a small number of their books, played a crucial role in forging a conservative political philosophy that we would recognize today. In the pages ahead I focus on those authors, books, and periodicals that had the most enduring influence on American conservatism. It was from this nucleus that the conservative movement that we know today was born.

This section is focused on American conservatism and thus will emphasize journalists and intellectuals actually born in the United States and living there during conservatism's formative years. This is not to say that the American conservative movement was not influenced by thinkers overseas. American conservatives also took inspiration from writers such as C. S. Lewis, T. S. Eliot, and Michael Oakeshott, but their thought will not be expounded upon in the pages ahead.

One curiously celebrated text, which is still considered a classic among conservatives, was Richard Weaver's *Ideas Have Consequences* (1948). No one familiar with Weaver's biography can question his tremendous impact on American conservatism. However, Weaver had a unique intellectual journey, and *Ideas Have Consequences*, his most renowned work, is far more radical and original than anything that can be found in the pages of the *Weekly Standard* or heard on Fox News. Whereas other conservatives championed a Burkean prudence or declared their affinity for classical liberalism, *Ideas Have Consequences* was a thundering assault on modernity itself.

There is a reactionary tendency among many on the right to look back fondly at a particular era and imply that we should turn back the clock to that period. Libertarians frequently praise the early years of the American republic, when limited government was taken for granted. Pat Buchanan clearly holds the 1950s in high esteem. Given the accolades that many of today's conservatives bestow on Ronald Reagan, they clearly view the 1980s as a golden age. Weaver looked much farther back for an example of a well-structured social order. According to Weaver, the West got off track in the fourteenth century, when William of Occam's nominalist philosophy triumphed over the Scholasticism of Thomas Aquinas, and it has followed a downward trajectory since that point.[39] To Weaver, the important question was whether universals have a truth independent of humans. He argued that the West had answered that question incorrectly, which explained civilization's slow-motion dissolution.

Weaver admired the social order of the Middle Ages. He was also a passionate defender of the American South, and his early work can be classified as part of the Southern Agrarian movement (which will be discussed in greater detail in chapter 3). Weaver argued that while the feudal ideas of man and society had been in retreat in the West for centuries, many of its elements were successfully transplanted to the American South, where they continued to thrive long after they had died out in Europe. Anachronistic ideals like chivalry persisted in this small corner of the world and even survived the destruction that came with the Civil War and Reconstruction. According to Weaver, the old South was "the last non-materialist civilization in the Western world."[40] Weaver further praised the South for "regarding science as a false messiah."[41]

In *Ideas Have Consequences*, Weaver lamented the decline of distinction and hierarchy, attacked equality as a "disorganizing concept,"[42] and expressed skepticism toward democracy. He further praised the US Constitution precisely because of its undemocratic nature.[43] More problematic for conservatives who would claim Weaver as their prophet were his assaults on modern capitalism, industrialism, and the bourgeoisie. The only chapter in *Ideas Have Consequences* that is congruent with contemporary conservative talking points was focused on private property, which Weaver dubbed "the last metaphysical right."[44] Weaver was a ferocious defender of tradition; he was indisputably a thinker on the right, but it is difficult to see how *Ideas Have Consequences* was a foundational text for today's conservatives. In his later years, however, Weaver embraced positions more congruent with the mainstream conservative movement.

Russell Kirk, whose best-known work is titled *The Conservative Mind* (1953), was perhaps the most important conservative thinker in the postwar era. In contrast to Trilling and others who dismissed the intellectual pedigree of conservatism, Kirk argued that contemporary conservatives possessed a rich intellectual history, and they were following the tradition of many powerful thinkers. He argued that conservatism, as he defined it, first appeared in 1790, when Edmund Burke published *Reflections on the Revolu-*

tion in France.[45] Kirk argued that Burke articulated a "politics of prescription" that continues to inspire conservatives. Burke rejected the notion that society should be ordered on principles derived from abstract thinking and instead vigorously defended habit and custom as representing the accumulated wisdom of mankind. At the same time, Burke understood the inevitability of change. He did, however, argue that change must proceed incrementally. According to Kirk, "Conservatism is never more admirable than when it accepts changes that it disapproves, with good grace, for the sake of a general conciliation; and the impetuous Burke, of all men, did most to establish this principle."[46]

Although many conservatives take it for granted that Burke represents the best possible guide for the right, not all of Kirk's contemporaries agreed. Not surprisingly, given the uncompromising stance taken in *Ideas Have Consequences*, Richard Weaver rejected Burke as a model in his book *The Ethics of Rhetoric* (1953). In this book, which is less frequently cited by conservatives today, Weaver assailed Burkean rhetoric as the "argument from circumstance," and as such it could provide no defense of principles:

> This argument merely reads the circumstances—the "facts standing around"—and accepts them as coercive, or allows them to dictate the decision. If one should say, "This city must be surrendered because the besiegers are so numerous," one would be arguing . . . from present circumstances. The expression "In view of the situation, what else are you going to do?" constitutes a sort of proposition-form for this type of argument. Such argument savors of urgency rather than perspicacity; and it seems to be preferred by those who are easily impressed by existing tangibles.[47]

In spite of Weaver's misgivings, the idea that American conservatives can trace their intellectual genealogy to Edmund Burke was apparently compelling and is now widely accepted by writers on the right and left. In *The Conservative Mind*, Kirk argued that there was an intellectual continuity from Burke to the present day, and he included within the Burkean ranks men such as John Adams, John Randolph of Roanoke, Alexis de Tocqueville, George Santayana, and T. S. Eliot.

Kirk was a fierce opponent of ideology as he defined it. According to Kirk, "The word ideology means political fanaticism, a body of beliefs alleged to point the way to a perfect society."[48] This was precisely what conservatism was supposed to guard against. According to Kirk, this did not imply that conservatives were unprincipled but rather that they were suspicious of anyone who claimed that a particular policy platform would lead to utopia.

Kirk's work was primarily important for providing the American right with a genuine intellectual lineage—though many on the right, beyond Weaver, disagreed with Kirk as to whom conservatives should turn for inspiration. Kirk provided conservatives with a defense against the charge that they were mere reactionaries, threatened by change and the loss of social status that change entailed. Kirk's "politics of prudence," however, was insufficient to form the basis of a conservative movement dedicated to the principles of limited government, traditional values, and strong national defense. When discussing the postwar American right, it is impossible to downplay the importance of the cold war and the perceived Soviet menace.

Although most figures on the American right before World War II expressed skepticism of foreign intervention and an overseas empire, later conservatives viewed communism and the Soviet Union as an existential threat, and thus isolationism was no longer a viable option. Communism's militant atheism, opposition to capitalism and private property, and stated goal of world domination caused many Americans on the right to view foreign affairs as the single most important issue in the United States. The creation of the Warsaw Pact in Eastern Europe, the rise of a communist regime in China, and the Soviet Union's successful testing of nuclear weapons only increased the right's panic over communism. Feelings toward the cold war eventually became a shibboleth for conservatives, and in many ways it was their primary means of delineating political friend from foe.

Murray Rothbard, who despised the right's militaristic turn, argued that the cold war obliterated the right-wing tradition of libertarianism in America:

> For the blight that destroyed the libertarianism of the Right-wing
> and effected its transformation was nothing less than hysterical
> anticommunism. It began with this kind of reasoning: there are two
> "threats" to liberty: the "internal" threat of domestic socialism, and
> the "external" threat of Soviet Russia. The external threat is the most
> important. *Therefore,* all energies must now be directed to battling and
> destroying that "threat." In the course of this shift of focus from statism
> to communism as the "enemy," the Right-wing somehow failed to
> see that the real "external" threat was not Soviet Russia, but a warlike
> foreign policy of global intervention, and especially the nuclear weapons

of mass destruction used to back up such a policy. And they failed to see that the main architect in organizing a foreign policy of global nuclear intervention was the United States. In short, they failed to see that both the "external" and "internal" threats of statism to liberty were essentially domestic.[49]

Many right-wing authors during this period were interested almost solely in foreign relations and the best means of combating the Soviet menace. Many of these writers were former communists. Whitaker Chambers, for example, had once served as a Soviet spy; he rose to prominence among conservatives when he named other Soviet agents in the United States, many serving in high-ranking positions in the State Department, most notably Alger Hiss, who had played an important role in the formation of the United Nations. Chambers's story of how he became a communist, why he abandoned communism and embraced Christianity, and the events of the Alger Hiss perjury trial were recounted in his book, *Witness* (1952), which is still considered a classic among conservatives despite its tremendous length.[50] Max Eastman was another former communist who later became a fervent anticommunist and ally of the conservative movement—though he eventu- *
ally broke with conservatism over the issue of religion. Frank Meyer, whose crucial influence on conservatism I will discuss shortly, was also a communist for much of his early life.

James Burnham was another leftist radical who turned against communism and joined the conservatives' ranks. His work focused primarily on foreign policy. Though most scholars likely know Burnham best for his classic work, *The Managerial Revolution* (1941),[51] he is best remembered by conservatives for his later book, *Suicide of the West* (1964), in which he argued that "Liberalism is the ideology of western suicide. When once this initial and final sentence is understood, everything about liberalism—the beliefs, emotions and values associated with it, the nature of its enchantment, its practical record, its future—falls into place."[52]

THE WEST IS DYING

George Nash noted the following about the relationship between the cold war and conservatism: "The effects of Communism and the cold war on conservatism may be divided into two categories: responses to threats from abroad, and responses to threats from within."[53] Conservatives increasingly made the case that the liberal response to the Soviet menace abroad was ineffectual. They became overtly hostile to the Democratic Party's handling of foreign affairs, which they contended allowed the creation of the Iron Curtain and did nothing to stop the fall of China. Thinkers like Burnham contended that mere containment was not enough; the communists needed to be pushed out of Eastern Europe. At home, the conservatives were increasingly concerned with communist infiltrators, a fear seemingly justified by Whittaker Chambers's revelations before the House Un-American Activities Committee. Conservatives became suspicious that the left in America was not just mistaken about how to conduct the cold war but was actively assisting America's enemies. Anticommunist fervor reached a peak in 1950 when Senator Joseph McCarthy, a Republican from Wisconsin, claimed that a large number of Soviet spies and sympathizers were working in the US government.

Among the prominent anticommunists on the right in the postwar years, there was a clear sense of foreboding, even a belief that an ultimate communist victory was probable or even inevitable. Whitaker Chambers remarked the following after breaking with communism: "I wanted my wife to realize one long-term penalty, for herself and for the children, of the step I was taking. I said, 'You know, we are leaving the winning world for the losing world.' I meant that, in the revolutionary conflict of the 20th century, I knowingly chose the side of probable defeat."[54] William F. Buckley described *Witness* as a book of "Spenglerian gloom."[55] Burnham argued in 1947 that if current policies continued, "the defeat and annihilation of the United States are probable."[56]

Fear of the Soviet Union was not sufficient for the creation of a coherent conservative movement, but it did help unite the various factions discussed to this point. Free-market libertarians, cultural traditionalists, and foreign policy hawks all despised communism, and this mutual loathing helped unite factions that otherwise had little in common. To form a coherent political platform, however, some means was necessary to unite these often conflicting elements of right-wing thought. More than anyone else, William F. Buckley was responsible for consolidating a single conservative movement from this loose constellation of right-wing intellectuals and journalists.

In 1951, while still in his midtwenties, Buckley published his controversial book, *God and Man at Yale*.[57] In this polemical work, Buckley discussed his experiences as an undergraduate student. He argued that the faculty at his alma mater aggressively pushed their secular and liberal agenda on students. (This is still a common refrain among conservatives.) Although the book was attacked by liberal reviewers across the nation,[58] it served to launch Buckley into the public spotlight. In 1955, Buckley published the first issue of *National Review*, which provided a national platform for a diverse group of right-wing authors. The original contributors included Whitaker Chambers, James Burnham, Frank Meyer, and Russell Kirk. In the first issue of *National Review*, Buckley provided the magazine's mission statement:

> Let's face it: Unlike Vienna, it seems altogether possible that did NATIONAL REVIEW not exist, no one would have invented it. The launching of a conservative weekly journal of opinion in a country widely assumed to be a bastion of conservatism at first glance looks like a work of supererogation, rather like publishing a royalist weekly within the walls of Buckingham Palace. It is not that, of course; if NATIONAL REVIEW is superfluous, it is so for very different reasons: It stands athwart history, yelling Stop, at a time when no one is inclined to do so, or to have much patience with those who so urge it.[59]

Before the creation of *National Review*, there were of course other periodicals that published right-wing authors, such as *American Mercury, Freeman*, and *Human Events*. However, *National Review* quickly overshadowed all of these other publications and became the premier journal of conservative opinion.

Bringing these disparate authors together in a single periodical did not resolve their many differences, and some conservative intellectuals, such as T. S. Eliot and the Southern Agrarian Allen Tate, refused to contribute.[60] A number of contributors were vocal critics of Russell Kirk, and the disputes between libertarians and traditional conservatives were never fully resolved. A number of works attempted to resolve the apparent contradictions on the American right in order to create some kind of meaningful consensus.

One important work in this tradition was Frank Meyer's *In Defense of Freedom: A Conservative Credo* (1962).[61] Meyer argued that in the United States, traditionalists and libertarians were natural allies. He noted that while traditionalists were right to emphasize virtue, true virtue is impossible in the absence of liberty: "Only if there exists a real choice between right and wrong, truth and error, a choice which can be made irrespective of the direction in which history and impersonal Fate move, do men possess true freedom."[62] In other words, the cause of individual virtue and cultural conservatism is best served by a limited government.

While Meyer labored to reconcile disparate elements of right-wing thinking, and thereby consolidate traditionalists and libertarians into a single intellectual tradition, he maintained his critical stance toward many other notable conservatives, particularly Russell Kirk. Like Weaver, Meyer rejected Kirk's arguments regarding prudence and calmly accepting organic change.

Meyer demanded an intransigent defense of individualism that was not dependent on the contemporary zeitgeist. It was largely due to his disagreements with Meyer that Kirk asked for his own name to be removed from the masthead of *National Review*, though he remained a contributor.[63]

Although the nascent conservative intellectual movement in the postwar years sought to unite many disparate strands of thought under one banner, many writers we now consider crucial to the development of the movement continued to eschew the term conservatism. As previously mentioned, Hayek completely rejected the term. Upon hearing himself described as a conservative in the pages of *National Review*, Frank Chodorov responded, "Anyone who calls me a conservative gets a punch in the nose."[64] The rejection of the term conservative was not limited to the radical libertarians sometimes included in this movement. Chambers similarly rejected the label, preferring to call himself a "man of the right."[65]

Others settled into the new conservative movement with a strong libertarian element more easily than one might have anticipated. Richard Weaver, given his traditionalism, may seem an odd ally of libertarians. However, in 1960 he made the following argument: "I maintain that the conservative in his proper character and role is a defender of liberty. He is such because he takes his stand on the real order of things and because he has a very modest estimation of man's ability to change that order through the coercive power of the state."[66]

The principles of contemporary conservatism were further solidified in 1960 at the inaugural meeting of Young Americans for Freedom (YAF). At this meeting, held at William F. Buckley's estate in Sharon, Connecticut, YAF adopted the Sharon Statement, which affirmed twelve "eternal truths." These principles included a libertarian defense of economic liberty and the Constitution's division of powers. However, three of these twelve principles were explicitly in favor of a strong national defense and an aggressive stance toward communism: "We will be free only so long as the national sovereignty of the United States is secure; that history shows periods of freedom are rare, and can exist only when free citizens concertedly defend their rights against all enemies"; "The forces of international Communism are, at present, the greatest single threat to these liberties"; and "The United States should stress victory over, rather than coexistence with, this menace."[67] It is interesting to note that the Sharon Statement had nothing to say about social issues, and it gave only a brief nod to religion. YAF went on to be a prominent force in American politics throughout the 1960s and organized chapters on college campuses throughout the United States.

To demonstrate the degree to which the cold war was the primary concern of many mainstream conservatives in the postwar years, we can look at Buckley's own words:

> The most important issue of the day, it is time to admit it, is survival. Here there is apparently some confusion in the ranks of conservatives, and hard thinking is in order for them. The thus-far invincible aggressiveness of the Soviet Union does or does not constitute a threat to the security of the United States, and we have got to decide which. If it does, we shall have to arrange, sensibly, our battle plans; and this means that we have got to accept Big Government for the duration—for neither an offensive nor a defensive war can be waged, given our present government skills, except though the instrument of a totalitarian bureaucracy within our shores.[68]

The Neoconservatives

Feuding on the right continued (indeed, many disputes within the mainstream conservative movement remain ongoing), but by the mid-1960s an intellectual conservative movement that we would recognize today had coalesced—though it continued to evolve. One major development after this period was the arrival of the so-called neoconservatives as major players in the conservative movement in the 1970s. Just as many of the most prominent figures in the postwar right in America were former communists, the first neoconservatives were drawn predominantly from the left, and many had been enthusiastic supporters of the civil rights movement, and before that the New Deal. They moved in a conservative direction after becoming disillusioned with liberal policies and new directions in left-wing thinking such as feminism, postcolonialism, and multiculturalism. As we will see in later chapters, most of the intellectual and political movements discussed in this book view the neoconservatives as the great villains in the story of the American right—if they even consider neoconservatives (or "neocons") to be conservative or right wing at all. Today, most people labeled as neoconservatives by others personally reject the label and do not see themselves as distinct from the broader conservative movement.[69] Irving Kristol was one prominent neoconservative who never backed away from the term:

> What, exactly, is neoconservatism anyway? I would say that is more a descriptive than a prescriptive term. It describes the erosion of liberal faith among a small but talented and articulate group of scholars

and intellectuals, and the movement of this group (which gradually gained many new recruits) toward a more conservative point of view: conservative, but different in certain important respects from the traditional conservatism of the Republican Party. We were, most of us, from lower-middle-class or working-class families, children of the Great Depression, veterans (literal or not) of World War II, who accepted the New Deal in principle, and had little affection for the kind of isolationism that then permeated American conservatism. We regarded ourselves originally as dissident liberals—dissident because we were skeptical of many of Lyndon Johnson's Great Society initiatives and increasingly disbelieving of liberal metaphysics, the view of human nature and of social and economic realities, on which those programs were based.[70]

Neoconservatives became primarily known for their aggressive stance on foreign policy. Indeed, it would not be an overstatement to say that this is the defining feature of neoconservatism as the term is used today. Neoconservatives are also more forthright in their rejection of economic libertarianism than many previous conservatives, are less interested in fighting the culture wars, and are more willing to denounce their ideological predecessors on the right.

One frequently hears the claim that neoconservatives were predominantly influenced by the political theorist Leo Strauss, a scholar who spent much of his career at the University of Chicago. Indeed, a number of prominent figures associated with neoconservatism studied directly under Strauss or acknowledged Strauss as an influence, including Allan Bloom, Irving Kristol, and Abram Shulsky. Anyone reading Strauss's work on political theory may think it odd that he is considered a godfather of any popular political movement; it is not immediately apparent why Strauss's work on Plato, Maimonides, or Machiavelli would lead one to favor, for example, the invasion of Iraq. Much of Strauss's work is difficult to read and understand, which makes his presumed influence on populist politicians and policy makers in Washington, DC, all the more inexplicable. As James Atlas noted in the *New York Times*, "At first glance, Strauss's work seems remote from the heat of contemporary politics. He was more at home in the world of Plato and Aristotle than in debates about the origins of totalitarianism."[71] It has been said both that Strauss "abhorred liberal democracy"[72] and that Strauss was a "friend of liberal democracy—one of the best friends democracy has ever had."[73]

Providing the "correct" interpretation of Strauss is beyond the scope of this book, as is an exhaustive examination of Straussian hermeneutics. A key reason the conservative movement embraced Strauss was his vigorous opposition to relativism, nihilism, and historicism.[74] Although Strauss attacked relativism, he did not do so in defense of biblical revelation—in fact, he wrote relatively little on theology. However, Strauss provided intellectual firepower for those conservatives who wished to dig in their heels in defense of immutable truths—though some scholars have argued that Christian traditionalists who believed Strauss's thought was congruent with their own are mistaken.[75] Strauss's attack on relativism was echoed by his student, Allan Bloom, in his 1987 best seller, *The Closing of the American Mind.*[76]

The degree to which conservative politicians and activists read Strauss and apply his ideas to practical politics is certainly debatable. However, Strauss and his ostensible influence on neoconservatives received a great deal of attention from popular media during the early 2000s. This was due to Strauss's thoughts on "esoteric" and "exoteric" readings of political writings. Strauss argued that we cannot assume that the words in a political text literally represent the views of the author. Out of fear of persecution, a political philosopher may have to write "between the lines."[77] Some opponents of the invasion of Iraq noted that many of the loudest cheerleaders for the war were influenced by Strauss and his students and therefore presumably embraced the Straussian argument that deception is warranted in order to achieve desired ends—in this case, deliberately providing misleading information about weapons of mass destruction in order to ensure the invasion of Iraq.[78]

A greater willingness to use the language of universal equality was another characteristic of the thinkers labeled neoconservative. Harry Jaffa, another student of Strauss, was an outspoken defender of Abraham Lincoln. He argued that the line in the Declaration of Independence, "all men are created equal," was not just a rhetorical flourish, but the primary motivation of the American Revolution. He further claimed that equality was fundamentally a conservative principle: "That men are by nature free and equal is the ground simultaneously of political obligation—of consent as the immediate source of the just powers of government—and a doctrine of limited government and of an ethical code. Because man is by nature a rational being, he may not rule over other men as if they were mere brutes."[79] By seeing equality as a fundamentally conservative principle, Jaffa argued that Lincoln was a conservative. This new tendency to equate equality and conservatism has also allowed other conservatives to claim that Martin Luther King Jr. "meets the very definition of an American conservative"[80]—never mind that

✳ FOX NEWS (NEO CON)

most conservatives, including the editorial board of *National Review*, were openly opposed to King while he lived. Jaffa's attitude toward equality was decidedly different from the attitude of the first generation of postwar conservatives. For example, Willmoore Kendall, a mentor of William F. Buckley at Yale who was also associated with *National Review* in its early years, rejected the notion that equality was an integral element of the American political tradition.[81]

FOX NEWS CROWD ✳

As with equality, the neoconservatives, and now conservatives more generally, frame themselves as enthusiastic promoters of democracy; they frequently promote democracy as a panacea for many of the world's ills. Such a position could not be more at odds with the views of the pre–World War II right in America, which was often ostentatiously elitist and skeptical of the masses.

U.S. IMPERIALISM TRUE

Neoconservatives soon proved to be fierce opponents of their critics on the right, as we shall see in later chapters. In the battle for the soul of the conservative movement, the neoconservatives were the clear victors. Although there is a tradition of conservative skepticism toward foreign interventionism, there were few prominent right-wing critics of the 2003 invasion of Iraq—by that time, the major conservative institutions, magazines, talk show hosts, and politicians had almost universally accepted the neoconservative vision of the United States as the promoter of democracy across the globe. Furthermore, when conservatives attack the left, they now usually frame their arguments in the language of equality—for example, they often argue that affirmative action is at odds with the goal of a truly color-blind society or discuss their liberal opponents as elitists who are out of touch with ordinary Americans. Although one might question the sincerity of their egalitarianism, it is undeniable that many conservatives have lately eschewed elitist rhetoric. With the possible exception of the gay marriage issue, today's conservatives rarely defend tradition for its own sake. Rather, when defending traditional institutions and values, conservatives typically rely on utilitarian arguments rather than a defense of tradition per se. We furthermore rarely hear anything akin to Richard Weaver's radical assault on modernity from leading conservative publications or institutions.

The Political Rise of the Conservative Movement

Up to this point, I have focused on the ideas that animated the conservative movement and the debates among American conservatives. We are primarily interested in these ideas, however, because they ultimately had real-world consequences when conservative Republicans won important elected offices. The rise of today's conservative movement as a political force in the United States was a slow process. Although a recognizably conservative intellectual movement gained prominence in the United States shortly after World War II, it took time for conservatives to become a dominant force within the Republican Party. Powerful voices within the GOP remained skeptical of the conservatives' cultural traditionalism, vigorous opposition to the welfare state, and overt hawkishness toward the Soviet Union. This battle reached a climax in 1964, when conservatives rallied around Barry Goldwater's presidential campaign. In the Republican primary election of that year, the conservative Goldwater squared off against the moderate Nelson Rockefeller.

The struggle between Goldwater and Rockefeller was unusually heated for a primary election, where presumably all candidates are on the same side in the end. Rockefeller dropped out of the race after losing California to Goldwater. At the Republican National Convention, where Goldwater accepted the party's nomination, the conservatives made no attempt to reconcile with the moderate and liberal wing of the party, and Rockefeller was actually booed. For his part, Rockefeller refused to support Goldwater in the general election against President Johnson.

Goldwater's uncompromising tone was embraced by conservative Republicans. *National Review* was enthusiastic about Goldwater, and many prominent conservatives helped Goldwater prepare his speeches, including Russell Kirk and Harry Jaffa.[82] Goldwater's 1960 manifesto, *The Conscience of a Conservative*, was actually ghostwritten by L. Brent Bozell III,[83] an editor and columnist for *National Review*. Goldwater further enjoyed popularity among young conservatives on college campuses. Young Americans for Freedom expended tremendous energy organizing for Goldwater.[84]

Republican candidates are now generally expected to run to the right during primary elections, then move back to the center in order to win the general election. Goldwater, however, never backed down from his conservative stances. Goldwater suggested that the Tennessee Valley Authority should be sold to the public sector and that Social Security should be voluntary, and he made it clear that he opposed new civil rights legislation.[85] During the primaries, Goldwater expressed a willingness to use nuclear weapons to win the Vietnam war—though he later clarified that he was not advocating such a strategy. He further did not even distance himself from the charge of extremism, noting in his acceptance speech, "Extremism in defense of liberty is no vice!"[86]

Goldwater's open zealotry failed to resonate with a majority of voters, and

Johnson was able to successfully portray him as a dangerous radical. He was crushed in the general election. Goldwater won only six states and less than 40 percent of the popular vote. It is frequently noted that Goldwater's conservative positions cost him the general election. Although it is almost certainly true that his uncompromising position as a standard-bearer for the right did not help his cause, he probably had little chance of winning regardless of his campaign decisions. Lyndon Johnson assumed the presidency less than a year before the 1964 presidential election as a result of Kennedy's assassination. It is unlikely that the American public would have opted for a new president, regardless of whom the Republicans nominated. Had Goldwater won, the United States would have had three different presidents over the course of two years. That being the case, one can argue that Goldwater had nothing to lose by running on his true positions; at least it provided conservatives an opportunity to openly make their argument before the nation.

In any event, the failed Goldwater campaign ultimately proved a boon to the conservative movement in America. For one, it introduced Ronald Reagan—who had not yet entered politics—to a national audience. His speech, "A Time for Choosing," given in support of the Goldwater campaign, established Reagan as a rising star among conservative Republicans, and he went on to win the California governor's race in 1966.

The Goldwater campaign also proved to be a major source of funds for the nascent conservative political movement. During the 1964 campaign, large sums from thousands of supporters poured in for Goldwater. It turned out that many of these donors were willing to give again, as the conservative activist Richard Viguerie suspected. Using the donor lists he acquired after 1964, Viguerie went on to raise millions of dollars for conservative candidates and organizations.[87] Viguerie used his direct-mail fund-raising skills to grow conservative groups such as the National Rifle Association, the National Right to Work Legal Defense Foundation, and the newspaper *Human Events.*[88]

The conservative movement was also assisted by the perceived failures of liberalism in America. Concurrently with Johnson's landslide presidential victory, the Democrats secured a massive advantage in the House of Representatives and the Senate. This gave the Democrats a free hand to implement their preferred policies at home and abroad. During this period, Johnson oversaw the passage of the Voting Rights Act, the creation of Medicare, and an immigration reform that abolished national quotas. The cultural disruptions of the 1960s, however, caused the Democrats' liberal agenda to stall.

Although the American public demonstrated its skepticism of Goldwater's extreme brand of conservatism in 1964, by the end of the decade, they were equally (if not more) concerned with excesses from the left. New schisms between the moderate and extreme left weakened the liberal movement in the United States. Given that Lyndon Johnson was responsible for escalating the Vietnam war, many of his most vocal critics came from the antiwar left. The growing antiwar movement split the Democratic Party. Some Democrats continued to support the war, and the more radical factions of the antiwar movement alienated many Americans—even some who may have agreed that the war was misguided and poorly executed.

Throughout the 1960s and 1970s, Americans were polarized by racial politics, and this polarization increased as more vigorous efforts to ensure racial equality—such as busing—were implemented. This was also an era in which a liberal Supreme Court made a number of unpopular decisions concerning the rights of criminal defendants, with *Miranda v. Arizona* and *Gideon v. Wainright* being two prominent examples. Race riots in the late 1960s stoked further anxieties among Americans, who were increasingly attracted to the party of law and order. The new Republican coalition was dominated by the group Nixon called the "silent majority," who were opposed to the party of "abortion, amnesty [for those who evaded the draft], and acid."[89]

The issue of civil rights had long threatened to split the Democratic coalition that had dominated American politics since 1932. This split finally materialized in the 1960s. The civil rights movement, supported by a Democratic president, caused an enormous number of white Southerners to abandon the party they had reliably supported since the Civil War. Although Goldwater lost the 1964 election by a landslide, he was the first Republican to win a majority of states in the Deep South, earning the electoral votes of South Carolina, Georgia, Alabama, Mississippi, and Louisiana. In 1968, the Democrats lost every Southern state but Texas; the rest supported Nixon or the segregationist George Wallace. Although Lyndon Johnson won 61 percent of the popular vote in 1964, in 1968, 57 percent of the country supported either Nixon or Wallace.[90]

It is impossible to overstate the degree to which racial politics played a role in undermining the Democratic majority that had dominated the United States since the New Deal. As Kevin P. Phillips, author of *The Emerging Republican Majority*, wrote in 1969:

> The principal force which broke the Democratic (New Deal) coalition
> is the Negro socioeconomic revolution and liberal Democratic

ideological inability to cope with it. Democratic "Great Society" programs aligned that party with many Negro demands, but the party was unable to defuse the racial tension sundering the nation. The South, the West, and the Catholic sidewalks of New York were the focal points of conservative opposition to the welfare liberalism of the federal government; however, the general opposition which deposed the Democratic Party came in large part from prospering Democrats who objected to Washington dissipating their tax dollars on programs which did them no good.[91]

The GOP also began making major inroads in Western states. Although Goldwater won his home state of Arizona, he lost all other states in the West. The Democratic dominance of the West ended shortly thereafter. Although today we think of California as a bastion of liberalism, Southern California was for a period a focal point of the conservative movement. Reagan began his political career as the governor of California, and Orange County was once considered the epitome of Nixon Country. From 1968 to 1988, Republicans won California, and its considerable number of Electoral College votes, in every presidential election.

Beyond their new strength in the South and West, Republicans also enjoyed the electoral support of the new Christian right in America. After World War II, Americans took a new interest in religion. In 1940, less than half of the US population belonged to a church. By 1955, 60 percent of Americans were church members.[92] This increase in religious observance benefited a conservative movement that was often explicitly Christian. The religious right became particularly incensed by *Roe v. Wade* and the nationwide legalization of abortion. Christian conservatives, who bristled at the myriad of indicators that society was becoming decadent and morally corrupt, became some of the most reliable supporters of the Republican Party.

The Republican ascendency was stalled by Watergate and Nixon's resignation, and Jimmy Carter was able to successfully win much of the South in his 1976 presidential campaign. However, in 1980, Ronald Reagan won a landslide victory and immediately began implementing conservative policies, such as a major military buildup and tax cuts.

Whether it was due to Reagan's personal charisma or the policies themselves, his efforts were rewarded with an even-more resounding electoral victory in 1984, and his vice president, George H. W. Bush, won the 1988 presidential election with relative ease. The Republican Party's electoral dominance appeared to be weakening when Bill Clinton won the 1992 presidential election, once again providing the Democrats control over the White House, the House of Representatives, and the Senate. Part of that victory, however, can be ascribed to Clinton's record as a Southern governor and his insistence that he was a moderate Democrat, as well as the substantial number of votes earned by the Reform Party candidate Ross Perot.

There was a major Republican resurgence in 1994, when Newt Gingrich led the so-called Republican Revolution. For the first time in decades, the Republican Party held majorities in both the House and Senate. The new Republican Congress further thought it had a mandate from the electorate to push hard for conservative policies, as stated in the Contract with America. Although the Democratic president, who exhibited considerable political skill, was able to block many Republican efforts, he nonetheless signed several major conservative bills, such as the Personal Responsibility and Work Opportunity Reconciliation Act of 1996.

After the bitter and narrowly won 2000 presidential election, George W. Bush sat in the White House and enjoyed Republican majorities in the House and Senate.[93] Like Reagan, Bush positioned himself as a conservative Republican, and he set out to implement conservative policies—such as additional tax cuts. The terrorist attacks of September 11, 2001, gave conservative hawks the opportunity to launch an invasion of Iraq, which they had desired for many years.[94] After Bush's successful reelection campaign in 2004, the future looked bright for conservatives. Hugh Hewitt, a prominent conservative talk show host, went so far as to argue that a permanent Republican majority was in reach.[95]

Conservative confidence after the 2004 presidential election proved unwarranted. Since that time, the GOP has suffered a number of important electoral setbacks, notably losing Congress in 2006 and the presidency in 2008. The Republicans had some impressive successes in the 2010 and 2014 midterm elections, but there are now a number of demographic trends that threaten to doom the party to permanent minority status, as we will see later in this volume.

Conclusion

After a brief discussion of the meaning of right wing, as I define the term, this chapter examined the birth and evolution of American conservatism. The American conservative intellectual movement is relatively young, and a conservatism that we would recognize today can be traced back no further than the early 1950s. I also argued that conservatism has continued to evolve, and it was through this process of slow evolution that various elements of conservative thought eventually became established as conservative doctrine in the United States.

UGH!

At present, the neoconservatives remain a dominant power within the Republican Party and the broader conservative movement. In the concluding chapter, we will see that the neoconservatives may have ultimately won a Pyrrhic victory, as conservatism in America presently faces the greatest challenges of its short history. The next chapter, however, will describe how the mainstream conservative movement shed itself of dissenters of the right who opposed the movement's ideological evolution.

Defining Conservatism's Boundaries

A HISTORY OF CONSERVATIVE PURGES

After the creation of a coherent conservative ideology in the years after World War II—the loose association of traditionalist and libertarian values that was later defined as "fusionism"—the organized conservative movement almost immediately began the task of defining who was and who was not a proper conservative. There have always been debates between prominent conservative intellectuals and public figures. These debates are often vigorous and acrimonious, but they rarely end with a major figure on the right being denounced and shunned. However, public efforts by conservatives to distance themselves from those who stray too far from the ideological mainstream have occurred with some frequency since the dawn of the movement. Often the targets of these purges were respected figures with a large audience. This chapter will examine some of the more high-profile examples of conservatives banished from the movement for ideological reasons.

Although I use the loaded term purge to describe the periodic housecleaning that occurs within the intellectual conservative movement, I am not sympathetic to all of the figures who have suffered this fate. Indeed, it would be impossible to have fond feelings for all of these intellectuals, political leaders, and journalists, given the degree to which they differed from each other. I am furthermore not arguing that it was a mistake for the organized conservative movement to shed itself of some or all of these individuals and groups. Doing so may have been politically smart and morally right. I leave it to the reader to make that decision in every individual case.

I should also clarify what I mean when I use the term organized conservatism—a phrase that appears numerous times in this volume. There is obviously not a single hierarchical structure called conservatism. Every major conservative institution and publication is presumably independent from all the others as well as independent from the Republican Party. This legal independence, however, does not preclude widespread cooperation and agreement. This cooperation and organization across the mainstream American right is now facilitated by groups like Americans for Tax Reform, led by Grover Norquist. This organization hosts a weekly "Wednesday Meeting" attended by prominent conservatives in Washington, DC, in order to facilitate coordination within the conservative movement.[1] The groups that regularly attend this meeting are leaders of what Norquist calls the Leave Us Alone Coalition.[2] Although there is not a single organization called conservatism, it is fair to speak of a single entity called the conservative movement. This movement is led by think tanks such as the Heritage Foundation and the American Enterprise Institute, publications like *National Review* and the *Weekly Standard,* centers of higher learning like Hillsdale College, Patrick Henry College, and Liberty University, advocacy groups like the National Rifle Association and the National Right to Work Legal Defense Foundation, the hosts of popular programs on the Fox News Channel, newspaper columnists like George Will and David Brooks, and AM radio hosts such as Rush Limbaugh and Glenn Beck.

Although organized conservatism and the Republican Party must be conceptually disaggregated and may at times even find themselves at odds, the two are now more aligned than was once the case. Although the conservative movement has tied its fortunes to the Republican Party for many decades, the congruence between ideology and partisanship in both Congress[3] and in the electorate[4] has never been higher. That is, very few people define themselves as conservatives and also vote for the Democratic Party, nor do many self-described liberals vote for the Republican Party. The congruence between ideology and partisanship has given the organized conservative movement additional power within the Republican Party—there is no longer a strong faction of liberal Republicans pushing back against conservative demands.

The pages that follow will detail some of the better-known successful efforts of the organized conservative movement to police the boundaries of acceptable right-wing thought in the United States. The rest of this chapter will describe those groups and individuals who were considered outside the boundary of mainstream conservative thought, and the efforts on the part of the mainstream conservative movement to distance itself from these groups and individuals. In some cases, this was as simple as firing a relatively obscure journalist from a conservative magazine; in other cases, this involved the stigmatization of leaders with tens of thousands of followers or of presidential candidates who came close to securing the Republican nomination.

The late paleoconservative columnist and author Samuel T. Francis gave his own account of how these purges typically occurred. He argued that when the leading voices of the conservative movement faced a threat from the right, they formed a temporary alliance with the left and presented a united front against fellow conservatives who were attempting to advance dangerous ideas. This left those targeted with no potential ideological allies and no major outlets for spreading their ideas. Such efforts were beneficial to the leaders of organized conservatism, as occasional purges protected them from those who would challenge their dominance of the ideological movement, and it benefited the left because it further restricted the boundaries of acceptable right-wing criticism of social trends and public policy. Francis argued that this purging occurred with increasing frequency after the ascendency of the neoconservatives:

> The movement that came to be known in the 1970s as neoconservatism, largely northeastern, urban, and academic in its orientation, is now the defining core of the "permissible" Right—that is, what a dominant Left-liberal cultural and political elite recognizes and accepts as the Right boundary of public discourse. It remains legally possible (barely) to express sentiments and ideas that are further to the Right, but if an elite enjoys cultural hegemony, as the Left does, it has no real reason to outlaw its opponents. Indeed, encouraging participation in the debate fosters the illusion of "pluralism" and serves to legitimize the main Leftward trend of the debate. Those outside the permissible boundaries of discourse are simply "derationalized" and ignored—as anti-Semites, racists, authoritarians, crackpots, crooks, or simply as "nostalgic," and other kinds of illicit and fringe elements not in harmonic discord with the *Zeitgeist* and therefore on the wrong side of history. That is

where the de facto alliance of the Left and neoconservative Right has succeeded in relegating those who dissent from their common core of shared premises such as journalist Patrick J. Buchanan and anyone else who seriously and repeatedly challenges their hegemony.[5]

For the most part, this chapter deals with purges of figures to the right of the mainstream conservative movement. This chapter does not discuss prominent figures who broke from the American right—or were rejected by the right—because they were too liberal or moderate. Although the conservative movement has not always been kind to dissenters on the left, one could argue that it has been particularly aggressive in attacking opponents to the right, bestowing pariah status on those that threaten to move the conservative movement in a dangerous direction. Multiple writers have argued that William F. Buckley played a unique part in policing the boundaries of conservatism. David Frum, for example, stated that "the epic of American conservatism since 1945" was Buckley's "purging" the conservative movement of undesirable elements.[6] Many of the examples that follow will show that this is not an unreasonable description of Buckley's role in the conservative movement.

The Rise and Fall of the John Birch Society

Not long after an organized intellectual movement we would recognize as contemporary conservatism arrived on the political scene, a number of right-wing organizations and individuals began competing for dominance in the public arena. We have already mentioned Young Americans for Freedom, founded in 1960. This organization, which was strongly influenced by William F. Buckley, played a crucial role in organizing the conservative movement. However, YAF was not the first postwar movement on the right to attract thousands of followers across the United States.

In 1958, retired candy manufacturer and fierce anticommunist Robert H. W. Welch Jr. founded the John Birch Society (JBS), named after an American intelligence officer and Christian missionary killed by supporters of the Chinese Communist Party. Welch was an especially committed anticommunist and unusually paranoid about communist subversion—which is no small statement, given the period in which he rose to national prominence. Indeed, Welch's insistence that a communist conspiracy already controlled the highest levels of government was largely responsible for the demise of his organization as a powerful force in the United States.

Although the JBS preceded other famous organizations designed to organize conservative activists, such as Young Americans for Freedom, it was not the first grassroots anticommunist organization in the United States. The Christian Anti-Communism Crusade, for example, was several years older. Welch, however, had a unique gift for salesmanship and organization—skills he learned in his career in the private sector. It is actually somewhat difficult to precisely categorize the JBS's organizational structure. Although it presented itself as a grassroots organization, it was also intensely hierarchical, and individual chapters had little discretion regarding their activities. Ironically, the structure of the JBS was not wholly dissimilar from the structure of the Communist Party. Most important decisions regarding the organization's direction were made by Welch himself.[7] Unlike much of the organized conservative movement, Welch was convinced that his group needed to be independent of the Republican Party.[8] Although Welch and his organization were openly enthusiastic about some Republican figures such as Barry Goldwater, unlike most contemporary conservative groups, the JBS did not immediately line up behind whoever happened to be the Republican presidential candidate.

Within just a few years, the JBS had tens of thousands of members, though precise numbers are impossible to determine.[9] Although the JBS maintained a home office in Belmont, Massachusetts, it organized local chapters throughout the United States, and it hired paid coordinators to maintain communication between chapter leaders and Welch.[10] Jonathan M. Schoenwald, who has conducted important research on the origins of American conservatism, argued that the JBS was unique in the degree to which ordinary members were active and aggressive: "Being a JBS member was not like being a member of the ACLU or the ADA; those liberal groups did not expect their members to do much more than contribute money and perhaps periodically write to a senator or representative. Joining the JBS was entirely different; although some people merely renewed their memberships annually, the majority was active on one level, if not several."[11] Also, unlike most grassroots conservative efforts in the United States today, there were apparently few efforts on the part of the JBS to coordinate with other groups on the right—though they did provide subscriptions to other conservative publications. The group is now most famous for its outrageous accusations regarding communist conspiracies. Although many conservatives, such as Russell Kirk, openly favored Senator Robert Taft over Dwight Eisenhower in the 1952 Republican presidential race, Welch saw Eisenhower's victory in nearly apocalyptic terms and warned his followers not to trust Richard Nixon, who was the vice president at the time:

Nixon always brings to my mind the old gag that a wife is a person who helps you to get over all the troubles you wouldn't have had if you had never married; or the somewhat more elegant version that diplomats help us to solve our problems that never would have arisen if there were no diplomats. But for the dirtiest deal in American political history, participated in if not actually engineered by Richard Nixon in order to make himself Vice-President (and to put Warren on the Supreme Court as part of that deal), Taft would have been nominated at Chicago in 1952. It is almost certain that Taft would then have been elected President by a far greater plurality than was Eisenhower, that a grand rout of the Communists in our government and in our midst would have been started, that McCarthy would be alive today, and that we wouldn't even be in this mess that we are supposed to look to Nixon to lead us out of.[12]

Whereas other conservatives were merely contemptuous of liberal Republican Nelson Rockefeller, Welch was convinced Rockefeller was "definitely committed to trying to make the United States a part of a one world socialist government."[13] Inflammatory rhetoric of this type ultimately led the rest of the organized conservative movement to distance itself from Welch and the JBS, and ultimately to condemn the organization entirely. William F. Buckley and *National Review* played an important role in undermining the JBS, but it is often forgotten that Buckley and Welch were on friendly terms for some time. Welch donated money to Buckley in the early years of *National Review*, and the two men were on good terms until at least 1961—though they had already openly disagreed on the extent to which the highest levels of government were controlled by a communist conspiracy.[14] Throughout the early 1960s, the JBS remained influential. When Barry Goldwater was poised to win the Republican nomination, however, and the conservatives were finally about to see one of their own at the top of the ticket, the extremist and unhinged rhetoric of Welch and his followers became too embarrassing for the conservative movement to tolerate.

Buckley was later open about his efforts to bring down the JBS. In fact, in 2003 he wrote a novel, *Getting It Right*, about the end of the JBS and Ayn Rand's Objectivist movement (which I will discuss shortly) and the triumph of his own brand of conservatism.[15] Toward the end of his life, Buckley wrote a short piece detailing the efforts to bring down the JBS without alienating the group's tens of thousands of members.[16] In early 1962, long before Goldwater announced his candidacy, Goldwater, Buckley, Russell Kirk, and William Baroody (the head of the American Enterprise Institute) met to discuss the issue of the JBS. All at the meeting were in general agreement that the JBS needed to be "excommunicated" from the conservative movement, but Goldwater did not know how to distance himself from the group without losing support from its members. According to Buckley, Goldwater declared, "Every other person in Phoenix is a member of the John Birch Society. . . . I'm not talking about Commie-haunted apple pickers or cactus drunks, I'm talking about the highest cast of men of affairs."[17] The task of denouncing Welch and his organization fell to Buckley, who wrote a lengthy essay for *National Review* titled, "The Question of Robert Welch."[18] In this essay, Buckley condemned Welch's tendency to accuse high-ranking leaders of both political parties of direct, knowing involvement in a communist conspiracy. Goldwater subsequently endorsed Buckley's essay in a letter to the editor published in the following issue.

In his opening shot against the JBS, Buckley made it clear that his problem was specifically with Welch, not with the organization—though obviously the two could not really be disaggregated. In 1965, however, after Goldwater's disastrous defeat, Buckley struck against the JBS with greater force. In his syndicated column, "On the Right," Buckley pointed out that absurd remarks from the JBS were not limited to Welch.[19] Other conservative organizations, such as the American Conservative Union, also severed ties with the society.[20]

Welch's paranoia is generally discussed as the catalyst for his organization's marginalization by the broader conservative movement. However, Welch's personality was not the only thing at odds with *National Review*–style conservatism. Welch and the JBS were also assaulted for their skepticism about American involvement in Vietnam, as such a stance indicated that the JBS threatened to steer the American right in an isolationist direction. James Burnham attacked the JBS for this reason in 1965—a time when most American conservatives remained fully committed to the Vietnam war:

And there is a third factor operating in the Birch movement, since it began spreading a bit over the country, that has had some influence in getting JBS members to accept the grotesque conclusions that Mr. Welch reaches on the Vietnam war and on the country's other foreign activities. Mr. Welch himself may not have anticipated this factor when he started out, but there are frequent signs that he now is not only well aware of its existence in his ranks but ready to give expression to it and even, in his own manner, to exploit its possibilities. I refer to the isolationist tradition that survives in many parts of this country, though it no longer gets much recognition even from many of those who still share it.[21]

Finding itself without allies in the rest of the respectable conservative movement and few friends within the Republican Party, the influence of the JBS waned throughout the 1960s and the 1970s. The organization still exists and remains committed to the theory that communist conspiracies threaten the independence of the United States. In fact, the organization still maintains that the "smear attacks" against the organization originated in Moscow.[22] In 2002, John F. McManus, president of the JBS, wrote a book titled *William F. Buckley: Pied Piper for the Establishment*, which asserted that Buckley was largely responsible for the nation's statist, leftward turn and that blamed him for the degree to which the conservative movement had become ineffectual.[23] However, the JBS's influence, even within the conservative movement, is now small if not nonexistent.

Although the contemporary reader will likely find Robert Welch's comments about the communist conspiracy bizarre and perhaps even unhinged, it is important to remember the social context in which the JBS was a powerful political force. Fear of Soviet subversion was rampant in American society in the 1950s and 1960s. In terms of paranoia, the difference between Welch and Senator Joseph McCarthy was one of degree, not kind. Buckley was furthermore not a consistent opponent of anticommunist fearmongering—he actually coauthored a book defending McCarthy.[24] Thus, it may not be fair to characterize Buckley and his allies as reasonable and thoughtful conservative counters to the irresponsible and radical members of the JBS.

Whether Welch actually was far more radical than other prominent conservatives of his era, the decline of the JBS demonstrated the ability of the organized conservative movement to draw borders around itself and determine who fell outside of these parameters. This series of events also demonstrated the personal power wielded by Buckley on such questions. Again, while American conservatives have never been ideologically uniform, they soon established a tradition of declaring certain people and opinions out of bounds. We see another example of this in the conservative movement's contentious relationship with one of the more eccentric offshoots of libertarianism: Objectivism.

Ayn Rand and the Objectivists

Robert Welch and the JBS did not differ from most other conservatives on questions regarding the characteristics of a good society. Welch was a conservative Protestant in favor of traditional values and opposed to economic collectivism. Welch's personal paranoia, rather than ideology, was the primary source of contention between Welch and other conservatives. At about the same time that Welch appeared as one of the primary standard-bearers for grassroots conservatism in the United States, a new ideological movement— which stood on fundamentally different metaphysical grounds than mainstream conservatism—threatened to take the American right in a totally new direction. The rise and fall of Ayn Rand and her Objectivist movement was a unique chapter in the history of the right in the United States.

Ayn Rand, whose real name was Alisa Rosenbaum, was born in Russia in 1905. Her parents were wealthy Russian Jews living in St. Petersburg. Like many others in Russia's upper class, the Rosenbaum family lost its social status as a result of the Bolshevik revolution, though Rand was able to attend Petrograd State University. She studied screenwriting after completing her undergraduate degree, and she told Soviet authorities that she wished to study American filmmaking—claiming that she would return and assist the Russian film industry—in order to secure her permits to leave the country.[25] Rand arrived in the United States in 1926 and became an American citizen in 1931. Her background was different in virtually every way from the other early major figures of American conservatism, which perhaps makes the stark differences between their worldviews more explicable.

Rand's philosophy, which she later called Objectivism, was individualistic and materialist. It openly celebrated selfishness as a moral good. According to Rand's philosophy, "Man exists for his own sake. . . . The pursuit of his own happiness is his highest moral purpose. . . . He must not sacrifice himself to others, nor sacrifice others to himself."[26] Rand thoroughly rejected all forms of collectivism and mysticism, including Christianity. Rand's outspoken atheism did not make her an unusual figure in the American right in the interwar years. Many writers during this period were equally skeptical of religion. Rand felt a particularly strong affinity for H. L. Mencken, telling him in a 1934 letter that he was "one whom I admire as the greatest representative of a philosophy to which I want to dedicate my whole life."[27] By the time a coherent conservative movement formed in the 1950s and 1960s, however, the association between religion and ideology in the United States was much stronger, and conservatives were less willing to align themselves with militant atheists.

Rand's first novel, *We the Living*, was published in 1936. The novel, set in postrevolutionary Russia, was semiautobiographical. Like her later works, the novel was a vehicle for her anticollectivist arguments. Beyond her literary efforts, Rand also engaged in political activism in the 1940s, and she built relationships with prominent libertarians such as Isabel Patterson and Ludwig von Mises; the latter strongly influenced Rand's economic views.[28] Rand finally reached a large audience for her views with the 1943 publication of *The Fountainhead*. This novel clearly explained Rand's individualist philosophy and ethical system despite providing little commentary on contemporary political events or public policies.

As a result of her new fame, Rand began to draw many young libertarians into a group, ironically called the Collective.[29] This group, which included future chairman of the Federal Reserve Alan Greenspan, was dedicated to the principles of Objectivism. Rand presented her philosophy most clearly to the world in *Atlas Shrugged*, her magnum opus, published in 1957. This dystopian novel, which brought her to new heights of wealth and fame, also further clarified the philosophical distinctions between Rand's Objectivism and the nascent conservative movement.

Although the plot of *Atlas Shrugged* focused on the struggle between heroic, selfish capitalists and power-hungry, parasitic collectivists, it also directly attacked all forms of religion:

> For centuries, the mystics of the spirit had existed by running a protection racket—by making life on earth unbearable, then charging you for consolation and relief, by forbidding all the virtues that make existence possible, then riding on the shoulders of your guilt, by declaring production and joy to be sins, then collecting blackmail from the sinners. We, the men of the mind, were the unnamed victims of their creed, we who were willing to break their moral code and to bear damnation for the sin of reason—we who thought and acted while they wished and prayed— we who were moral outcasts, we who were the bootleggers of life when life was held to be a crime—while they basked in the moral glory for the virtue of surpassing material greed and of distributing in selfless charity the material goods produced by—blank out.[30]

Although her economics were conventionally libertarian, and on foreign policy she was actually rather hawkish compared to others on the libertarian right,[31] her open celebration of selfishness and Nietzschean hostility to Christianity put her at odds with mainstream conservatives, many of whom

RAND, HAYEK, + MISES - JEWS

directly tied their political views to their Christian worldview. The organized conservative movement does not generally shun potential supporters based on a religious litmus test—many prominent conservatives in the early years of the movement were religious skeptics. However, the mainstream right has never been tolerant of open hostility toward Christianity. The most important salvo against Rand from the right was a review of *Atlas Shrugged* by Whittaker Chambers in *National Review*.[32] By publishing this review, Buckley signaled to the world that American conservatism was fundamentally opposed to Rand's philosophy, despite being in agreement on many policy issues.

Chambers had previously made it clear that he viewed the cold war in explicitly religious terms, and he went so far as to say that communism can only be rejected on religious grounds: the "crux of this matter is whether God exists. If God exists, a man cannot be a Communist, which begins with the rejection of God. But if God does not exist, it follows that communism, or some suitable variant of it, is right."[33] In his review of *Atlas Shrugged*, Chambers pulled no punches, describing it as a "remarkably silly book" that "deals wholly in the blackest blacks and the whitest whites."[34] He further attacked the forthright atheism of the novel and noted that Rand's materialism demonstrated that she had more in common with Marx, whom she hated, than with conservatives. Other prominent conservatives, such as Russell Kirk, also attacked Rand in the pages of *National Review*.[35]

Although Rand claimed to have never read this review, her followers were outraged, and the review spurred much debate on the American right. Rand received support from a number of prominent libertarians such as Ludwig von Mises, John Chamberlain, and Murray Rothbard (who had previously been critical of Rand).[36] To blame the divide between conservatives and Rand and her followers entirely on the religious intolerance of conservatives would be unfair, as Rand herself was notoriously hostile toward those with whom she disagreed—even if they agreed on most issues. Rand, for example, openly despised F. A. Hayek, a fellow secular Jew and supporter of free-market capitalism influenced by Mises, as a result of a disagreement on epistemological issues.[37]

In his history of American conservatism, George Nash argued that the feud between Rand and her detractors ended with Rand's unambiguous defeat:

When the furor over Ayn Rand eventually subsided, it became clear that Chambers . . . had won: Objectivism did not take conservatism by storm. As William F. Buckley Jr. reflected in the early 1960s, Rand's "desiccated philosophy" was inconsistent with the "conservative's emphasis on transcendence," while her harsh ideological fervor was profoundly distasteful. Rand herself was similarly aware of the unbridgeable gap. *National Review*, she declared in 1964, was "the worst and most dangerous magazine in America"; its mixture of religion and capitalism represented a sullying of the rationally defensible (freedom and capitalism) with mystical, unconvincing obscurantism.[38]

When Rand died in 1982, Buckley—who on more than one occasion wrote uncharitable obituaries for his deceased political opponents[39]—declared final victory over Rand's ideology: "Ayn Rand is dead. So, incidentally, is the philosophy she sought to launch. It died stillborn."[40] Although Rand never did become the official voice of the American right, she was an influential figure, and she continues to inspire readers. Former Republican vice presidential nominee Paul Ryan, for example, has credited Rand with informing many of his views.[41]

Mel Bradford

In the two cases we just considered, it is difficult to say whether the purged elements were to the left or the right of the mainstream conservative movement. The members of the JBS were in general agreement with mainstream conservatives on most of the issues of the day. Rand was certainly less willing to accept the welfare state as a political necessity than were most conservatives, which might indicate that she was to the right of the organized conservative movement on economic issues. Today we tend to associate secularism with the left. However, while Rand's uncompromising atheism put her at odds with the increasingly religious conservative movement in America, she was certainly part of the Nietzschean, atheist right.

As the twentieth century continued to progress, the conservative movement put a greater emphasis on drawing clear boundaries as to just how far to the right a group or individual could wander and remain welcome within the mainstream conservative tent. This was particularly true when it came to issues related to race and ethnicity; the major voices of the conservative movement have now apparently determined that they will not defend fellow conservatives who cross certain boundaries on racial issues. Again, this is not to say that the conservative movement has embraced a progressive agenda on race; however, it has attempted to make it clear that some positions are no longer tolerated within the respectable right. Although many liberals may think that conservatives have been insufficiently vigorous in their efforts to drive out racists, anti-Semites, and conspiracy theorists, it cannot be said that the mainstream conservative movement does not occasionally engage in housecleaning of this type.

The question is why the conservative movement made this about-face on the issue of race. It is worth remembering that during the pivotal years of the civil rights movement the major voices of American conservatism—including Barry Goldwater and *National Review*—were openly against legislation such as the Civil Rights Act. Some of the most prominent early conservatives defended the social order of the antebellum South. However, after the victory of the civil rights movement in the 1960s, a new group of conservatives was willing to make peace with federal efforts to promote racial equality and preferred to focus their efforts on other issues. Some of the leading conservative writers of this period became vocal opponents of racism—though they continued to express skepticism of new federal efforts, such as affirmative action, to combat racial inequality. As noted in chapter 1, the prominent neoconservative scholar Harry Jaffa aggressively made the case that Abraham Lincoln was a conservative in his day and should serve as an inspiration for contemporary conservatives.

All of this led to a tension within the conservative movement between the neoconservatives and the more traditional Southern conservatives. Within conservative circles, the ideological gap between the neoconservatives and the older generation of conservatives was well known, but it was not particularly problematic given that the two groups did not interact very much. They had different recognized intellectual standard-bearers and separate publications—*Chronicles* became the primary vehicle for what would eventually become called paleoconservative thought, and *Commentary* was the neoconservatives' most important magazine. Mark Gerson, a prominent neoconservative, noted, "Until the 1980s, the neoconservatives and the paleoconservatives did not have much occasion to speak with one another. The descendants of Lionel Trilling and the descendants of Richard Weaver resided in completely different worlds. Their one mutual friend, William F. Buckley, felt no need to bring them together. Quite simply, the neoconservatives and the paleoconservatives traveled in different circles, and this, presumably, was acceptable to both groups."[42] The tension between neo- and paleoconservatives first erupted into open hostility when M. E. "Mel" Bradford was selected by President Reagan to serve as the chairman for the National Endowment for the Humanities (NEH) in 1981. It was also at this time that Buckley ceased to act as a neutral liaison between these two groups, choosing to back the neoconservative position—an act he repeated on more than one occasion.

Bradford had academic credentials appropriate for the position. He earned his PhD in English from Vanderbilt University and went on to teach at numerous prestigious universities.[43] He also published or edited more than a dozen books. As a devoted Southern conservative, his appointment to the NEH was backed by a number of conservative senators at the time, such as Jesse Helms. Like Richard Weaver a generation before him, Bradford was a vocal defender of the social traditions of the American South and was part of the same intellectual tradition—in fact, Bradford wrote his doctoral dissertation under Donald Davidson, one of the most prominent Southern Agrarians. Unlike Weaver, however, Bradford faced formidable hostility from within conservative ranks. Specifically, Bradford's open sympathy for the Confederacy and hostility toward Abraham Lincoln—Bradford had actually compared Lincoln to Hitler—put him at odds with Irving Kristol, the foremost public intellectual associated with neoconservatism. Kristol had his own candidate in mind for the position at NEH: William Bennett.[44]

Other major conservative figures joined in the attack on Bradford, including George Will, who wrote a fiery denunciation of Bradford in the *Washington Post*, declaring that Bradford possessed a "profoundly mistaken moral judgment."[45] Bradford, who was also a former George Wallace supporter, would certainly have also faced hostility from liberal Democrats, but attacks from other conservatives sunk his prospects. The neoconservatives succeeded in their campaign against Bradford in part because Buckley and Edwin Feulner, president of the Heritage Foundation, decided to back Kristol in the dispute and called for Reagan's withdrawal of Bradford as a candidate.[46]

Not all conservatives were pleased with the growing strength of the neoconservatives within the movement. The traditionalist conservatives opposed to the neoconservatives attempted, on multiple occasions, to strike back and reclaim the movement they felt rightly belonged to them. There was particular hostility to the degree to which the neoconservatives felt justified in setting the boundaries of acceptable conservative thought—after all, the neoconservatives were new to the movement and in many cases were refugees from the left. Stephen J. Tonsor, a conservative opponent of the neoconservatives, made the following remarks in 1986:

> It has always struck me as odd, even perverse, that former Marxists have been permitted, yes invited, to play such a leading role in the

Conservative movement of the twentieth century. It is splendid when the town whore gets religion and joins the church. Now and then she makes a good choir director, but when she begins to tell the minister what he ought to say in his Sunday sermons, matters have been carried too far. I once remarked to Glenn Campbell of the Hoover Institution that had Stalin spared Leon Trotsky and not had him murdered in Mexico, he would no doubt have spent his declining days in an office in Hoover Library writing his memoirs and contributing articles of a faintly neoconservative flavor to *Encounter* and *Commentary*.[47]

These internal struggles within the conservative movement were little noticed by much of the public, mostly because the paleoconservatives were largely irrelevant by the mid-1980s—so much so that prominent neoconservatives did not feel it necessary to respond to paleoconservative critiques.[48] The most important battles between the neoconservatives and the paleoconservatives in their struggle to define the American right were still to come, however. In the early 1990s, the paleoconservatives found a champion to rally behind: Pat Buchanan. Before discussing Buchanan and his movement, however, we should discuss another even more controversial figure on the right who sought to change the direction of the conservative movement.

The Rejection of David Duke

In many respects, the 1980s was a period of transition for the American right. This was the period in which many of the major leaders of the GOP and the leading organs of the conservative movement declared their final surrender on civil rights. This does not mean that they did not continue to battle the left on a number of fronts regarding racial issues, but when it comes the key battles of the 1960s, the conservative movement acknowledged that it could not reverse broad social trends—and many even began arguing that the right had been on wrong side of history during that key period. Although conservatives remained intransigent on issues like busing, and most opposed racial affirmative action, there were fewer voices calling for a repeal of landmark legislation such as the Civil Rights Act. President Reagan signed the Martin Luther King Day holiday into law in 1983, despite the objections of many Republicans—though many states refused to acknowledge the holiday, or gave it a different name, for many years thereafter. Although Reagan vetoed the bill to place sanctions on apartheid South Africa, his veto was overridden by Congress. Race was clearly a major issue for many Republicans in Congress such as Jesse Helms, and the party clearly continued to rely on white racial anxiety for votes. However, the conservative movement, broadly speaking, was trying to move beyond the more transparent racism that was once common within its ranks.

Although the demographic profile of the United States began to change remarkably in the 1980s, largely as a result of the changes in immigration law that occurred in the 1960s, most conservatives did not publicly decry demographic change as such. Although immigration restrictionism was a predominantly right-wing phenomenon, few notable conservatives openly decried mass immigration specifically because it was changing the racial and ethnic profile of the country. Instead, many leading conservatives noted that America was founded on ideas rather than a specific racial ethnicity, and thus a more diverse nation was not necessarily a threat to the conservative project. David Frum noted the following about mainstream conservative thought during this period:

> Most conservatives at least professed to be unalarmed about this gradual transformation of the country. They claimed that America was a nation founded upon a "proposition"; anyone who assented to the American proposition could become an American. The editorialists at the *Wall Street Journal* effusively welcomed the new arrivals. Bill Bennett claimed that the new immigrants made better citizens than many of the Anglos whose families had lived here for 200 years, and that the blame for any difficulties posed by immigration fell upon the weak-willed elite that failed to insist upon prompt assimilation.[49]

We should of course not overstate the degree to which conservatives were on board with racial egalitarianism by the 1980s, or even today. It has been argued that Reagan's political success can be attributed to his use of dog-whistle racism, which activated the racial anxieties of whites without crossing the line into open racism. In a 1981 interview, Lee Atwater, then an advisor to President Reagan, described the evolution of conservative discourse on race, noting that, while the rhetoric had changed, the underlying sentiments had not:

> You start out in 1954 by saying, "Nigger, nigger, nigger." By 1968 you can't say "nigger"—that hurts you. Backfires. So you say stuff like forced busing, states' rights and all that stuff. You're getting so abstract now [that] you're talking about cutting taxes, and all these things you're

talking about are totally economic things and a byproduct of them is [that] blacks get hurt worse than whites.

And subconsciously maybe that is part of it. I'm not saying that. But I'm saying that if it is getting that abstract, and that coded, that we are doing away with the racial problem one way or the other. You follow me—because obviously sitting around saying, "We want to cut this," is much more abstract than even the busing thing, and a hell of a lot more abstract than "Nigger, nigger."[50]

It is beyond the scope of this work to determine whether the conservative movement's change in racial rhetoric was due to a genuine change in attitudes or a response to changes in what was deemed acceptable in American discourse on race. However, it is undeniable that by the 1980s, GOP leaders and the conservative movement more generally had moved away from explicitly racist remarks and were embarrassed by those who failed to stick with the new program. This new tone of the American right was directly challenged by a former grand wizard of the Ku Klux Klan (KKK), David Duke, who briefly served in the Louisiana legislature as a Republican and came close to winning a US Senate seat in 1990.

Although Southern politicians have always been the most aggressively hostile to federal efforts to promote racial equality, Duke was uniquely open about his racist and anti-Semitic views. One of the first groups Duke ever joined was the National Socialist Liberation Front, a neo-Nazi group, and his views on race remained strongly influenced by Hitler's racial doctrines, though he later denied that he was a Nazi.[51] He also joined the KKK at the age of seventeen and later started a group on the Louisiana State University campus called the White Youth Alliance. He severed his ties with the KKK in 1980 and established a new organization, the National Association for the Advancement of White People.[52] Although this group lacked the notoriety and size of the KKK, leading a group with a more innocuous name was part of his effort to appeal to a more mainstream audience, and he began to downplay his more extremist past. In an interview with the *New York Times*, Duke did not apologize for his earlier associations, but he indicated that his views had evolved as he matured: "There are many liberals today who were radical leftists in their younger days. . . . I'm a conservative who might have been considered a radical rightist in my younger days."[53]

William Moore argued that Duke's views had never changed. Rather than change his views to be more mainstream, he repackaged them to make them more appealing to a mainstream audience: focusing on affirmative action and welfare policies that he perceived disproportionately benefited blacks at the expense of whites.[54] His strong electoral support in his campaigns in the late 1980s and early 1990s indicates that he was quite successful in his efforts.

Duke narrowly won election to the Louisiana state legislature as a Republican in 1989, after his unsuccessful bid for president as the candidate for the openly racist Populist Party the year before. The Republican Party scrambled to find a response to Duke, and the weak reaction of the Louisiana Republican Party gave Duke additional traction. In his 1990 run for a US Senate seat, Duke won almost 44 percent of the vote. In 1991, he ran unsuccessfully for governor of Louisiana, winning 39 percent of the vote.

At the height of his popularity, David Duke put the Republican Party in a quandary. In both his Senate and gubernatorial bids, he had secured the party's nomination through the democratic primary process. To overtly reject him, the Louisiana Republican Party risked alienating their electoral base. On the other hand, his prominence was an embarrassment to the Republican Party nationwide, which was trying to move away from overt racial hostility. In an interview given shortly before the 1991 election for governor, William A. Nungesser, chairman of the Louisiana Republican Party, summed up the Duke candidacy as follows: "It's a nightmare for us."[55]

President George H. W. Bush was unequivocal in his opposition to Duke. In an attempt to block Duke, the White House persuaded the incumbent governor, Buddy Roemer, to switch his party affiliation from Democrat to Republican. However, Roemer was unpopular among Louisiana Republicans, particularly for his decision to veto an antiabortion bill passed by the legislature. Roemer did not win the party's endorsement, which went to Clyde Holloway. Roemer came in third in the first round of voting, leaving the race between Duke and the Democratic candidate, Edwin Edwards. The GOP then had to decide whether it would endorse the open racist running under their party's banner, or the Democrat. The White House remained overtly opposed to Duke and denied that Duke was truly a Republican. In an interview before the election, John Sununu, Bush's chief of staff, said, "David Duke is not the Republican nominee. He is an individual that has chosen to call himself a Republican. The President is absolutely opposed to the kind of racist statements that have come out of David Duke now and in the past."[56] Bush personally made similar remarks: "When someone has a long record, an ugly record of racism and of bigotry, that record simply cannot be erased by the glib rhetoric of a political campaign. So I believe David

Duke is an insincere charlatan. I believe he's attempting to hoodwink the voters of Louisiana, I believe he should be rejected for what he is and what he stands for."[57]

Ben C. Toledana, writing in *National Review*, further explained the problem Duke represented:

> State Representative David Duke is also running as a registered
> Republican. A year ago, over six hundred thousand people (44 per
> cent of those who went to the polls) voted for Duke for the US Senate
> against longtime incumbent Bennett Johnston. Why would anyone
> vote for Duke for any office? His KKK background is well known.
> Even his own campaign literature can't be any more specific about his
> occupation than "internationally published author," lecturer, and State
> Representative. Duke is surely a press-made person, someone who, if he
> had been ignored, would be no bigger than a wart on a gnat's posterior.
>
> Yet David Duke has become a significant factor in Louisiana and
> beyond. Even George Bush, on a good day, would have difficulty finding
> fault with Duke's platform: "no tax increases; balance the budget; reduce
> the size of government; get tough on crime; reform the welfare system;
> end unjust affirmative action and quotas; reform education; protect
> the environment; and care for the senior citizen." The problem is not
> with the proposals but with the proponent. But there are lots of angry,
> frustrated, and undiscerning people who are desperate for a spokesman,
> even if it's David Duke.[58]

William F. Buckley echoed these sentiments shortly thereafter: "How to Treat David Duke never seemed much of a problem until just now. The way to treat him, surely, was as a sometime wizard of the Ku Klux Klan. A fellow-traveler of Nazism. Someone, in a word, who belongs in Coventry, not in the State House in Baton Rouge." Buckley continued, "Suppose he is elected governor of Louisiana. If David Duke is still in any palpable way a racist of the KKK stripe, let alone the Nazi stripe, then our problem becomes one of huge magnitude."[59]

The Republican Party—and the conservative movement more generally—was saved considerable embarrassment when Duke lost his gubernatorial bid by a landslide margin. Although a Democrat won the election, the Republican Party was not saddled with Duke occupying a prominent place in American politics. One could fairly accuse many conservatives of hypocrisy for their emphatic rejection of Duke—and many liberals have done so.

After all, one could argue that Bush tapped into similar racial sentiments in his infamous Willie Horton advertisements during his 1988 presidential campaign. Furthermore, Duke's actual policy platform was virtually indistinguishable from other conservative Republicans—at least when it came to domestic policy. One could argue that Duke's real problem was that he had a long record of articulating his racist positions explicitly, rather than in coded messages designed to activate racial anxieties among whites. However, Duke's repudiation by the major voices within the conservative movement and the Republican Party made it clear they would not allow explicit racists to be prominent standard-bearers for conservatism in America.

David Duke again attempted to enter national politics when he ran in the 1992 Republican presidential primaries. He performed dismally, winning few votes in the states in which he ran. In that year, he was overshadowed by another conservative, one with much greater political skill, who also challenged the Republican establishment.

Pat Buchanan's Failed Insurgence

Although most conservatives view the Reagan years as a golden age of the American right, the neoconservatives had a right to feel particularly triumphant. The internal division on the right regarding who Reagan would appoint as NEH chairman had minimal consequences regarding actual public policies—in fact, Bennett resigned that position a few years later to serve as Reagan's secretary of education. However, this event demonstrated which conservative faction held the greatest sway over the GOP and thus had the greatest influence over policy.

As noted above, many American conservatives were resentful of the neoconservatives. Although the paleoconservatives were clearly disgruntled by their growing influence, other right-wing groups were similarly distrustful of the neoconservatives. Many libertarians were skeptical of the neoconservatives, for various reasons. The liberal or even Marxist roots of many leading neoconservative intellectuals raised obvious red flags for many radical antistatists. The neoconservatives were much more willing to accommodate a generous welfare state, provided it was a conservative welfare state. This position was stated directly by Irving Kristol:

> The idea of the welfare state is in itself perfectly consistent with a
> conservative political philosophy—as Bismarck knew, a hundred years
> ago. In our urbanized, industrialized, highly mobile society, people
> need governmental action of some kind if they are to cope with many

of their problems: old age, illness, unemployment, etc. They need such assistance; they demand it; they will get it. The only interesting political question is: *How* will they get it?[60]

This willingness to declare defeat on an issue that had largely defined the right since the 1930s was a step too far for many of the more forceful antistatists. Although it is commonly said that neoconservatives were liberals who had been mugged by reality, there was some justifiable suspicion that the neoconservatives had never actually changed their positions. That is, that they occupied the same ideological space in the 1970s and 1980s that they had occupied in the 1950s and 1960s, but "the Left had moved further Left."[61] As a result of the radical student movements and the left's new antiwar stance, those American liberals who did not follow this leftward drift unexpectedly found themselves ideologically closer to the Republican Party than the Democratic Party. Although conservatives certainly welcomed any trend that increased the size of their coalition, many were frustrated that these newcomers demanded that the conservative movement reshape itself in their image.

There was another element of neoconservatism that caused many traditional conservatives to bristle: its ostentatiously Jewish character. Most of the prominent early neoconservatives were Jews from New York such as Kristol, Sidney Hook, Norman Podhoretz, and Nathan Glazer. The six-day war in 1967 proved to be a turning point for many future neoconservatives. The American left's failure to stand up for Israel in that conflict convinced many that the conservative movement would be a more reliable friend to the Jewish state than the left. It would be inaccurate to say that Jewish conservatives were the only element of the American right that was uniquely concerned about Israel; the rising evangelical movement—which included many who believed that Israel was to play a pivotal role in fulfilling biblical prophesies—also considered unequivocal American support for the Jewish state nonnegotiable. That being said, many traditional conservatives were concerned that the neoconservatives were more loyal to Israel than the United States. Although prominent neoconservatives were open about the degree to which their religion and ethnicity informed their political preferences, their critics on the right who condemned them on these grounds became suspected of anti-Semitism.

The closest the neoconservatives' foes on the right came to wrestling back control of the conservative movement and the GOP came in 1992 and 1996, when Patrick J. Buchanan managed to cobble together a coalition of unlikely ideological allies, united primarily by their hostility to neoconservatism. Although the hostility between neoconservatives and other conservative factions was apparent in the early 1980s, they remained united, for the most part, in their strong support for Ronald Reagan. This unity did not survive the presidency of his successor, George H. W. Bush.

Many conservatives were suspicious of Bush before he ever became president, and to secure the Republican nomination he had to reassure both economic and religious conservatives that he was a true conservative on all fronts, most notably making the promise, "Read my lips: no new taxes."[62] Less than a year into Bush's presidency, the Berlin Wall came down, and the issue that had united the right for four decades, including those who might have otherwise been inclined toward isolationist attitudes, was gone forever. The end of the cold war allowed for a renewed debate on the American right regarding the proper role of the United States in world affairs.

Buchanan had previously been a consistent cold warrior—he had served in the Nixon and Reagan administrations. When the cold war ended, however, Buchanan called for the dismantling of the American empire, calling for a foreign policy of "America First—and Second, and Third."[63] This put him squarely at odds with neoconservatives who openly called for a "Pax Americana" and "global hegemony."[64] President Bush's reaction to Iraq's invasion of Kuwait in 1990 demonstrated that Bush's vision of American foreign policy vision was aligned with that of the neoconservatives. Bush's rhetoric further reinforced this point: "Out of these troubled times, our fifth objective—a new world order—can emerge: a new era—freer from the threat of terror, stronger in pursuit of justice, and more secure in the quest for peace."[65] This kind of rhetoric was particularly troubling to the kind of conservatives who possessed a nostalgic vision of the United States as a commercial republic free from "entangling alliances," to use George Washington's phrase.

The demise of the Soviet Union also coincided with a change in Buchanan's views toward Israel. During the cold war, Buchanan was an enthusiastic supporter of Israel. During the run-up to the gulf war, however, Buchanan expressed concern that the United States was being manipulated into a war that served Israeli interests rather than those of the United States: "There are only two groups that are beating drums right now for war in the Middle East, and that is the Israeli Defense Ministry and its 'Amen' corner in the United States."[66]

Buchanan's sentiments did not apparently find widespread support, and George H. W. Bush had high approval ratings at the end of the gulf war. Nonetheless, Buchanan's remarks received approval from many libertarians who encouraged him to run in the 1992 presidential primaries, which he did.[67] Buchanan also found support from more conventional conservatives, such as Joseph Sobran, then an editor at *National Review,* and the columnist Sam Francis, both of whom I will discuss shortly.

Buchanan also enjoyed new support as a result of Bush's backtracking on his promise not to raise taxes, again raising questions as to his commitment to conservative principles. Bush was further hampered by an economic decline. Buchanan's populist opposition to free-trade agreements such as the North American Free Trade Agreement (NAFTA) also played well among working-class primary voters. Buchanan failed to win any states in the 1992 primaries—which was not completely unexpected, given that his opponent was the incumbent president—but he did perform much better than expected in New Hampshire.

Buchanan also made opposition to mass immigration a key point of his campaign. Although the organized conservative movement had for some time claimed that it supported a color-blind society and emphasized that whatever concerns it had with immigration were not due to changes in the nation's racial and ethnic makeup, by the 1990s this claim was being put to the test. The demographics of states like California were changing rapidly, in part because of President Reagan's decision to sign a bill granting amnesty to a large portion of the nation's undocumented immigrants in 1986. Besides Buchanan's quixotic presidential runs, there were other political events in the 1990s that indicated that many Americans were concerned about the present wave of immigration, with the anti-immigrant Proposition 187, passed in California in 1994, being the most prominent example. In Buchanan, the nativist wing of the conservative movement had found a figure to rally behind.

The surge of support for Buchanan was a source of particular concern for neoconservatives, both because they disagreed with his positions on several key issues—notably foreign policy—and because they suspected he harbored anti-Semitic sentiments. Prominent neoconservatives began to build a case that Buchanan was motivated by anti-Semitism and even fascistic tendencies.[68] In his defense, Buchanan argued that he did not meet the definition of an anti-Semite in the sense that he harbored a hatred of Jews. Instead, he argued that the anti-Semitism charge was being thrown about in an attempt to intimidate him and smear his reputation. Joshua Muravchik, writing in *Commentary,** responded to this claim, arguing that there was sufficient evidence to demonstrate that Buchanan was an anti-Semite according to Buchanan's own definition:

PAT WAS CORRECT

* *NEOCON*

There may be no authoritative definition of the term [anti-Semitism]. But when a man falsely maintains that he is the victim of a "preplanned orchestrated smear campaign" by the Anti-Defamation League; when he is hostile to Israel; when he embraces the PLO despite being at adamant odds with its political philosophy; when he implies that Jews are trying to drag America into war for the sake of Israel; when he sprinkles his columns with taunting remarks about things Jewish; when he stirs the pot of intercommunal hostility; when he rallies to the defense of Nazi war criminals, not only those who protest their innocence but also those who confess their guilt; when he implies that the generally accepted interpretation of the Holocaust might be a serious exaggeration—when a man does all these things, surely it is reasonable to conclude that his actions make a fairly good match for the first, not the second, of Patrick J. Buchanan's two definitions of anti-Semitism.[69]

As was the case in the Mel Bradford incident, *National Review* weighed in on this debate between different conservative factions, again siding with the neoconservatives. The December 31, 1991, issue of *National Review* ran only one article, "In Search of Anti-Semitism," written by William F. Buckley. The article dealt both with Buckley's own efforts to root out anti-Semitism in American intellectual life and the accusation that Buchanan and his main supporter at *National Review*, Joseph Sobran, were anti-Semites. In the article, Buckley refrained from directly accusing either men of harboring a hatred for the Jews. He did, however, note the following: Buchanan is "a Gentile who said things about Jews that could not reasonably be interpreted as other than anti-Semitic in tone and substance."[70]

The accusation of anti-Semitism, which *National Review* tepidly endorsed, did not spell the end of Buchanan as a force in the conservative movement. In fact, in early 1992, the *National Review* actually endorsed Buchanan in the Republican primaries—to the outrage of many neoconservatives, both Jewish and Christian. They gave this endorsement largely because of the many problems the magazine's editors had with Bush.[71] After securing the Republican nomination, Bush received Buchanan's endorsement, and Buchanan was allowed to speak at the Republican National Convention, giving his now-famous "culture war" speech. Although the speech was initially well received, some conservatives subsequently blamed Buchanan's ferocious right-wing populism for Bush's loss.[72]

Buchanan and the paleoconservative movement he represented made one final political resurgence during the 1996 Republican presidential primaries. In the crowded primaries that year, Buchanan stood out as the candidate furthest on the right on cultural issues such as immigration and abortion. He also maintained his isolationism in foreign policy and populist opposition to free trade. Buchanan won a plurality of the vote in New Hampshire, Louisiana, Alaska, and Missouri. With the exception of Delaware and Arizona, which were won by Steve Forbes, moderate Republican Bob Dole won every other state. Dole lost badly in the general election, but the mainstream conservative movement had apparently rid itself of Buchanan and his supporters permanently.

Pat Buchanan remained a popular columnist and has since written a number of best-selling books, but he never again played a prominent role in the Republican Party. In his third-party run for president in 2000, he earned less than 1 percent of the popular vote. Buchanan's hope that grassroots American conservatives secretly opposed the ideological stances of the neoconservatives and would vote against them if they had a conservative alternative was proven mistaken. President George W. Bush was at least as committed as his father to free trade, and even more militant in foreign affairs. The conservative movement had again coalesced into a unified front.

Other Paleos: Joseph Sobran and Sam Francis

To my knowledge, the primary leaders of the conservative movement never excoriated and shunned a politician or political writer simply for having supported Pat Buchanan in 1992 or 1996. However, although support for Buchanan per se was not necessarily problematic, many of those who did offer him support had a record of making similarly inflammatory remarks that put them at odds with the mainstream conservative movement. This section will deal with two such figures, who found themselves increasingly isolated from the rest of the movement in the 1990s as the boundaries of acceptable conservative discourse continued to narrow.

Joseph Sobran was the best-known case of a conservative writer losing his position as a result of racist or anti-Semitic tendencies during this period. Sobran is a particularly interesting case because of his status within the conservative intellectual movement; he was a senior editor of *National Review* in the 1980s and a personal friend of William F. Buckley's. He was also known as a skilled stylist and was well liked by his colleagues. He had, however, a long record of making controversial statements about race, had a number of questionable personal connections, and regularly skirted the line between acceptable criticism of the relationship between Israel and the United States and outright anti-Semitism. His status within the movement, however, kept him protected from attacks from neoconservatives far longer than would have likely been the case had he been just another syndicated columnist.

Sobran was one of Buckley's protégés, and it was largely thanks to Buckley that he was able to begin his career as a writer.[73] In 1986, Buckley warned Sobran that his writing was increasingly giving the impression that he harbored a dangerous obsession with Israel.[74] Sobran did himself no favors by making anti-Israel remarks that were factually incorrect. According to Mark Gerson, Sobran at one point made the following, completely untrue, assertion: "Israel is a deeply anti-Christian country; it has even eliminated the plus sign from math textbooks because the plus sign (yes: +) looks like a cross! Yet because Israel depends on American Christians for tax money and tourism, it is has to mute this theme for foreign consumption."[75] Sobran further raised eyebrows with a 1986 column in which he enthusiastically praised a little-known magazine called *Instauration* that was openly racist and anti-Semitic.[76]

The neoconservatives were quick to attack Sobran, and it is in some ways remarkable that he was able to maintain his relationship with the flagship journal of the conservative movement for such a long time. Midge Decter, a neoconservative writer and the spouse of Norman Podhoretz, told Buckley in the mid-1980s that Sobran was a "crude and naked anti-Semite."[77]

Buckley did not believe Sobran was personally anti-Semitic, but he stated that a fair reading of his work could give that impression. Sobran refused to back down, however, and he disregarded Buckley's warnings. Buckley later asked Sobran to call him and read to him over the phone any future columns he intended to publish on the issue of Israel and the Middle East.[78] In 1990, Sobran sent Buckley two pieces for *National Review* that Buckley refused to publish. Sobran subsequently resigned as a senior editor, though he continued to submit articles on cultural issues to the magazine.[79] Sometime thereafter, Sobran ceased to write for *National Review*. When asked if there was anything Sobran could do in order to resume writing for the magazine, Buckley responded that it was no longer possible for *National Review* to have any affiliation with Sobran.[80] Although he continued to write, Sobran ceased to have a national platform to express his views. He was clearly bitter about his firing; he viewed his departure from *National Review* as a sign that the magazine was fully committed to neoconservatism.[81]

Sobran was not the only high-profile conservative writer to lose access to the major conservative publications. Sam Francis's downfall is also worth noting as an example of conservatives shunning one of their own. Whereas many of the figures who were once influential conservatives and were subsequently disavowed later became bitter critics of American conservatism, Francis was interesting in that he was a vocal critic of the American conservative movement long before he found himself locked out of the primary conservative publications.

Francis had a long relationship with the conservative movement. Upon completion of his PhD in English history, he went to work at the Heritage Foundation. He subsequently joined the staff of Senator John East of North Carolina. In the late 1980s he joined the *Washington Times* as an editorial writer. He also wrote a number of articles for *National Review* during this period. Francis was unique among paleoconservatives in that his critique of American culture was not based on his personal religious sentiments. The conservative writer James Burnham had an important influence on Francis's thinking—indeed, Francis wrote a book on Burnham's thought.[82] Like Burnham, Francis had a strong interest in the study of power and authority divorced from religious or other metaphysical arguments. Unlike many conservatives, Francis did not oppose a strong government, but he wanted to change who controlled the state.

In 1993, while still employed at the *Washington Times*, Francis published a book titled *Beautiful Losers: Essays on the Failure of American Conservatism*. In this book he took aim at all the elements of the conservative movement he disliked, and neoconservatives in particular. He noted that the "neos" were culturally separated from ordinary American life and had no connection with the white Protestants in the South and Midwest who were the natural base of the conservative movement:

> Of the twenty-five conservative intellectuals whose photographs appeared on the dust jacket of George H. Nash's *The Conservative Intellectual Movement in America Since 1945*, published in 1976, four are Roman Catholic, seven are Jewish, another seven (including three Jews) are foreign born, two are southern or western in origin, and only five are in any respect representative of the historically dominant Anglo-Saxon (or at least Anglo-Celtic) Protestant strain in American history and culture (three of the five later converted to Roman Catholicism).[83]

Francis became a vocal opponent of mass undocumented immigration in the 1980s.[84] This was not an unusual position for a conservative to take. However, while most conservatives rely on rhetoric regarding the rule of law or perhaps the challenges associated with assimilation when criticizing

immigration, Francis was open about opposing immigration specifically because it was changing the racial and ethnic makeup of the nation. His can-
didness on this issue set him apart even from other paleoconservatives like
Buchanan. Francis further had little respect for the contributions that nonwhites had made to the development of American civilization: "It is very
well to point to black cotton-pickers and Chinese railroad workers, but
the cotton fields and the railroads were there because white people wanted
them and knew how to put them there."[85] It is unsurprising that Francis was
viewed as an embarrassment to much of the conservative movement, and it
did not take long before his opponents found sufficient reason to push him
out of his position at the *Washington Times.*

YES

In 1994, Francis gave a speech at a conference sponsored by American
Renaissance, which is designated a hate group by the Southern Poverty Law
Center. In attendance was a young conservative named Dinesh D'Souza,
then a scholar at the American Enterprise Institute. D'Souza later recounted
the conference in a column for the *Washington Post:*

> Another popular speaker was Samuel Francis, a southern conservative
> who writes for the *Washington Times.* A lively controversialist, Francis
> began with some valid complaints about how the Southern heritage is
> demonized in mainstream culture. He went on, however, to attack the
> liberal principles of humanism and universalism for facilitating "the war
> on the white race." At one point he described country music megastar
> Garth Brooks as "repulsive" because "he has that stupid universalist
> song, in which we all intermarry." His fellow whites, he insisted, "must
> reassert our identity and solidarity, and we must do so in explicitly racial
> terms through the articulation of racial consciousness as whites. . . .
> The civilization that we as whites created in Europe and America could
> not have developed apart from the genetic endowments of the creating
> people, nor is there any reason to believe that the civilization can be
> transmitted to a different people.[86]

FRANCIS
WAS ★
RIGHT
HERE

Francis was fired from the *Washington Times* shortly thereafter. He continued to write for a number of smaller publications like *Chronicles* and edited the journal *Occidental Quarterly*—also categorized as a white nationalist
journal by the Southern Poverty Law Center. Having lost his respectability
within the mainstream conservative movement, Francis became even more
explicit and radical in his racial views. His syndicated column was dropped

by all mainstream publications except the *Pittsburgh-Tribune Review,* which also dropped him in 2004 after he wrote a column attacking interracial sex.[87]

Iraq and the Attack on "Unpatriotic Conservatives"

Throughout the 1980s and 1990s, most conservative purges were aimed at individuals whose public statements on race, religion, and ethnicity failed to evolve with a societal zeitgeist that was increasingly in favor of racial equality and intolerant of open racists. Few have argued that the conservative movement was morally or politically wrong to shed itself of such people. Perhaps more will be troubled, however, by the mainstream conservative reaction to dissenters on the issue of the war on terror and the invasion of Iraq.

In the 2000 presidential election, Governor George W. Bush did not present himself as a foreign policy crusader dedicated to spreading democracy throughout the world via military force. Indeed, Bush explicitly campaigned on a "humble" foreign policy platform and rejected "nation building."[88] Whatever Bush's personal views on foreign policy at the start of his administration, his cabinet was from the beginning filled with hawks such as Dick Cheney and Donald Rumsfeld. The terrorist attacks of September 11, 2001, presented the hawkish neoconservatives with an unprecedented opportunity to implement their vision of US foreign policy—which included regime change in Iraq, despite the fact that Iraq had played no role in the attacks on America.

The mainstream conservative movement was in nearly complete agreement with these policies, and books such as *An End to Evil* (2004) by David Frum and Richard Perle and *The Case for Democracy* (2004) by Natan Sharansky and Ron Dermer were warmly received by conservative commentators. During the early years of the Iraq war, most vocal critics of the conflict were on the left. There were a number of conservative opponents of the conflict, however, and they were furiously denounced by leading voices on the American right.

Shortly after the Iraq war began, David Frum wrote a cover story in *National Review* titled "Unpatriotic Conservatives," which provided a list of the major figures on the right that opposed the conflict. The essay opened by expressing surprise that any self-described conservatives could be opposed to the conflict: "From the very beginning of the War on Terror, there has been dissent, and as the war has proceeded to Iraq, the dissent has grown more radical and more vociferous. Perhaps that was to be expected. But here is what never could have been: Some of the leading figures in this antiwar movement call themselves 'conservatives.'"[89] Much of the essay was spent denouncing figures who had already been rejected by the mainstream conservative movement: Pat Buchanan, Sam Francis, Joseph Sobran, and other paleoconservatives. But the essay also attacked conservative figures that had genial relationships with the conservative movement up to that point, such as Robert Novak and Scott McConnell.

There were likely cases of conservatives with misgivings about the war choosing not to voice their concerns out of fear for their standing within the movement. Although we cannot know for certain the number of conservatives who chose to keep their feelings to themselves, there is anecdotal evidence that this occurred. For example, Damon Linker, then an associate editor for the religious conservative journal *First Things*, was discouraged from publishing an article making a conservative case against invading Iraq because doing so would give him a "reputation for being unreliable."[90]

There were other venues for antiwar conservative writers—notably the *American Conservative*, which was founded specifically to provide a platform for such voices. However, this magazine and various websites such as AntiWar.com had far less reach than established magazines like *National Review* and the *Weekly Standard*, the television station Fox News, think tanks such as the American Enterprise Institute, or talk radio show hosts such as Rush Limbaugh. In the early years of the Iraq war, the mainstream conservative movement was united in its enthusiastic embrace of George W. Bush and the war on terror.

It would be inaccurate to describe the conservative reaction to antiwar critics on the right as a purge. To my knowledge, no major figure in the conservative movement lost his or her job just for opposing the war. The reality is that most such critics had already been excommunicated by the mainstream movement or had never been a part of it to begin with. This is curious. There were many reasons why one might have opposed the invasion of Iraq on conservative grounds—indeed, given the degree to which conservatives are skeptical of the federal government's competence domestically, there was a surprising faith among conservatives in the ability of Washington to fundamentally transform Iraq and the rest of the Middle East. Yet with few exceptions (such as Novak), the mainstream conservative movement was fully on board with the project. Most of those antiwar dissenters on the right had already been dismissed by the movement as racists, anti-Semites, or general cranks. The mainstream conservative movement may have been right to reject such people. However, the leaders of the movement, and prominent figures within the GOP, may have been mistaken for their failure to seriously engage with the conservative critiques of the Iraq invasion in 2003 and before. When the neo-Wilsonian vision of foreign policy embraced by virtually all of the conservative movement led to a bloody quagmire in Iraq, conservatism in America suffered a blow to its reputation from which it has not yet recovered.

By 2004, many conservatives admitted that they had underestimated the challenges associated with the occupation of Iraq, and some figures, including George Will and William F. Buckley, admitted that the entire enterprise may have been a mistake.[91]

The Final (?) Expulsion of the Openly Racist Right

Much of this chapter dealt with the efforts of the conservative movement to distance itself from open and even suspected racists. However, those figures and institutions on the right that sincerely wish to rid the conservative movement of its racist elements have an apparently Sisyphean task. Every few months, it seems, a new case emerges in which a prominent—or not so prominent—conservative crosses the boundary into explicitly racist territory. After media exposure, this person is either fired from his or her position or resigns. Critics on the left are then able to use this as evidence that the conservative movement—and by extension, the Republican Party— remains a hotbed of racism, in spite of conservative claims to the contrary. A few recent examples, which occurred in rapid succession in 2013, will illustrate this.

In early 2013, *National Review* fired one of its popular contributors, John Derbyshire, over racially inflammatory remarks made at a different online venue, *Taki's Magazine*. Written in the context of the George Zimmerman trial, when a number of black authors were explaining the talks they had with their own children about the realities of racism in America, Derbyshire provided his own "non-black" version of the "the talk."[92] In the essay, Derbyshire described how he would speak to his own children about race, noting in particular the tendency of many blacks to engage in antisocial behavior. He specifically warned the reader to stay away from "concentrations of blacks not all known to you personally," as well as "heavily black neighborhoods."

National Review was swift to condemn Derbyshire for his remarks and publicly stated that the magazine would no longer publish his work. In explaining his decision, *National Review* editor Rich Lowry described Der-

68 *Chapter Two*

byshire's essay as "nasty and indefensible." He stated that the column constituted a "kind of resignation."[93] This was followed by a new headache for *National Review* when critics pointed out that one of the magazine's blogs also published work by Robert Weisberg, who had previously been an invited speaker at an American Renaissance conference. Lowry then also dismissed Weisberg and thanked the magazine's critics for pointing out Weisberg's other activities; his affiliation with American Renaissance had apparently been unknown to the magazine.[94]

One can argue that *National Review's* dismissal of Derbyshire came surprisingly late. His now-infamous essay in *Taki's Magazine* was only marginally more racially charged than his earlier work, including work he published for *National Review*. Furthermore, the magazine subsequently published an essay by Victor Davis Hanson titled "Facing the Facts about Race" that was similar to Derbyshire's column in many respects.[95] This led Camille Dodero to ask in *Gawker*, "Just how racist do you have to be for *National Review* to fire you?"[96]

Other conservative groups faced similar attacks for the comments made by their employees. In 2013, the Heritage Foundation came under fire when it was discovered that one of its policy analysts, Jason Richwine, had written his doctoral dissertation on the subject of IQ and immigration.[97] Specifically, Richwine argued that the United States should consider the mean IQ of a country when determining the number of immigrants from that country the United States will allow. His thesis was built on controversial research indicating that different human populations have different average levels of intelligence, and that this has economic and social implications. Although Richwine apparently made his case with sufficient scholarly rigor to earn his PhD from Harvard, when the subject of his early research became widely known, it proved embarrassing for Heritage. Although the Heritage Foundation supports restrictionist immigration policies, it generally attempts to make its case using nonracial arguments. Richwine resigned from his position shortly after the controversy began. It is worth noting that although—to my knowledge—Richwine has not subsequently found full-time employment within the organized conservative movement, some conservatives disagreed with how Heritage reacted to the scandal. Richwine was defended in *National Review*, for example.[98] The magazine also provided Richwine a platform to tell his side of the story.[99]

Another recent scandal involved one of Senator Rand Paul's prominent staff members. Rand Paul is the son of former congressman Ron Paul, who spent his career in Congress arguing for libertarian principles. One of Rand

Paul's aides was a former radio show host and newspaper columnist named Jack Hunter. Hunter cowrote Paul's book, *The Tea Party Goes to Washington* (2011). During his time working with Paul, Hunter's work was conventionally libertarian—opposed to the militant internationalism of the neoconservatives abroad and opposed to government intervention in the economy at home. However, in his earlier career, he had a record of making controversial statements. During his career in radio, Hunter called himself "the Southern Avenger," praised John Wilkes Booth, advocated secession, and insulted Spanish-speaking immigrants.[100] Hunter apologized for his earlier remarks and noted that his views had since evolved considerably. In an interview with the *Daily Caller*, Hunter remarked, "There's a significant difference between being politically incorrect and racist. I've also become far more libertarian over the years, a philosophy that encourages a more tolerant worldview, through the lens of which I now look back on some of my older comments with embarrassment."[101] Although Paul defended Hunter from charges that he was a white supremacist, Hunter nevertheless resigned from Paul's staff to avoid causing any additional embarrassment for the Kentucky senator.[102]

None of these preceding examples demonstrate definitively that the conservative movement is now completely inhospitable to racists. Critics on the left can correctly note that all of the people discussed in this section were perfectly welcome in the conservative movement until they were exposed, and it is unlikely that their colleagues were completely unaware of their views before that exposure. There is furthermore no way to know how many prominent conservatives harbor similar sentiments but have effectively couched their views in neutral language, providing them plausible deniability to charges that they are racists, anti-Semites, or white supremacists. It is also worth noting that the major institutions within the conservative movement have not been consistent in denying pundits and analysts with a history of racist remarks with new venues to express their views. However, these examples do demonstrate the mainstream right's continued willingness to jettison people who cross certain boundaries when it comes to discourse on race. The mainstream right in America appears to have determined that, at least publicly, it favors racial egalitarianism and disagrees with the left only on the means by which racial equality can be achieved.

This chapter did not provide an exhaustive list of figures on the right who were shunned by the organized conservative movement in America. There were additional minor figures, such as Revilo P. Oliver and others associated with *American Mercury*, who were ultimately rejected by conservatives for their anti-Semitism. On that note, it is worth mentioning that even Russell Kirk was targeted by the neoconservatives for remarks that he made in the late 1980s and early 1990s regarding Israel and US foreign policy. In a speech he gave at the Heritage Foundation in 1988, Kirk expressed his mixed feelings regarding neoconservatives. Although Kirk acknowledged their many accomplishments, he also condemned their "infatuation with ideology." He also noted that "it seemed as if some eminent Neoconservatives mistook Tel Aviv for the capital of the United States."[103] Kirk repeated this line in a later speech, and further suspicions were raised about Kirk as a result of his enthusiastic support for Pat Buchanan. A major public falling-out between the organized conservative movement and the author of *The Conservative Mind* would have been quite an embarrassment. However, Kirk died in 1994, sparing organized conservatism from the awkwardness such a scandal would have generated.

Will the Conservative Movement Maintain Control of Itself?

The preceding pages demonstrated the impressive ability of the mainstream conservative movement to define what ideas, groups, and individuals can properly be described as conservative. By doing so, they kept more radical—or simply different—right-wing voices from reaching a larger audience or exercising major influence on the Republican Party. It is not immediately clear that it will maintain that ability in the years ahead. William F. Buckley died in 2008. There is not presently a figure who commands such universal respect among conservatives, or one who has the power to almost single-handedly excommunicate figures from the conservative movement. This void has been noted by commenters on the left and right.

Writing in the *New York Times*, David Welch, a former research director for the Republican National Committee, argued that the rise of the Tea Party movement as a force in American politics was possible precisely because there is no longer a figure like Buckley to control the tone of the American right:

> In the 1960s, Buckley, largely through his position at the helm of
> *National Review*, displayed political courage and sanity by taking on
> the John Birch Society, an influential anti-Communist group whose
> members saw conspiracies everywhere they looked.
>
> Fast forward half a century. The modern-day Birchers are the Tea
> Party. By loudly espousing extreme rhetoric, yet holding untenable

beliefs, they have run virtually unchallenged by the Republican leadership, aided by irresponsible radio talk-show hosts and right-wing pundits. While the Tea Party grew, respected moderate voices in the party were further pushed toward extinction. Republicans need a Buckley to bring us back.[104]

Geoffrey Kabaservice, writing in the *New Republic*, also argued that Buckley would have opposed the more outrageous recent stances of the Tea Party movement and the Republican Party in general:

Buckley felt that outlandish stances discredited conservatism by making it seem "ridiculous and pathological," as he wrote to a supporter who had criticized his editorial. They allowed the media to tar all conservatives as extremists, and turned off young people. He insisted that conservatism had to expand "by bringing into our ranks those people who are, at the moment, on our immediate left—the moderate, wishy-washy conservatives" who comprised the majority of the Republican Party. "If they think they are being asked to join a movement whose leadership believes the drivel of Robert Welch," he warned, "they will pass by crackpot alley, and will not pause until they feel the embrace of those way over on the other side, the Liberals." Buckley consistently maintained that conservatism was the "politics of reality."

Needless to say, it is not a keen grasp of reality that distinguishes the politics of the Tea Party. The many Tea Partiers who fail to distinguish between liberalism and socialism are only repeating the errors of the Birchers, whom Buckley criticized for their "neurotic oversimplifications." In his later years, Buckley believed that the Republican failures in Iraq stemmed from a similar tendency to engage in ideological wishful thinking instead of hard analysis. He also cautioned against the tendency of conservatives to transform the cautious insights of supply-side economics, for example, into theological certainties, and to move toward ever more narrow and rigid definitions of doctrinal acceptability. Fanaticism and obsession, he believed, ultimately represented a surrender of individual freedom. As the high priest of the conservative movement, Buckley had latitude to advance unorthodox proposals such as the legalization of marijuana without being condemned for apostasy, but he also sought similar indulgence for other conservative thinkers.[105]

Not everyone agrees with these descriptions of Buckley. Other writers on both the left and the right have suggested that contemporary conservatism is still pursuing Buckley's goals and using his tactics. In *American Spectator,* a conservative magazine, Jeremy Lott argued that the Tea Party was using the same long-term strategy championed by Buckley, even when it meant sacrificing short-term partisan gains.[106] Criticizing conservatism from the left, Rick Perlstein argued that it is a myth that Buckley, or anyone else, ever reined in the "crazier" impulses of the American right, and trends we see within the conservative movement today are merely a continuation of precedents set decades ago.[107]

Even if one can accurately describe William F. Buckley as having kept the American conservative movement on a relatively short leash, it is unclear whether it would even be possible for a similar figure to emerge today. The means of communication have changed dramatically. In the 1950s and 1960s, it required a considerable capital investment to start a professionally managed magazine capable of reaching a national audience. Dissenters on the right who were excommunicated by the small number of publications that served as the official voice of American conservatism had no way to again reach a large audience. There were, of course, a number of smaller publications that remained available to thinkers on the more radical right in the second half of the twentieth century, such as the openly anti-Semitic *American Mercury* mentioned earlier, but these had a small number of subscribers and were not available on most newsstands. There was furthermore a qualitative, aesthetic difference between mainstream publications and more radical periodicals. No one could pick up a pamphlet published by a radical right-wing organization and mistake it for a respectable publication.

This is no longer the case. Print-based conservative media has experienced a long-term decline. *Human Events,* one of the oldest conservative newspapers, ceased publishing its print edition in 2013.[108] There was even some recent speculation that a libel suit could bring down *National Review,*[109] which has never been a profitable magazine—though the claims that *National Review* was on the verge of shutting down were premature.

The rise of alternative media is a major reason no single publication, think tank, or public figure will likely never again serve as a powerful ideological gatekeeper, on the left or the right. Although starting a print magazine is expensive, starting a professional-looking website is not. Aesthetically, a mainstream conservative website may be no superior to a fringe group's website. The undiscerning reader may not be able to tell which sites offer mainstream conservative views and which sites provide commentary far to the right of anything written at the *Weekly Standard* or uttered by a Republican candidate. If the reader finds these arguments compelling, he or she can easily follow a trail of URLs to similar material. Further, websites are easily accessed by anyone with a computer and an Internet connection. Someone with an inclination to read more radical perspectives no longer needs to seek out obscure books and publications and have them sent in the mail. This proliferation of online political material has also apparently made the threat of excommunication by the mainstream conservative movement less financially threatening. John Derbyshire, for example, is still paid for his weekly columns at *Taki's Magazine* and VDARE.com. A few years before, *National Review*'s decision to cease publishing Ann Coulter's work due to an anti-Muslim article she wrote after the 9/11 terrorist attacks (specifically, she wrote, "We should invade their countries, kill their leaders and convert them to Christianity") does not seem to have harmed her career as a writer and speaker.[110]

The many difficulties the Republican Party will face in the decades ahead, as I will outline in the concluding chapter, may also weaken the power of the organized conservative movement. Although the movement achieved impressive victories since its formation in the early 1950s, its ability to continue doing so is likely to wane. If the conservative movement continues to aggressively pursue the same policies it has supported for decades, and if it continues to falter in its efforts to implement those policies, its credibility will likely diminish, even among those who are naturally sympathetic.

It is possible that a slow decline in the power of organized conservatism in America will usher in a new era of progressive hegemony in American politics. However, it is also conceivable that organized conservatism's weakness will open up new space for right-wing ideological movements that have long lived on the fringe. Although progressives may view some of these alternative right-wing ideologies as a superior alternative to the conservative movement they have known for seven decades, they may find others much more frightening, should they ever find a large base of popular support.

I do not claim that this is inevitable. As others have noted, the end of the conservative movement has been incorrectly predicted many times before. Nor do I claim to know what, if any, kind of right-wing ideological movement will fill the void if *National Review*–style conservatism loses its credibility and influence. It is, however, worth our time to explore these dissident right-wing movements that have long waited to emerge from the darkness and take a place in popular political discourse. The rest of this book is dedicated to that task.

Small Is Beautiful

LOCALISM AS A CHALLENGE TO

LEFT AND RIGHT

This chapter examines the loose constellation of intellectuals, activists, and popular writers who advocate a return to smaller-scale communities and economies. They often emphasize the damage caused by the nation's relentless drive toward urbanization and suburbanization. They bemoan the degree to which Americans no longer possess geographic roots and note that this has led to a decline in strong, meaningful social ties—or, to use a term more commonly used in contemporary social science, a decline in social capital. These thinkers are often just as hostile to economic globalization and the demise of local economies as they are to the growing power of government in Washington, DC. They emphasize the importance of limits in an age obsessed with perpetual growth. In other words, this chapter is about the political philosophy of localism and its critique of contemporary American politics, economics, and culture.

Although I use the term localist throughout this chapter, I should note that many of the thinkers described in the pages ahead never used this word themselves; some preferred the terms agrarian, communitarian, or simply conservative to describe their political philosophies. However, I contend that each scholar, journalist, and public intellectual discussed in the forthcoming pages focused primarily on the same kind of issues, often reaching similar conclusions, which justifies my decision to combine their thinking under a single umbrella term.

One might object to the inclusion of a chapter on localism in a book on right-wing thought. Many of the people I describe in this chapter would not classify themselves as right wing or even as conservatives; some view themselves as cultural critics on the left. I do, however, believe the intellectuals and pundits whose work emphasizes the deracination of small, tight-knit communities in our era of global capitalism and centrally administered states can be described as right wing as I have defined the term. In my categorization, all major left-wing movements view universal equality as the ultimate normative ideal. All ideological movements that believe some other value or values should trump the drive toward greater equality and that will oppose the left when its policies threaten these values I categorize as right wing. *RIGHTLY SO*

On its face, one might expect the left to view localists as the most innocuous ideological category discussed in this book. Given the degree to which localists provide trenchant critiques of the warfare state and thoughtfully discuss the alienating and environmentally destructive effects of global capitalism, they surely have many things to say with which readers on the left can agree. However, the localist perspective is generally viewed with suspicion. Phrases like "states' rights" and "local autonomy" have been used to justify many of the policies, such as racial segregation, that the left, and much of the right, considers a shameful aspect of American history. Following the policy preferences of localists to their logical conclusion would furthermore require dismantling national programs and legislation designed to foster greater equality across the United States. Thus, writers and intellectuals within this ideological camp must perpetually defend themselves against charges that they are simply providing camouflage for other, less progressive motives.

This chapter will provide a survey of the disparate literature that influences localists today. We will see that this ideological current built its intellectual foundation on a wide range of work in economics and sociology, and in many ways it does not fit neatly within the standard left–right dichotomy of American politics.

I should note that compared to other chapters in this volume, it was difficult to determine which figures from this ideological camp are most influential and therefore deserving of our attention. Compared to other political philosophies, localism is not presently a strong and organized force in

American culture and politics. It has no prominent think tanks or politicians explicitly promoting its ideals. Thus, a group's or individual's inclusion in this chapter is based largely on my own subjective evaluation. Those whose works are frequently cited by contemporary localists, who wrote influential books, or who have a large number of readers and admirers today are discussed in detail here. This chapter does not provide an exhaustive coverage of all the figures who have made cogent arguments in favor of this political philosophy, however, and at the end of this chapter I will provide some suggested additional readings.

Agrarianism and the South in the Early Twentieth Century

It is not surprising that some of the earliest and most influential critics of government centralization, economic globalization, and urbanization came from the South. The Civil War and Reconstruction certainly left many Southern whites suspicious of federal power, and the leveling force of industrialization threatened the traditional agricultural economy of the region and the stratified social hierarchy with which it was associated. This does not mean that defenders of the traditional Southern way of life were simply sentimental reactionaries. In response to these trends, a group of Southern poets and intellectuals formed a literary and ideological movement designed to protect the mores of the South from what they perceived to be the more destructive aspects of modernity.

The best-known and influential writers and scholars from this intellectual tradition were known as the Southern Agrarians, and they evolved out of a discussion group at Vanderbilt University in the 1920s known as the Fugitive Poets. This was a period in which modernization was disrupting Southern society on a massive scale. Although legal and illegal efforts to maintain the system of racial hierarchy throughout the South remained rigidly in place at that time, other aspects of modernity were undermining traditional social norms. Railroads had spread across the region, thousands of Southerners had abandoned the countryside and small towns and moved to big cities, and more than a million Southerners—both black and white—had left the South entirely in the preceding decades.[1] During this period, the folkways of the Old South appeared to be on a path toward complete extinction. The Agrarians were determined to provide an intellectual basis for thwarting these seemingly inevitable trends without devolving into mere sentimentalism.

In 1930, the Twelve Southerners produced their manifesto, *I'll Take My Stand: The South and the Agrarian Tradition*. The book was a compilation of twelve essays on subjects such as religion, education, and economics. Some of the authors, such as Allen Tate, Donald Davidson, and John Crowe Ransom, were already well known as poets and critics, whereas others had not achieved widespread acknowledgement. Although they were not all in the same geographic location, they all knew each other and held similar cultural and political convictions. Throughout the book, the authors attacked both American materialism and puritanism, and they provided a spirited defense of the defeated and maligned Old South. They decried the degree to which the South was increasingly coming to resemble the industrial North in terms of economics and social fluidity.

The book did not call for secession or a new civil war, declaring that the idea was "finished in 1865."[2] To them, the real question was, "How far shall the South surrender its moral, social, and economic autonomy to the victorious principle of Union?"[3] The book was predominantly a critique of the ideology of unrestrained economic growth and the unrelenting march of industrialism, and it argued that this led to many social evils such as unemployment, the obsessive accumulation of superfluous goods, and a coarsening of human interactions. They presented agrarianism as an alternative to industrial civilization:

MUCH WORSE TODAY (21ST CENT.)

> Opposed to the industrial society is the agrarian, which does not stand in particular need of definition. An agrarian society is hardly one that has no use at all for industries, for professional vocations, for scholars and artists, and for the life of cities. Technically, perhaps, an agrarian society is one in which agriculture is the leading vocation, whether for wealth, for pleasure, or for prestige—a form of labor that is pursued with intelligence and leisure, and that becomes the model to which other forms approach as well as they may. But an agrarian regime will be secured readily enough where the superfluous industries are not allowed to rise against it. The theory of agrarianism is that the culture of the soil is the best and most sensitive of vocations, and that therefore it should have the economic preference and enlist the maximum number of workers.[4]

A LA LUDOVICI

I'll Take My Stand offered little in the way of a policy platform. It did not provide a series of reforms that would ensure the revival of an agrarian society in the South or elsewhere. The authors admitted this potential short-coming and instead offered their work as a vision of what a well-ordered society would look like.

Much of what the Twelve Southerners had to say about the alienating and isolating effects of industrial capitalism will be familiar to capitalism's critics on the modern left. The Agrarians were, however, in no way progressive as we use the term today. This is particularly glaring when we consider the issues of race, segregation, and slavery. When discussing slavery in the nineteenth century, the authors downplayed the institution as a catalyst for the conflict between North and South;[5] they even defended slavery as a necessary means of protecting society from the "menace" posed by free blacks.[6]

Agrarianism was most influential during the 1930s, well before the arrival of the conservative movement as we know it today. Buckley-style conservatism, which valued free-market capitalism both as a good in its own right and because it provided the industrial means of winning wars overseas, did not integrate the agrarian critique of industrialization into its policy platform. Given that many of the prominent conservatives in the postwar years were lifelong urbanites, they were less willing to embrace the agrarian's claim that only small villages and towns could foster genuine communities. Further, while conservatives in the postwar years believed that the United States and the Soviet Union represented two diametrically opposed economic systems, *I'll Take My Stand* argued that capitalism and communism were cut from the same industrializing cloth:

> Indeed, even now the Republican government and the Russian Soviet Council pursue identical policies toward the farmer. The Council arbitrarily raises the value of its currency and forces the peasant to take it in exchange for his wheat. This is slightly legalized confiscation, and the peasants have met it by refusing to grow surplus wheat. The Republicans take a more indirect way—they raise the tariff. Of the two policies, that of the Russian Soviet is the more admirable. It frankly proposes to make of its farmers a race of helots.[7]

There were many irreconcilable differences between postwar conservatism and Southern Agrarianism, and the Agrarians were marginalized by the end of World War II. Some prominent Agrarians never showed much interest in the postwar conservative movement. Allen Tate, for example, refused to write for *National Review*.[8] Some conservatives, such a Peter Viereck, returned the hostility, noting, "At their worst, [the Agrarians'] writings of

Buckley

the 1930's, and again in the 1950's, are merely a futile, back-to-1788 kind of conservatism, reflecting not the organic traditions of genuine conservatism but the lifeless ones of a contrived synthetic substitute. They are the Nescafé of conservatism."[9]

The relationship between Agrarianism and the new conservative movement was not entirely hostile, however. Russell Kirk, for example, was a well-known admirer of the Agrarians, though he was not a Southerner. The figure who did the most to bridge the gap between the Southern Agrarians and the postwar conservatives was Richard Weaver. Weaver was a native Southerner and strongly influenced by Agrarianism—he completed his master's thesis under John Crowe Ransom. In 1942, Weaver completed his dissertation, which later became his book, *The Southern Tradition at Bay.* As noted in the first chapter of this book, Weaver was an open admirer of the feudal order in the antebellum South, and this shows in his most famous work, *Ideas Have Consequences.* However, although Weaver was open in his admiration of the South, he also sought to universalize the ideals of the Old South. Also unlike the original Agrarians, Weaver eventually abandoned all hostility toward capitalism; he served as an editorial advisor for the *New Individualist Review*, a libertarian economics journal.[10] For these reasons, it would be incorrect to label Weaver's later work as part of the larger Agrarian intellectual tradition, a point made cogently by Weaver's friend and fellow conservative, Willmoore Kendall.[11]

Weaver was also less aggressively racist than many of the earlier Agrarians. In fact, he wrote curiously little about race at all. In 1957 he did write an essay for *National Review* decrying the push for racial integration.[12] However, this essay was less focused on defending segregation than on questioning the motives of those who championed forced integration. He argued that the push for civil rights for blacks was really an attack on private property and part of the larger effort to create a mass, undifferentiated society more amenable to a communist economic system. His writings on race were less openly racist than those of many of his colleagues at *National Review*, including William F. Buckley. Weaver died, however, before the greatest racial upheavals of the 1960s occurred, so there is no way to know how he would have reacted to these developments. As the twentieth century continued to progress, the original Twelve Southerners began to diverge on racial questions. Robert Penn Warren, for example, later became open to the idea of racial integration, whereas Donald Davidson remained a dedicated segregationist to the end.

The Southern Agrarians were an influence for many later conservatives, such as Mel Bradford and Thomas Fleming. However, it is not possible to fully disentangle the other ideas in *I'll Take My Stand* from its position on race, and for this reason few thinkers who desire a mainstream audience cite the work favorably. Although agrarianism, and localism more generally, are treated with suspicion because of their long association with racism and segregation, other writers have tackled many of the same issues from a perspective divorced from racial politics.

Wendell Berry: Kentucky Poet, Farmer, and Localist

Because of their openly reactionary attitudes toward race, the Twelve Southerners who wrote *I'll Take My Stand* are now rarely taken seriously as social critics. Another Southerner, born a generation later, picked up the banner of agrarianism and articulated its message in a manner that was racially neutral, or even antiracist. Wendell Berry was born in 1934 in rural Kentucky. Throughout his life he has been a poet, novelist, essayist, and farmer, and from his small agricultural community he emerged as a trenchant social critic. He earned degrees from the University of Kentucky in the 1950s and taught English at New York University in the early 1960s before returning to Kentucky, where he has since remained.

Like the other figures discussed in this chapter, Berry is concerned with the proper scale of human institutions. He believes the overall national economy should consist of many small local economies and that cities should not be larger than the surrounding local agriculture can sustain. He is distressed by the growth of agribusiness at the expense of small farmers, and as a Kentuckian, he is particularly incensed by the mining industry, which he claims cares little about the environmental degradation that results from strip mining.

Like Thomas Jefferson, Berry's ideal America is an agrarian republic, and he believes economic policies should favor small-scale economic enterprises. He is suspicious of the increasing concentration of power in the executive branch and skeptical about the bureaucracies that implemented welfare policies.[13] He is similarly skeptical of the warfare state and has been a vocal critic of the war on terror.[14]

Berry argued that small size and rootedness are both indispensable attributes of community: "If the word community is to mean or amount to anything, it must refer to a place (in its natural integrity) and its people. It must refer to a placed people. Since there obviously can be no cultural relationship that is uniform between a nation and a continent, 'community' must mean a people locally placed and a people, moreover, not too numerous to have a common knowledge of themselves and their place."[15] Berry thus believes in pluralism in the sense that the nation consisted of multiple coherent communities that differed from each other in significant ways, rather than pluralistic in the sense that large urban centers are pluralistic because they contain large numbers of people belonging to different racial, ethnic, and religious groups. To Berry, the diverse, tolerant metropolitan area cannot foster true community, and he supports the right of local cultures to separate themselves from the trends of industrialization and globalization.[16]

Berry is also a skeptic of many forms of technological innovation; he even had favorable things to say about the Luddites who destroyed textile machines because of the threat that they posed to their livelihood.[17] To Berry, new technologies, even if they increased economic efficiency, can be harmful if they disrupt communities. He described Americans' belief in limitless growth and innovation as "Faustian economics."[18] *LAISSEZ FAIRE*

One can immediately see the connection between Berry's thought and the earlier Southern Agrarian tradition. Indeed, Berry acknowledged that *I'll Take My Stand* had a profound effect on this thinking.[19] Unlike the Vanderbilt Southern Agrarians of the 1930s, however, Berry is a consistent anti-racist—though to be fair, many of the original Twelve Southerners also abandoned their attachment to segregation later in life. However, Berry's thoughts on race differ from those of contemporary progressives. He argues that racism is a symptom of a larger cultural sickness. Berry argues that slavery did not originate out of the belief that blacks were an inferior race. Instead, slavery began because people wanted to be "free from the obligations of stewardship."[20] Racist theories then followed in order to provide a justification for this practice. *{ NOTE*

Berry also expressed a negative view of the Great Migration of blacks from the Southern countryside to the urban centers of the North in the early twentieth century. While living in the rural South, American blacks possessed a number of useful skills, and many had the capacity to be competent farmers. Rather than encourage their migration into urban slums, racial conciliation would have been better achieved by policies that helped Southern blacks become owners of small farms. Although civil rights legislation has improved the political standing of American blacks, "their economic status has become more dependent, consumptive, and degraded than it was before."[21] Berry was skeptical of forced busing as a tool of school integration—not because he opposed the integration of schools but because "busing tends to distract attention from the much more widespread phe-

ANTI-BUSING

nomenon of segregation by economic subdivision."[22] He furthermore views busing as a further source of community disintegration; busing students from great distances necessarily broke the ties between teachers and the local community.

To Berry, the solution to the race problem was the rediscovery of community. And unlike the Twelve Southerners, Berry argued that the antebellum South never developed true communities as he understood the term, as "community, properly speaking, cannot exclude or mistreat any of its members."[23] He further believes that there are ways government could foster genuine community as he understood the term:

> Is this something that the government could help with? Of course it is. Community cannot be made by government prescription and mandate, but the government, in its role as promoter of the general welfare, preserver of the peace, and forbidder of injustice, could do much to promote the improvement of communities. If it wanted to, it could end its collusion with the wealthy and the corporations and the "special interests." It could stand, as it is supposed to, between wealth and power. It could assure the possibility that a poor person might hold office. It could protect, by strict forbiddings, the disruption of the integrity of a community or a local economy or an ecosystem by any sort of commercial or industrial enterprise, that is, it could enforce proprieties of scale. It could understand that economic justice does not consist in giving the most power to the most money.[24]

Robert Nisbet and *The Quest for Community*

Southerners were certainly overrepresented in the ranks of right-wing critics of modernity that focused on the problems associated with global capitalism and centralized government. Thus, it was not always clear the degree to which their defense of traditional mores was motivated by racial animus—though Wendell Berry is a clear exception to this. Other scholars, from non-Southern backgrounds, raised similar critiques, divorced from the rhetoric of racial hierarchy. Robert Nisbet, born in California in 1913, was one of the most erudite of these social critics. Nisbet is widely acknowledged as one of the most influential conservative intellectuals of the postwar period. He earned his PhD in sociology in 1939 and went on to help found the department of sociology at the University of California at Berkeley.

The Quest for Community, published in 1953, was Nisbet's first important book—and arguably his most important book. Like the Agrarians, Nisbet lamented the loss of community in modern life. Nisbet was quite specific in his description of community, and he made it clear that it meant something other than just one's neighborhood or municipality: "By community, I mean something that goes far beyond local community. The word . . . encompasses all forms of relationship which are characterized by a high degree of personal intimacy, emotional depth, moral commitment, social cohesion, and continuity in time."[25] A key idea running throughout Nisbet's work—including his later book, *Twilight of Authority* (1975)—is that the central state grows when intermediate institutions decline. Before the modern era, there were multiple sources of authority in the West. Increasingly, however, a greater share of power was assumed by the central state:

> At present time we are suspended, so to speak, between two worlds
> of allegiance and association. On the one hand, and partly behind us,
> is the historic world in which loyalties to family, church, profession,
> local community, and interest association exert, however ineffectually,
> persuasion and guidance. On the other is the world of values identical
> with the absolute political community—the community in which all
> symbolism, allegiance, responsibility, and sense of purpose have become
> indistinguishable from the operation of centralized power. In the
> Western democracies we have moved partly into the second, but not
> wholly out of the first. In this suspended position lie both our danger
> and our hope—our hope because we have not yet become anesthetized
> into moral passivity; our danger because manifestly these sources have
> become weakened and the spell of the political community has become
> ever more intense.[26]

Like many writers of his era, Nisbet was concerned with the totalitarian impulse, but he did not view democracy per se as a foolproof inoculation against totalitarianism. Nisbet argued that the unitary view of democracy and the pluralistic view of democracy must be conceptually disentangled. The unitary view of democracy, congruous with Rousseau's notion of a General Will, called for an end to all previous social loyalties—such as loyalties to regional and local authorities—and the "construction of a scene in which the individual would be the sole unit, and the State the sole association, of society."[27] According to this view, all other intermediate institutions fracture society and serve as a hindrance to social harmony. According to Nisbet, while a state built on this philosophical foundation may have all of the formal attributes of democracy such as political equality, it also creates

[handwritten margin note: ✷ NOTE]

"conditions of social dislocation and moral alienation."[28] Nisbet argued that democracy in this conception is no guarantor of freedom.

In contrast, the pluralistic view of democracy understands the importance of institutions and sources of authority that stand between the individual and the unitary state, and these institutions stand as the primary bulwark against totalitarianism. In an atomized society in which individuals live in a state of isolation, the attractiveness of a powerful central state as a source of meaning and belonging will grow. Smaller-scale institutions, which grow organically from the family, common interest, and social needs, are the best protection against the totalitarian impulse: "Only in their social interdependences are men given to resist the tyranny that always threatens to arise out of any political government, democratic or otherwise. Where the individual stands alone in the face of the State he is helpless."[29]

Nisbet's work was warmly received by conservatives, and many conservatives today claim him as an important influence. Ross Douthat, a conservative columnist at the *New York Times*, described *The Quest for Community* as "arguably the most important work of conservative sociology."[30] During his life, he wrote frequently for *National Review*, and he eventually left academia to take a position with the American Enterprise Institute. However, Nisbet remained somewhat aloof from the conservative movement and played little role in the debates that shaped the movement's direction.[31]

Nisbet's contemporary readers can see why Nisbet and the organized conservative movement kept each other at arm's length. Compared to many other prominent conservatives, Nisbet was more consistent in his condemnation of a unitary, powerful, and centralized state. Specifically, he abhorred the centralizing effect of war and its impact on families and communities. During war, institutions that stand between the individual and the state represent a dangerous source of inefficiency, and states thus have a compelling interest to weaken them. Wars also lead to drastic social dislocations. He lamented the fact that hawks on the right were categorized as conservative and reminded readers that before World War II, "conservatives had been steadfastly the voices of non-inflationary military budgets, and of an emphasis on trade in the world instead of American nationalism."[32]

Nisbet's critique of capitalism also makes it harder to place his work in an ideological movement that hails free-market capitalism as an absolute good. Although Nisbet was not an opponent of the free market and was certainly no socialist, he believed the rise of labor unions was an important, beneficial development, as unions represented a new form of intermediate organization.[33] He agreed with Joseph Schumpeter's analysis of corporate capitalism, noting that the rise of massive corporations owned by impersonal shareholders decreases the number of actual business owners and ultimately undermines the bourgeois order necessary for maintaining capitalism.[34]

Much of Nisbet's work now appears remarkably prescient, and Robert Putnam's book, *Bowling Alone* (2000) demonstrated that the decline in social capital that Nisbet lamented has only continued since the early 1950s. Indeed, *The Quest for Community* was written during a period when American civic life appeared—in retrospect—remarkably robust.

Christopher Lasch: Communitarian Socialist   BETTER INDIVIDUALIST

The localist perspective cuts across traditional ideological boundaries to a degree not found in the other political philosophies discussed in this book. Where most of the figures previously discussed can be categorized on the political right, or at least as conservatives of some sort, Christopher Lasch never presented himself as anything other than a man of the left. Equality was always one of his major concerns. He considered himself a socialist and a populist, and he was strongly influenced by both Marx and the Frankfurt School. Other influences, however, included Amitai Etzioni, a founder of communitarianism.[35] Lasch was also a powerful critic of the managerial liberalism that dominated American society during his lifetime, and much of his thought has been appropriated by contemporary localists. Despite his left-wing economic views, much of his social criticism echoed the critiques of traditionalist conservatives and even paleoconservatives; according to Paul Gottfried, by the time of his death, Lasch "might have been moving to the right of Pat Buchanan on many social issues."[36]

Lasch studied at Harvard and Columbia. He spent most of his academic career as a professor of history at the University of Rochester. Lasch first came to national attention for his best-selling book, *The Culture of Narcissism* (1979). This book covered a great variety of topics, including art, sports, the family, bureaucracy, and politics. Although Lasch remained firmly on the left, he argued that the left's energies were increasingly misdirected. Whereas the radical left was still railing against the "authoritarian personality," such a personality was no longer dominant in the postmodern world.[37] In its place was the now-dominant narcissist, who did not try to force his GREED values on others because he had no real values of his own aside from the desire to acquire goods. The narcissist has no real grounding in the past and no real social connections in the present. Lasch argued that the emergence of this personality type was the inevitable and reasonable response to contemporary social trends.

Lasch was concerned by changes in family structure, especially the degree to which child rearing was increasingly the responsibility of "surrogate parents responsible not to the family but to the state, to private industry, or to their own codes of professional ethics."[38] He further lamented the permissiveness exhibited by modern parents, as well as the growing obsession with authenticity. Lasch believed the family was the bedrock of a decent society, and the outsourcing of parental duties and the absence of parental authority was resulting in a generation of narcissistic adults. These trends were amplified by the pervasiveness of advertising and a culture that celebrates consumption and hedonism.[39]

Although he was a populist in favor of greater equality, Lasch was also critical of welfare liberalism, as it undermined individuals' sense of personal and moral responsibility, allowing them to treat their every misfortune as the inevitable result of social circumstances. Because liberals had abandoned the old republican ideals of discipline, responsibility, and self-denial, they had no grounds to oppose the culture of immediate gratification that modern capitalism requires. Further, while the demise of feudalism and authoritarian priests and kings presumably ushered in a new era of egalitarianism, Lasch argued that American capitalism had simply transferred earlier forms of authority to the authority of corporations and the managerial class:

> A new ruling class of administrators, bureaucrats, technicians, and experts has appeared, which retains so few of the attributes formerly associated with the ruling class—pride of place, the "habit of command," disdain for the lower orders—that its existence as a class goes unnoticed. The difference between the new managerial elite and the old proportioned elite defines the difference between a bourgeois culture that now survives only on the margins of industrial society and the new therapeutic culture of narcissism.[40]

Lasch also criticized welfare programs for alleviating some of the social harms associated with capitalism without addressing its major underlying problems. The paternalistic welfare state kept issues such as growing inequality from leading to radical political reforms. It furthermore fosters a childlike dependence on bureaucracies while simultaneously encouraging people to follow their worst impulses. The end result is a society that is simultaneously helpless and self-indulgent. The bureaucratic professionals who operate the welfare state additionally have little incentive to solve social problems, as social problems lead to greater demand for their services—and indeed have every reason to create new sources of discontent.[41]

Lasch was no mere reactionary longing for the return of a paternalistic aristocracy. However, he did point out the present-day elites lack some of the positive attributes possessed by the elites they displaced—indeed, they "retain many of the vices of aristocracy without its virtues."[42] Wealthy families were once rooted to a particular community, often retaining their status as local elites for many generations. As important members of their communities, it was understood that they had certain civic obligations.[43] Their sense of noblesse oblige was certainly motivated by self-interest, but their philanthropy nonetheless connected their lives to those less fortunate in their community. This was a key point in Lasch's final book, *The Revolt of the Elites and the Betrayal of Democracy* (1995).

Lasch argued that the United States was an increasingly bifurcated society, with elites controlling both the nation's economy and politics. The new upper class is largely defined by its separation from the rest of society, and because they presumably reached their status via merit rather than birth, they feel little sense of personal responsibility toward their communities. The wealthy sink their capital into "private and suburban schools, private police, and private systems of garbage collection; but they have managed to relieve themselves, to a remarkable extent, of the obligation to contribute to the national treasury."[44] He similarly was less antagonistic toward Middle America than his fellow liberals. Lasch acknowledged that much of the lower middle class in the United States exhibited "racism, nativism, anti-intellectualism, and all the other evils so often cited by liberal critics."[45] However, he also faulted the left for not recognizing this class's positive elements: "Its moral realism, its understanding that everything has its price, its respect for limits, its skepticism about progress."[46]

Although similarly concerned with the decline of community, Lasch rejected the Agrarian critique of urbanization, noting that a healthy civic society is just as possible within cities as in small towns and rural areas, and cities had further fostered new forms of civil associations such as the labor union. The problem, for Lasch, was not with cities per se:

> The best minds have always understood that town and country are complementary and that a healthy balance between them is an important precondition of a good society. It was only when the city became a megalopolis, after World War II, that this balance broke down. The very distinction between town and country became

meaningless when the dominant form of settlement was no longer urban or rural, much less a synthesis of the two, but a sprawling, amorphous conglomeration without clearly identified boundaries, public space, or civic identity.[47]

Although skeptical of capitalism, Lasch was also concerned by the decline of religion, particularly among elites whose attitude toward religion "ranges from indifference to active hostility."[48] Although Lasch does not appear to have been personally religious, he argued that religion was indispensable to maintaining a decent society. He did not, however, have positive feelings toward the religious right. Like liberals who turned to the therapeutic state to ameliorate the damage caused by capitalism, the religious right similarly failed to address the root causes of societal decline: "Adherents of the new religious right correctly reject the separation of politics and religion, but they bring no spiritual insights to politics. They campaign for political reforms designed to discourage homosexuality and pornography, say, but they have nothing to tell us about the connection between pornography and the larger consumerist structure of addiction maintenance."[49] Like the religious right, Lasch was concerned by the breakdown of the traditional family and the degree to which children were now raised by day care workers, but he argued that this was an inevitable result of a free-market culture that devalued unpaid work, such as taking care of one's own children.[50]

As a critic of both market and centralized-state solutions to social problems, Lasch sought to formulate a third way. He turned to populism as a potential alternative. He preferred it to the communitarianism of thinkers such as Amitai Etzioni and Alan Wolfe:

> Populism, as I understand it, is unambiguously committed to the principle of respect. . . . Populism has always rejected both the politics of deference and the politics of pity. It stands for plain manners and plain, straightforward speech. It is unimpressed by titles and other symbols of exalted social rank, but it is equally unimpressed by claims of moral superiority advanced in the name of the oppressed. It rejects a "preferential option for the poor," if that means treating the poor as helpless victims of circumstance, absolving them of accountability, or excusing their derelictions on the grounds that poverty carries with it a presumption of innocence. Populism is the authentic voice of democracy. It assumes that individuals are entitled to respect until they prove themselves unworthy of it, but it insists that they take

responsibility for themselves. It is reluctant to make allowances or to withhold judgment on the ground that "society is to blame." Populism is "judgmental," to invoke a current adjective the pejorative use of which shows how far the capacity for discriminating judgment has been weakened by the moral climate of egalitarian "concern."[51]

As part of his populist views, Lasch was clearly in favor of limiting wealth: "Luxury is morally repugnant, and its incompatibility with democratic ideals, moreover, has been consistently recognized in our political culture. The difficulty of limiting the influence of wealth suggests that wealth itself needs to be limited."[52]

N LIKE EXCEPT USE OF DEMOCRATIC

Like Nisbet on the right, Lasch is acknowledged as an important thinker on the left. Like Nisbet, Lasch's presumed ideological allies have shown little interest in incorporating his thought into their discourse. It is not difficult to see why. The apparent contradictions in his thought, as well as his tendency to take aim at both the left and right, left him with few disciples who could embrace every element of his thought. Feminists bristle at Lasch's cultural conservatism, particularly his attitude toward family.[53] Although economic progressives share Lasch's concerns about inequality, they are generally less skeptical about the welfare state. Nor have mainstream progressives shared his concern about the rootlessness of today's elites. In fact, books like Richard Florida's *The Rise of the Creative Class* (2002) openly celebrate the creation of wealthy, liberal enclaves largely disconnected from the rest of American society.[54] *GATED COMMUNITIES*

Localist Economists in the Age of Globalization

Economists, by the nature of their field, are concerned with the issue of efficiency. Their method of analysis further tends to treat human beings as though they are interchangeable, rational utility maximizers. This tends to be true whether they approach economics from a left-wing or a right-wing perspective. Opponents of economic centralization—both in the form of government and multinational corporations—can name few prominent economists among their numbers. I do, however, wish to highlight two important economists who defended the interests of the economy's smaller players, such as small farmers and shopkeepers, against both socialist economic reforms and the leveling force of global capitalism: Wilhelm Röpke and E. F. Schumacher.

YES

Wilhelm Röpke may seem an odd addition to this chapter. He was hostile to all forms of collectivism and strongly influenced by Ludwig von Mises, which may make it easier to categorize him as a libertarian than as a localist. He furthermore was one of the architects of Germany's amazing economic rebound after World War II. However, Röpke was also a strong proponent of a decentralized economy and wary of the effects of large corporations and monopolies. For these reasons, he continues to exert a major influence on localist thinkers.

Röpke was born in Germany in 1899 and experienced firsthand the upheavals of twentieth-century Europe. He served with distinction in World War I before earning his doctorate in 1921. He was an early critic of National Socialism, and he thus fled Germany after the Nazis took power. He moved to Turkey in 1933 and to Switzerland in 1937. In Switzerland, Röpke discovered what he considered a humane economic model, one that possessed a thriving market economy, decentralization, diversity without ethnic conflict, free trade, and economic self-reliance.[55] Among the Swiss, Röpke further found evidence that a modern economy does not necessarily have to destroy traditional communities and social arrangements.[56]

Röpke wrote of the virtues of a free economy at a time when continental Europe was under the control of two totalitarian systems, and he was equally critical of communists and Nazis for their brutality and their centrally planned economies. Although a staunch proponent of free trade between nations, he was less skeptical of the state than the Austrian School economists who were the predominant intellectual force opposed to socialism and planned economies at that time. Like many of the scholars and public intellectuals considered in this chapter, Röpke was convinced that intermediate forms of order, which stand between the individual and the state, were necessary to maintain a free society.

After years in exile, writing of the benefits of a free society at a time when the future appeared to belong to totalitarians of one stripe or another, Röpke found himself in a position to shape the economic system of Germany. Although his decision to leave Germany harmed his academic career in the 1930s, his long-standing opposition to the Nazis gave him great credibility at the conclusion of the war. In the years immediately after the war, the German economy remained under strict government control, leading to shortages, inflation, and a barter economy. Röpke argued that all of these policies needed to be undone if Germany was to become a free and prosperous society, and his writings strongly influenced the nascent Christian Democratic Union, the center-right political party that was the primary opponent of the Social Democrats.[57] In 1948, many of Röpke's preferred policies were implemented by Ludwig Erhard, who later became the chancellor of Germany and was inspired by Röpke's writings. The end of price and wage controls and the reintroduction of a sound currency were largely credited as catalysts for the so-called German economic miracle.

Although Röpke continues to inspire many libertarian thinkers, and during his lifetime he was a collaborator with libertarians such as Friedrich von Hayek, he warrants inclusion in this chapter because of the many ways he broke with standard libertarian doctrine. Whereas libertarians emphasize individual autonomy and sovereignty, Röpke focused on community. Like other figures in this chapter, Röpke opposed the "enmassment" of society.[58] He was distressed by the degree to which urbanization, proletarianization, and overpopulation were turning people into undifferentiated particles:

> People live in mass quarters, superimposed upon each other vertically and extending horizontally as far as the eye can see; they work in mass factories or offices in hierarchical subordination; they spend their Sundays and vacations in masses, read books and newspapers printed in millions and of a level that usually corresponds to these mass sales, are assailed at every turn by the same billboards, submit, with millions of others, to the same movie, radio, and television programs, get caught up in some mass organization, flock in hundreds of thousands as thrilled spectators to the same sports stadiums. Only the churches are empty, almost a refuge of solitude.[59]

Röpke argued that this state of affairs was unhealthy for both individuals and society, as it destroyed organic communities and paved the way for collectivism.

As a bulwark against mass society, Röpke favored a strong middle class, widespread property ownership, and the decentralization of state powers. He opposed the displacement of small farmers by gigantic agribusinesses, as well as the growing need for women to enter the workforce. He rejected the secular rationalism of many of his libertarian contemporaries, arguing that liberty developed naturally in places like the town hall meetings of colonial America and the cooperatives established by Swiss peasants.[60] Also unlike most libertarians, Röpke was not always critical of government intervention in the economy; in fact, it was sometimes necessary to guarantee a good society. He therefore rejected both true laissez-faire capitalism and a capitalism that accepted state policies that only benefited the oligarchs. Although he was a firm believer in economic freedom, he also recognized that unbridled capitalism could weaken communities and lead to a society of lonely, atomized individuals with nowhere to turn but the national government to solve social problems.

To allow for necessary state intervention in the economy without further promoting a mass society inclined to totalitarianism, Röpke turned to federalism, with broad powers delegated to smaller states, as well as other intermediate institutions that stand between the individual and the central state: "This is where federalism and local government clash with political centralization. It is here that the friends of the peasantry, the crafts, and middle classes, as well as the small firms and of widely distributed private property and the lovers of nature and of the human scale in all things part company with the advocates of large-scale industry, technical and organizational rationality, and giant cities."[61] Besides the centralization of government, Röpke also opposed the centralization of the economy into the hands of monopolists, thus favoring state action to break up monopolies whenever they appeared.[62] He further favored policies that would reverse the trend toward urbanization and lead to greater property and home ownership, though not in a manner that would encourage urban sprawl.[63]

Also unlike most of the leading libertarians of his day, Röpke was a deeply religious Protestant. He argued that "the ultimate source of our civilization's disease is the spiritual and religious crisis which has overtaken all of us and which each must master for himself. Above all, man is *Homo religiosus,* and yet we have, for the past century, made the desperate attempt to get along without God, and in the place of God we have set up the cult of man, his profane or even ungodly science and art, his technical achievements, and his State."[64]

Although Röpke is considered an architect of Germany's postwar economic rebound, many of his preferred policies were ignored. Although Germany developed a federal system, it never did follow the path of radical decentralization that Röpke proposed; the growth of big cities was not halted or reversed, and the largest and most influential industries were not broken up. It is largely those elements of his thought that were never translated into public policy that most inspire contemporary localists.

It is worth noting another German-born economist who sought to formulate an economic policy that respected community while acknowledging the realities of the modern economy. E. F. Schumacher was born in 1911. He moved to England before World War II and was a protégé of John Maynard Keynes. Like Röpke, Schumacher was influential after the war, assisting Germany with its economic recovery while working as an advisor for the

British Control Commission. Over time he became increasingly critical of Keynesian economics.

Schumacher became deeply concerned by what he called the "idolatry of giantism,"[65] and he called for an economic system on a human scale. His best-known work was his 1973 book, *Small Is Beautiful: A Study of Economics as if People Mattered.* Like other figures considered here, he noted that the modern economy and modern transportation tended to break ties of community and make people "footloose":

> Everything in the world has to have a *structure*, otherwise there is chaos. Before the advent of mass transport and mass communications, the structure was simply there, because people were relatively immobile. People who wanted to move did so; witness the flood of saints from Ireland moving all over Europe. There were communications, there was mobility, but no footlessness. Now, a great deal of structure has collapsed, and a country is like a big cargo ship in which the load is in no way secured. It tilts, and all the load slips over, and the ship founders.[66]

Societies in which most people are rooted to a geographic location are also societies in which people possess a clear sense of their place in the world. Schumacher argued that mass mobility "produces a rapidly increasing and ever more intractable problem of 'drop-outs,' of people who, having become footloose, cannot find a place anywhere in society. Directly connected with this, it produces an appalling problem of crime, alienation, stress, social breakdown, right down to the level of family."[67]

As the title of his book suggests, Schumacher was deeply concerned with the question of size. Unsurprisingly, Schumacher rejected the notion that nations must be large and businesses must be gigantic in order to be prosperous, and he provided many examples demonstrating his point. However, he did not think that everything must be small, noting that "man needs many different structures, both small ones and large ones, some exclusive, some comprehensive."[68] The important point for Schumacher was that different activities have different appropriate scales:

> We need both freedom and order. We need the freedom of lots and lots of small, autonomous units, and, at the same time, the orderliness of large-scale, possibly global, unity and coordination. When it comes to action, we obviously need small units, because action is a highly

personal affair, and one cannot be in touch with more than a very limited number of persons at any one time. But when it comes to the world of ideas, to principles or to ethics, to the indivisibility of peace and also of ecology, we need to recognize the unity of mankind and base our actions upon this recognition. Or to put it differently, it is true that all men are brothers, but it is also true that in our personal relationships we can, in fact, be brothers to only a few of them, and we are called to show more brotherliness to them than we could possibly show to the whole of mankind.[69]

WALL
STREET
GANG

Schumacher criticized modern economists for their obsession with quantifiable metrics such as gross national product, which tell us little about the quality of individual lives. He thought that economists had lost both the ability to recognize qualitative distinctions and to acknowledge the reality of limits to growth. Schumacher further argued that the maxim "everything has its price" leads to the devaluation of things people cherish for noneconomic reasons. In contrast to contemporary economic thought, Schumacher suggested "Buddhist economics" as a viable alternative.[70]

According to Schumacher, the Buddhist approach toward work and the accumulation of goods is fundamentally at odds with the approach taken by modern economists. Whereas Western economists view labor as a disutility that must be compensated for in the form of wages, "The Buddhist point of view takes the function of work to be at least threefold: to give a man a chance to utilize and develop his faculties; to enable him to overcome his ego-centredness by joining with other people in a common task; and to bring forth the goods and services needed for a becoming existence."[71] This view of work and production does not value the creation of goods for their own sake, nor does it oppose wealth per se, but it does reject the economists' assumption that "a man who consumes more is 'better off' than a man who consumes less."[72] This attitude toward economics also places a higher value on smaller, self-sufficient communities that consume only the resources needed to ensure basic needs are met. It rejects the extravagant waste of both renewable and nonrenewable resources in the quest for ever more consumption.

MAIN
STREAM
CONS
HOSTILE

Although Schumacher may have had much to say with which social conservatives could agree, his outspoken environmentalism, his critique of consumerism, and his concerns about giant corporations would find a limited audience among a conservative movement that predominantly looked toward libertarians for economic policy. For this reason, he had a much greater impact on environmentalists on the left than on the mainstream right. However, one can also hear echoes of Russell Kirk and other traditionalists in Schumacher's thought, and he remains an inspirational figure to localists today.

Rod Dreher: Crunchy Conservative

The localist movement, to the extent that it can even be called a movement, has received little attention from the mainstream right in recent years. Given the conservative movement's love for the free market and acceptance of—to use Joseph Schumpeter's term—creative destruction, it is little wonder that it pays little heed to warnings against excessive consumerism and sprawling suburbs. At a time when conservative magazines regularly defend Walmart from all criticisms[73] and Sarah Palin works to safeguard Americans' inalienable right to drink forty ounces of sugary soda in a single sitting,[74] it is no surprise that the movement has taken little interest in the rhetoric of limits. However, during the Bush years, Rod Dreher, then a writer at *National Review*, openly embraced the localist cause, attempting to formulate a set of communitarian principles he called crunchy conservatism.

Born in 1967, Dreher was raised in the rural South, though he did not remain there. He has spent much of his adult life in New York City and Dallas, Texas. Although a religious traditionalist—he started as a Methodist, then became a Roman Catholic, and is now an Orthodox Christian—Dreher embraced many lifestyle choices typically associated with the environmentalist left—buying organic fruits and vegetables from a local co-op, for example. He was further frustrated when conservatives in a Southern city refused to consider whether any limits should be placed on land development.[75] In defense of his brand of conservatism, Dreher published his manifesto, *Crunchy Cons*, in 2006, though he had presented his ideas on the subject in an earlier *National Review* cover story.

Unlike other figures in this chapter, Dreher did not make a point to emphasize how he differed from mainstream conservatives on issues of policy. In fact, he emphasized the degree to which the crunchy cons were conventionally conservative:

> We don't believe it's the government's job to guarantee social equality, only equality before the law and, within reason, equality of opportunity. Guns don't bother us (unless they're in the hands of criminals), and neither, as a general rule, does capitalism (unless it, too, is in the hands of criminals). We prefer Fox News to CNN, think of Lucianne

Goldberg as America's very own gimlet-eyed Auntie Mame, and count ourselves as members in good standing of the Vast Right Wing Conspiracy. . . . We honor the military, and are not embarrassed to say that this is the best country in the world—and we don't qualify that with a "but . . ." We proudly fly the flag on our front porch.[76]

Although not particularly different from other conservatives in the voting booth, Dreher argued that crunchy conservatives had a fundamentally different approach to life than other conservatives. In the opening pages of the book, he listed ten principles that crunchy cons believed. For example, they believe "culture is more important than politics," and "conservatism that does not recognize the need for restraint, for limits, and for humility is neither helpful to individuals and society nor, ultimately, conservative." Dreher was also clear that he did not have a list of public policies that would incubate the cultural developments he wished to see. Instead, he called on conservatives to reevaluate the way they were living their individual lives: "Politics and economics will not save us. If we are to be saved at all, it will be through living faithfully by the Permanent Things, preserving these ancient truths in the choices we make in everyday life."[77]

Throughout the book, Dreher cited conservatives such as Russell Kirk as inspirations, but he also acknowledged the influence of Schumacher and the left-wing author and journalist James Howard Kunstler. He shared social conservatives' hostility toward the lack of sexual restraint in contemporary America, but he criticized them for their relative silence on the issue of material acquisitiveness, noting that greed is no less a sin than lust.[78] Like other writers discussed in this chapter, Dreher is fond of small-town living, and he extolled agrarian values throughout *Crunchy Cons*. He did not, however, argue that crunchy conservatives needed to flee from cities to farms and small towns; at the time the book was written, Dreher was living in Dallas, though he has since moved back to a small town in Louisiana. He insisted that "anybody can live the crunchy-con way, no matter where you are."[79]

Although less critical of the conservative movement than any other writer discussed in this chapter, the conservative reaction to *Crunchy Cons* was mixed. Because of his close ties with the mainstream conservative movement, Dreher's critiques could not be simply ignored by conservatives, as is generally the case for writers such as Berry and Schumacher. Writing in the *National Review Online*, Jonah Goldberg argued that crunchy conservatives should not be disaggregated from the rest of the conservative movement, and in *Crunchy Cons*, Dreher simply confirmed what liberals inaccurately believe about conservatives.[80] According to Goldberg: "Crunchy conservatism reeks with the implication that mainstream conservatives really are the caricatures and stereotypes the left claims." He further criticized Dreher for his emphasis on superficial lifestyle choices, such as food preferences, rather than more substantive subjects. Writing in *American Spectator*, Florence King was even more critical, noting that Dreher was simply echoing the older liberal critique of American capitalism:

> If this all sounds familiar, it is. Except for its hosannas to homeschooling as a means of strengthening the family, *Crunchy Cons* is a back-to-the-future trip to the 1950s when similar books were all the rage. Reading Dreher is like re-reading *The Organization Man*, *The Lonely Crowd*, *The Affluent Society*, and all the various Split-Level-this and Two-Car-that alienation scenarios that poured off the presses during the Eisenhower years. The only one it does not resemble is *The Crack in the Picture Window*, which was mordantly funny.[81]

Since publishing *Crunchy Cons*, Dreher's work has become decidedly more critical of the mainstream conservative movement, and his ideas about how proper conservatives should distance themselves from American culture have grown more radical. He now proposes what he calls the Benedict Option, which entails creating communities that are largely withdrawn from the increasingly degenerate modern world.[82] Dreher now works as a blogger for the *American Conservative*.

Bill Kauffman: Front Porch Anarchist

The final figure in this chapter is well known to many libertarians, but Bill Kauffman's ferocious defense of small-town living and traditional values makes him a somewhat unusual figure within the libertarian movement. He has also been associated with the paleoconservative movement, but he describes himself as an anarchist and a "placeist." He counted the late Gore Vidal among his friends[83] and has written glowingly of Dorothy Day, Eugene Debs, Gene McCarthy, and George McGovern. He is also a lifelong Democrat, and he served as aide to New York senator Daniel Patrick Moynihan. Throughout his career he has extolled the virtues of Middle America. His work builds on many of the ideas discussed throughout this chapter.

Kauffman has described himself as a "reactionary radical" and is an un-

usual figure in that his sources of inspiration cut across ideological boundaries. His 2006 book *Look Homeward, America* was a description of those figures from American history he considered ideological fellow travelers:

> These reactionary radicals—a capacious category in which I include
> Dorothy Day, Carolyn Chute, Grant Wood, Eugene McCarthy,
> Wendell Berry, and a host of other cultural and political figures—
> have sought to tear down what is artificial, factitious, imposed by often
> coercive forces and instead cultivate what is local, organic, natural, and
> family-centered.
>
> In our almost useless political taxonomy, some are labelled "right
> wing" and others are tucked away on the left, but in fact they are
> kin: embodiments of an American cultural-political tendency that
> is wholesome, rooted, and based in love of family, community, local
> self-rule, and a respect for permanent truths. We find them not at the
> clichéd "bloody crossroads" but at fruitful conjunctions: think Robert
> Nisbet by way of Christopher Lasch, or Russell Kirk by way of Paul
> Goodman. Think, always, of things looking homeward.[84]

Although skeptical of the state, Kauffman is also a critic of how capitalism
and popular culture is leading to the homogenization of American life. His
2002 book *Dispatches from the Muckdog Gazette* told the story of his decision
to return to his home city of Batavia, New York, after living in Washington,
DC, and Southern California.[85] The book was an ode to the virtues of small
towns at a time when moving to one of the largest metropolitan areas in
the nation is considered a necessary precursor to success. Although Americans have always celebrated the nation's restless spirit, first crossing the Atlantic to form the initial European colonies, followed by the conquest of the
American West, and the current enthusiasm for metropolitan areas filled
with transplants from elsewhere, Kauffman attacked the cult of mobility:
"Mobility is a great sickness crippling America, withering its civic life and
deadening its spirit. But it remains undiagnosed, its symptoms mis-ascribed,
for only the mobile have microphones and cameras and printer's ink."[86] To
Kauffman, true civil society requires a sense of rootedness.

Like others within this intellectual milieu, Kauffman is a vocal critic of
American foreign policy. Like Nisbet, Kauffman decries the effect of war on
community: "War kills the provinces. . . . It drains them of their cultural life
as surely as it takes the lives of eighteen-year-old boys. I have written previously about how almost every healthy, vigorous cultural current of the 1930s

was terminated by US entry into the Second World War."[87] Like many nonin-terventionists who are not political progressives, Kauffman reminds readers of the older, antiwar conservatives who exerted influence before the postwar conservative movement. His 2008 book *Ain't My America* documents the "long, noble history of anti-war conservatism and middle-American anti-imperialism."[88] Although in contemporary discourse it often seems that support for military intervention overseas is the one hallmark of conservatism, Kauffman argues that traditionalist conservatives were once the most incisive critics of imperial ambitions. Kauffman listed conservative objections to virtually every American war and geographic expansion, including the War of 1812 and the Louisiana Purchase. He described Lincoln's opposition to the Mexican-American War as the future president's "finest moment,"[89] and he noted that the Anti-Imperialist League, which opposed the annexation of the Philippines after the Spanish-American War, largely based their opposition on conservative grounds.[90] He further noted that conservative Republicans were the most vocal opponents of America's involvement in both world wars.

Conclusion

This being but one chapter in a larger volume on nonliberal critiques of the conservative movement and American society, it was not possible to provide a thorough discussion of all the major proponents of agrarian and localist thought in the twentieth and twenty-first centuries. The decision to focus on the figures presented in this chapter rather than others was necessarily based on my own subjective evaluation of who remains relevant and influential. Other experts on this subject may object to several omissions or may argue that I incorrectly included figures that properly belong in another ideological category.

To partially remedy the shortcomings of this chapter, I want to briefly recommend a few other authors and books that the interested reader may find useful. For the reader interested in short essays and blog posts from contemporary localists, the website Front Porch Republic (http://www .frontporchrepublic.com/) is a useful resource. For a more thorough discussion of agrarian thought in the United States in the twentieth century, I suggest Allan Carlson's 2000 book *The New Agrarian Mind*.[91] This book discusses the Vanderbilt Southern Agrarians and Wendell Berry, but it also provides insights into the thought of lesser-known figures such as Liberty Hyde Bailey and Louis Bromfield.

The economic principles of distributism also served as an inspiration for many localists and agrarians. Distributism is largely based on Catholic social teachings and argues for widespread property ownership as an alternative to both monopolistic capitalism and state ownership of the means of production. Its primary twentieth-century proponents were G. K. Chesterton and Hilaire Belloc. Distributism strongly influenced Schumacher, who was a Catholic convert.

There are also figures associated with mainstream liberalism who have raised critiques regarding the alienating effects of modern life. *The Lonely Crowd*, written by David Riesman, Nathan Glazer, and Reuel Denney and published in 1961, discussed the rise of cosmopolitan, "other-directed" people who are "at home everywhere and nowhere."[92] There was also a renewed interest in declining community life among well-known commentators across the political spectrum after Robert Putnam published *Bowling Alone* in 2000. The localist critique of mass culture and contemporary capitalism is also occasionally reminiscent of the work of critical theorists such as Theodor Adorno.

At this time it would be difficult to claim that anything resembling a large localist movement exists in the United States. Although both parties will pay occasional homage to the principles of local control and autonomy, they are rarely consistent on this issue. On both the mainstream left and the mainstream right, localist arguments are typically made when it suits their ideological preferences. On issues such as abortion, legalized marijuana, the right to discriminate, and the regulation of businesses, few on the right or the left consistently champion the right of communities to determine their own policies.

It is not entirely surprising that an ideology of radical decentralization has not translated into a unified, mass-based organization with a single coherent platform. Different groups struggling for greater local, state, or regional autonomy or even secession often have very different ideological foundations, and thus working together is challenging and sometimes impossible. The neo-Confederate League of the South, for example, has very different criticisms of the national government in Washington, DC, than the champions of the Second Vermont Republic or the Cascadian independence movement. The localists' critiques of both monopolistic capitalism and bureaucratic efforts to alleviate poverty and inequality further hamper their efforts to find allies on either the left or the right. The localist critique of contemporary America has also been largely dismissed for its sentimental attachment to a bygone era and its choice to ignore the oppressive elements of small-town and rural life. To the extent that localism is influencing

American life, it often does so in the realm of economics rather than politics. There is presently a strong movement in support of locally produced agriculture, for example.

Whatever the validity of the localist critique of American politics, economics, and culture, the trend of "footlooseness" appears to be continuing unabated. Americans remain a highly mobile people, though geographic mobility declined somewhat as a result of the economic recession of 2007–2009.[93] Rural areas continue to have a difficult time retaining young people, particularly college-educated young people, as Patrick J. Carr and Maria J. Kefalas demonstrated in their 2009 book, *Hollowing Out the Middle: The Rural Brain Drain and What It Means for America.*[94] The reality may be that present economic conditions make high levels of mobility a necessity for most Americans, even those who prefer the comforts of rootedness and smaller-scale communities.

4

Godless Conservatism

THE CHALLENGE OF THE SECULAR RIGHT

Although this book is predominantly about right-wing ideological currents that differ fundamentally from the mainstream conservative movement on major issues of policy, the group considered in this chapter is somewhat different. On most issues, the activists and journalists described in the pages that follow are conventionally conservative. Being a religious skeptic or atheist does not preclude a person from wanting a lower capital gains tax or favoring a strong national defense. However, since the postwar period, conservatism in America has had a transparently religious quality; indeed, some conservatives have argued that conservatism and religion are impossible to disentangle. For this reason it is easy to understand why secular Americans do not always feel at home in the conservative movement.

INCLUDING OL

We might therefore think of secular conservatives as conservatives who reached their political conclusions by other means. Rather than developing policies around a religious view about the nature of humanity, secular conservatives have argued that conservatives can justify their worldview and public policy preferences on a purely rational basis. This chapter will discuss the often-contentious relationship between the conservative movement and nonbelievers and explain the secular case for conservatism.

Religion and the Early Conservative Movement

As previously noted, before the mid-twentieth century, there was not an obvious connection between religion and the political spectrum. Neither William Jennings Bryan nor H. L. Mencken would have seen how the New Testament leads to free-market economics, for example. Part of the connection between religion and economic views surely grew from communism's overt hostility toward religion. Religious believers had no choice but to reject Bolshevism, even if they had little interest in free-market economics as such, and their rejection of doctrinaire communism surely also spurred skepticism toward less extreme varieties of socialism. Later, the growth of the counterculture in the United States, which was almost exclusively left wing, drove religious Americans into the conservative camp.

It is also true that many of the founders of American conservatism as it is currently understood were devout religious believers. Some saw the cold war in explicitly religious terms. This was articulated most forcefully by Whittaker Chambers, who was a communist spy before converting to Christianity. As noted in chapter 2, to Chambers, religion was the only grounds for rejecting communism, and if atheists are correct, then communism is the only reasonable political order. To Chambers, communism was not principally an economic system. Instead, it was principally a vision of human life without God, "the vision of man's liberated mind, by the sole force of its rational intelligence, redirecting man's destiny and reorganizing man's life and the world."[1]

Although Russell Kirk cited many religious nonbelievers in *The Conservative Mind* (1953), in other works he was also clear that belief in "an enduring moral order" was a necessary characteristic of conservatives.[2] Kirk further noted that religion must be the foundation for any civilization:

> For culture comes from the cult. For the past three centuries, the cult of our civilization—that is, the Christian religion—has been declining in power. The principle reason for this decay has been the growth of the anti-cult of scientism, which is by no means the same thing as natural science. John Locke's religious rationalism has trickled down, among great many of the educated or half-educated of our own time, to perfect indifference or positive hostility toward a transcendent religion. And so the culture itself, the core of which was faith, begins to fall to pieces.[3]

It is interesting to note that although the base of the Republican Party is Protestant, Roman Catholics were heavily overrepresented among the intellectuals and journalists who founded the movement. William F. Buckley and L. Brent Bozell Jr. were Catholics. Russell Kirk and Frank Meyer both converted to Catholicism. Although tensions between Catholics and Protestants were still politically relevant in the United States after World War II, this did not apparently prove a stumbling block for the nascent conservative movement.

Of course, many of the most important figures in the early conservative movement were not religious at all. This was particularly true of the libertarians who shaped much of conservatism's economic direction. Secular Jews such as Milton Friedman and Ludwig von Mises were overrepresented among the economists who inspired conservatism. However, their thoughts on religion were apparently considered irrelevant to a conservative movement looking for an intellectual defense of the free market. Further, most of these thinkers did not have a problem working alongside religious conservatives. Hayek argued that religion was an indispensable buttress to a healthy society:

> Like it or not, we owe the persistence of certain practices, and the civilization that resulted from them, in part to support from beliefs which are not true—or verifiable or testable—in the same sense as are scientific statements, and which are certainly not the result of rational argumentation. . . . They did help their adherents to "be fruitful and multiply and replenish the earth and subdue it" (Gen. 1:28). Even those among us, like myself, who are not prepared to accept the anthropomorphic conception of a personal divinity ought to admit that the premature loss of what we regard as nonfactual beliefs would have deprived mankind of a powerful support in the long development of the extended order that we now enjoy, and that even now the loss of these beliefs, whether true or false, creates great difficulties.[4]

Other secular proponents of a free society, however, were less willing to compromise with proponents of a free society on the issue of religion. Ludwig von Mises, for example, was much more openly critical of religion than Hayek. We saw in chapter 2 that Ayn Rand's militant atheism cost her support from conservatives who may have been otherwise persuaded by her message. This was apparently a critical distinction to many early conservatives. One did not have to believe in a personal god to have a place in the movement, but there was no room for people who openly despised religion. William F. Buckley articulated the following position: "Can you be a conservative and believe in God? Obviously. Can you be a conservative and not believe in God? This is an empirical essay, and so the answer is, as obviously, yes. Can you be a conservative and despise God and feel contempt for those who believe in Him? I would say no."[5]

Besides Rand, other writers who might otherwise have long remained affiliated with the conservative movement found this too great a litmus test. One such figure had served as one of the original contributing editors for *National Review*: Max Eastman. Like Whittaker Chambers and Frank Meyers, Eastman was a former communist. Unlike others who ultimately rejected communism and became religious believers, Eastman maintained his unabashed atheism. Despite agreeing with William F. Buckley on most political issues, he found that the overt religiosity of the magazine required him to remove his name from the masthead. He explained his decision to Buckley in a letter to the editor:

There are too many things in the magazine—and they go too deep—that directly or casually side-swipe my most earnest passions and convictions. It was an error in the first place to think that, because of political agreements, I could collaborate formally with a publication whose basic view of life and the universe I regard as primitive and superstitious. That cosmic, or chasmic, difference between us has always troubled me, as I've told you, but lately its political implications have been drawn in ways that I can't be tolerant of. Your own statement in the issue of October 11 [1958] that Father Halton labored "for the recognition of God's right to His place in Heaven" invited me into a world where neither my mind nor my imagination could find rest. That much I could take, although with a shudder, but when you added that "the struggle for the world is a struggle, essentially, by those who mean to unseat Him," you voiced a political opinion that I think is totally and dangerously wrong.[6]

Although Eastman was certainly not the only prominent nonbeliever (OL) within the conservative movement, few others broke with organized con- yes servatism over the issue of religion. With the rise of the evangelical right as a political force in the 1970s, it became even clearer that Christian conservatives were the base of the Republican Party. Without their support, there was not a sufficient electoral coalition to elect Republicans and no real means of enacting any conservative policies, even those policies with no religious basis. Most prominent conservatives, regardless of their private beliefs, have since offered little criticism of evangelical Christianity. Jewish neoconservatives, for example, have apparently had little discomfort with a conservative movement principally supported by faithful evangelical Protestants.

Religion and US Politics Today

At present, the relationship between religiosity and ideological inclination can be seen both among elites and within the electorate. Whereas the principal religious divide in the United States during its first 150 years or so was between Protestants and Catholics (and Jews, to a lesser extent), today the key divide is between those who attend worship services with great frequency and those who attend services rarely or have no religion at all.[7] The relationship between religiosity and politics is strongest among non-Hispanic whites; among other racial and ethnic groups, religion is a weaker predictor of vote choice. Observant white Christians are perhaps the most important element of the Republican electoral coalition and are the main constituents of conservative politics.

The power of the religious right, even within the Republican Party, has weakened since 2004, when it could claim credit for securing the presidential reelection of one of their own: George W. Bush. The most prominent evangelical leaders of that time are now deceased (Jerry Falwell, D. James Kennedy), elderly (Pat Robertson is now in his mid-eighties), or disgraced (Ted Haggard), and there is not currently a group of conservative evangelicals who exhibit comparable influence within the Republican Party. The Tea Party is typically more concerned with economic issues than with social issues. Nonetheless, religion remains a key political fault line in American politics.

The difference in party affiliation among the religious and the less religious or nonreligious is partly attributed to differences in policy preferences. This is particularly true on culture war issues such as abortion and gay marriage.[8] There are, of course, religious Americans who support both abortion rights and gay marriage and secularists who oppose them, but the correlation between religious beliefs and attitudes toward these contentious policy issues remains strong.

Unfortunately for the Republican Party, religious observance has been on a steady decline for more than two decades in the United States, as I will discuss further in the concluding chapter. If religious observance continues to decline and religion remains such a strong predictor of party identification and ideology, then conservatism will weaken further as a political force in the United States. It is not necessarily true, however, that many key elements of conservative thought require a religious justification.

Is There a Secular Case for Conservatism?

It is unsurprising that the leaders of the conservative movement frequently cite the American founding fathers as sources of authority and inspiration. Much of the conservative movement treats the founding documents of the United States, such as the Declaration of Independence and the Constitution, with a near-religious reverence. For this reason, it is similarly unsurprising that today's conservatives look for evidence that the prominent leaders of the American Revolution and the framers of the Constitution shared their religious convictions. After all, if conservatism as it is understood in the American context is based primarily on both a Christian worldview and the insights of the original American patriots, then the founding fathers were surely Christians themselves. The reality, of course, is more complicated.

It is beyond my expertise to definitively declare what the founding fathers "really believed." However, there is ample evidence that many of the most important political figures in early US history were not precursors to Jerry Falwell. It is true that the overwhelming majority of Americans were Christians in the late eighteenth and early nineteenth centuries. However, the religiously unconventional were certainly overrepresented among the most influential early American leaders.

Many books have been written on this subject, arguing both for and against the notion that the founding fathers were pious Christians. Willmoore Kendall, one of the most erudite conservatives of his day, made a strong argument for the former position, pointing out the continuities between the explicitly religious Mayflower Compact and the more secular Declaration of Independence and Bill of Rights.[9] The preponderance of evidence, however, indicates that many of the figures most celebrated by contemporary conservatives were privately secular, or at least unconventional in their Christianity. Brooke Allen made this case persuasively in her 2006 book *Moral Minority*.[10]

Allen provided exhaustive evidence that Benjamin Franklin, George Washington, John Adams, Thomas Jefferson, James Madison, and Alexander Hamilton were all religious skeptics of varying degrees. Washington was generally silent about matters of religion, but his actions indicated that religion was not particularly important to him. Although he attended religious services regularly while serving as president, he refused to take Communion. When the preacher informed Washington that this set a bad example for others in the congregation, Washington's response was to cease attending services on the days that the sacrament was distributed.[11] Thomas Jefferson's rejection of biblical revelation is well known. John Adams similarly rejected basic Christian doctrine such as the concept of the Trinity and was an open Unitarian.[12]

Throughout American history, many presidents celebrated by today's conservatives would fail their religious litmus test. Although it is unclear what Abraham Lincoln personally believed about religion, it is true that he never joined a church, and many of his writings as a young man seem to indicate skepticism about religion. However, his obvious knowledge of the Bible and his frequent references to God in his speeches indicates that he was not hostile to Christianity. There was and remains considerable debate as to Lincoln's personal beliefs about religion. Allen C. Guelzo argued that Lincoln subscribed to his own brand of "Calvinized deism," and it is clear that Lincoln believed in some form of divine providence.[13] However, unlike George W. Bush and other recent Republican presidents, Lincoln apparently did not feel the need to ostentatiously explain his personal religious beliefs. A later Republican president was more open about his lack of conventional Christian beliefs. William Howard Taft was a Unitarian and never hid his lack of belief in the divine nature of Christ.

Although these examples may make evangelical Christians uneasy, they do indicate that the principles many conservatives embrace, such as limitations on government and the separation of powers, do not require a theological justification. The doctrine of original sin is one argument that conservative Christians rely on in order to justify their support for limited government: because mankind's nature is fixed, state-led efforts to reshape human behavior are doomed to fail. In contrast to some Enlightenment thinkers, proponents of this view contend that human beings are not a blank slate that can be molded by their social circumstances. In other words, religion provides the justification for what Thomas Sowell called the restrained vision of humanity. However, such arguments do not necessarily require a religious foundation, as many secular conservatives have argued.

From the absence of God (or multiple gods), it does not follow that human nature is infinitely malleable; our choice is not between the fatalistic belief in original sin and the belief that well-managed social institutions can correct all human shortcomings. One can also argue that human behavior,

including unfortunate human weaknesses, are largely hardwired by biology. ENR
Attributes such as greed, self-centeredness, ethnocentrism, violence, and
the impulse to believe in the supernatural may be a part of basic human nature as a result of natural selection; if these traits provided a reproductive advantage in ancient times, human beings still have these traits, and thus there
are limits to the efficacy of social interventions designed to correct them.[14]
For this reason, the secular conservative Anthony Daniels (who often writes
under the pen name Theodore Dalrymple) has argued that "the traditional
religious view is in some respects more accurate than the supposedly scientific, secularist view."[15]

This emphasis on the biological foundations of human behavior does not
just indicate that all human beings have limited potential but also indicates
that humans will differ in their capacities. People will differ in their levels
of intelligence, discipline, and time preference as a result of genetic inheritance, just as they differ in their heights. Some of these differences will have
social consequences, such as economic inequality. As long as people differ in
these traits—and there is presently no meaningful way to remove these differences—inequality will remain a persistent element of society. If there was
an immediate, total redistribution of wealth, inequality would nonetheless TOTALI-
eventually reemerge unless an aggressive state constantly enforced equality. TARIAN

Secular conservatives, like religious conservatives, argue that we have to
accept certain human attributes, such as material greed and ambition, as
"sown into the nature of man"[16] and design our social institutions in such a
way that causes the least harm. Thus, conservatives of all religious inclina-
tions tend to favor Madisonian arguments about political institutions that
weaken the dangers of ambition—such as separation of powers—and economic arrangements—such as capitalism—that channel greed in a socially
useful direction.

Secular Conservatives Today

At present, there are few prominent figures on the mainstream right who   I AM
are actively hostile to religion. Most atheist and agnostic conservatives ap-   NOT
parently have little problem making common cause with the religious con-   MAIN-
servatives. In recent years, however, many well-known conservatives have   STREAM
openly admitted their lack of belief. There has also been some recent push-
back from secular conservatives against religious conservatives who pro-
claim themselves as the only true conservatives. ONLY TRUE FAITH   A
The columnist George F. Will is the most prominent conservative writer   NEO-
to openly admit his rejection of religion. Will has been a prominent con-   CON.

WILL: A NEVER
TRUMPER NEO-CON,

DERBYSHIRE
A VIRTUAL ATHEIST

servative public intellectual since the 1970s, but for most of that time he said little about his own religious beliefs. Given his opposition to abortion, for example, one might have inferred that he was a conventional Christian. Will first publicly acknowledged his agnosticism in 2008 during an interview on the *Colbert Report*,[17] though he had hinted at his secularism in an earlier column that criticized intelligent design, a theory that rejects natural selection as an argument for the development of new species.[18] He finally spoke specifically about his lack of religion in an article in *National Affairs*. In this essay, Will did not claim to be hostile to religion, but he did declare that when asked his particular religion, he had to respond, "none."[19] He did, however, argue that nonbelieving conservatives should be friendly toward the religious:

> In fact, religion is central to the American polity precisely because religion is not central to American politics. That is, religion plays a large role in nurturing the virtue that republican government presupposes because of the modernity of America. Our nation assigns to politics and public policy the secondary and subsidiary role of encouraging, or at least not stunting, the flourishing of the infrastructure of institutions that have the primary responsibility for nurturing the sociology of virtue. American religion therefore coexists comfortably with, but is not itself a component of, American government.[20]

One reason Will's lack of religious convictions has not led to greater tension within the conservative movement stems from his general agreement with organized conservatism on the issue of abortion. Will does not appear to care very much about abortion per se, but he has stated that he believes *Roe v. Wade* was decided incorrectly. There are nonreligious arguments against abortion, as one can argue that life begins at some point before the end of the first trimester even if God does not exist, and some secular conservatives have made such arguments.[21]

This has not been true of all secular conservatives. Charles Krauthammer, also a secular conservative, argued that the pro-life movement needed to drop its focus on criminalizing early term abortions.[22] John Derbyshire, who wrote frequently for *National Review* before writing his infamous racially charged column in *Taki's Magazine*, was an even more vocal critic of the pro-life movement. Although Derbyshire was once a regular churchgoer, he ceased attending services in 2004, and in the following years he became more open about his lack of religion.[23] In a 2006 review of Ramesh

Ponnuru's pro-life manifesto, *Party of Death*, Derbyshire referred to the pro-life movement as a "cult" and a "frigid and pitiless dogma."[24] Derbyshire appears to be somewhat of an outlier, however, and few mainstream conservatives have been so aggressively critical of the pro-life movement.

Although atheist and agnostic conservatives are for the most part willing to respect the religious convictions of their believing political comrades, schisms do occasionally erupt. In early 2014, a controversy erupted when the group American Atheists announced its plan to attend the Conservative Political Action Conference (CPAC), the most important annual gathering of conservative leaders and activists in Washington, DC, sponsored by the American Conservative Union (ACU). The group had arranged to have a booth at the conference. This led to an immediate and angry reaction from many religious conservatives, most notably L. Brent Bozell III, president of the Media Research Center: *X-TIAN FANATIC*

> The invitations extended by the ACU, Al Cardenas and CPAC to American Atheists to have a booth is more than an attack on conservative principles. It is an attack on God Himself.
> American Atheists is an organization devoted to the hatred of God. How on earth could CPAC, or the ACU and its board of directors, and Al Cardenas condone such an atrocity?[25]

HOW CAN A PERSON HATE SOME-THING THAT DOES NOT EXIST?

In response to this criticism, the ACU backed down and uninvited American Atheists, though the group did attend the conference despite lacking a booth. In response, Charles C. W. Cook, an atheist conservative and staff writer for *National Review*, argued that atheism and conservatism were certainly not incompatible and that the conservative movement should make a greater effort to reach out to atheists. He went on to note that the same temperament that led to his atheism also led to his political conservatism:

> As it happens, not only do I reject the claim that the two positions are antagonistic, but I'd venture that much of what informs my atheism informs my conservatism also. I am possessed of a latent skepticism of pretty much everything, a hostility toward the notion that one should believe things because they are a nice idea, a fear of holistic philosophies, a dislike of authority and of dogma, a strong belief in the Enlightenment as interpreted and experienced by the British and not the French, and a rather tenacious refusal to join groups. Occasionally, I'm asked why I "believe there is no God," which is a reasonable

question in a vacuum but which nonetheless rather seems to invert the traditional order of things. After all, that's not typically how we make our inquiries on the right, is it? Instead, we ask what evidence there is that something is true. Think, perhaps, of how we approach new gun-control measures and inevitably bristle at the question, "Why don't you want to do this?"[26]

✗ Heather Mac Donald is perhaps the most vocal opponent of the Christian right's effort to place a religious litmus test on fellow conservatives. Mac Donald is a fellow at the Manhattan Institute and a contributing editor of *City Journal.* She regularly appears on Fox News and writes for conservative publications such as *National Review* and the *Wall Street Journal.* Unlike most figures associated with the mainstream right, however, Mac Donald has never shied away from fights with religious believers, and she has challenged the argument that values and morality require a belief in the supernatural. She has lamented elsewhere that the number of religious believers in the United States is "depressingly high."[27]

Many secular conservatives are respectful of religious belief. For example, the secular conservative S. E. Cupp has written a book vigorously defending American's right to religious freedom, even in the public arena.[28] Heather Mac Donald, however, has felt little need to defer to people who believe things that are, in her view, preposterous. She has noted on multiple occasions that petitionary prayer is a ridiculous practice.[29] She is further frustrated that so few of her fellow secular conservatives ever challenge the religious right.

At this point, it is not possible to discuss secular conservatism as a movement. There are a number of reasons for this. To begin with, the secularists on the right discussed in this chapter differ relatively little from typical religious conservatives on actual issues of policy, with occasional exceptions when it comes to issues such as abortion and gay marriage. Thus, they have little reason not to remain in a political coalition with more devout coideologues, even if it means enduring opening prayers and frequent invocations of God. They furthermore must acknowledge that a right-wing coalition that does not include religious believers would be very small. The 2012 American National Election Survey indicated that only about 5 percent of respondents both claimed that they were conservative or very conservative and that religion was "not important" in their life. Exit polls in the 2012 presidential election indicate that 70 percent of people with no religion supported Obama.[30]

Other secularists have not been vocal in their opposition to religion because although they do not personally believe, they argue that religion is, on the whole, a positive element in society. Anthony Daniels (writing as Theodore Dalrymple), for example, has argued "that it is impossible for us to live decently without the aid of religion."[31] He has further stated that "to regret religion is to regret Western Civilization."[32]

There is an additional reason some secular conservatives have chosen not to openly attack religious belief: religion is probably not going away. One proponent of this view is the atheist conservative and science blogger Razib Khan. Khan has long been interested in religion as a natural phenomenon and has argued repeatedly that human beings have a natural propensity for religious belief: "[Religion] is a natural phenomenon, it emerges simply from the structural biases of our minds and the modal paths of our lives. . . . You can't get away from God, he simply repackages himself in new forms, whether it be Crystals, as a Goddess, or as Kim Jong-il."[33] Thus, Khan is skeptical that zealous New Atheists such as Richard Dawkins or Sam Harris will successfully usher in a new era of enlightened, postreligious thought.

Although Khan argues efforts to eradicate religion will fail, he does not believe nonbelieving conservatives have a responsibility to keep quiet about their lack of religious convictions. In 2008 he began the website Secular Right (http://secularright.org/), which has since provided an outlet for a number of conservatives with no religious beliefs, including Mac Donald and Derbyshire. Rather than promote atheism or attempt to start a new movement, the site's writers make the case that conservative politics are not contingent on religion:

> We believe that conservative principles and policies need not be grounded in a specific set of supernatural claims. Rather, conservatism serves the ends of "Human Flourishing," what the Greeks termed *Eudaimonia*. Secular conservatism takes the empirical world for what it is, and accepts that the making of it the best that it can be is only possible through our faculties of reason.[34]

Conclusion

The conservative movement and the Republican Party with which its fortunes are tied face a serious challenge regarding religion. The religious are a key component of the Republican coalition and make up much of the conservative movement's leadership. A conservatism that was outwardly hostile toward the religious—or even simply chose to ignore religious arguments—would have a very small constituency. It is also true that religious observance is on the decline, and if this trend continues, then conservatives must increasingly make their case in nonreligious terms to remain politically relevant at the national level. The conservative columnist Kathleen Parker has argued that evangelicals are largely to blame for recent Republican electoral defeats:

> As Republicans sort out the reasons for their defeat, they likely will overlook or dismiss the gorilla in the pulpit.
> Three little letters, great big problem: G-O-D.
> I'm bathing in holy water as I type.
> To be more specific, the evangelical, right-wing, oogedy-boogedy branch of the GOP is what ails the erstwhile conservative party and will continue to afflict and marginalize its constituents if reckoning doesn't soon cometh.
> Simply put: Armband religion is killing the Republican Party. And, the truth—as long as we're setting ourselves free—is that if one were to eavesdrop on private conversations among the party intelligentsia, one would hear precisely that.[35]

It may be that the power of the religious right within the conservative movement and the Republican Party has been overstated. For example, it was widely assumed that Mitt Romney could never become the Republican presidential nominee because of evangelicals' hostility to Mormons.[36] However, these fears were apparently unfounded, as Romney won the nomination in 2012, and evangelical white Christians did turn out to vote for him.[37] This may not prove much, however. Whatever the theological differences between Mormons and evangelicals, politically they are similar. Mormons are, on average, some of the most consistent Republican voters, and Romney ran as a conventional social conservative. It is doubtful that evangelicals would turn out in great numbers for an openly secular candidate.

The American conservative movement faces a great challenge in the years ahead. Can it make its case to a secular audience without simultaneously losing support from the religious right? This will not be an easy problem to resolve, but this chapter has demonstrated that conservatism does not necessarily require a religious foundation. Although a thorough discussion of this issue is outside the scope of this book, I should also note that contemporary liberalism is not necessarily incompatible with religion, even evangelical Christianity.

Pundits and politicians have rightly questioned whether conservatism can successfully appeal to secular Americans. It is not a certainty, however, that conservatism will remain an attractive ideology for the religious. The association between religiosity and reactionary politics is relatively recent. One does not have to look far back to see examples of religion motivating radical politics as well. No one could fully understand the abolitionist movement of the nineteenth century without also understanding the Puritan religious fervor within many Northern states. As I noted above, William Jennings Bryan saw no contradiction between his Christian faith and his populist economic platform. Nor did his voters.

Aside from a handful of cultural issues and, for certain varieties of Christian dispensationalists, devotion to Israel, there is little direct connection between the writings in the New Testament and the mainstream conservative policy platform. Indeed, the inherent egalitarianism of Christianity could be interpreted in a way that implies the need for economic redistribution. Some prominent leaders on the evangelical left have made this very argument. Jim Wallis, a leading progressive evangelical, has long criticized the religious right, but he believes that we have entered the post–religious right era and that evangelicals will once again become the leading proponents of progressive social change.[38]

It is too early to tell whether Wallis will ultimately be proven correct. The relationship between religiosity and political behavior has not weakened in recent years, but it is possible that a new generation of evangelical Christians will be open to certain progressive policies. A political realignment in which the left becomes the ideology of the religious and the right becomes the natural home of secular Americans seems unlikely, and a rapprochement between secular progressives and theologically conservative evangelicals would surely require many compromises from both sides—compromises many do not appear willing to make. Still, given the relatively fluid relationship between politics and religion in American history, the possibility cannot be dismissed entirely.

Ready for Prime Time?

THE MAINSTREAM LIBERTARIANS

Compared to mainstream conservatism, libertarianism is a coherent ideological tradition, based on simple principles of self-ownership and nonaggression. This does not mean that libertarians are a united front in American politics. Indeed, there are probably more schisms and subcategories within libertarianism than within conservatism. Self-described libertarians disagree with one another on a wide range of policy and philosophical issues. Many chapters in this volume could have been dedicated to the varieties of libertarian thought. In the interest of space, I have chosen to disaggregate libertarians into just two categories: radical libertarians unwilling to make any compromises with the state or make common cause with conservatives, and libertarians willing to engage with the broader conservative movement in the interest of making marginal changes that advance their interests. The latter category will be the focus of this chapter.

The divide between libertarians that I emphasize in this chapter and the next roughly corresponds to the divide between libertarians who favor a minimal state (minarchists) and those who believe mankind requires no states whatsoever (anarchists). However, the two divisions do not perfectly overlap. There are minarchists who utterly reject the conservative project and have no interest in working with the broader conservative coalition. There have also been anarchists who enthusiastically supported certain Republican candidates, viewing such candidates as a vehicle for promoting antistatism.

What Is Libertarianism?

Before beginning our discussion of either brand of libertarianism, it is important to establish some basic principles on which virtually all libertarians agree and explain how libertarianism fundamentally differs from conservatism. There has always been a major tension within the American conservative movement. It perpetually finds itself having to find the correct balance between liberty and order. Born in revolution, led initially by patriots seeped in Enlightenment thinking, the United States has no true reactionary tradition. Thus mainstream conservatives cannot fully abandon the Enlightenment and classical liberalism without also turning their back on their own country's political traditions—nor have they, for the most part, attempted to do so. However, conservatives also break from some elements of laissez-faire, classical liberal thinking. For example, they typically subscribe to traditional religious beliefs and recognize that the state has at least some role to play in maintaining social norms.

Libertarians do not have a similar tension; they consider themselves as the true heirs of the classical liberal tradition. Indeed, as we saw in chapter 1, some prominent libertarians—such as F. A. Hayek—rejected the term libertarian and preferred to simply call themselves liberals. Libertarians further generally view themselves as the true successors of the American Revolution. As Brian Doherty put it, "The libertarian vision is all in Jefferson. Read your Declaration of Independence: We are all created equal; no one ought to have special rights and privileges in social relations with other men. We have, inherently, certain rights—to our life, to our freedom, to do what we please in order to find happiness."[1]

A key foundation of libertarianism is the nonaggression principle. Murray Rothbard described this principle as follows: "The libertarian creed rests upon one central axiom: that no man or group of men may aggress against the person or property of anyone else. This may be called the 'nonaggression axiom.' 'Aggression' is defined as the initiation of the use or threat of physical violence against the person or property of anyone else. Aggression is therefore synonymous with invasion."[2]

Libertarians also generally agree on the principle of self-ownership: "The right to self-ownership asserts the absolute right of each man, by virtue of his (or her) being a human being, to 'own' his or her own body; that is, to control that body free of coercive interference."[3] Thus libertarians reject any external effort to restrict what individuals can put in their bodies (prohibitions on drug use), the amount of money they can charge for their labor (minimum wage laws), the right to worship or not worship, however they see fit (efforts to enforce religious norms or outlaw religious practices), or to interfere with how individuals use their private property. This principle has an impressive intellectual pedigree, as it can be traced to John Locke, who stated, "Every man has a *property* in his own *person*. The *labour* of his body and the *work* of his hands, we may say, are properly his."[4]

Libertarians believe in cooperation. Indeed, they argue that human flourishing is impossible in the absence of cooperation, but they emphasize that cooperation must be voluntary and based on the principles of private property. Ludwig von Mises compared the spontaneous cooperation promoted by classical liberals with the state-mandated cooperation demanded by socialists:

> Now we wish to consider two different systems of human cooperation under the division of labor—one based on private ownership of the means of production, and the other based on communal ownership of the means of production. The latter is called socialism or communism; the former, liberalism or also (ever since it created in the nineteenth century a division of labor encompassing the whole world) capitalism. The liberals maintain that the only workable system of human cooperation in a society based on the division of labor is private ownership of the means of production. They contend that socialism as a completely comprehensive system encompassing all the means of production is unworkable and that the application of the socialist principle to a part of the means of production, though not, of course, impossible, leads to a reduction in the productivity of labor, so that, far from creating greater wealth, it must, on the contrary, have the effect of diminishing wealth.[5]

Libertarian writings are dominated by discussions of economics. Indeed, libertarianism can be thought of as an economic theory, and many of the most ferocious debates within libertarianism focus on the relative merits of different economic methods, such as whether some of the key assumptions of neoclassical economics are fundamentally flawed.[6] The same cannot be said of mainstream conservatism, and many of the most influential early conservative books (such as *Ideas Have Consequences* and *The Conservative Mind*) said little about how modern economies should be organized. In contrast, much of twentieth-century libertarianism was simply a restating of the arguments made by nineteenth-century liberal economists such as Frédéric Bastiat and Carl Menger. However, twentieth-century libertarians also made their own contributions to economic and political theory.

Robert Nozick is perhaps the libertarian thinker best known by contemporary political philosophers. Before Nozick's 1974 work, *Anarchy, State, and Utopia,* political scientists and philosophers in academia paid little attention to libertarian theory. Although the book probably changed few of Nozick's colleagues' minds, it did demonstrate that libertarian arguments needed to be taken seriously. *Anarchy, State, and Utopia* provided one of the most powerful and influential defenses of the minimal state and is considered one of the more compelling attacks on John Rawls's influential work, *A Theory of Justice,* a book that remains a major inspiration for contemporary progressives. Nozick explained his argument and their implications early in the work:

> Our main conclusions about the state are that a minimal state, limited to the narrow functions of protection against force, theft, fraud, enforcement of contracts, and so on is justified; that any more extensive state will violate persons' rights not to be forced to do certain things, and is unjustified; and that the minimal state is inspiring as well as right. Two noteworthy implications are that the state may not use its coercive apparatus for the purpose of getting citizens to aid others, or in order to prohibit activities to people for their *own* good or protection.[7]

This quotation in many ways perfectly sums up the libertarian argument. The work also makes a number of additional arguments that commonly appear in libertarian rhetoric, such as the claim that "redistributive justice" via taxation is analogous to slavery: "Taxation from earnings is on par with forced labor . . . taking the earnings of *n* hours labor is like taking *n* hours from the person; it is like forcing the person to work *n* hours for another's purpose."[8]

Although libertarians are in general agreement about basic premises such as the nonaggression principle, they differ on how these principles should be put into practice. For example, most people accept that individual human beings will not always recognize the property rights of others or other people's right to self-ownership. How should libertarians respond to predatory groups of individuals? Most libertarians argue that a state of some form is necessary to protect individual rights, but other state actions—whether to promote equality or to discourage individuals from engaging in behavior that harms only themselves—are unjustified and are themselves a violation of individual rights. Other libertarians go a step further, however, and reject even this minimalist state, arguing that even law enforcement and national defense can be conducted without a unitary state with a monopoly on justified violence.

Although one might expect that ideologues dedicated to radical individualism will find it difficult to engage in any form of collective action, libertarians have a long history of organizing academic groups and activist organizations. The Mont Pelerin Society, founded in 1947, was an early academic organization dedicated to promoting classical liberal ideals. Throughout the society's history, it has claimed many Nobel Prize winners as members, including Milton Friedman, F. A. Hayek, James Buchanan, and George Stigler. Dozens of libertarian journals have sprung up since World War II, both academic (*Quarterly Journal of Austrian Economics, Journal of Libertarian Studies, Independent Review*) and for a popular audience (*Reason, Inquiry, Liberty*). Libertarians have also founded dozens of think tanks at the national and state level (including, to name just a few, the Cato Institute, the Institute for Humane Studies, the Ludwig von Mises Institute, and the Foundation for Economic Education).[9] Libertarians created the most successful and long-lasting third party in American history. Libertarians are, however, prone to internal squabbling over (what appear to outsiders as) minor philosophical or policy differences—though the same could probably be said of any ideological movement.

Among libertarians who agree that some form of state is necessary, there is nonetheless disagreement as to what policies constitute an unjust invasion of personal liberty. Do sovereign states have the right to restrict immigration, or, as Bryan Caplan has argued, are immigration restrictions no less unjust than state-enforced racial discrimination within a nation's borders?[10] Can the state provide any sort of social safety net, or should all charity be strictly voluntary? How should a nation respond to threats abroad? Is preemptive war always unjust? Libertarians have long debated these issues.

Libertarians have always had an ambiguous place within the conservative movement. Some conservatives have emphasized the degree to which the two philosophies are compatible. Ronald Reagan, for example, once famously stated, "If you analyze it I believe the very heart and soul of conservatism is libertarianism."[11] Not all conservatives agree on this point. Despite the efforts of Frank Meyer and others to demonstrate that there is no contradiction between the two political philosophies, most intellectuals on both sides of the divide recognize major points at which the two are at odds. Many libertarians, for example, rejected the conservative efforts to use the military to contain communism during the cold war and rejected the Bush doctrine of the war on terror. The issue of war and the military was sufficiently important to some libertarians that they rejected the notion that they could make common cause with conservatives.

This animosity occasionally went the other direction as well. Russell Kirk, for example, was critical of libertarians, though he also had some favorable things to say about them. Kirk argued that the libertarian obsession with unlimited freedom was unhealthy and if put into practice would undermine the cultural framework that made the American system of ordered liberty possible. To Kirk, libertarian was often a code word for libertine, and conservatives were right to reject their moral vision:

> The libertarians are rejected because they are metaphysically mad. Lunacy repels, and political lunacy especially. I do not mean that they are dangerous: nay, they are repellent merely. They do not endanger our country and our civilization, because they are few, and seem likely to become fewer. . . . There exists no peril that American public policies will be affected in any substantial degree by libertarian arguments; or that a candidate of the tiny Libertarian Party will ever be elected to any public office of significance: the good old causes of Bimetallism, Single Tax, or Prohibition enjoy a more hopeful prospect of success in the closing years of this century than do the programs of Libertarianism. But one does not choose as a partner even a harmless political lunatic.[12]

The idea that libertarians are simply hedonists who want to free themselves from all traditional moral norms has long haunted the movement, and not without reason. Many libertarians were associated with various countercultural movements in the 1960s and 1970s, and to this day, libertarians focus a great deal of their attention on the injustice of the war on drugs. Libertarians counter that they do not oppose religion or traditional moral values—many are traditionally religious and conservative in their private lives—but they do oppose the state when it tries to coerce people into living up to a specific moral standard. Nonetheless, many conservatives have expressed suspicion that libertarians are primarily interested in drugs and sex. Conservative author Dinesh D'Souza made the following remarks when *Reason* hosted a "secular Christmas party":

Many libertarians are basically conservatives who are either gay or druggies or people who generally find the conservative moral agenda too restrictive. So they flee from the conservative to the libertarian camp where much wider parameters of personal behavior are embraced. To the sensible idea of political and economic freedom many libertarians add the more controversial principle of moral freedom, the freedom to live however you want as long as you don't harm others.[13]

Conservatives who would completely reject libertarianism on moral grounds face a problem. Most of the important economic theories to which mainstream conservatives subscribe were developed by libertarians or classical liberals. If conservatives rejected the work of Friedrich Hayek and Milton Friedman on the grounds that they were "metaphysically mad," they would have little respectable economic scholarship to justify their preferred economic policies. Thus conservatives have a habit of appropriating libertarian thought when it suits them and rejecting it when it does not. Conservative columnist Jonah Goldberg described conservatism's relationship with libertarianism as follows: "I always compared libertarians to the Celtic warrior-tribes often employed by British kings. They are incredibly useful as allies in battle, but you wouldn't want them to actually run things."[14]

Libertarians are divided on whether they should be willing to accept their status as a junior partner in the conservative movement. It is true that conservatives occasionally give libertarian economic views a thoughtful hearing, and some Republicans even try to implement libertarian economic ideas. But conservatives are also willing to ignore all other advice that libertarians provide. Some libertarians, understandably, find the divide between themselves and conservatives too great to join the conservative coalition. On the other hand, explicit, radical libertarianism has a limited appeal in the United States. The conservative movement, and the Republican Party it backs, perhaps represents the only chance libertarians have to see any of their policy preferences made into law.

For decades, many libertarians have been working closely with the conservative movement, pushing for antistate policies where they can, and occasionally making marginal gains. The leaders of the conservative movement have surely benefited from their scholarship and activism, even if they have typically ignored libertarian critiques of the warfare state and government efforts to promote individual virtue.

Libertarians who have worked within the mainstream right may shortly find themselves rewarded for their patience. Thanks to recent imbroglios abroad, supported wholeheartedly by neoconservatives, the traditional hawkishness of the conservative movement has likely been discredited in many people's eyes. Libertarian critiques of American foreign policy may finally get a hearing from other groups on the right. The declining religiosity in the United States may further weaken the power of social conservatives to dictate domestic policy within the conservative movement, making space for libertarian arguments regarding social policy. To regain lost electoral ground in the decades ahead, the Republican Party may find itself necessarily taking a libertarian turn.

Describing all of the internal philosophical and political debates within the libertarian movement is beyond the scope of this project. Nor, in the interest of space, will it be possible to thoughtfully discuss every important libertarian intellectual of the last seven decades. The rest of this chapter highlights many of the most important libertarian intellectuals and institutions that have often been associated with the larger conservative movement since World War II.

Conservatism's Favorite Libertarian: Milton Friedman

Although the conservative movement was happy to appropriate the arguments of many influential mid-twentieth-century libertarians, the relationship between libertarians and conservatives was often strained. Although Hayek was willing to work with conservatives, he made it abundantly clear that he was not one of them. Although many conservatives admired Ayn Rand's literary talents and embraced her antiredistributionist rhetoric, her aggressive hostility to religion caused a permanent rift between mainstream conservatism and her Objectivist movement—a movement that always considered itself distinct from libertarianism but nonetheless shared most of its views on public policy. Some libertarians were more willing to work directly with the conservative movement and viewed it as a vehicle for pushing their antistate agenda. Milton Friedman is the most notable figure in this category. As Brian Doherty noted, "Friedman . . . always tried, while remaining radical in his goals, to work within and among the institutions whose gears mesh with the wheels of the 'real world'—focusing his energy on the GOP, not the LP [Libertarian Party]; on *Newsweek* and not the movement magazine *Liberty*."[15]

Friedman is somewhat unusual within the libertarian movement in that he spent part of his career working for federal bureaucracies and he had a direct, meaningful impact on public policy in both the United States and abroad. During World War II, Friedman worked in the tax research division of the US treasury. While there, he helped develop the tax withholding system for the federal income tax—an aspect of Friedman's career that many libertarians criticize. Friedman earned his doctorate from Columbia University in 1946 and spent most of his teaching career at the University of Chicago. He continued to work after his retirement from the University of Chicago in 1977, later moving to California to take a position at the Hoover Institution at Stanford University. He also continued to advise governments, both formally and informally, for many years.[16]

Friedman established himself as a leading libertarian thinker in the United States with the publication of *Capitalism and Freedom* in 1962. The book is widely acknowledged as having a great influence on both conservatives and libertarians.[17] Compared to other dense, lengthy classic libertarian texts of the postwar period—such as *Human Action* by Ludwig von Mises (more than 800 pages) and *Man, Economy, and State,* by Murray Rothbard (more than 1,000 pages)—*Capitalism and Freedom* was not an extended doorstop book. The most recent paperback edition is barely 200 pages long.[18] The work is also rather straightforward, and noneconomists should have little difficulty following Friedman's arguments.

Although comparatively short, *Capitalism and Freedom* covers a vast number of topics, such as the folly of occupational licensing, the case for free trade, Friedman's thoughts on control of the money supply, and the case for a "negative income tax" as an alternative to the present welfare system. Friedman also argued that free-market capitalism was a solution to racial discrimination. He argued that discriminating against individuals on the basis of noneconomic characteristics—such as religion or race—is economically inefficient, and in the absence of state-mandated restrictions, the unfettered free market will punish those who engage in such irrational discriminatory practices:

> It is often taken for granted that the person who discriminates against others because of their religion, color, or whatever, incurs no cost by doing so but simply imposes costs on others. This view is on par with the very similar fallacy that a country does not hurt itself by imposing tariffs on the products of other countries. Both are equally wrong. The man who objects to buying or working alongside a Negro, for example, thereby limits his range of choice. He will generally have to pay a higher price for what he buys or receive a lower return for his work. Or, put the

other way, those of us who regard color of skin or religion as irrelevant can buy some things more cheaply as a result.[19]

One of the reasons Friedman was so influential was because he worked tirelessly to develop actual policies that were both hospitable to libertarian principles and had a realistic chance of being implemented. Friedman played a role in the abolition of the draft while working for President Nixon's Commission on an All-Volunteer Armed Force. Friedman stated that his role in this policy innovation was the most satisfying moment of his career.[20] He was also an early proponent of vouchers as an alternative to the current public school system. "School choice" has since become a popular Republican talking point.[21]

Friedman also had some influence on Pinochet's dictatorial regime in Chile, a fact frequently noted by many of Friedman's detractors on the left. Friedman gave a series of talks in Chile in the mid-1970s, and even had a brief meeting with Augusto Pinochet. He subsequently wrote Pinochet a letter in which he offered his advice on how to halt inflation and grow the economy.[22] Friedman argued that Chile's subsequent economic success was a real-world demonstration of the superiority of free markets, though other economists have challenged Friedman's interpretation.[23]

Friedman's status as an economist reached new heights in 1976 when he was awarded the Nobel Prize. This was a period in which libertarian economic ideas were becoming increasingly mainstream—Hayek had won the same prize two years earlier. Friedman received more public attention in 1980 when he, along with his wife, Rose, hosted the ten-part television series, *Free to Choose*, on PBS. In the series, which was also a book by the same name, the Friedmans made the case that capitalism had a strong track record for promoting human flourishing, whereas central planning always ended in disaster.

Friedman received the Presidential Medal of Freedom in 1988 and continued to work until his death at the age of ninety-four in 2006.

Funding a Movement: The Koch Brothers

Compared to other ideological groups on the right discussed in this volume, libertarians have attained a level of academic respectability. Although most social science departments are dominated by scholars that are left of center, the impressive number of Nobel prizes claimed by libertarian economists requires their opponents to take them seriously. The libertarian intellectual movement in America has an additional advantage over other right-wing groups that break from conservative orthodoxy: funding. Although many prominent philanthropists, as well as small donors, have helped fund the mainstream libertarian movement, none has achieved the level of influence of the Koch Family Foundations.

As of 2013, Koch Industries, based in Wichita, Kansas, was the nation's second-largest privately owned company, with annual revenue of more than $100 billion.[24] Koch is primarily known for its oil refineries and pipelines, though it also owns cattle ranches, as well as companies that manufacture fertilizer and consumer goods. Charles and David Koch collectively own 84 percent of the company. For decades, they have used their considerable wealth to promote libertarian causes.

The Kochs have been funding libertarian academic scholarship and activism since the 1970s. Rather than simply pouring money into lobbying activities (though they do engage in traditional lobbying), a great deal of the Koch fortune has been spent on organizations dedicated to promoting ideas, both within academia and among the general public. Perhaps most notably, Charles Koch provided the initial funding for the Cato Institute in 1977. Koch money also helped support the Libertarian Party—David Koch was the vice presidential nominee for the party in 1980. Koch's presence on the ticket allowed him to bypass campaign finance laws, and he spent more than $2 million on the campaign.[25] Since David's failed run for vice president, the Kochs have been less conspicuous in the public arena, but they have continuously given generously to libertarian causes. Brian Doherty explained the logic of the Koch family's philanthropic strategy:

> One longtime Koch lieutenant characterized the overall strategy
> of Koch's libertarian funding over the years with both a theatrical
> metaphor and Austrian capital theory one: Politicians, ultimately, are
> just actors playing out a script. The idea is, one gets better and quicker
> results aiming not at the actors but at the typewriters, to help supply the
> themes and words for the scripts—to try to influence the areas where
> policy percolate from: academia and think tanks. Ideas, then, are the
> capital goods that go into building policy as a finished product—and
> there are insufficient libertarian goods at the top of the structure of
> production to build the policies libertarians demand. Support that the
> Kochs have given to, for example, a think tank such as the Cato Institute
> or an organization that finds and supports young academics, such as
> the Institute for Humane Studies, is a means to increase the amount of

libertarian capital goods in order to create more of the ultimate political consumer good of libertarian policy.[26]

As part of the effort to promote libertarian "capital goods," the Charles Koch Foundation spends generously on programs in higher education and provides resources to libertarian scholars. The foundation provides research fellowships to undergraduate students, and it funds professors who develop new courses that educate students in libertarian or classical liberal ideas. The Koch Summer Fellow Program and the Koch Associate Program are designed to foster the next generation of libertarian think-tank employees. Koch money also led to the creation of the Mercatus Center at George Mason University.[27] The Mercatus Center, currently directed by Tyler Cowen, a libertarian professor and author, conducts academic research with real-world policy applications.

In recent years, the Kochs have received much attention as a result of their spending on grassroots advocacy organizations. In 1984, they founded Citizens for a Sound Economy (CSE), a group focused on organizing small-government activism. CSE had some success in the 1990s organizing against some of President Bill Clinton's policy initiatives. In 2004, CSE split into two new organizations, FreedomWorks and Americans for Prosperity. The latter group has been extraordinarily successful in organizing the economic conservative movement at the grassroots. Americans for Prosperity has both a large office in Washington, DC, and thirty-four state-level chapters. According to its website, Americans for Prosperity has more than 2.3 million activists.[28] The group played a major role in organizing the opposition to the Affordable Care Act, and it spent more than $40 million during the 2010 election cycle, which ended with Republicans regaining their majority in the House of Representatives.[29] As a result of this success, the Koch brothers have found themselves increasingly in the public spotlight, and they are frequently criticized by their ideological opponents.

A key critique of groups like Americans for Prosperity is that they represent so-called AstroTurf, rather than true grassroots, political involvement.[30] Groups like this spend great sums of money to generate the appearance of public support for economic libertarianism. Some liberal critics argue that the Tea Party movement is largely a sham orchestrated by corporate interests. Although the people who attend Tea Party rallies are sincere, their energies are being directed toward specific efforts that advance a corporate agenda. George Monboit provided one of the many progressive critiques of Americans for Prosperity and related organizations in the *Guardian*:

Most of these bodies call themselves "free-market thinktanks," but their trick . . . is to conflate crony capitalism with free enterprise, and free enterprise with personal liberty. Between them they have constructed the philosophy that informs the Tea Party movement: its members mobilise for freedom, unaware that the freedom they demand is freedom for corporations to trample them into the dirt. The thinktanks that the Kochs have funded devise the game and the rules by which it is played; Americans for Prosperity coaches and motivates the team.[31]

As the Tea Party movement became increasing influential in the early years of the Obama administration, progressive critics of the Kochs became increasingly vitriolic, though there is little evidence that this criticism is leading to a decrease in their spending. Americans for Prosperity, for example, spent millions of dollars on Wisconsin governor Scott Walker's 2012 recall election, leading Democratic National Committee chairwoman Debbie Wasserman-Schultz to declare, "Democrats were up against nothing short of an avalanche of secret, out-of-state and corporate special interest money amounting to a massive $31 million war chest for Governor Walker compared to just $4 million on our side." She went on to note, "In fact, the Koch brothers alone gave twice as much money to Scott Walker as the total amount of money raised by his opponent Tom Barrett."[32]

Not all criticism of the Koch brothers comes from the left, however. They have had critics within the mainstream conservative and the libertarian movements for decades. In 1979, *National Review* published a scathing article on the Cato Institute and the Koch Foundation, largely criticizing them for their noninterventionist foreign policy stance.[33] The criticisms from libertarians are more interesting; they largely stem from a falling-out between Murray Rothbard and his colleagues at the Cato Institute. Rothbard was critical of the Koch's brand of libertarianism, which downplayed the ideological movement's more extreme rhetoric in order to gain greater respectability and popularity.

Rothbard went on to join the Ludwig von Mises Institute, founded by Lew Rockwell in 1982. Rothbard and the scholars associated with the Mises Institute have since been vocal critics of the Koch brothers and the organizations they fund; they refer to the constellation of Koch-funded libertarian groups as the Kochtopus.[34] Rothbard and other libertarians faulted the Kochs for their insufficient radicalism and their rejection of Austrian economics. The next chapter will provide a more detailed discussion of Rothbard's anarchocapitalist thought.

The Cato Institute

Libertarians have a deserved reputation for wonkishness, which makes it unsurprising that one of the most influential think tanks on the right is libertarian in its orientation. As mentioned previously, the Cato Institute was formed in 1977 thanks to funding from Charles Koch. Ed Crane, who served as president of Cato until 2012, proposed the idea to Koch in 1976, and the organization opened its doors shortly thereafter in San Francisco. Murray Rothbard was one of Cato's first board members. The institute is named after *Cato's Letters*, a series of pamphlets distributed during the Revolutionary War.

The launching of a magazine, *Inquiry*, was an early Cato initiative. The magazine was clearly libertarian in its policy prescriptions, but it deliberately packaged its message in such a way to appeal to readers on the left, focusing on peace and civil liberties.[35] Cato also conducted seminars, public policy research, and a radio program titled *Byline*.

In its early years, Cato was generally Austrian in its economic views and amenable to Rothbard's anarchistic sensibilities; the next chapter will provide a more thorough discussion of Austrian economics. Over time, however, Cato's overall tone began to change. The institute hired its first non-Austrian economist, David Henderson, in 1979. Rothbard critiqued Cato's waning radicalism in a series of articles published in *Libertarian Forum*, leading to his break with the institute.[36] Cato moved from California to Washington, DC, in 1982, further undermining the institute's antiestablishment credibility to many radical libertarians.

Cato's work on economic issues such as social security, the national budget, environmental regulations, and welfare has heavily influenced Republican legislators, and it is understandable that commentators frequently speak of Cato as a conservative organization analogous to the Heritage Foundation. Many prominent Republicans were known for having a warm relationship with Cato. According to Nina J. Easton, writing in the *Los Angeles Times* in 1995, "On any given day, House Majority Whip Tom DeLay of Texas might be visiting for lunch. Or Cato staffers might be plotting strategy with House Majority Leader Dick Armey, another Texan, and his staff. Cato's constitutional law briefs cross the desks of conservative Supreme Court justices and their clerks."[37] However, the Cato Institute remains thoroughly libertarian on most issues and has been critical of Republicans on many occasions. For example, Cato has been generally noninterventionist in its foreign policy stance, which caused some friction with its occasional allies on the right. For example, it vigorously opposed the 1991 gulf war, causing it to lose funding from the conservative Olin Foundation.[38] Cato similarly supports drug legalization and liberalizing immigration reforms, both of which are opposed by most social conservatives.

Although the Cato Institute has long had a cozy relationship with the broader conservative movement and the Republican Party, it also emphasizes the degree to which it is nonpartisan and dedicated to libertarian principles. Indeed, we can easily find many additional examples of Cato criticizing Republicans. During George W. Bush's years in office, for example, Cato excoriated Republicans for their profligate spending.

It would be an exaggeration to say that Cato has always been consistent in its dedication to peace. For example, in a 2001 policy report, Cato published an article titled, "Terrorism's Fellow Travelers." The article attacked those who argued American foreign policy was to blame for the September 11, 2001, terrorist attacks, and it used rhetoric that would not have seemed out of place in the *Weekly Standard*: "The external threat now properly dominates our attention as Americans—who first crushed fascism, then contained and outlasted communism—prepare once more to confront the totalitarian menace."[39] Although Cato did oppose the invasion of Iraq, once it had occurred, Tom Palmer, a senior fellow at Cato, wrote in support of military efforts to defeat the insurgency, noting that "defeating [the terrorists] requires both bullets and a vision."[40]

Although Cato could not have begun without the Koch brothers, the think tank has recently had a contentious relationship with its most wealthy benefactors. In 2012, Charles and David Koch filed a lawsuit for control of Cato. For many years, control of the institute was divided between four shareholders: the Kochs, Cato president Ed Crane, and William Niskanen. When Niskanen died, the Kochs believed they had the option to buy his shares, but the institute argued that those shares belonged to Niskanen's widow.[41] Many libertarians believed the future direction of the Cato Institute was at stake in the lawsuit. Justin Logan, the director of foreign policy studies at Cato, worried that the Kochs wanted to transform Cato into a partisan organization focused on helping other Koch-backed groups and abandon its nonpartisan criticisms of American foreign policy and military spending:

> So what does all of this mean for foreign policy? The implications
> seem clear. Given the Koch brothers' stated desire to turn Cato into a
> research arm of Americans for Prosperity, Cato's foreign policy would
> in the best case be abolished and in the worst case would be influenced

by people like John Hinderaker, who was nominated to Cato's board despite calling himself a "neocon" and describing George W. Bush as "a man of extraordinary vision and brilliance approaching to genius." Other neoconservative Republican partisans like Charles Krauthammer have served as keynote speakers at recent Koch confabs. To the extent Cato had foreign policy output at all, it would be used to ratify the foreign-policy decisions made by the Republican political elite. The quality of those decisions in recent decades has been terrible, and I, for one, could not act in such a role.[42]

Later in 2012, the Kochs and Cato reached an agreement in which the shareholders' agreement was dissolved and Ed Crane stepped down as president. The agreement was apparently amenable to all parties, and it helped assuage fears that a "Koch-ified Cato" would lose all credibility as a source of independent libertarian scholarship.[43]

Reason

Like the mainstream conservative and progressive movements, libertarians have relied heavily on magazines and periodicals to spread their ideas. Libertarians have created a dizzying number of publications and pamphlets over the last fifty years. Most of these were short-lived, had a small circulation, or both. The longest lasting and most influential of these was *Reason*. Interestingly, its origins were no less humble than many of the now-forgotten libertarian publications, and at its founding in 1968 there was little reason to expect it would eventually become the most important libertarian journal of opinion.

When *Reason* began, it was just another obscure mimeographed newsletter with an inconsistent publication schedule. *Reason* was founded by Lanny Friedlander, who began the magazine in his undergraduate dorm room at Boston University. Under Friedlander's leadership, the magazine never had more than a few hundred subscribers. In 1970 Friedlander sold the magazine to a group of fans and contributors, and as a result of mental health problems, he largely vanished from the public eye. At the time of his death in 2011, he had played no role in the magazine for several decades, and he had largely been forgotten by the libertarian movement.[44]

Reason's circulation experienced a substantial increase in the 1970s. By the early 2000s it had tens of thousands of monthly subscribers, and its website received millions of monthly visits.[45] *Reason* readers will notice a number of ways in which it differs from other libertarian periodicals. Although it discusses economic issues, it is approachable for nonexperts who may have little knowledge or interest in subjects like Austrian praxeology or other technical economic jargon. It also focuses heavily on cultural issues. Finally, *Reason* has a generally upbeat tone, and it focuses more on libertarian successes than failures. Although the state has continued to grow, *Reason* emphasizes the many fronts on which libertarians have won important victories: price and wage controls have been discredited; the gay liberation movement has changed the cultural landscape and many alternative lifestyles enjoy widespread tolerance; there are fewer wars and fewer war casualties; the Soviet Union is gone and economic freedom is increasing worldwide.

In 2008, *Reason* published an article arguing that America was on the verge of a "Libertarian Moment":

> We are in fact living at the cusp of what should be called the Libertarian Moment, the dawning not of some fabled, clichéd, and loosey-goosey Age of Aquarius but a time of increasingly hyper-individualized, hyper-expanded choice over every aspect of our lives, from 401(k)s to hot and cold running coffee drinks, from life-saving pharmaceuticals to online dating services. This is now a world where it's more possible than ever to live your life on your own terms; it's an early rough draft version of the libertarian philosopher Robert Nozick's glimmering "utopia of utopias." Due to exponential advances in technology, broad-based increases in wealth, the ongoing networking of the world via trade and culture, and the decline of both state and private institutions of repression, never before has it been easier for more individuals to chart their own course and steer their lives by the stars as they see the sky. If you don't believe it, ask your gay friends, or simply look who's running for the White House in 2008.[46]

Although *Reason*'s general positivity is in stark contrast to other libertarian publications that see America as always slouching toward fascism or communism, its open celebration of increasing social liberalism has led to criticism from both traditional conservatives and other libertarians. In 2003 *Reason* published an article celebrating "35 heroes of freedom"—people responsible for making the world "groovier and groovier." Although the list included several well-known libertarian figures, such as Milton Friedman and F. A. Hayek, others on the list were more controversial: Larry Flynt (who "brought tastelessness to new depths, inspiring an unthinkable but revealing coalition between social conservatives and puritanical feminists—

and helping to strengthen First Amendment protections for free expression along the way"), Madonna ("The Material Girl led MTV's glorious parade of freaks, gender-benders, and weirdos who helped broaden the palette of acceptable cultural identities and destroy whatever vestiges of repressive mainstream sensibilities still remained"), and Dennis Rodman ("As a cross-dressing, serially pierced, tattoo-laden, multiple National Basketball Association championship ring holder, the Worm set an X-Men-level standard for cultural mutation").[47]

Articles like this did little to assuage the conservative fear that libertarians were predominantly focused on breaking down traditional social norms rather than on returning to limited, constitutional government. Kevin Michael Grace argued that *Reason*'s focus on sexual liberation demonstrated the juvenile nature of the publication, and argued that if we look at other spheres of life, then the United States has certainly not become freer in recent decades: "The world may be freer since 1968, but *Reason*'s editors do not live in the world, they live in the United States. And only a fool or liar would deny that America is much less free than it was 35 years ago. There is no sphere of human activity that American governments do not seek to regulate—except the sexual sphere."[48]

Fighting for Liberty Inside the Republican Party: The Paul Family

There are many reasons for libertarians to feel optimistic about the future of their ideological movement. The trend toward greater social tolerance—and hence less desire to use the state to enforce social conformity—appears to be continuing unabated. At the same time, consistent government failures continue to undermine trust in the state. Young Americans in particular are exhibiting greater distrust in government.[49] Although antiwar libertarians certainly lamented Bush's misadventure in Iraq, the end result of that conflict was an electorate increasingly skeptical of the use of American force abroad. In 2013, for example, the American public showed little interest in the Syrian civil war, in spite of hawkish arguments that the United States needed to intervene in that conflict. Libertarian scholars and activists cannot claim credit for all of these developments; some of these trends in opinion would surely have occurred in the absence of an organized libertarian movement. However, if the American electorate really is turning in a more libertarian direction, some of the credit must go to the most prominent spokesmen for libertarian ideas. In recent years, no proponent of libertarian ideas has had a greater reach than former Texas congressman Ron Paul.

Ron Paul served in the United States Congress as a Republican during three different periods. He was first elected to fill a vacancy in 1976 via special election, though he was subsequently defeated by his Democratic opponent in the general election. In 1978, he won his seat in a rematch against the Democratic opponent, and he held it until 1985—he did not seek reelection in 1984. He returned to Congress in 1997 and held his seat until his retirement in 2013.

Although many Republican elected representatives happily embrace libertarian rhetoric but immediately abandon libertarian ideals once they begin the actual business of governing, Ron Paul was unusual for his consistency. Even among libertarians, Ron Paul is something of a radical. He is an ardent supporter of Austrian economics, crediting Hayek and Mises for shaping his economic views, and he was friends with Murray Rothbard.[50] He was first motivated to get involved in politics by the policies implemented during the Nixon administration: price and wage controls and the decision to take the US dollar off of the gold standard.[51] Before his political career, Paul had served as a flight surgeon in the United States Air Force and later ran his own private practice in obstetrics and gynecology.

Although Paul served in Congress as a Republican throughout his political career, he abandoned the party in the 1980s, arguing that Republicans and Democrats differed little on the issues that mattered to him: "Ronald Reagan has given us a deficit 10 times greater than we had with the Democrats."[52] Paul ran for president as a member of the Libertarian Party in 1988, winning less than 1 percent of the popular vote. Paul considered another run in 1992, but he opted to support Pat Buchanan in the Republican primaries instead.[53]

After his 1997 return to Congress, Paul earned the nickname Dr. No for his penchant for voting against bills—even bills that were seemingly innocuous. He voted against providing earthquake relief to India, for example, and against giving a congressional medal to Mother Teresa. A story in *Texas Monthly* explained Paul's legislative philosophy:

> He quickly made a name for himself as the ultimate constitutional
> dogmatist: If it wasn't written in plain language in the Constitution,
> which allocated only a few specific powers to the federal government,
> he didn't believe in it. In Paul's view, government should provide for
> national defense, ensure fairness under the law, guarantee personal
> liberty—and get out of the way. That includes abortion, which he sees
> as murder, but he believes that the proper authority to deal with it is the

state, not the federal government. What galls him more than anything else is the sheer size of government. He likes to remind people that in 1909 the cost of government at all levels came to 7.7 percent of the total domestic economy. Today that figure is 50 percent.[54]

Paul ran for the Republican presidential nomination in 2008 and enjoyed impressive success despite his many disagreements with the party and the mainstream conservative movement; Paul was from the beginning a vocal opponent of the invasion of Iraq. He raised large sums of money on the Internet, and he had a large following on social media.[55] Unfortunately for Paul, online enthusiasm did not translate into real-world votes in the Republican primaries. His platform of abolishing the Federal Reserve, returning to the gold standard, legalizing drugs, and dismantling much of the American military apparently had little appeal to the average Republican primary voter. Paul finished fifth in the important Iowa caucus and fifth in the New Hampshire primary, ending any real chance he may have had to secure the nomination. He had fourteen total delegates pledged at the Republican National Convention in 2008, leaving Paul a distant fourth behind John McCain, Mike Huckabee, and Mitt Romney. He was not given an opportunity to speak at the convention.

Although Paul's lack of success among the Republican Party faithful is not surprising, it is also worth noting that some libertarians were ambivalent about Ron Paul. As a devoted Southern Baptist, Paul is personally more culturally conservative than many libertarians. Paul is also wary of free-trade agreements such as NAFTA and international bodies such as the World Trade Organization, not because he opposes free trade, but because such agreements represent government "managed trade."[56] Ron Paul is also a favorite of 9/11 conspiracy theorists and has consistently warned against plans to construct a "NAFTA superhighway." Some libertarians have thus argued that Paul is not helping the movement escape the stereotype that it is a hotbed of paranoid crackpots. In 2007, *Reason* published an article about Paul, asking, "Is he good for the libertarians?": "Still, many libertarians are either ambivalent or actively unhappy with Paul's campaign and the public attention it has gotten. They feel either that Paul is not libertarian enough in all respects, or are unhappy with linking libertarianism to certain aspects of Paul's rhetoric, focus, or past." The article, however, ultimately concluded that libertarians should support Paul in spite of their misgivings.[57]

The most damaging attacks against Ron Paul were based on a series of newsletters published under his name starting in the late 1970s. Although these newsletters were always libertarian in their policy prescriptions, they also included a great deal of racially charged language. In the *New Republic*, James Kirchik documented some of the more controversial elements of these newsletters, which included attacks on Martin Luther King Jr. They also predicted that the 1990s would be a period of tremendous racial violence and urged readers, "If you live in a major city, and can leave, do so. If not, but you can have a rural retreat, for investment and refuge, buy it." The newsletters also blamed "'civil rights,' quotas, mandated hiring preferences, set-asides for government contracts, gerrymandered voting districts, black bureaucracies, black mayors, black curricula in schools, black tv shows, black tv anchors, hate crime laws, and public humiliation for anyone who dares question the black agenda" for playing a role in instigating the 1992 Los Angeles riots.[58]

The most controversial and heavily criticized passages from Ron Paul's newsletters were written during a period when many libertarians, such as Ron Paul's friend and former staffer Lew Rockwell, were advocating a so-called paleolibertarian political strategy—a strategy I will discuss in greater detail in the next two chapters. For his part, Paul denied that he personally wrote any of these articles, or was even aware of all of their content at their time of publication. He apologized for their content, but without acknowledging that he had any role in what was being written in his newsletters, and to this day, no one has openly taken credit for writing the newsletters. In recent years, Paul's rhetoric has always been racially neutral, and his salvos against the war on drugs often note that drug laws are racially discriminatory. Nonetheless, Paul continued to receive criticism for articles written for publications that had his name in their titles. *Reason*, for example, criticized Paul for not taking greater responsibility for the racist and homophobic remarks that appeared in his newsletters; to truly take "moral responsibility" for the content of his newsletters would require "openly grappling with his own past—acknowledging who said what, and why. Otherwise he risks damaging not only his own reputation, but that of the philosophy to which he has committed his life."[59]

Ron Paul ran in the Republican presidential primaries again in 2012, again winning no states and few delegates. He left Congress in 2013. Although Paul never had a realistic shot at becoming president of the United States, he helped create the infrastructure of a libertarian movement that continues to be influential in Republican politics. After Paul's failed 2008 presidential bid, the energies of his movement were subsequently channeled into groups like the Campaign for Liberty, a nonprofit that argues for both a noninterventionist foreign policy and unfettered capitalism. In Congress, Ron Paul's role as the Republican Party's libertarian purist has largely been filled by Justin Amash, a member from Michigan who was first elected in 2010. The most influential successor to Ron Paul, however, is his son, Rand Paul, who was elected as one of Kentucky's representatives to the US Senate in 2010.

[handwritten margin note: VOTED TO IMPEACH TRUMP]

Like his father, Rand was previously employed as a doctor; he worked as an ophthalmologist in Bowling Green. Although he apparently shares his father's libertarian principles, Rand has been a more pragmatic legislator and actually works toward legislative accomplishments. He achieved national fame for his filibuster of a vote to confirm President Obama's nominee for director of the CIA, John Brennan. The Obama administration's drone policy was the catalyst for the filibuster.[60] The filibuster, which was assisted by other Tea Party favorites such as Ted Cruz, lasted for more than twelve hours. Brennan was eventually confirmed, but the stunt cemented Paul as a major figure in the Senate and brought new national attention to the issue of drone strikes.

Although Rand Paul has a higher profile, and a higher office, than his father ever achieved, many libertarians who embraced Ron Paul are skeptical of Rand. Rand, for example, rejects the term libertarian and prefers to call himself a "constitutional conservative."[61] Rand Paul further alienated some libertarians by endorsing Mitt Romney as the Republican Party's nominee in 2012, even though his father was still technically a candidate.[62] Rand has furthermore been more flexible in his stance against military interventions. He has also been generally conservative on issues such as abortion, gay marriage, and immigration.

In spite of some libertarian misgivings, Rand Paul is by far the most libertarian member of the US Senate. He is furthermore discussed as a presidential candidate who may have a genuine shot at winning the Republican Party's nomination in 2016. For this reason, most prominent libertarians have been relatively respectful in their criticisms of Rand. David Boaz, executive vice president of the Cato Institute, for example, stated, "I wish he was better on the gay marriage issue, and I'm a little concerned with his position on immigration. But I think when you combine his positions on economic issues with his views on foreign interventionism, and the surveillance state, you have a much better libertarian profile than I see in any other leading politician."[63]

Libertarian Youth Organizations

Youth organizations play a prominent role in most ideological movements, and many contributed to the transformation of the American political landscape in the postwar years. The left-wing Students for a Democratic Society (SDS) was the best known of these groups, but groups on the right exercised similar influence. Young Americans for Freedom (YAF) played a critical role in shaping the American conservative movement; it also demonstrated the major tension between libertarians and conservatives. As noted in chapter 1, Young Americans for Freedom was founded in 1960 under the leadership of William F. Buckley. The organization was a "fusionist" from the start. That is, it embraced Frank Meyer's argument that liberty and cultural conservatism were natural allies. It thus incorporated many libertarian and conservative ideas, which is made apparent in the group's founding document, the Sharon Statement.

YAF played an important role in securing Barry Goldwater's nomination and had a large membership throughout the 1960s—far more members than SDS. However, the unsteady coalition between conservatives and libertarians ultimately fell apart in 1969. The dramatic story of this schism was told in detail by Jerome Tuccille in his 1970 book, *Radical Libertarianism: A Right Wing Alternative.*[64] As the 1960s progressed, YAF was home to a growing contingent of libertarians with no interest in either social and religious traditionalism or in militant anticommunism. Culturally it had more in common with the New Left than with the conservatives. Some prominent radical libertarians, such as Karl Hess and Murray Rothbard, urged libertarian members of YAF to leave the organization altogether and form a new group. Rothbard, for example, wrote an open letter to the YAF convention making this point: "Why don't you get out, form your own organization, breathe the clear air of freedom, and then take your stand, proudly and squarely, not with the despotism of the power elite and the government of the United States, but with the rising movement in opposition to that government."[65]

The traditional conservatives in YAF also indicated that they wanted the radical libertarians to leave their organization, or at least acquiesce to the group's conservative leadership on major issues. At the 1969 YAF convention in St. Louis, all of the scheduled speakers were mainstream conservatives, such as Buckley. Karl Hess came to the convention, but he was informed that he would not be given a chance to officially address the organization. Hess's son then announced that a miniconvention for libertarians would be held outside after Buckley's speech. The conservatives were apparently surprised by the number of libertarian dissidents at the conference, as approximately a quarter of all attendees showed up to hear Karl Hess deliver his message. Hess encouraged the radical YAFers to split off from YAF and instead work independently or with New Left organizations such as the SDS.[66]

Although the conservatives in YAF embraced the war in Vietnam, one of the libertarian attendees openly burned a draft card on the floor. By the end of the convention, the participants were thoroughly polarized. Although the conservative faction of YAF maintained control of the organization and passed a resolution condemning the radicals, the convention demonstrated that the ideological chasm between the conservatives and the radical libertarians was unbridgeable. Tuccille ended his book by optimistically predicting that young libertarians and right-wing anarchists would forge a powerful new alliance with the left:

> Some of the radicals have split off entirely from YAF; others will remain on an individual basis and continue to proselytize among the conservative ranks. The most important thing to emerge from the convention is that, for the first time, the most influential forces on the Libertarian Right will be working to establish an open and working coalition with the New Left in their common struggle to resist the abuses of the United States government.[67]

The dream of a grand new coalition between libertarians and the New Left never materialized. Although libertarians and leftists could agree that the Vietnam war was unjust and that African Americans had legitimate complaints against an abusive government, the left never showed much interest in laissez-faire capitalism, which is unsurprising, as the New Left had a strong Marxist element. The prospects for such an alliance were further weakened by the decline of the countercultural left as a major force in American politics in the 1970s. In 1969, the same year as the disastrous YAF convention in St. Louis, SDS fell into disarray. What remained of SDS was largely coopted by the left-wing terrorist group, the Weather Underground Organization, which preached violent revolution. By the early 1970s, it was clear that the American electorate was tired of militant student radicals, whether they were left wing or libertarian. Rather than the dawn of a revolution, the early 1970s were dominated by Nixon's bourgeois Silent Majority.

YAF still exists, though it is no longer particularly influential. Although it was never completely disbanded, it had few large chapters and was largely out of the public eye during the 1990s and first decade of the twenty-first century. In 2011 the group officially merged with Young America's Foundation, an organization that is predominantly focused on bringing conservative speakers to college campuses. At this point, the only national conservative youth organization with chapters on most college campuses is the College Republicans, an organization that is explicitly focused on promoting Republican candidates. The fact that young conservatives' energy is focused primarily on groups like the College Republicans and the Young Republicans is yet another indication of the degree to which organized conservatism and the GOP are now inextricably linked and perhaps even interchangeable.

The most significant right-wing organizations on college campuses that are not explicitly partisan are libertarian in their orientation. Two such organizations deserve mention here: Young Americans for Liberty (YAL) and Students for Liberty (SFL). YAL, led by executive director Jeff Frazee, was a continuation of the group Students for Ron Paul, which formed in 2008 in support of Paul's presidential campaign. According to its website, YAL has more than 500 chapters and 160,000 activists nationwide.[68]

Although libertarian, YAL is decidedly nonantagonistic toward conservatives. It generally eschews the term libertarian and instead calls itself pro-liberty. Many of the group's talking points are conventionally conservative, and its statement of principles includes phrases such as "the God-given natural rights of life, liberty, and property set forth by our Founding Fathers."[69] In some respects, YAL is continuing the fusionist tradition developed by Frank Meyer. Its list of "strategic partners" includes conventionally conservative groups such as the Intercollegiate Studies Institute and Young America's Foundation, as well as openly libertarian organizations such as the Cato Institute and the Mises Institute. However, whereas the early conservative movement heavily emphasized the need for a massive military to confront communism and rejected libertarians who disagreed, YAL is decidedly and openly noninterventionist on foreign policy. YAL is comparatively quiet on social issues; it does not appear to have a formal position on marriage equality, for example.

YAL regularly holds conferences that host well-known libertarian and conservative speakers. The 2013 YAL National Convention provided a platform for Ron Paul and representatives from the Cato Institute, the Institute for Humane Studies, and the Charles Koch Institute, but it also provided speaking time for more conventional conservatives such as Ted Cruz and representatives from the Heritage Foundation and the Leadership Institute.

Students for Liberty is the other large libertarian youth organization worth noting. The organizational structure of SFL differs from YAL. SFL is not chapter based, and it does not have a formal roster of members. SFL is also more openly liberal on social issues. SFL president and cofounder Alexander McCobin described gay marriage as "the civil rights issue of the 21st century."[70] Although McCobin noted that there was plenty of room for people who were socially conservative in their private lives within the liberty movement, he is unequivocal in his opposition to any state-led efforts to legislate moral behavior. In response to critical remarks made by Ann Coulter regarding the libertarian movement, he made it clear that there were some issues that true libertarians considered settled and no longer worth discussing:

> We know what's up for debate, and so we also know what's not. The justifications for and limits on intellectual property? Up for debate. Racism? Not up for debate. Deciding which government agencies should be abolished, privatized, reformed, or maintained? Up for debate. State-sponsored discrimination against individuals based on their sexuality? Not up for debate. Austrian versus Chicago economics and their responses to Keynesianism? Up for debate. Ann's claim that liberals are out to destroy the family? That's so clearly absurd that it's in stand-up comedy territory.[71]

The issue of the Civil Rights Act, which clearly put some restrictions on how businesses could use their private property, has long been debated among libertarians. SFL is unequivocally supportive of this legislation. McCobin favorably cited a libertarian scholar who argued that the Civil Rights Act, even its provisions that deny private businesses the right to discriminate, was just and should not be repealed.

These libertarian youth organizations are still relatively new on the political scene. It remains to be seen whether YAL and SFL alumni will eventually enjoy the same kind of influence that former YAFers enjoyed in the 1970s, 1980s, and 1990s. Nor is it clear that they will be successful in ultimately gaining control of the mainstream right. However, the liberty movement can perhaps be encouraged that many, perhaps most, of the energetic young activists on the right are decidedly libertarian in their views, and today's young activists will eventually take on prominent leadership roles in the conservative movement's leading institutions and within the GOP.

Is the Tea Party Libertarian?

I mentioned in chapter 1 that I do not consider the Tea Party movement sufficiently different from the mainstream conservative movement to classify it as one of the right-wing alternatives to conservatism discussed in this volume. However, given the publicity this populist movement has received in recent years, it does deserve a mention here. Specifically, it is worth asking whether the Tea Party can be described as a libertarian movement. In my view, the answer is no, but the Tea Party is animated by certain libertarian sentiments.

A problem with any discussion of the Tea Party stems from its deliberately nonorganized and nonhierarchical structure. There is no single Tea Party headquarters with an executive director giving marching orders. That does not mean that there are not powerful moneyed interests pouring money into the Tea Party. Tea Party supporters argue that the movement was a spontaneous populist uprising that arose in response to a bloated government. Opponents describe it as a corporate-funded AstroTurf campaign. As Ronald Formisano argued in his 2012 book, *The Tea Party: A Brief History*, it is both: "So what is the answer to the question . . . 'Astroturf or Grassroots Populism?' The simple answer is that the Tea Parties have been created by both kinds of populism, in part by the few—the corporate lobbyists from above—but also from the passionate many expressing real grassroots populism."[72]

Juan Williams of Fox News argued that the Tea Party was a natural outgrowth of Ron Paul's failed 2008 presidential campaign, lending plausibility to the argument that the movement is fundamentally libertarian.[73] Tea Party organizations tend to focus on economic issues rather than social issues. Many of the most prominent organizations affiliated with the Tea Party, such as Americans for Prosperity and FreedomWorks, rely heavily on Koch money. All of this indicates that the Tea Party is a libertarian movement.

However, while groups like FreedomWorks and the Tea Party Patriots may prefer to focus on taxes and the size of government, the disorganized and amorphous nature of the Tea Party movement means that local Tea Party organizations are free to focus on anything they choose. When the social networking site, Tea Party Nation, organized its first conference, it included speakers who focused primarily on social issues such as gay marriage and abortion.[74] Although prominent Tea Party leaders, such as Tea Party Express cofounder Sal Russo, have been proponents of liberalizing immigration reforms,[75] many self-described Tea Partiers are vocal opponents of such policies; a coalition called the Tea Party Immigration Coalition, for example, warned Republican National Committee chairman Reince Priebus that they would consider voting for a third party if the Republican Party backed amnesty for undocumented immigrants.[76]

Polling data further indicates that the typical Tea Party supporter is not qualitatively different from the average conservative Republican. Vanessa Williamson, Theda Skocpol, and John Coggin described the demographic profile of Tea Party as not all that different from that of the Republican Party's most enthusiastic supporters: "Older, white, and middle class is the typical profile of a Tea Party participant. Between 55 and 60 percent of supporters are men; 80–90 percent are white; and 70–75 percent are over 45 years old."[77] They further found that the Tea Party supporters they profiled were not antigovernment zealots or libertarian purists; they generally supported policies like Social Security and Medicare. For all of these reasons, I reject the notion that the Tea Party can be considered an ideological movement in any way separate from the mainstream conservative movement.

Conclusion

The libertarian movement has enjoyed great success in recent years, and those libertarians that have worked closely with the mainstream right now possess greater influence within the conservative movement than ever before. The rhetoric on the right has become increasingly libertarian in its tone, and the Republican Party will have to conform to this tone to keep libertarians satisfied.

Of all the dissident right-wing ideologies in the United States, none can compare to libertarians when it comes to funding, access to lawmakers, or platforms in prominent publications and television shows. Libertarians are increasingly well organized, and they seem to have a great deal of youthful enthusiasm behind them—at least when we compare this movement to the others examined in this volume. Whether or not libertarianism will displace traditional conservatism as the general ideology of the Republican Party remains to be seen; it would be premature to predict such a change in the near future. Nonetheless, libertarians have reasons for optimism, as they occupy an important role within the mainstream American right.

Not all libertarians or anarchists on the right are satisfied with simply having a voice within the broader conservative movement. Many such intellectuals, activists, and journalists have no interest in making marginal changes to federal policy or getting a respectful hearing from the Republican leadership. Many fundamentally reject America's two-party system—

and even the legitimacy of the American government. To some of these radicals, the state's existence is a moral outrage, and electing a handful of Republicans who occasionally prattle about the Constitution hardly counts as a victory. The ideas of these radical libertarians will be the focus of the next chapter.

Enemies of the State

RADICAL LIBERTARIANS

In the previous chapter I noted two characteristics of the mainstream libertarian movement: an acceptance of the state's legitimacy and a willingness to engage with the broader conservative movement. This chapter considers libertarian thinkers and activists that lack one or both of these characteristics. Anarchist is the better-known term for those who deny the need for a state. Unfortunately, the word anarchist has been appropriated by too many disparate groups to convey very much information. There is a variety of left-wing anarchism, which technically denies the legitimacy of the state, at least as it currently exists, but which also calls for communal ownership and equality. Noam Chomsky, for example, could be classified as this kind of anarchist. This variety of anarchism cannot, in my estimation, be characterized as right wing, and therefore it is outside the scope of this book. Beliefs about private property are the key dividing lines between anarchists on the left and anarchists on the right. Right-wing anarchists—who can also be called anarchocapitalists—reject the state but insist on the right to private property. This chapter will consider various right-wing antistatists in American history.

Not everyone in this chapter rejects the state entirely. In this chapter we also consider the Libertarian Party (LP), the longest-lasting third party in American history. The LP has greatly differed in its tone and strategy over time. In some periods it was openly radical in its antistatism; at other times it sold itself as the party of low-tax liberalism—that is, for economic conservatism but social progressivism. I consider it here, rather than in the preceding chapter, because by its very existence it makes the case that libertarians are not just one more constituency in the GOP's electoral coalition. The LP argues that libertarians need a completely separate vehicle for advancing their agenda.

This chapter will begin by considering some of the many debates that have occurred among libertarians. There are a number of key fault lines within libertarianism, and these divides can often be used to disaggregate radical libertarians and right-wing anarchists from their more moderate and accommodating ideological brethren. It will also briefly explain the intellectual tradition known as Austrian economics, a favored economic method utilized by many academic antistatists.

Key Divisions within Libertarianism

In discussing the divide between mainstream or pragmatic libertarians and radical libertarians or right-wing anarchists, I should again note that these two categories often overlap, and there are often important disagreements within these two libertarian camps. That being said, there are a number of ways in which radical libertarians typically break with mainstream libertarians. The importance of utilitarian arguments is one such schism.

When conversing with a mainstream libertarian about the trade-off between liberty and equality, the libertarian will often argue that this is a false choice. That is, liberty will also lead to greater equality; see Milton Friedman's argument about racial discrimination and the free market in the previous chapter for an example. These libertarians will similarly argue that freedom is also the best way to ensure widespread prosperity and social harmony. In the eyes of these libertarians, liberty is to be valued because it also provides a series of additional benefits.

This argument is potentially problematic for libertarians. The statement that greater liberty will lead to greater equality and prosperity can be tested empirically. Libertarians are generally confident that real-world data vindicate their arguments, but in cases where the evidence is mixed or even contrary to libertarian predictions, libertarians are faced with a quandary. If libertarians justify their position with utilitarian arguments and those arguments ultimately fail to persuade, then they have no additional arguments to make and must concede the position to their statist opponents.

The best libertarians can do in this scenario is argue that their ideas did not fail; they were simply never correctly or fully implemented. This may be a fair and accurate argument, but it is probably not persuasive; those making such arguments are not entirely dissimilar from communists who argued that the collapse of the Soviet Union was in no way an indictment of socialist economics. For this reason, radical libertarians and anarchists such as Murray Rothbard argued that liberty is morally justified based on natural rights, not because it leads to a greater average utility within society:

> There were two critically important changes in the philosophy and ideology of classical liberalism which both exemplified and contributed to its decay as a vital, progressive, and radical force in the Western world. The first, and most important, occurring in the early to mid-nineteenth century, was the abandonment of the philosophy of natural rights, and its replacement by technocratic utilitarianism. Instead of liberty grounded on the imperative morality of each individual's right to person and property, that is, instead of liberty being sought primarily on the basis of right and justice, utilitarianism preferred liberty as generally the best way to achieve a vaguely defined general welfare or common good. There were two grave consequences of this shift from natural rights to utilitarianism. First, the purity of the goal, the consistency of the principle, was inevitably shattered. For whereas the natural-rights libertarian seeking morality and justice cleaves militantly to pure principle, the utilitarian only values liberty as an ad hoc expedient. And since expediency can and does shift with the wind, it will become easy for the utilitarian in his cool calculus of cost and benefit to plump for statism in ad hoc case after case, and thus to give principle away.[1]

Rothbard went on to argue that utilitarians are weak allies in the struggle for liberty because utilitarians are virtually never radicals: "There have never been utilitarian revolutionaries."[2] The tendency of libertarians to become wonkish technocrats, focused on making marginal changes to existing policy, ensures that they represent no real threat to state power. The question of whether liberty should be justified on the basis of natural rights, utilitarianism, or some other foundation is not new. We will see that these questions divided individualists in the nineteenth century as well.

The issue of war and national defense remains a division within libertarianism. Recall that the original, Buckleyite conservative vision, which sought to fuse libertarianism and traditionalism into a single political movement, insisted on a hard line against communism and the Soviet Union. Libertarians were welcome in the movement, as long as they accepted the necessity of a massive American Empire capable of rolling back, or at least containing, the Soviet threat. Some self-described libertarians, such as Frank Meyer, saw no problem with this. Other libertarians, however, were opposed to a powerful national government, even if the Soviet Union represented a genuine threat. There is a tradition within libertarianism that rejects the mainstream conservative notion that the American military defends American freedoms. Such libertarians instead echo Randolph Bourne's statement, "War is the health of the State."[3]

Some of the libertarian critique of America's role in the cold war was spurred by the libertarian critique of Soviet economics. As we will see shortly, Ludwig von Mises, who strongly influenced twentieth-century libertarianism, relentlessly argued that socialism would be impossible to effectively implement. If this is true, there was never any real danger that the Soviet Union or its satellites would conquer the world. Indeed, by expressing so much fear about communism, conservatives who favored free markets indicated a lack of faith in their own economic system.

The war on terror again opened a rift within libertarianism, as some libertarians supported, and even championed, the invasions of Afghanistan and Iraq. They surely represented a minority among all libertarians, but their number was sufficient for Randy E. Barnett, himself a prowar libertarian, to assure readers of the *Wall Street Journal* that not all libertarians were antiwar. Barnett summed up the respective arguments as follows:

> Many libertarians, and perhaps most libertarian intellectuals, opposed the war in Iraq even before its inception. They believed Saddam's regime neither directly threatened the US nor harbored or supported the terrorist network responsible for Sept. 11. They also feared the risk of harmful, unintended consequences. Some may also have believed that since the US was not attacked by the government of Iraq, any such war was aggressive rather than defensive in nature.
>
> Other libertarians, however, supported the war in Iraq because they viewed it as part of a larger war of self-defense against Islamic jihadists who were organizationally independent of any government. They viewed radical Islamic fundamentalism as resulting in part from the corrupt dictatorial regimes that inhabit the Middle East, which have effectively repressed indigenous democratic reformers. Although opposed to nation building generally, these libertarians believed that a strategy of fomenting democratic regimes in the Middle East, as was

done in Germany and Japan after World War II, might well be the best way to take the fight to the enemy rather than solely trying to ward off the next attack.[4]

War, however, is qualitatively different from other policy issues, and Barnett was attacked quite aggressively in libertarian outlets like LewRockwell.com[5] and AntiWar.com.[6] In recent years, as the shock of 9/11 has further receded and the promises of the Iraq invasion were left unfulfilled, the number of prowar libertarian voices has dwindled. Few self-described libertarians still defend Bush's execution of the war on terror or join neoconservatives in damning the Obama administration for being insufficiently hawkish.

Libertarians also differ on the subject of immigration. On its face the answer to what a libertarian immigration policy looks like is simple: libertarianism demands open borders. The Cato Institute has long published scholarly reports documenting the economic and other benefits of high levels of immigration, and it has openly backed efforts to loosen existing immigration restrictions. In recent years, Bryan Caplan has been one of the most forceful libertarian proponents of completely open borders.[7] Tyler Cowen, Caplan's colleague at George Mason University and president of the Mercatus Center, has also expressed support for a generous immigration policy, though not open borders.[8] Libertarians typically argue for open immigration using both economic and moral arguments. On the economic side, immigration is said to stimulate growth and be a boon to both the immigrants and native-born citizens. Perhaps more importantly, immigration restrictions can be plausibly viewed as a violation of the nonaggression principle and no less a violation of libertarian principles than minimum-wage laws.

Not all libertarians accept these arguments. Milton Friedman, for example, expressed ambivalence about open borders. He was not against the free movement of peoples per se, but he was concerned that a libertarian immigration policy could not coexist with a welfare state: "It is one thing to have free immigration to jobs. It is another to have free immigration to welfare. And you cannot have both."[9] However, immigration restrictionists who use this quote to argue that Friedman was really one of them are mistaken: Friedman was in favor of high levels of immigration; he just did not believe that immigrants should be able to immediately receive welfare.

Other libertarians have been more hostile to open-borders arguments, though they are a minority within libertarianism. For example, in 2006, *Liberty* published a cover story titled "The Fallacy of Open Immigration," written by the magazine's editor, Stephen Cox. In his essay, which generated much discussion among libertarians, Cox argued that the economic benefits that resulted from massive unskilled immigration have been overstated.[10] He further argued that such a policy is ultimately counterproductive for libertarians as long as democracy is in place, given that, on average, immigrants tend to prefer statist policies. Finally, he argued that there is no right to immigration, and most people who claim there is such a right do not really believe it; if immigration were truly a right, then there could literally be no just form of immigration control whatsoever, a position that even few libertarians embrace.

Interestingly, another libertarian opponent of open borders is also one of the most radical libertarians considered in the volume: Hans-Hermann Hoppe. Hoppe, whose thought will be considered in greater detail later in this chapter, is a consistent anarchist, and in the stateless world he envisions, immigration as we currently understand the term will not be an issue. In the meantime, however, he rejects mainstream libertarian ideas about open borders. In a stateless world, literally all property will be private property, and private property implies the right to exclude. In a stateless world, there will likely be much less mobility, largely because there will not be the overproduction of goods such as public roads. To Hoppe, as long as states exist, liberal immigration policies do not represent an increase in individual freedom so much as yet another example of forced integration:

> States, as will be recalled, are also promoters of forced domestic integration. Forced integration is a means of breaking up all intermediate social institutions and hierarchies (in between the state and the individual) such as family, clan, tribe, community, and church and their internal layers and ranks of authority. In so doing the individual is isolated (atomized) and its power of resistance vis-a-vis the state weakened. In the "logic" of the state, a good dose of foreign invasion, especially if it comes from strange and far-away places, is reckoned to further strengthen this tendency. And the present situation offers a particularly opportune time to do so, for in accordance with the inherently centralizing tendency of states and statism generally and promoted here and now in particular by the US as the world's only remaining superpower, the Western world—or more precisely the neoconservative-socialdemocratic elites controlling the state governments in the US and Western Europe—is committed to the establishment of supra-national states (such as the European Union) and ultimately one world state. National, regional or communal

attachments are the main stumbling block on the way toward this goal. A good measure of uninvited foreigners and government imposed multiculturalism is calculated to further weaken and ultimately destroy national, regional, and communal identities and thus promote the goal of a One World Order, led by the US, and a new "universal man."[11]

Hoppe's remark about "forced integration" brings us to another important issue within libertarianism, and one of the more important progressive critiques of libertarians. When mainstream libertarians present themselves to the public, they typically focus on policy preferences that are congruent with much of the American electorate—issues such as marijuana legalization and lower taxes. However, in order to be consistent with their own stated principles, libertarians in power would presumably need to promote policies that are wildly unpopular, such as the complete dismantling of Social Security. More importantly, they would need to reopen debates that are considered closed. For example, it is difficult to reconcile libertarian principles with legislation such as the Civil Rights Act, though, as I noted in the last chapter, some have made the effort. For many libertarians, there is a qualitative difference between requiring states to treat all races equally and banning private businesses from discriminating on any grounds they choose. Although discrimination may be immoral and bad business, choosing not to hire a person or sell them a product, even if that choice was motivated by racism, does not violate the nonaggression principle. On the other hand, it is a violation of property rights when the government steps in and tells business owners that they must hire someone or sell that person a product. Libertarians who remain consistent on this issue can find themselves in an awkward situation, as it is often assumed that any objection to the Civil Rights Act must be motivated by racial animus. Indeed, early in his political career, Rand Paul found himself in trouble for voicing the standard libertarian view that people have a right to discriminate, even though he personally considers such discrimination immoral.[12]

Among mainstream libertarians who are careful to distance themselves from racist positions, the solution is simply to focus on other issues and make it clear that the repeal of antidiscrimination laws is at the bottom of their to-do list, if it is part of the libertarian agenda at all. Such libertarians also generally acknowledge that laissez-faire was an insufficient solution to problems generated by generations of slavery and discrimination. This seems to be the general stance of most of the writers associated with the Cato Institute[13] and *Reason*,[14] for example. Of course, while it is possible to be a sincere racial egalitarian and oppose civil rights legislation on libertarian grounds, it is also clear that not all libertarians are racial egalitarians. Both Hoppe and Rothbard have made remarks that are well outside the bounds of acceptable discourse on race in the contemporary United States, as we will see later in this chapter. But first we will explore antistate thought in America that preceded the birth of contemporary libertarianism.

Nineteenth-Century American Anarchists

When we consider the American precursors to contemporary libertarians, we immediately think of the radicals of the American Revolution, such as Thomas Paine and Thomas Jefferson. We often forget that there was a radical antistate and individualist-anarchist tradition in American thinking that continued throughout the nineteenth century and influenced later American libertarians and anarchists on the right. In this section, I will discuss three such figures: Josiah Warren, Lysander Spooner, and Benjamin Tucker.

Josiah Warren was, according to his biographer, the first American anarchist. He influenced anarchist and classical liberal thinking in the United States, as well as in Europe, notably that of Herbert Spencer and John Stuart Mill. In 1833, Warren began publishing *Peaceful Revolutionist*, a journal of anarchist thought.[15] Warren was an early proponent of communes that existed free from state interference, and he experimented with new community types that relied on his own idiosyncratic economic theories and his principle of individual sovereignty.[16] Warren argued that goods were worth exactly how much labor went into creating them, rather than the subjective value of the potential buyer. He expounded these theories in his 1849 short work, *Equitable Commerce*. Rather than price goods on the basis of "what they will bring," Warren argued that goods should be priced on the basis of their cost to the producer: "Cost, then, is the only rational ground of price, even in the most complicated transactions."[17] Warren's experimental communities, such as Utopia, Ohio, and Modern Times, New York, were reasonably successful compared to other experiments in communal living in the nineteenth century, though they ultimately ended in failure.

Lysander Spooner, who remains a celebrated figure within libertarian circles, is another radical individualist from this period. Born in 1808, Spooner was a legal theorist and political philosopher. He is best known for his work as an abolitionist, and his 1845 book, *The Unconstitutionality of Slavery*, was an important work of legal scholarship that made the case that, properly interpreted, the Constitution clearly banned slavery.[18] Although he was always opposed to slavery, he was also against the Civil War and critical of Lincoln. He noted that most other countries in the world successfully abolished the slave trade without resorting to brutal warfare, and he argued that abolitionism was only a pretext for more sinister motives.[19]

Among libertarians, Spooner is best remembered for his 1870 pamphlet, *No Treason: The Constitution of No Authority*. In this short work, which relied on arguments based on theories of natural rights, Spooner argued that the United States government was an utterly criminal organization, possessing no legitimate authority. To Spooner, there was no qualitative difference between a robber who steals your money and a government that taxes you. Indeed, the robber may be morally superior in that he does not claim to be working for your benefit when he appropriates your wealth.

According to Spooner, if government has any legitimacy, it must be based on the principle of consent; the Civil War, which ended with the South forced into a political union with the North, demonstrated that the government did not rely on consent to justify its existence. Spooner further argued that the existence of democratic institutions did not resolve this problem or give the state additional cover for violating individual rights.[20] The fact that a majority supports a position does not ensure that the position is just.

Spooner's view of what constituted the "consent of the governed" was far more radical than what Jefferson and others suggested. To Spooner, if a government really is to justify its existence on the basis of consent, then it must literally have the consent of every single individual it would claim to rule. If there are any exceptions to this, then the government cannot honestly be said to rest on consent.

After Spooner, Benjamin Tucker was the next important American individualist anarchist in the nineteenth century. Tucker was inspired by Warren and by the French anarchist Pierre-Joseph Proudhon; he was a devoted individualist anarchist by the time he was eighteen. He is best known as the publisher of the journal *Liberty*, which was published between 1881 and 1908. Like Warren, Tucker subscribed to a labor theory of value,[21] a fact that puts these thinkers at odds with classical liberal economists that would later be so influential in radical libertarian and right-wing anarchist circles. Tucker can also largely take credit for introducing German individualist Max Stirner to an American audience, and within the pages of *Liberty*, various contributors discussed the merits of Stirner's ideology of egoism and the importance of natural rights as a foundation for individualist ideologies.[22] Tucker himself came to reject natural rights as the basis for his political philosophy, rejecting the arguments of predecessors like Spooner.

We saw from the history of *National Review* that a single periodical can play an important role in shaping an ideological movement. *Liberty* played such a role in the individualist anarchist movement in the United States. Wendy McElroy has written extensively on Tucker's achievements:

> After 1865, radical individualism existed as an extreme faction within various other reform movements such as freethought, free love, and the labor movement. Although the basis of a systematic philosophy existed in the writings of theorists such as Warren and Spooner, it lacked cohesion. Not until Tucker's publication of *Liberty* did radical individualism become a distinct, independent movement functioning in its own name and seeking its own unique goals.
>
> This consolidation was the primary accomplishment of *Liberty*. It discussed and integrated ethics, economics, and politics to build a sophisticated system of philosophy. For three decades it provided a core around which a revitalized movement could flourish. During those years Tucker issued an unremitting flood of pamphlets and books promoting individualist thought.[23]

Although Tucker and his journal helped generate an intellectually coherent ideological movement, that movement never became a powerful political force in the United States. There was no significant constituency for individualist anarchism at the start of the twentieth century, and the movement died out with little acknowledgment. The final issue of *Liberty* was published in 1908, at the start of a century characterized by growing state power and totalitarianism throughout much of the world.

There is a clear distinction between the nineteenth-century radical individualists and twentieth-century anarchocapitalists: the two groups differ tremendously on the subject of economics. To contemporary readers, it can almost be taken for granted that a stateless society would also be a society of laissez-faire capitalism. After all, without a state, who would interfere with the market? To the nineteenth-century individualists, and to many left-wing anarchists today, socialism and anarchism were not incompatible. Tucker, for example, considered himself a socialist.[24] Given these economic views, one may question whether there is truly intellectual continuity between this brand of anarchism and radical libertarians and anarchists today.

Murray Rothbard argued that the individualist anarchism of Spooner and Tucker was similar to the views of contemporary libertarians in many important respects.[25] However, Rothbard's brand of anarchism broke with nineteenth-century individualist anarchism in a number of ways, the issue of land ownership and private property being the most important. According to the earlier individualist anarchists, private property should only be recognized if an individual is actually and personally using a specific piece of land; such a stance would have important consequences, notably that it would no longer be possible for anyone to rent land to others. Rothbard considered this and other economic ideas expounded by Spooner and Tucker to be based on entirely fallacious reasoning. In spite of these misgivings, however, Rothbard argued that "Lysander Spooner and Benjamin R. Tucker were unsurpassed as political philosophers and that nothing is more needed today than a revival and development of the largely forgotten legacy that they left to political philosophy."[26]

Austrian Economics

As noted in the previous chapter, libertarians are typically divided in their opinion of Austrian economics. This divide also generally corresponds to differences in their radicalism; radical libertarians typically have a high estimation of Austrian (or Misesian) economics. Mainstream libertarians generally eschew the Austrian method in favor or more traditional economic methods. Carl Menger, who lived from 1840 to 1921, is generally credited as the father of Austrian economics. Menger is best known for his development of the subjective theory of value. Menger argued that goods do not have an objective measurable value, but each individual will subjectively estimate the value they expect to derive from the good. This economic theory has important consequences, as Menger's disciples, such as Friedrich von Weiser and Eugen Böhm von Bawerk, later showed.

Perhaps the key idiosyncrasy of Austrian economics is its take on mathematical and statistical analyses of economic phenomena, which leaves economists from the Austrian tradition definitively at odds with other economists. The Austrian tradition rejects statistical economics. Thomas Taylor explained this logic in *An Introduction to Austrian Economics* (1980):

> Austrian economic analysis is carried out largely on the basis of theoretical, deductive reasoning; empiricism has little place in Austrian economic theory. . . . Economic phenomena, originating from a social environment, are deemed by the Austrians too complex and variable to permit the kind of experimental analysis that the physical scientists use. Accordingly, Austrian theory is opposed on methodological grounds to mathematics as a tool of economic analysis. Conceptual understanding,

not quantitative relations, is seen as the only meaningful basis of economic science. Menger, the father of the Austrian school, insisted on and followed this qualitative orientation throughout his works, as did his successors.[27]

Whereas much of contemporary economics relies primarily on the use of modern statistical techniques to test hypotheses, Austrian school economics can be better described as an exercise in applied logic. Austrians begin with a series of a priori assumptions—such as the assumption that individual behavior is purposive—and then make predictions about individual behavior. Austrians are fond of thought experiments, such as speculating on the behavior of one individual on a desert island and how that person's behavior will change as new individuals are added to the island's population and they begin to interact.

Besides their rigid stance on methodology, Austrians are best known for their theory of the trade cycle. Austrian school economists argue that the boom-and-bust cycles of the economy result from the expansion of credit and the money supply through the practice of fractional reserve banking. The expansion of credit results in an inflationary boom. This period of robust economic growth is always short lived, however, as the expansion of credit must necessarily come to a halt at some point, followed by a run on the banks and an economic contraction. According to Austrian logic, in the absence of government interference, busts will also be short lived. The economic contraction and reduction of the money supply will make goods in a country less expensive and exports from that country more attractive, leading to a new period of economic growth.

Rothbard and other Austrian economists made the case that economic downturns have become much more severe because of the strong relationship between banking and the government.[28] In a purely private banking system, fractional reserve banking would be uncommon. It is only when private banks are able to work in unison with a state-sponsored central bank that we see the now-familiar business cycle. The central bank allows individual private banks to extend their own liabilities much further than any prudent banker would dare consider in a purely private system.

Whereas mainstream commentary typically cites malfeasance or shortsightedness on the part of private business as the catalyst for economic downturns, Austrian school economists argue that the disruptive business cycle is the result of state interference in the economy, particularly on the issue of credit and interest rates. This is the reason why economists from the Austrian tradition are so critical of the Federal Reserve. Austrians also generally argue that the Great Depression was so severe precisely because the government was compelled to do something. Had the state taken a laissez-faire approach to that depression, rather than propping up shaky banks and businesses, the economic downturn would have been painful, but short.

Two names are predominantly associated with Austrian economics in the twentieth century: Ludwig von Mises and Friedrich Hayek. Mises was an early and important critic of socialism; he made the case that an efficient socialist economy was impossible. Born in 1881 in the Austro-Hungarian empire, Mises wrote some of the most important works in the Austrian economic tradition. *Socialism*, which was first published in 1922, was one of the most powerful critiques of Marxist economic theory ever written. In this work, Mises argued that socialism was doomed to fail because it lacked a price mechanism for making economic calculations.[29]

Hayek, born ten years later than Mises, is best known for his 1944 book, *The Road to Serfdom*, which argued that central planning will always lead to totalitarianism. It further argued that fascism and socialism had common roots—a view that was at odds with the popular interpretation of fascism as a capitalistic response to the socialist threat. To Hayek, all forms of collectivism were qualitatively similar:

> In many ways this puts the basic issue very clearly. And it directs us at once to the point where the conflict arises between individual freedom and collectivism. The various kinds of collectivism, communism, fascism, etc., differ between themselves in the nature of the goal towards which they want to direct the efforts of society. But they all differ from liberalism and individualism in wanting to organise the whole of society and all its resources for this unitary end, and in refusing to recognise autonomous spheres in which the ends of the individuals are supreme. In short, they are totalitarian in the true sense of this new word which we have adopted to describe the unexpected but nevertheless inseparable manifestations of what in theory we call collectivism.[30]

Hayek noted that central planning was inherently undemocratic, and therefore "democratic socialism, the great utopia of the last few generations, is not only unachievable, but that to strive for it produces something so utterly different that few of those who now wish it would be prepared to accept the consequences."[31] To Hayek, a planned economy would necessarily require the suppression of dissent, and thus a planned economy and freedom are incompatible even if some democratic forms are maintained.

Although I included the discussion of Austrian economics in the chapter on radical libertarianism, I should be clear that believing that Austrian school economists have made important contributions to economic thought does not guarantee that one will become a libertarian, radical or otherwise. Today's radical libertarians, on average, tend to be more inclined to embrace Austrian economic thinking than the more mainstream economic ideas of Milton Friedman. However, Hayek himself was not particularly radical, at least by libertarian standards. He was certainly no anarchist. He directly expressed support for government roads, government subsidies for science, art, and entertainment, unemployment benefits, and some form of social security; for these reasons, he was excoriated by more extreme libertarians, Murray Rothbard in particular.[32]

Other radical libertarians have criticized Hayek. Walter Block, another anarchocapitalist economist, argued that Hayek was too weak and hesitant in his defense of liberty and free markets. Although Hayek makes a strong case against totalitarian central planning, Block pointed out the many cases of government intervention that Hayek approved. Block concluded: "There is little doubt that Hayek deserves his reputation as a defender of economic freedom—but only compared to his contemporaries who, with only a few honorable exceptions, were almost totally immersed in interventionistic philosophy."[33] Hayek was also less ideological in his rejection of econometrics than Mises and his successors, which may explain why he is held in higher esteem among contemporary mainstream economists than other Austrians.[34]

Although Austrian economics is popular among libertarians, it has its critics, even within the libertarian intellectual movement. Bryan Caplan, for example, rejects Austrian economics and embraces mainstream neoclassical economics. Although he acknowledges the contributions of key Austrian scholars such as Mises, he argues that the Austrians' principled rejection of mathematics and econometrics is misguided.[35] As evidence of this, Caplan pointed out the many great contributions made by non-Austrian academic economists since 1949 and the relatively few contributions made by purist Austrian school economists since that time.

Austrian economics enjoyed a brief resurgence in popular interest in recent years, both due to Ron Paul's presidential campaigns (Paul's economic views were shaped by Mises) and because of the economic recession that began in 2007. Economic thinkers influenced by the Austrian school were able to plausibly claim that they predicted the crash and that it was playing out precisely as Austrian theory said it would; indeed, Austrians had been warning of a housing crash in the years leading up to the recession.[36] In spite of receiving greater-than-usual attention in recent years, there is little indication that Austrian economics is going to earn greater respect from mainstream academic economists. Economics is now a thoroughly quantitative discipline, and thus economists who reject the premises of modern econometrics cannot publish in the leading economics journals.

Murray Rothbard

Although Hayek was Mises's most celebrated protégé and the only Austrian school economist to win the Nobel Prize, his most radical student, who played a crucial role in the American libertarian movement, was undoubtedly Murray Rothbard. Born in the Bronx in 1926, most of Rothbard's upbringing was spent in a leftist social milieu.[37] Nonetheless, he went on to become one of the most influential anarchists of the right in US history. While in college, Rothbard was a statistics major for a time.[38] He eventually rejected modern econometrics and fully embraced the Misesian economic method.

While still a young man, Rothbard became a part of what he would later call the old right—that loose collection of antistatists discussed in this volume's first chapter. Unfortunately for Rothbard, that movement was ending as an intellectual and political force in American life just as he was maturing as an intellectual. The militantly anticommunist, Buckleyite conservative movement ultimately triumphed over the isolationist tradition on the right.

Rothbard spent much of his life attempting to build an independent libertarian movement, and he looked for ideological allies wherever he could. Rothbard was unique among libertarians, however, in his choices of potential associates. Rothbard quickly determined that the mainstream conservative movement was not interested in liberty or opposing the state, and he instead sought supporters on the New Left and later from the ranks of paleoconservatives.

Rothbard was also, perhaps surprisingly, an admirer of Senator Joseph McCarthy. Rothbard had a unique view on McCarthy and McCarthyism. Liberals hated McCarthy both for his anticommunist views and for his methods. Conservatives shared McCarthy's distaste of communism, but many were uncomfortable with his populist demagoguery—or at least claimed they were uncomfortable after McCarthyism died out as a political force. In contrast, Rothbard disliked McCarthy's goals[39]—as a committed noninterventionist, Rothbard was wholly against cold warriors—but admired his methods. Rothbard believed McCarthy's populism could and should be emulated by radical antistatists:

> But there was another reason for my own fascination with the McCarthy phenomenon: his populism. For the '50s was an era when liberalism—now accurately termed "corporate liberalism"—had triumphed, and seemed to be permanently in the saddle. Having now gained the seats of power, the liberals had given up their radical veneer of the '30s and were now settling down to the cozy enjoyment of their power and perquisites. It was a comfortable alliance of Wall Street, Big Business, Big Government, Big Unions, and liberal Ivy League intellectuals; it seemed to me that while in the long run this unholy alliance could only be overcome by educating a new generation of intellectuals, that in the short run the only hope to dislodge this new ruling elite was a populist short circuit. In sum, there was a vital need to appeal directly to the masses, emotionally, even demagogically, *over the heads* of the Establishment. . . . It seemed to me that this is what McCarthy was trying to do; and that was largely his appeal, the open-ended sense that there was no audacity of which McCarthy was not capable, that frightened the liberals, who, from their opposite side of the fence, also saw that the only danger to their rule was in just such a whipping up of populist emotions.[40]

Although a consistent noninterventionist, and thus opposed to the conservative movement on the key issue of foreign policy, Rothbard did not initially have a particularly hostile relationship with Buckley and others at *National Review*. Rothbard was a friend of Frank Meyer, and he contributed many articles to the magazine. For a time, there was even a possibility that Rothbard would begin writing a regular economics column for *National Review*.[41] The relationship between Rothbard and the mainstream conservative movement did not remain friendly. As the cold war became less cold throughout the 1950s and conservative rhetoric became, in Rothbard's view, increasingly bloodthirsty and reckless, he became an increasingly outspoken critic of the conservative movement, and Buckley became increasingly hostile toward Rothbard and his associates.[42] Rothbard eventually concluded that opposing the Soviets was literally the only thing that animated the conservative movement.[43]

By the mid-1950s, with the old right eclipsed by the new conservative movement, Rothbard was without a home in the political mainstream. At this time he became personally acquainted with Ayn Rand. Although they always had disagreements on policy, Rothbard appreciated Rand's moral vision; both Rand and Rothbard were opposed to utilitarian arguments for libertarianism. However, Rothbard found Rand's outrageous claims of total originality in her thinking preposterous, and he believed her views on economics demonstrated her ignorance of the subject.[44] The two got along well after the publication of *Atlas Shrugged* in 1957, which Rothbard told her was "the greatest novel ever written."[45] But Rothbard ultimately broke with Rand and her circle. His initial optimism that they could serve as a vanguard for a new individualist movement was dashed by Rand's megalomania and the cultish atmosphere of her Collective.

Rothbard continued looking for other potential political allies. Having rejected the new conservative movement as hopelessly statist, and wanting nothing to do with Rand's Objectivist movement, he turned to the New Left in the hope that the countercultural and antiestablishment sentiments on the left could be turned against the state itself. Rothbard was impressed by the New Left's radicalism; he believed that much of it was motivated by libertarian sentiments, even if many young leftists of the period claimed ideological affinity for totalitarians such as Mao.

Rothbard become involved with a number of leftist organizations and publications, and joined the Peace and Freedom Party in the late 1960s. He also contributed to *Ramparts,* the premier journal of the New Left. In an essay published in that magazine, "Confessions of a Right-Wing Liberal," Rothbard explained to his readers that his position had always been consistent, but America had changed around him:

> Twenty years ago I was an extreme right-wing Republican, a young and lone "Neanderthal" (as the liberals used to call us) who believed, as one friend pungently put it, that "Senator Taft had sold out to the socialists." Today, I am most likely to be called an extreme leftist, since I favor immediate withdrawal from Vietnam, denounce US imperialism, advocate Black Power and have just joined the new Peace and Freedom Party. And yet my basic political views have not changed by a single iota in these two decades!
>
> It is obvious that something is very wrong with the old labels, with the categories of "left" and "right," and with the ways in which we customarily apply these categories to American political life. My personal odyssey is unimportant; the important point is that if I can

move from "extreme right" to "extreme left" merely by standing in one place, drastic though unrecognized changes must have taken place throughout the American political spectrum over the last generation.[46]

Rothbard found an ally with a comparable ideological trajectory in Karl Hess. Hess was a former aide and speechwriter for Barry Goldwater who ultimately rejected the conservative movement and was thoroughly radicalized by the end of the 1960s. Although a part of left-wing organizations such as SDS, Hess described himself as a libertarian, notably in his lengthy essay, "The Death of Politics," published in *Playboy* in 1969, and like Rothbard, he believed that groups like SDS would ultimately move in a more libertarian direction.[47]

Rothbard's dream that the New Left would evolve into a revolutionary libertarian vanguard was never realized. The radical libertarians had for the most part broken with conservative groups like the YAF by the end of the 1960s, but they did not succeed in coopting and transforming the New Left, which by then was also beginning to fizzle out. Some of Rothbard's ultimate disappointment surely stemmed from the degree to which he and the New Left movement were temperamentally incompatible.

Although he was a radical ideologue, Rothbard was also thoroughly middle class and respectable in his demeanor and lifestyle. As Rothbard's biographer, Justin Raimondo, noted: "Rothbard was a man of the Old Culture: he believed it was possible to be a revolutionary, an anarchist, *and* lead a bourgeois life. Respectably dressed, if a bit rumpled, in his signature bow tie, white shirt, and jacket, Rothbard was immune to the blandishments of the sixties youth culture, preferring the odes of Cicero to the howls of Alan Ginsberg and the music of the Baroque to that of the Beatles."[48] In this respect, Rothbard was decidedly different from Hess, who made a conscious effort to demonstrate his radicalism in his appearance.

Rothbard also found that members of the New Left counterculture, even those who described themselves as libertarians, typically had little interest in lengthy, scholarly lectures on Austrian school praxeology or other aspects of libertarian theory building. The schism between the academic Rothbard and his followers, and the more impatient libertarian left opened up at a libertarian conference held in New York City in late 1969. Rothbard was insistent on the importance of theory and ideology. In the absence of a well-defined and consistent political philosophy, a political movement could be coopted and redirected. Unfortunately for Rothbard, relatively few left libertarians were interested in discussing laissez-faire capitalism in a lecture hall when they had the option of engaging in more radical direct action. At the 1969 conference, Hess used his time at the podium to call for an assault on Fort Dix, which was nearby. Many of the attendees responded to Hess's call, and they marched out of the building, opting to get tear gassed outside of Fort Dix rather than sit through additional scholarly panels.[49]

Rothbard's experience with the New Left counterculture, as well as the flakey weirdness of many libertarians and their tendency to indulge in survivalist fantasy or New Age silliness, left him more convinced that libertarianism needed to be respectable and appeal to ordinary Americans. In 1975, as part of an annual "wish list" for the movement, he condemned the cultural proclivities of his fellow libertarians:

> On psychobabble. Wouldn't it be great? A whole year of nothing, not a word, not a peep, about "open relationships," "growing as a person," "getting in touch with your feelings," "opening up a space," "non-authoritarian relations," "living free," and all the rest of the malarkey. But, then, what in the world would all of the psycholibertarians have to talk about? Well yes, that would be an interesting experiment indeed. Either they would have to painfully make their way to developing an interest in history, current affairs, economics, political philosophy— in short, the real world, or else they would have to descend into blissful silence (blissful, that is, for the rest of us).[50]

Rothbard's writing also became more ostentatiously antiegalitarian as he grew older. In 1971, he published an open defense of inequality in *Modern Age*, a mainstream conservative journal, titled, "Freedom, Inequality, Primitivism, and the Division of Labor." In this essay, he attacked the concept of equality head on, rather than indirectly on utilitarian grounds or on the basis of practicality.[51] To Rothbard, equality was itself an evil concept. Rothbard later declared that egalitarianism is ultimately a "revolt against nature," and until the right challenged the principle of equality on moral, rather than practical, grounds, the left would have an advantage in all political battles:

> Suppose, for example, that it has come to be adopted as a universal ethical goal that all men be able to fly by flapping their arms. Let us assume that "pro-flappers" have been generally conceded the beauty and goodness of their goal, but have been criticized as "impractical." But the result is unending social misery as society tries continually

to move in the direction of arm-flying, and the preachers of arm-flapping make everyone's lives miserable for being either lax or sinful enough not to live up to the common ideal. The proper critique here is to challenge the "ideal" goal itself; to point out that the goal itself is impossible in view of the physical nature of man and the universe; and, therefore, to free mankind from its enslavement to an inherently impossible and, hence, evil goal. But this liberation could never occur so long as the anti-armfliers continued to be solely in the realm of the "practical" and to concede ethics and "idealism" to the high priests of arm-flying. The challenge must take place at the core—at the presumed ethical superiority of a nonsensical goal. The same, I hold, is true of the egalitarian ideal, except that its social consequences are far more pernicious than an endless quest for man's flying unaided. For the condition of equality would wreak far more damage upon mankind.[52]

After breaking entirely with the left, Rothbard again became part of the effort to create a genuinely independent libertarian movement. In the mid-1970s, he and his ideological comrades were assisted by a much-needed infusion of funding from the Koch brothers. As noted in the previous chapter, Rothbard played an important early role in the Cato Institute; Rothbard actually chose the institute's name. However, as noted in the previous chapter, his active involvement with Cato ended over ideological and strategic disputes. Beginning in the 1980s, Rothbard was affiliated with the newly formed Ludwig von Mises Institute.

It was also in the 1980s that Rothbard began to push a decidedly different strategy for libertarians. Having failed to convert the New Left to the libertarian movement, and aware that the loose collection of free spirits who described themselves as libertarians were too few in number to achieve real political power, he urged libertarians to focus their efforts on middle class America—the very same people who supported the mainstream conservative movement he hated. He increasingly made common cause with traditionalists who were also cast out of the mainstream right, becoming an important figure within the John Randolph Club and an enthusiastic supporter of Pat Buchanan. In the paleoconservative movement, which will be discussed in greater detail in the next chapter, Rothbard saw an opportunity to build a new antistate coalition.

It was also during this period, unsurprisingly, that Rothbard made his most controversial statements about race. While in the 1960s and 1970s Rothbard had praised black militants, in the 1990s Rothbard was defending

David Duke and echoing much of his rhetoric. In an article about the campaign against Duke, Rothbard explained the logic of right-wing populism, which needed to focus its energies on attacking existing elites who benefit from contemporary social arrangements:

> The basic right-wing populist insight is that we live in a statist country and a statist world dominated by a ruling elite, consisting of a coalition of Big Government, Big Business, and various influential special interest groups. More specifically, the old America of individual liberty, private property, and minimal government has been replaced by a coalition of politicians and bureaucrats allied with, and even dominated by, powerful corporate and Old Money financial elites (e.g., the Rockefellers, the Trilateralists); and the New Class of technocrats and intellectuals, including Ivy League academics and media elites, who constitute the opinion-moulding class in society. In short, we are ruled by an updated, twentieth-century coalition of Throne and Altar, except that this Throne is various big business groups, and the Altar is secular, statist intellectuals, although mixed in with the secularists is a judicious infusion of Social Gospel, mainstream Christians.
>
> . . .

Libertarians have often seen the problem plainly, but as strategists for social change they have badly missed the boat. In what we might call "the Hayek model," they have called for spreading correct ideas, and thereby converting the intellectual elites to liberty, beginning with top philosophers and then slowly trickling on down through the decades to converting journalists and other media opinion-moulders. And of course, ideas are the key, and spreading correct doctrine is a necessary part of any libertarian strategy. It might be said that the process takes too long, but a long-range strategy is important, and contrasts to the tragic futility of official conservatism which is interested only in the lesser-of-two-evils for the current election and therefore loses in the medium, let along the long, run. But the real error is not so much the emphasis on the long run, but on ignoring the fundamental fact that the *problem is not just intellectual error.* The problem is that the intellectual elites benefit from the current system; in a crucial sense, they are part of the ruling class. . . . Any libertarian strategy must recognize that intellectuals and opinion-moulders are part of the fundamental problem, not just because of error, but because their own self-interest is tied into the ruling system.[53]

Much of Rothbard's right-wing populist platform was often explicitly or implicitly racial: "Abolish affirmative action, set aside racial quotas, etc., and point out that the root of such quotas is the entire 'civil rights' structure, which tramples on the property rights of every American. . . . Take Back the Streets: Crush Criminals. And by this I mean, of course, not 'white collar criminals' or 'inside traders' but violent street criminals—robbers, muggers, rapists, murderers. Cops must be unleashed, and allowed to administer instant punishment, subject of course to liability when they are in error. . . . Get Rid of the Bums. Again: unleash the cops to clear the streets of bums and vagrants. Where will they go? Who cares?"[54] Rothbard also favorably reviewed Charles Murray's controversial book, *The Bell Curve*, which included several chapters arguing that racial differences in intelligence can partially explain racial inequality. He argued that such research was necessary because it defends the free market from the charge that it is inherently discriminatory:

> If and when we as populists and libertarians abolish the welfare state
> in all of its aspects, and property rights and the free market shall be
> triumphant once more, many individuals and groups will predictably
> not like the end result. In that case, those ethnic and other groups
> who might be concentrated in lower-income or less prestigious
> occupations, guided by their socialistic mentors, will predictably
> raise the cry that free-market capitalism is evil and "discriminatory"
> and that therefore collectivism is needed to redress the balance. In
> that case, the intelligence argument will become useful to defend the
> market economy and the free society from ignorant or self-serving
> attacks. In short; racialist science is properly not an act of aggression
> or a cover for oppression of one group over another, but, on the
> contrary; an operation in defense of private property against assaults
> by aggressors.[55]

Although many 1960s radicals subsequently changed their views, Rothbard is interesting in that he transitioned from supporting the Black Panthers to supporting Pat Buchanan without—as far as I am aware—also undergoing a fundamental transition in his worldview. He was always on the lookout for the social group he believed represented the greatest threat to state power, and tried to focus its energies in a libertarian direction. In each case, it is fair to say, he failed. New Left groups like SDS collapsed without ever turning truly libertarian or anarchistic. The paleoconservative movement that Rothbard supported at the end of his life (he died in 1995) never did achieve real political power, and in many crucial ways rejected the libertarian vision.

Hans-Hermann Hoppe

In many radical libertarians' eyes, Murray Rothbard remains the paragon of erudite radicalism. However, his brand of right-wing anarchism did not disappear entirely after his death. A number of other economists continue to embrace his Austrian school methods and have reached similar conclusions. There is insufficient space in this chapter to examine each of these intellectuals, but one in particular deserves special attention. Hans-Hermann Hoppe, who earned a PhD in economics in Germany, viewed Rothbard as his primary mentor and the two worked in the economics department at the University of Nevada, Las Vegas.

In his preferred economic methods, Hoppe is similar to Mises and Rothbard. However, he is notable for applying these economic ideas to theories of government. Like Rothbard, Hoppe is an anarchist. However, assuming that states will continue to exist for the foreseeable future, Hoppe attempted to discern which form of government will be least destructive. His most important work on this subject was *Democracy: The God That Failed.*[56] As the title suggests, Hoppe breaks with many other libertarians on the question of the ideal form of government. According to Hoppe, if you must have a government at all, it certainly should not be democratic.

Hoppe's analysis of government was focused on the economic concept of time preference. Time preference is an issue considered by both neoclassical economists and Austrian economists, but the subject is particularly important to scholars from the latter tradition. The premise of time preference is that a person will only hold off on consuming a good today if doing so leads to an increase in future goods. Every person will have a different willingness to forgo contemporary consumption in order to achieve future benefits. However, some institutional arrangements are more conducive to deferring consumption than others. This applies to individual economic actors in their own transactions, but also to the rulers of states.

When a nation is ruled by a monarchy, the monarch may plausibly view the nation as his private property—private property that can be passed to the monarch's heirs. This leads monarchs to take a long view when it comes to economics, demographics, and politics. They wish the see the nation's capital stock increase, and they are willing to forgo present consumption in pursuit of that goal:

The institution of private government ownership systematically shapes the incentive structure confronting the ruler and distinctly influences his conduct of government affairs. Assuming no more than self-interest, the ruler tries to maximize his total wealth, i.e., the present value of his estate and his current income. He would not want to increase current income at the expense of a more than proportional drop in the present value of his assets. Furthermore, because acts of current income acquisition invariably have repercussions on present asset values (reflecting the value of all future expected asset earnings discounted by the rate of time preference), private ownership in and of itself leads to economic calculation and thus promotes farsightedness.[57]

This is decidedly not the case in democracies, where the rulers cannot claim the nation as their own property. Democratic rulers have a limited period in which they can benefit from the state they control, and thus their time preference is going to be high and they have strong incentives to be shortsighted in their policies. Although a democratic leader can use the nation's resources for his or her own advantage, this leader does not personally own these resources, and thus has no interest in their long-term value: "Instead of maintaining or even enhancing the value of the government estate, as a king would do, a president (the government's temporary caretaker or trustee) will use up as much of the government resources as quickly as possible, for what he does not consume now, he may never be able to consume. In particular, a president (as distinct from a king) has no interest in not ruining his country."[58]

In contrast to other political theorists, Hoppe argued that democracies are more likely to engage in tyrannical practices because citizens in a democratic system have a false sense of personal efficacy. In a democracy, the ruled incorrectly believe they have a personal say in how they are governed, and thus are more willing to accept burdens such as heavy taxes or military conscription. In a monarchy, subjects are perfectly aware of their status, and are more likely to resist expansions of the state's prerogatives.[59]

According to Hoppe, democracy is also responsible for the horrors of modern warfare. In contrast to theorists arguing that democracies are inherently peaceful, Hoppe suggests that wars between two monarchies are less destructive than wars between nations with democratic institutions. There are a number of reasons for this. Wars between monarchs are not typically ideological in nature. They stem from a desire to increase the monarch's territory or gain some other tangible benefit. A massive war that destroys cities and farmland benefits no one, and thus should be relatively uncommon. Because such wars are also private affairs between competing monarchies, there will also be a greater distinction between combatants and noncombatants.[60]

In contrast, in democratic societies, the distinction between the great mass of people and the state is nonexistent, and with the demise of that distinction the difference between combatant and noncombatant also falls away:

> In blurring the distinction between the rulers and the ruled, a
> democratic republic strengthens the identification of the public with a
> particular state. Indeed, while dynastic rule promotes the identification
> with one's own family and community and the development of a
> "cosmopolitan" outlook and attitude, democratic republicanism
> inevitably leads to nationalism, i.e., the emotional identification of
> the public with large, anonymous groups of people, characterized in
> terms of a common language, history, religion and/or culture and in
> contradistinction to other, foreign nations. Interstate wars are thus
> transformed into national wars. Rather than representing "merely"
> violent dynastic property disputes, which may be "resolved" through
> acts of territorial occupation, they become battles between different
> ways of life, which can only be "resolved" through cultural, linguistic, or
> religious domination and subjugation (or extermination).[61]

Although Hoppe makes it clear that he prefers monarchy to democracy, his true preference is a completely stateless society.[62] He has discussed how ~~ALL~~ such a society would function, and reading Hoppe's work demonstrates ~~KINDS~~ the tremendous diversity of libertarian thought. Whereas the writers at *Reason* magazine praise figures such as Larry Flynt and Madonna for making America "groovier," Hoppe makes it clear that his utopia is no hedonistic bastion of tolerance and openness. Although there would not be a central state to enforce moral norms, such norms would nonetheless exist and covenant communities must be ruthlessly intolerant of those who deviate. Communities based on private property rights should not only have the right to expel people in order to protect the social order, but they must do so in order to avoid degenerating back toward state socialism. He further argued that libertarianism is actually incompatible with counter-cultural attitudes, and decried libertarianism's "unusually high numbers of abnormal and perverse followers."[63] In order to restore private property rights and truly erode the

state, libertarians must actually be "radical and uncompromising conservatives."[64] He insisted that libertarians must always favor the right to discriminate, even on the basis of race, and further argued that as long as states exist,
states should have the right to restrict or completely ban foreign immigration.[65]

YES

Unsurprisingly, Hoppe's unconventional views were shared by few of his
colleagues in academia, and toward the end of his teaching career a student
complained about his conduct in the classroom. Specifically, in 2004 he said
that homosexuals tend to have a higher time preference than heterosexuals
because they typically do not have children; he was ultimately absolved of
any wrongdoing.[66] Hoppe retired from teaching in 2008.

Lew Rockwell and the Ludwig von Mises Institute

Whereas the Cato Institute is the center of mainstream, Beltway libertarianism, the Ludwig von Mises Institute is the intellectual epicenter of the
radical libertarian movement in the United States, and it provides an institutional outlet for Austrian school economists. The Mises Institute was
founded in 1982 by Lew Rockwell, who had been friends with Murray Rothbard since 1975; it was Rothbard who convinced Rockwell that the state is
an unnecessary institution.[67] Rockwell also worked with Ron Paul early in
Paul's political career, serving as one of Paul's congressional aides.

In the late 1970s and early 1980s, Rockwell was concerned that Mises's
influence on economic thinking and libertarianism was beginning to wane,
and for this reason was inspired to form the Ludwig von Mises Institute.[68]
During his time in Washington, DC, Rockwell had been unimpressed with
think tanks, libertarian or otherwise, calling them a "scam."[69] He initially
had difficulty securing funding for his organization, as few corporate donors were interested in radical antistate thinking or Austrian economics,
and traditional sources of funding for libertarians groups—the Kochs in particular—wanted nothing to do with the enterprise. The fact that Rothbard
was an early important figure in the Mises Institute guaranteed that the Institute would have to get by without Koch funding.[70]

In spite of initial difficulties, the Mises Institute opened in 1982 in Auburn, Alabama—far from the corridors of American power, or even a major
metropolitan area, though adjacent to Auburn University.[71] The Institute
published the first issue of the *Review of Austrian Economics* in 1986, which
ultimately became the *Quarterly Review of Austrian Economics*. The Institute
provides a venue for the most high profile scholars from the Austrian tradi-

tion, including economists like Hans-Hermann Hoppe and Walter Block, as well as historians such as David Gordon, Thomas Woods, and Ralph Raico. The Institute holds regular seminars for undergraduate and graduate students to learn about the Austrian economic method, and keeps important texts from influential Austrian scholars in print; it also provides many of the works for free on its website as PDFs.

Beyond the Mises Institute, Rockwell is probably best known among libertarians for the website, LewRockwell.com, which began in 1999. The site has published articles by hundreds of writers, and is one of the world's most visited libertarian websites. Not everyone who writes for the site, however, can be accurately described as libertarian. Antiwar conservatives, such as Pat Buchanan, are also published at LewRockwell.com. Rockwell also hosts a regular podcast with likeminded guests on the site. The site includes fairly conventional libertarian analysis of contemporary issues, but also includes original articles about disaster preparation and alternative medicine.

Unsurprisingly, scholars affiliated with the Mises Institute have made radical comments that are not always well received. Libertarians generally find liberals congenial to their arguments when they focus on marijuana legalization, open borders, peace, and social tolerance. However, when libertarians—including many Mises Institute scholars—follow their own arguments to their logical conclusions and argue against child labor laws and civil rights legislation, as well as for the right of secession and discrimination, libertarians are no longer treated respectfully as a superior alternative to mainstream conservatives. Rand Paul, for example, was recently criticized in the *New York Times* for his father's affiliation with the Mises Institute.[72]

Rockwell's most significant contribution to libertarian political strategy was his push for "paleolibertarianism," which sought to build a mainstream libertarian coalition based on culturally conventional but politically disenchanted middle class Americans. There was a brief period in the 1990s in which it appeared that radical libertarians and traditionalists could find sufficient common ground to organize a serious challenge to the political status quo in the United States. The story of this unsuccessful movement will be told in greater detail in the next chapter.

The Libertarian Party

I was ambivalent as to whether to include the LP within the chapter on mainstream or radical libertarianism. On the one hand, the LP has not consistently pushed an extremist antistate message, both for the practical purposes of growing the party and due to the philosophical positions of some of its leaders. When it comes to its actual candidates and policy platforms, in recent years the LP has not been particularly radical. Many of its presidential candidates were once fairly conventional Republicans, and the party has largely abandoned anarchocapitalism. Furthermore, by virtue of being a political party, the LP implicitly endorses the electoral system in the United States. On the other hand, because it is a separate party, the LP necessarily rejects the notion that its supporters are just another part of the conservative movement and the GOP's electoral coalition. This stance alone indicates that the party represents a particularly radical brand of libertarianism.

1972

The LP was largely founded on the efforts of David Nolan, a former Republican. Like many libertarians, Nolan gave up on the organized conservative movement after the disastrous YAF conference of 1969.[73] In 1971, Nolan and his colleagues began the process of organizing the new party, and the LP was officially born in 1972. Its first national convention was held in June of that year, and John Hospers, a philosophy professor at the University of Southern California, was the first LP presidential candidate.

Murray Rothbard was a surprising early critic of the LP. Nolan had hoped Rothbard would serve as the party's first presidential candidate, but Rothbard reminded his readers that the Peace and Freedom Party, which had far more followers and activists than the fledgling LP, never achieved anything of significance and quickly fell apart.[74] If the New Left had never successfully created a new political party, then surely libertarians, who were much smaller in number and less well organized, had no chance of breaking into electoral politics. At the very least, a libertarian political party was premature. Rothbard ultimately chose to involve himself in the LP, however, and he played an important role in the party in the late 1970s and 1980s.

The LP's first presidential run was no less disappointing than Rothbard anticipated. Even if there was a massive amount of grassroots support for libertarianism in the electorate, getting a new party on the ballot in every state is incredibly difficult; the fact that the LP organized so shortly before the 1972 presidential election assured that it would be impossible to make it onto enough state ballots to secure the presidency even if Hospers won every state in which he was a choice. In the end, Hospers was only able to make it onto the ballot in two states, and he earned far less than 1 percent of the total popular vote.

Although its effect on the outcome of the 1972 presidential race was minimal, the LP ticket did make electoral history in that year. Hospers did not win the popular vote in any state, but he did win the support of a single bad-faith elector in the electoral college. Although state delegates to the electoral college are expected to vote as their state voted, federal law does not force them to do so. After the election, Roger MacBride, one of the electors from Virginia, refused to vote for Nixon and instead gave his support to Hospers and his running mate, even though Hospers was not even on the ballot in Virginia. Hosper's running mate was Theodora Nathan, and thanks to MacBride, Nathan was the first woman and the first Jewish person to receive a vote in the electoral college.

In spite of its weak showing in its first year, the LP persevered. Like any political party, the LP struggled with factionalism within the party. Although libertarianism is presumably based on a few simple axioms, we already have seen that, in practice, self-described libertarians have disagreed with one another on virtually every important issue. A key point of disagreement, however, is between the anarchists and the minarchists. Could the LP officially call for something other than total privatization on issues like defense, the courts, or the police without permanently alienating the anarchist wing of the party? The solution, which helped keep the party together, was the 1974 Dallas Accord. At the LP convention in Dallas, Texas, it was unofficially determined that, in the interest of party unity and political organizing, the party would not take an official stand on whether or not states could ever be just and legitimate.[75]

The LP has never been able to satisfy all of its members and potential supporters. The key question of radicalism versus gradualism never really went away. A number of radicals ran for office on the Libertarian ticket for state-level offices—Jerome Tuccille ran for governor of New York in 1974—but its presidential candidates tended to be less extreme and presumably more electable. In 1976, Roger MacBride was the nominee. The party was somewhat more successful that time, making the ballot in thirty-two states and earning 173,000 votes.[76]

It was in 1980 that the LP both enjoyed its greatest success and infuriated its more radical members. This was the year in which Ed Clark ran for president on the LP ticket, and David Koch was on the ticket as the vice presidential candidate. As noted in the previous chapter, the presence of Koch on the ticket gave the LP the advantage of additional funding; because it was his own campaign, Koch was less limited in his ability to spend money. This year was also notable because of the degree to which Clark ran a moderate campaign, describing his libertarian ideology as "low-tax liberalism."[77] This irritated many more radical libertarians, who believed Clark was selling out libertarian principles in order to make the LP more palatable to voters. Over the course of the campaign, Clark occasionally took positions that were less economically libertarian than Ronald Reagan's proposals.[78] In spite of misgivings from party radicals, the LP did comparatively well in 1980, winning more than 900,000 votes, or more than 1 percent of the popular vote, for the first time in its history. This was the largest number of votes earned by a LP candidate until 2012, when the LP won over a million votes.

In spite of the relatively successful showing by a moderate candidate in 1980, the radical wing of the LP secured one of its own as the party's nominee in 1984: David Berglund.[79] Unfortunately for the party, Berglund was unable to build on Clark's foundation. In 1984, the LP won far fewer votes than it won in 1980. Subsequent LP candidates have varied in their radicalism and proper placement on the ideological spectrum. Ron Paul was the nominee in 1988, and he performed better than Berglund, but still won less than 1 percent of the popular vote. The party received between one quarter and one half of 1 percent throughout the 1990s and early 2000s.

In the two most recent presidential elections, the LP ran high-profile former Republicans as candidates. In 2008, Bob Barr, a former Republican member of Congress from Texas, was the nominee. Barr was an interesting choice in that his record in Congress was not particularly libertarian; he had previously supported the Patriot Act and voted to approve the Iraq war, for example. Barr ultimately won about 0.04 percent of the popular vote.[80] Gary Johnson, former Republican governor of New Mexico, was the party's nominee in 2012 after failing to secure the Republican Party's presidential nomination. He had a more consistent libertarian record than Barr, and he had more success on Election Day. His 0.99 percent of the popular vote was the largest share earned by a LP candidate since 1980.[81]

Against the State and Individual Liberty?

As noted earlier, a conservative critique against libertarianism is that it is motivated purely by selfishness and hedonism. Although some libertarians may be motivated by the desire to take drugs, have unconventional sex, and pay few taxes, few would describe this impulse as the basis for their political philosophy. Many of the figures discussed in this chapter, such as Hoppe, clearly bristle at the state of contemporary culture, and they blame the state for bringing deleterious cultural revolutions about. In fact, one could argue that some (though few) libertarians oppose the state because it is not repressive enough. That is, in the absence of a centralized state, other forms of order would emerge—forms of order that are less tolerant of moral decadence and extreme individualism than the current order. This brand of right-wing anarchism is completely divorced from the liberal tradition.

We see this brand of libertarianism on display in the small national anarchist movement. This movement is against the centralized state but in favor of racial separatism and tribalism. The movement calls for a stateless society made up of homogenous, self-ruling communities—communities that may or may not subscribe to liberal values such as tolerance. This movement, which borrows many of its aesthetic sensibilities from the anarchist left, has yet to garner a major following. Its leading theoretician is Troy Southgate. Jack Donovan, a right-wing blogger and author, has called for what he describes as anarchofascism.[82] He wishes to see the tribal unity that fascism presupposes, but he does not believe it can be implemented from the top. Instead, he wishes to see the world once again free from the state and instead dominated by male gangs: "When the body of the people is released from the head of the sovereign, chaos will ensue. In that chaos, men will find themselves. They will stop looking to the State for help, and start looking to each other. Together, men can create smaller, tighter, more localized systems."[83]

Observers of contemporary libertarianism will also see the occasional *FORMER JBS* combination of religious fervor with antistatism. Gary North, who is an associate scholar at the Mises Institute, is both a libertarian and a Christian theocrat. He has argued, for example, that the Bible directly calls for free-market capitalism.[84] North is a Christian Reconstructionist, and as such, he argues that "the whole law of God, including, but not limited to, the Mosaic case laws is the standard by which individuals, families, churches, and civil governments should conduct their affairs."[85] This theocratic vision differs from others, however, in that it does not call for high levels of centralization, such as we see in Islamic theocracies today. Rather than a unified theocratic government led by a single religious leader or group of leaders, this vision calls for "a decentralized social order where civil government is only one legitimate government among many other governments, including family government and ecclesiastical (church) government."[86] North and those who share his political and theological views thus envision a society that both lacks a powerful centralized government and implements the harshest elements of Old Testament law.

These anarchists and radical libertarians who are both on the right and completely outside of the liberal tradition are few in number and without

GOING NOWHERE

any meaningful influence. I am not suggesting that other, more prominent radical libertarians secretly harbor these views. I mention these ideas simply to note one may oppose the state for reasons other than a passion for individual liberty.

Conclusion

This chapter, and the chapter that preceded it, demonstrates the paradoxical nature of libertarianism. Virtually all libertarians agree on a small number of simple axioms (nonaggression and self-ownership), yet the libertarian movement is rife with factionalism and fierce disagreement. These disagreements are often deeper than ephemeral questions of strategy or tone. Both radical anarchists and low-tax liberals claim the title of libertarian, which further confuses the issue. There is also the important question of whether libertarians can or should be considered a part of the larger mainstream right in the United States and whether libertarians should be treated as a totally distinct ideological category or even an ideology on the left.

Rothbard and others found long ago that libertarians and leftists were unsuitable allies; while they could make common cause on particular issues, their fundamental worldviews were simply too different for any long-term alliance to form. Thus the question has generally remained whether libertarians should form an alliance with conservatives or insist on going their own way. In recent years, however, there has been some talk of a rapprochement between libertarianism and the left. This conversation began largely as a result of an article that Brink Lindsey wrote in the *New Republic* in 2006, "Liberaltarians."[87] Lindsey, who at that time worked for the Cato Institute, noted that progressives and libertarians have more in common with each other than is generally acknowledged. He argued that the two camps could cooperate more in the future. Lindsey pointed out the degree to which the contemporary conservative movement had moved even further away from libertarian principles during the Bush presidency, and thus conservatives and libertarians should stop pretending that they hold a similar worldview. He further noted that it is time for contemporary liberals to embrace the free market, as free markets have unquestionably been a primary catalyst for progressive social changes in recent decades.[88]

Lindsey's arguments were given a respectful hearing from other libertarians, and Will Wilkinson, a fellow Cato Institute scholar, shared Lindsey's hope that progressives and libertarians could find new common ground.[89] Now that the cold war is over and communism no longer represents a legitimate threat, much of the tactical justification for a libertarian–conservative alliance is gone. However, in recent years there has been less talk of a new fusionism between libertarians and progressives. Since President Obama's election, the Democratic Party has shown little sympathy for libertarian ideas, and the mainstream right is again becoming comparatively antistatist; although I do not consider the Tea Party a libertarian movement, its primary institutions have certainly expressed many libertarian ideas. Although mainstream conservatives and libertarians may disagree on a number of key issues, to the extent that libertarians remain in any larger coalition, it is a good bet that libertarians will continue to seek alliances on the right.

7

Nostalgia as a Political Platform

In chapter 2, which discussed the conservative movement's frequent purges, we saw that many of the scholars and journalists ultimately rejected by the mainstream right can be properly classified as part of the paleoconservative movement. In that chapter I discussed the specific comments that cost many of these figures their mainstream respectability. However, it would be unfair to only examine those passages that indicated that paleoconservatives were primarily motivated by racism or anti-Semitism, though some critics may plausibly argue that racial animus was a key motivating factor for many paleoconservatives. Thinkers from this ideological tradition have a much larger body of work, and their ideas deserve a more comprehensive examination.

Despite making an impressive showing in the 1990s, paleoconservatism presently appears to be a spent force. Unlike the mainstream right or the libertarian movement, it does not have any powerful, well-funded research institutes. Nor does it enjoy support from any billionaire benefactors. Although many of the most important paleoconservative intellectuals and journalists are still alive and working, few have access to mainstream publications or other media venues, nor is there a younger generation of prominent paleoconservative activists eager to carry on the ideological tradition.

Before moving forward, it will be useful to have a working definition of the term paleoconservative. The term is relatively young, first entering into the American political lexicon in the 1980s.[1] Many have described paleoconservatives as the lingering remnant of the old right that was influential before the rise of the contemporary conservative movement in the 1950s. On the basis of this definition, paleoconservatives may be considered the ideological descendants of H. L. Mencken, Albert Jay Nock, and Garet Garrett. Joseph Scotchie, who wrote the most comprehensive book on the paleoconservative movement, actually uses the terms paleoconservative and old right interchangeably.[2] Although this is not an unreasonable description, I do not agree with it, as it implies that today's paleoconservatives are more elitist and libertarian than is probably the case.

One of the few things we can say definitively about all paleoconservatives is that they dislike neoconservatives and believe they had an invidious effect on the American right; they typically assert that the neoconservatives are not, in fact, conservative at all. Southerners are overrepresented in the paleoconservative ranks, but it is not a Southern nationalist movement. Paleoconservatives have been typically more likely to use racially inflammatory language than mainstream conservatives, and they are generally restrictionist in their immigration policy preferences, but it would also be incorrect to treat paleoconservatism and white nationalism as interchangeable. Paleoconservatives are generally less hawkish than other conservatives, but they are divided on whether the United States conducted the cold war in a just and reasonable manner. George Nash described the paleoconservative movement as follows: "Fiercely and defiantly 'nationalist' (rather than 'internationalist'), skeptical of 'global democracy' and entanglements overseas, fearful of the impact of Third World immigration on America's Europe-oriented culture, and openly critical of the doctrine of free trade, Buchananite paleoconservatism increasingly resembled much of the American Right *before* 1945: before, that is, the onset of the Cold War."[3]

Paleoconservatism is noticeably gloomy and negative. As Justin Raimondo noted in *Chronicles*, "Surely, the defining characteristic of the paleoconservative temperament is disgust—with the current state of the country, the culture, and (most of all) the 'official' conservative movement."[4] Indeed, it would be accurate to say that paleoconservatives have spent more time critiquing the right—particularly the neoconservative right—than the left. To be fair, this animosity was returned. As noted in chapter 2, many of the figures discussed in this chapter were excommunicated from the conservative movement and airbrushed from the movement's history books.

Despite its insistence that it represents "permanent things," the reality is that the conservative movement in America has evolved as social circumstances changed. For example, the mainstream conservative movement now tries to distance itself from what prominent conservative leaders said about civil rights in the 1960s. It is not implausible to imagine that within a few decades the movement will try to disassociate itself from the anti–gay marriage stance it promoted during the Bush years, and perhaps even claim that acceptance of gay marriage represented a victory for conservatives. From a Burkean standpoint, there is nothing wrong with a political party or political movement evolving with the times. Such evolution is surely necessary for practical purposes. Russell Kirk argued that the acceptance of change is an essential conservative principle.

We might think of paleoconservatives simply as conservatives who simply refuse to get with the times. That is, as the rest of the movement changes, they remain right where they are ideologically and in their policy preferences. As time goes on, those conservatives who refused to keep up with the zeitgeist become too distant from their former allies to maintain any kind of formal association, and they find themselves shunned. Different figures associated with paleoconservative thought are politically frozen in different eras, and thus they do not always agree with one another. Their one shared characteristic is bitterness toward an ostensibly right-wing movement that throws inconvenient professed allies to the wolves.

In a 1993 essay attempting to make sense of the paleoconservative movement, Chris Woltermann argued that the movement would simply not exist without its chief antagonist, neoconservatism, and paleoconservatives are predominantly defined by their disagreements with neoconservatives.[5] To Woltermann, the key points of contention between these groups are "commitment to individual human rights and enthusiasm for private power. . . . Although paleoconservatives appreciate individual rights, they assign primacy to private powers as the source of such rights."[6] The two groups also differ in their attitudes toward modernity. Few neoconservatives express an open desire to turn back the clock to any specific period of history, even when they lament certain contemporary trends. Many paleoconservatives, however, reject many of the premises of the modern world, which actually makes them "profoundly countercultural."[7]

In the pages that follow, I will describe the ideas that motivated this group of anachronistic figures on the right. We will see that there was a general continuity between the paleoconservatives and the old right, but the paleoconservatives also provided their own new analysis of American social and economic trends. Unlike libertarians, paleoconservatives are not bound by a set of logical axioms, and thus they have disagreed on many important issues. We will also consider the efforts to forge a new right-wing alliance between paleoconservatives and radical libertarians, and their failed effort to dislodge the mainstream conservative movement as the hegemonic force on the right.

Remnants of the Old Right

Like many libertarians, the paleoconservative movement can plausibly describe itself as the intellectual heir of the old right that opposed the New Deal and Roosevelt's push for war against the Axis powers. But paleoconservatives and libertarians, on average, differ in their opinions on many key policies. Thus, if they are both claiming the old right as their ideological ancestor, one or both of them must be mistaken. The reality, however, is that the old right was never a coherent ideological category. As we saw in chapter 1, the old right was really a loose confederation of social critics united in little else than opposition to Roosevelt. Figures like Mencken and Nock were not in the business of writing policy platforms or leading a grassroots revolt; their dispositions were not well suited for such a task. The degree to which many of the most celebrated figures of the old right were secular further undermines the argument that paleoconservatives were simply a continuation of this older right-wing tradition. The paleoconservative movement was openly conservative on cultural issues and relied heavily on religious rhetoric. To my knowledge, Sam Francis was the only prominent paleoconservative thinker who was not personally religious, and he never lambasted Christianity as such.

Nonetheless, it is clear that many right-wing intellectuals from the interwar period did influence the paleoconservative movement, particularly on issues of war and peace. One particularly important writer, whose thought is echoed by more contemporary figures like Pat Buchanan, was John T. Flynn. Like many figures on the right during the late 1930s and early 1940s, Flynn was part of the America First Committee and opposed American entry into World War II. Flynn made the case that Roosevelt had put the United States on a path toward fascism and that waging a war against Germany, Italy, and Japan would only expedite the process. Flynn argued that the most ardent opponents of fascism overseas were laying the groundwork for fascism at home.[8]

Garet Garrett was another important antiwar figure on the right who influenced both libertarians and later paleoconservatives. Garrett, like many paleoconservatives decades later, argued that conservative efforts to block revolutionary change are now futile. The revolutionaries have already succeeded: "There are those who still think they are holding the pass against a revolution that may be coming up the road. But they are gazing in the wrong direction. The revolution is behind them. It went by in the Night of Depression, singing songs to freedom."[9] Garrett continued:

> You do not defend a world that is already lost. When was it lost? That you cannot say precisely. It is a point for the revolutionary historian to ponder. We know only that it was surrendered peacefully, without a struggle, almost unawares. There was no day, no hour, no celebration of the event—and yet definitely, the ultimate power of initiative did pass from the hands of private enterprise to government.
>
> There it is and there it will remain until, if ever, it shall be reconquered. Certainly government will never surrender it without a struggle.[10]

Up to this point, contemporary antiwar libertarians would have few points of disagreements with old right thinkers. However, there is a major issue on which paleoconservatives and libertarians disagree, and on this issue the paleoconservatives are continuing an older right-wing tradition that today's libertarians reject. Paleoconservatives, in contrast to both libertarians and mainstream conservatives, are generally protectionist and skeptical of free-trade agreements. Although conservatives typically laud free trade as an indispensable part of American capitalism, they tend to forget that the Republican Party was aggressively protectionist and in favor of heavy tariffs for the first several decades of its existence. At the time, it was assumed that protectionism was necessary in order to foster young industries in the United States. America's growth as an economic powerhouse in the late nineteenth century indicates that these policies were not unsuccessful.

Protectionism now has few supporters. Unions, which are generally associated with the left, remain skeptical of new free-trade agreements, but the Democratic Party has recently been generally supportive of free trade. In 2014, President Obama signed legislation designed to expedite the creation of new trade agreements, though not without some resistance from his fellow Democrats. Among mainstream economists, barriers to trade represent an inefficiency that denies nations the ability to make best use of their comparative advantages and ultimately harms all parties but a few special interests. Libertarian economists have decried protectionism for more than a century. Frédéric Bastiat famously mocked protectionism by noting that if we really believe in protectionist principles, we should block out the sun for the benefit of candlestick makers. Paleoconservatives were therefore some of the last significant supporters of old-fashioned protectionism.

Mel Bradford

As noted in chapter 2, M. E. "Mel" Bradford was the preferred choice of many traditionalists for the position of chair of the National Endowment for the Humanities during the Reagan administration. Compared to the lofty positions occupied by neoconservatives during the Reagan years, the NEH chairship was a relatively modest bone for the president to throw a group that was still an important element within the conservative coalition. Nonetheless, the neoconservatives successfully maneuvered one of their own, Bill Bennett, into that position. This set off a heated exchange between neoconservatives and that group on the right that was just beginning to be called paleoconservative. Chapter 2 briefly mentioned some of the reasons for neoconservative hostility toward Bradford: antipathy toward Lincoln and sympathy for the Confederacy, as well as support for George Wallace during his presidential campaigns. However, that chapter said little about Bradford's thought.

Bradford's views were deeply linked to his personal identity as a Southerner. Although he is now best known for his views on history and politics, Bradford was not a historian or a political scientist; he earned his PhD in English from Vanderbilt University, and much of his scholarly research was focused on the work of William Faulkner. Bradford also had a strong interest in the intentions of the men who wrote the US Constitution, and near the end of his life he wrote a book on the subject.

Like the Southern Agrarians who preceded him, Bradford defended the hierarchical nature of the traditional South; he argued that it represented a more harmonious and natural social order than the order associated with the North's industrial capitalism. He described the South at its best as "a patriarchal world of families, pre- or non-capitalist *because* familial, located, pious, and 'brotherly'; agrarian in order not to produce the alienated, atomistic individual to whom abstractly familial totalitarianism can appeal; classically republican because that system of government best allowed for the multiplicity that was the nation while at the same time permitting the agrarian culture of families to flourish unperturbed."[11]

Bradford courted controversy with his work for much of his career, but his philosophical disputes with the neoconservative scholar Harry Jaffa are still well remembered. Jaffa and Bradford sparred over the issue of equality and how it relates to conservatism. Their respective positions on this issue are still worth reading because they represent such a critical fault line in right-wing thought. Unlike most conservatives of his day, who believed equality was a noble ideal but who argued that inequality should be allowed for utilitarian reasons, Bradford attacked egalitarianism head-on.

To Bradford, the "cult of equality" was anathema to true conservatism.[12] In his view, the line from the Declaration of Independence, "all men are created equal," was clearly a rhetorical flourish and was never intended as a dogma; if one reads that phrase in the context of the larger document, it is impossible to infer that Jefferson was arguing for egalitarianism. In contrast to other conservatives, such as Jaffa, Bradford argued that the American Revolution was not particularly revolutionary and that it was not motivated by a passion for equality. Bradford further argued that Abraham Lincoln's understanding of Jefferson's thought was not just mistaken but also represented a "millenarian infection" that promised to result in an "endless series of turmoils and revolutions."[13] Bradford was not the first conservative to make these arguments; his statements on equality, the Declaration of Independence, and Lincoln were similar to arguments made by Willmoore Kendall a few decades before. The fact that Bradford was controversial even among conservatives demonstrates the degree to which the mainstream conservative movement had evolved on these questions since it was founded.

Bradford praised conservatives and libertarians for rejecting the progressive demand for equality of results, but he criticized them for accepting the doctrine of "equality of opportunity" because accepting even this more mild brand of egalitarianism opened the door for ever-greater demands of equality. Further, while Christians can rightly speak of spiritual equality before God, this form of equality does not have political implications.[14]

As an aside, Bradford's intransigence on many issues—such as equality, on which he is considered on the wrong side of history by most contemporary Americans—reveals a key point about conservatism. At its most simplistic, conservatism can be described as simply a defense of the status quo, whatever that may be. Thus, at the end of the 1980s, doctrinaire communists in the Soviet Union could be described accurately as conservative. In this formulation, conservatism has no fixed meaning but rather is defined entirely by the current social situation.

This, of course, is something of a problem for traditionalists in most of the developed world, including the United States. Although American conservatives can claim victory on the question of whether central planning or the market leads to greater overall prosperity, on virtually every other front, conservatism has been in slow retreat. Social values that within living memory Americans took for granted have been completely upended. The various social revolutions that occurred since World War II are now firmly entrenched. Thus, if conservatism is simply defined as a defense of the established order, the defense of equality, social tolerance, and a large, powerful national government can now be described as conservative. Indeed, few on the mainstream right seriously propose undoing the left's most impressive victories of the last six decades. The one glaring exception is the constitutional right to abortion, which most important conservative institutions still officially oppose.

Paleoconservatives differ from their mainstream counterparts on this point. Among the prominent paleoconservatives, there was an open desire to reverse many social changes. Bradford was one of the more articulate proponents of this view, and he argued that the traditional right needed to take a more radical stand. Like Richard Weaver before him, Bradford was concerned with the issue of rhetoric, and he excoriated conservatives for allowing the left to define and redefine America's most important political values. In order to maintain respectability, conservatives have conceded key points to their ideological opponents. Conservatives furthermore allowed their vision for America to be preempted by "considerations of policy or the ephemera of 'management style.'"[15]

Bradford was an early critic of those newcomers to the conservative movement who, upon being welcomed into the conservative tent, insisted that conservatism be redefined to better match their own sensibilities. Bradford, in 1986, attacked the neoconservatives for this practice: "There are, to be sure, certain groups who have recently attached the conservative label to themselves who . . . so redefine our position that we can no longer hold it for our own." He further argued that these so-called conservatives "steal our identity and put it to uses at odds with its origins: to invert it into something foreign to itself, leaving those who are still conservatives in the familiar sense of the term no ground on which to stand."[16] In subsequent decades, this has been a common complaint of the paleoconservatives.

Bradford died in 1993, and his work is rarely discussed by mainstream conservatives; his failure to secure a position at the NEH is now generally considered just an unimportant footnote in the history of the conservative movement. To paleoconservatives, however, Bradford's story epitomizes the perfidy of neoconservatives.

Pat Buchanan

Perhaps no other figure discussed in this book is more openly sentimental about pre-1960s America than Patrick J. Buchanan. Whether he is talking about the decline of domestic manufacturing, the high levels of immigration, the right's thorough defeat in the culture wars, or the United States' military overreach, Buchanan clearly believes that America has become poorer, more degenerate, more imperialistic, and less free over the course of his lifetime. A sense of Spenglerian despondency is present in all of his recent books. Buchanan is also unusual among former and present presidential contenders in that he has long been a prolific author.

Pat Buchanan's political philosophy might be summed up by the title of this 1999 book, *A Republic, Not an Empire.* He clearly would like to see America return to a time when the federal government was small and there were no permanent foreign entanglements—a position that sets him apart from the mainstream conservative movement. Although not a pacifist of the libertarian or any other variety, Buchanan has argued that American foreign policy should exclusively service American interests rather than human rights or democracy abroad. On the basis of this standard, Buchanan takes a dim view of most of America's overseas conflicts throughout its history. He further rejects the notion that the United States ever truly had an isolationist period.

Beyond criticizing America's conducting of the Vietnam war and recent misadventures in the Middle East, Buchanan has more controversially challenged conventional wisdom about World War II. In *A Republic, Not an Empire,* Buchanan advanced the argument that Pearl Harbor was Japan's rational response to the economic warfare the United States was waging against Japan in the form of trade embargoes and asset seizures.[17] More recently, Buchanan attacked the accepted narrative about the European theater of the war. In *Churchill, Hitler, and the Unnecessary War* (2008), Buchanan argued against the notion that German aggression was solely responsible for the outbreak of war. According to Buchanan's interpretation of events, much of the blame for that devastating conflict must be ascribed to the Winston Churchill, who foolishly extended Poland a guarantee of security even though Britain could obviously not protect Poland from a German invasion.[18] Buchanan further rejected the notion that World War II was a straightforward, good-versus-evil struggle, noting that there were more than enough barbaric acts committed by the Allies—especially the bombing of civilians—to make such an interpretation untenable.

Not surprisingly, Buchanan was one of the most vocal voices on the right against the invasion of Iraq. He has similarly been warning against the current bellicose attitude toward Russia, arguing that the United States has been the true aggressor in Eastern Europe and that Russian anxieties about the eastward expansion of NATO are understandable. This expansion, according to Buchanan, is furthermore foolhardy, since the United States has no compelling national interest in the Baltic countries or any other part of Eastern Europe that has traditionally been part of Russia's sphere of influence.[19]

Buchanan was perhaps the last prominent figure on the American right to furiously denounce free-trade agreements out of principle. His stance on this subject shows that he rejects common interpretations of American economic history. When making their arguments about protectionist policies, proponents of free trade commonly point to the Smoot-Hawley Tariff, which was implemented shortly after the onset of the Great Depression. It is now conventional wisdom that this policy exacerbated an already painful economic situation. Buchanan, however, disagrees with this assessment. Buchanan has argued for more than two decades that protectionism did not intensify the Great Depression. In fact, according to Buchanan, "no nation has ever risen to pre-eminence through free trade."[20] Buchanan has more recently argued that free trade resulted in Britain's decline as the preeminent economic power in the world, and it is presently having the same effect in the United States.

Perhaps even more than foreign policy, Buchanan has long been incensed by American immigration policy. Specifically, Buchanan objects to the porous southern border of the United States, as well as the lack of will to end undocumented immigration and lower the high levels of legal immigration. He made immigration a key part of his platform in all three of his presidential runs, and he has since written several books focusing primarily on this issue. The first of these, *The Death of the West* (2002), discussed how the combination of low native birth rates combined with high levels of immigration is fundamentally changing the demographics of the United States. The book argued that this will ultimately break down the nation's cultural cohesiveness and threaten its political stability.

Buchanan and other paleoconservatives are certainly not alone on the right in their concern about immigration. However, Buchanan is notable for being such an early and aggressive proponent of immigration restriction. He was also an early voice warning Republicans that even if they agreed that immigration was good for the economy and desired by the party's wealthy donors, immigration would ultimately doom the party to permanent-minority status. All the work that he and others had done to build the powerful Republican coalition that put Nixon and Reagan in the White House was being undone by immigration:

> For a quarter century, Democrats were unable to pick the GOP lock on the presidency, because they could not shake loose the Republican grip on the white vote. With the exception of Lyndon Johnson's landslide of 1964, no Democrat since Truman in 1948 had won the white vote. What broke the GOP lock on the presidency was the Immigration Act of 1965.
>
> During the anti-Soviet riots in East Berlin in 1953, Bertolt Brecht, the Communist playwright, quipped, "Would it not be easier . . . for the government to dissolve the people and elect another?" In the last thirty years, America has begun to import a new electorate, as Republicans cheerfully backed an immigration policy tilted to the Third World that enlarged the Democratic base and loosened the grip that Nixon and Reagan had given them on the presidency of the United States.[21]

The accusation that mass immigration is a deliberate attempt by business elites and left-wing multiculturalists to "dissolve the people and elect another" is a common refrain among the more vigorous opponent opponents of immigration, particularly paleoconservatives. Brecht's remark, noted in the Buchanan quote above, is frequently quoted by other restrictionists, such as Peter Brimelow[22] and other writers associated with VDARE.com,[23] an anti-immigration website that also publishes Buchanan's columns. Brimelow himself was once an editor at *National Review* and during the 1990s wrote scathing attacks on American immigration policies.[24] Like other figures discussed in chapter 2 who attacked immigration using explicitly racial arguments, Brimelow's work is no longer published in mainstream venues.

Like many other paleoconservative restrictionists, Buchanan has openly acknowledged that part of the problem with contemporary immigration is that it is non-European. To my knowledge, he has never publicly declared that nonwhites are inherently inferior to whites or otherwise genetically unsuited to live in Western countries. However, he has on many occasions noted that these new immigrants are different—in important and negative ways—from the previous waves of immigrants who arrived in the eighteenth and early nineteenth century. This type of argumentation is not embraced solely by paleoconservatives. The late Samuel Huntington made similar arguments about immigration in his 2004 book, *Who Are We?*[25] The cultural argument against current mass immigration holds that the United States possesses a specific political culture—an Anglo-Protestant culture, to use Huntington's term—and the current waves of immigration threaten to permanently alter this culture.

Whereas previous immigrants made an aggressive effort to assimilate—and even if they did not, sheer distance from their country of origin made assimilation ultimately a foregone conclusion—today's immigrants, especially those from Latin America, maintain their emotional ties to their country of origin and have little desire to conform to the predominant cultural norms of the United States. According to Buchanan, "Unlike the immigrants of old, who bid farewell to their native lands when they boarded the ship, for Mexicans, the mother country is right next door. Millions have no desire to learn English or to become citizens. America is not their home; Mexico is; and they wish to remain proud Mexicans."[26]

It is not just immigration that threatens Buchanan's vision for America's culture. As a devout Catholic and cultural conservative, Buchanan has decried the long-term decline in religious observance in the United States. He argues that this is not just bad for Christianity in America but bad for the nation as a whole, regardless of the degree to which Christian doctrine conforms to reality. Buchanan argued that religion was a useful bulwark against the spread of Marxism in the West and that religious decline will usher in a new era of socialism.[27] Buchanan also ascribes the decline in religious observance to a host of negative social trends such as higher illegitimacy rates, abortion, cheating in all aspects of life (in academics, business, and marriage), and in the rise of suicides.[28]

Although all of Buchanan's recent books have had a gloomy tone, his 2011 book *Suicide of a Superpower* was perhaps Buchanan at his most despondent. In this work, he touched on all of the issues that he considered in his previous books: imperial overreach, unchecked immigration, the decline of religion, and the decimation of American manufacturing. The book's subtitle asked, "Will America survive until 2025?" Buchanan answers: probably not. To reverse America's decline, Buchanan suggested a number of policies that have a negligible probability of being enacted, such as a complete moratorium on immigration, the closure of most American military bases overseas, a radical decrease in government spending, economic protectionism, and an aggressive conservative counterattack in the culture wars.[29]

Suicide of a Superpower was not just Buchanan's most pessimistic book; it was also his most explicitly racial work. Some critics argued that the controversial fourth chapter of the book, titled "The End of White America," crossed the boundary from acceptable social criticism into outright racism. In this chapter, Buchanan argued that "tribal politics is not unusual, tribal politics is eternal."[30] As America becomes more diverse, Buchanan argues that we can reasonably expect that politics will become a zero-sum game of competing racial and ethnic groups. He also blamed political dysfunction in California directly on immigrants; he was also openly critical of homosexuality and the various groups that lobby for more gay rights.

Despite being disavowed by the mainstream conservative movement, Buchanan remained a mainstay on many television networks for many years after his last failed presidential bid. *Suicide of a Superpower*, however, appears to have ended Buchanan's run as a prominent political commentator. As a result of heated criticism, MSNBC terminated its relationship with Buchanan in 2012. Phil Griffin, president of the network, explained this decision by noting, "The ideas he put forth aren't really appropriate for national dialogue, much less the dialogue on MSNBC."[31] Unsurprisingly, Buchanan responded to these attacks, claiming he had been "blacklisted" by groups like the Anti-Defamation League and Color of Change—groups Buchanan claims lobbied for his firing. He argued that it was hypocritical for liberal groups to silence speakers with whom they disagree: "All the while prattling about their love of dissent and devotion to the First Amendment, they seek systematically to silence and censor dissent."[32]

Although no longer employed by MSNBC, Buchanan continues to provide political commentary on multiple radio and television programs, and he still writes a weekly column.

Thomas Fleming and *Chronicles*

Different trends within right-wing thought are generally associated with particular magazines. *National Review* has long been the flagship journal of the mainstream conservative movement. *Commentary*, and more recently the *Weekly Standard*, are the main voices of neoconservatism. The main venue for paleoconservative thought was and remains *Chronicles*, which is published by the Rockford Institute—perhaps the only paleoconservative think tank. Like the Mises Institute, the Rockford Institute is ostentatiously distant from the major metropolitan areas on the coasts; it is located in Rockford, Illinois.

The Rockford Institute was founded in 1976 by John Howard, but the figure most associated with the think tank and its journal is Thomas Fleming. Fleming, a classicist, earned his PhD at the University of North Carolina, Chapel Hill, where he met two like-minded graduate students and future collaborators: Clyde Wilson and Sam Francis.[33] Fleming's first foray into publishing was the short-lived *Southern Partisan Quarterly Review*, a journal intended to represent the Southern intellectual tradition that first appeared in 1979. Like many others in the paleoconservative ideological camp, much of Fleming's work is an open defense and celebration of the South. In his contribution to the 1982 edited volume, *The New Right Papers*, Fleming approvingly noted that many of the most socially conservative voices in Washington, DC, came from the South.[34]

Fleming argued that Northern conservatives solely interested in propping up the capitalist system are not conservative at all; in contrast, conservatism had a decidedly different, more authentic, meaning in the South:

ECONOMISM

It is obvious to anyone that many capitalist "conservatives" are nothing better than nineteenth century liberals with a hangover. Their libertarian ideas of freedom, expressed almost always in economic terms, are tempered only by the recognition that it takes force to keep the discontented masses in their place. However, when a Southerner *SOME TRUTHS HERE* calls himself conservative, he is usually thinking of a way of life, of a social order and a moral order for which the people of the 1860s went to war. He is more disturbed by the disintegration of the family than by rising interest rates. He believes in Free Enterprise and might even be happy to go to war to resist Soviet aggression, but he is not so delighted with the mobility and tawdriness of modern life, with the fast food and the fast buck artists who seem intent on turning the New South into a suburb of Chicago. He does not like to see family farms swallowed up by Agribusiness in the interest of progress and productivity. Above all, he knows the value of stability and the price of progress.[35]

In the above passage, we immediately recognize similarities between this brand of paleoconservatism and the localist ideology examined in chapter 4. Indeed, the two cannot always be easily distinguished, and writers associated with localism, such as Bill Kauffman, have written for *Chronicles* in the past. It is at this point that I should again note that there is not a fixed and consistent definition of paleoconservative, as Fleming himself has acknowledged. Fleming argued that paleoconservatism is a continuation of the interwar old right, whereas Paul Gottfried viewed paleoconservatism as the true heir of the 1950s conservative movement before it was hijacked by neoconservatives. Fleming further argued that paleoconservatism cannot be properly conceived of as a movement, an ideology, or a philosophy; it is an approach or style of political thinking and acting. It shares many of the concerns of earlier conservative thought—a respect for order, a love of personal liberty, and a willingness to learn from tradition, but it is both more coherent and a good deal more skeptical of propaganda and political mythology. Though perfectly willing to make compromises with political realities, palaeoconservatives are not willing to surrender their principles or their loyalties or their integrity for the sake of a job in Washington or a column in *The New York Times*.[36]

Although Fleming did not leave for a job in Washington or New York, he did leave the South in 1984 to take the position of managing editor of *Chronicles*. Under Fleming's leadership, *Chronicles* became the one of the first prominent journals on the right to stake out a clear and uncompromising stance against further mass immigration, for both economic and cultural reasons.[37] Hostility toward mass immigration—particularly undocumented immigration from the developing world—has been a common characteristic of paleoconservatism. Further, while the mainstream conservative movement is generally careful to limit its critique to unlawful immigration,[38] paleoconservatives have been openly opposed to high levels of legal immigration as well. Paleoconservatives are generally immune to the American tendency to romanticize Ellis Island and immigration; Chilton Williamson Jr., a former editor at *National Review* but now the senior book editor at *Chronicles*, wrote a book on immigration called *The Immigration Mystique: America's False Conscience* (1996), in which he argued against the various romantic myths Americans believe about immigration.[39]

Compared to Gottfried and other figures associated with the paleoconservative movement, Fleming claims to be less bitter and angry toward the neoconservatives.[40] Part of this surely stems from the fact that Fleming never had a career within the mainstream conservative movement to begin with, and one cannot be cast out of a club to which one never belonged. He is also less convinced that the conservative movement ever had much value, even before the movement was supposedly conquered by invading neocons.

In spite of always being somewhat aloof from the conservative movement, Fleming and *Chronicles* have come under attack from better-known institutions. One of most significant attacks on *Chronicles'* brand of paleoconservatism occurred when the Rockford Institute fired Richard Neuhaus, a Catholic priest and neoconservative who went on to edit *First Things*. Neuhaus apparently long had a contentious relationship with Fleming; he believed Fleming held racist and anti-Semitic views. After his break with the institute, he made these accusations publicly in the pages of *National Review*.[41] Fleming was again attacked in *National Review* in David Frum's infamous "Unpatriotic Conservatives" essay in 2003. Fleming retired from *Chronicles* in 2015.

The Rockford Institute was responsible for the creation of the John Randolph Club, which for a time served as a meeting ground for paleoconservatives and paleolibertarians—a subject that will be examined in greater detail in the pages ahead.

Samuel T. Francis

Samuel T. Francis was a unique figure within the conservative movement. Unlike many paleoconservatives who castigated the mainstream right after being shunned, Francis was highly critical of organized conservatism while he was still well regarded within the movement. He was personally secular and an integral player in one of the more openly religious and traditionalist ideological categories on the American right. As a disciple of James Burnham, Francis was a student of power, and power politics rather than principles was a key element in his major works.

Because of his fixation on elites and power, Francis never took the left's claim to support egalitarianism at face value. According to Francis, egalitarian rhetoric was just a cover for naked power politics. Equality was simply a "political weapon" that provided rhetorical justification for the rise of a new elite class:

> Egalitarianism, embedded in Progressivist environmentalist social theory, served to weaken and delegitimize the local, private, and small-scale class, government, and social institutions of nineteenth century bourgeois elite. Egalitarian environmentalism also served to legitimize the rise of a new elite composed of experts (managers) who could apply the skills and ideas of environmental amelioration. Despite the critique of egalitarianism, then, it flourished (and continues to flourish) not because of its intrinsic scientific or philosophical merits but because it serves the interests and aspirations of an elite that is dependent upon large, centralized government administering social engineering and therapeutic functions ostensibly intended to ameliorate social institutions.[42]

Although conservatives have always claimed to believe earnestly in the power of ideas, Francis insisted that the degree to which an idea was correct had little bearing on whether it would win out in the political arena. Developing powerful counterarguments to the left's doctrines was not a useful endeavor, as the truth of the left's propositions was beside the point.[43] As long as the current egalitarian orthodoxy served those in power, that orthodoxy would remain in place.

Unlike many conservatives, Francis was generally uninterested in theories of free-market capitalism or theological arguments for the Republican platform. Instead, Francis argued that the American white middle class could serve as a counterrevolutionary force that fought for its own interests without relying on a universalist, egalitarian justification. Much of his work was focused on developing a program for promoting the interests of the so-called Middle American Radicals, a group originally named by the sociologist Donald I. Warren. A key point about Middle American Radicals was that they were not opposed to the state per se; instead, they wanted the state to serve their needs, rather than the needs of other groups. These radicals viewed, correctly in Francis's estimation, government as being in favor of the very rich and the very poor, squeezing those in the middle; the poor, especially poor minorities, receive what they demand, and the managerial elites get good jobs, but the middle class ends up with the bill. In Francis's view, this white middle class is the truly disenfranchised group in the United States, but it cannot overturn the existing social order as long as the dominant liberal ideology is viewed as legitimate.

According to Francis, the hegemonic ideology within a nation will be determined by those who control the culture; therefore, the right is mistaken for single-mindedly pursuing political power via partisan politics. Francis argued that the right needed to study the ideas developed by Marxist theorist Antonio Gramsci. He posited that elites are able to direct American society "through their dominance of culture more than through their control of the means of production."[44] If Middle American Radicals wanted to truly retake their country, they needed to do more than vote for Republicans; they "must first make a long march through the institutions of culture before trying to wield political or economic power."[45] Real power would follow cultural hegemony. The Reagan Revolution failed to accomplish anything lasting because the right had completely neglected the cultural component of power. Even if conservative Republicans dominate every level of government, they will, at best, be fighting a failed rearguard action as long as the left controls the educational and entertainment institutions in the country. The great masses of people tend to internalize whatever messages they receive from the major cultural organs, and as long as the left plays a predominant role in shaping the culture, winning elections will accomplish little. ✓

Francis argued that Middle American Radicalism was conveyed in support for David Duke,[46] but its most powerful and compelling expression was in the candidacy of Pat Buchanan. According to Francis, what Middle America wanted was not more abstract thinking about the benefits of liberty or the moral basis of global democratic capitalism; they wanted a politician who fought for their interests and traditional American culture. To Francis, Buchanan was the best shot Middle America had to enjoy real power. He argued that Buchanan was the first Republican presidential candidate in many decades that genuinely represented Middle America on both the cultural and the economic fronts. Even after Buchanan's second defeat, he was hopeful that Buchanan was just a harbinger of the populist revolution to come.

Like other paleos, Francis was an acrimonious critic of the mainstream conservative movement; he viewed it as a hindrance to the radical agenda he wanted to see advanced. In part, this had to do with Francis's view on what constituted an authentic conservative; conservatives, according to Francis, should focus on "the survival and enhancement of a particular people and its institutionalized cultural expressions."[47] This brand of conservatism had nothing to do with capitalism—though it was not inherently anticapitalist—and had no interest in wars to spread democracy to other countries. It was economically nationalistic and thus suggested that the state should manage trade to benefit the country, rather than trusting that the free market's invisible hand will necessarily benefit everyone. Although he did not necessarily reject the label paleoconservative, Francis preferred to label his cause simply as right wing.[48]

Francis argued that the US government increasingly embraced the policies of anarchotyranny. In this system, the government does not punish the real criminals or rein in the most antisocial elements of society, but it does relentlessly bully the law-abiding and the innocent. As examples, he pointed to policies such as the Patriot Act, a law that undermines the liberties of ordinary Americans, which coexist with a de facto policy of open borders, in which any criminal or potential terrorist could enter the country unimpeded.[49]

Like many paleoconservatives, Francis was a proud Southerner, but he was opposed to all talk of a new secessionist movement. In fact, he called enthusiasm for secession an "infantile disorder." For Francis, there were several problems with secession. The big problem, of course, was that it was not feasible. However, even if it was possible, it would not solve any underlying problems. The elites in the South were culturally similar to the elites elsewhere, and an independent South would soon resemble the United States it had escaped. For Francis, the divide was not the Mason-Dixon Line but "between elite and non-elite." Rather than focus on geographic boundaries, Middle Americans across the continent needed to join together to overthrow the existing order.[50]

Sam Francis wrote on racial issues more frequently than other figures associated with the paleoconservative movement—a movement that, to say the least, was not known for its sensitivity to minority concerns. As noted in chapter 2, his long record of racially inflammatory remarks ultimately cost Francis his respectability and his ability to be published in mainstream venues, and it is not necessary to again repeat those statements. Given his record of racist remarks, it is worth considering whether Francis could properly have been described as a white nationalist. Both his critics on the left and some of his admirers on the white nationalist right claim he should be so labeled.[51] He certainly had affiliations that made such accusations more credible; he was a prominent leader of the Council of Conservative Citizens (which has been described as a hate group) and an editor of the *Occidental Quarterly*, which was a journal for intellectuals and journalists on the radical right.

BY WHOM?

Although Francis was certainly a racist as the term is generally used, I am not convinced that he could properly be described as a white nationalist. Although some watchdog groups that monitor racists apply the phrase white nationalist to any white person who makes racist remarks, I would use a narrower definition. In this book, I only describe as white nationalists those figures who want to create a nation in which citizenship is restricted exclusively to whites, either through the secession of a currently homogenous geographic unit or via ethnic/racial cleansing. To my knowledge, Francis never publicly advocated such a policy, even after losing access to all mainstream publishing venues and thus having little to lose. That being said, much of Francis's writing toward the end of his life was explicitly racial, and had he not died at the relatively young age of fifty-seven in 2005, he may have moved in a more expressly white nationalist direction.

The Paleo Alliance

Given that paleoconservatives and many libertarians both plausibly claim the same ideological heritage, why did conservative guardians of the old right tradition fail to seek allies on the libertarian right in the postwar years?

The cold war certainly provides part of the explanation. Whereas Rothbard and other radical libertarians opposed American bellicosity during the cold war from the beginning, the conservatives who later became paleoconservatives—such as Sam Francis and Pat Buchanan—were generally in favor of an aggressive stance against communism.[52] A key difference between the paleoconservatives and the mainstream conservative movement, however, was how they believed US foreign policy should develop after the cold war concluded. The paleoconservatives were apparently willing to accept the "totalitarian bureaucracies within our shores" to ensure the Soviet Union's ultimate defeat, but once the USSR closed up shop, they were prepared to return to a noninterventionist foreign policy.

Although many conservatives reveled in America's status as the world's only superpower, the end of the cold war also led many conservative hawks to rethink America's role in the world. United in their hostility to the warfare state, a new ideological coalition was forged. The short-lived alliance between paleoconservatives and certain culturally conservative libertarians began with a meeting between representatives from the Rockford and Mises institutes in 1989. When the parties at this meeting found that their similarities outweighed their differences, they next established the John Randolph Club, which first convened in 1990.[53] The various factions remained at odds on a number of issues—free trade being the most prominent—but for the time being, their mutual hostility to the mainstream right was more important than any other issue.

In a speech given at the John Randolph Club in 1992, Murray Rothbard famously declared that the end of the Buckleyite conservative movement [NEO CON] was at hand and that a new right-wing alternative was being born:

> Social democracy is still here in all its variants, defining our entire respectable political spectrum, from advanced victimology and feminism on the Left over to neoconservatism on the Right. We are now trapped, in America, inside a Menshevik fantasy, with the narrow bounds of respectable debate set for us by various brands of Marxists. It is now our task, the task of the resurgent right, of the paleo movement, to break those bonds, to finish the job, to finish off Marxism forever.
>
> One of the authors of the Daniel Bell volume says, in horror and astonishment, that the Radical Right intends to repeal the twentieth century. Heaven forfend! Who would want to repeal the twentieth century, the century of horror, the century of collectivism, the century of mass destruction and genocide, who would want to repeal that?

Well, we propose to do just that. With the inspiration of the death of the Soviet Union before us, we now know that it can be done. With Pat Buchanan as our leader, we shall break the clock of social democracy. We shall break the clock of the Great Society. We shall break the clock of the welfare state.

We shall break the clock of the New Deal. We shall break the clock of Woodrow Wilson's New Freedom and perpetual war. We shall repeal the twentieth century.

One of the most inspiring and wonderful sights of our time was to see the peoples of the Soviet Union rising up, last year, to tear down in their fury the statues of Lenin, to obliterate the Leninist legacy. We, too, shall tear down all the statues of Franklin D. Roosevelt, of Harry Truman, of Woodrow Wilson, melt them down and beat them into plowshares and pruning-hooks, and usher in a twenty-first century of peace, freedom, and prosperity.[54]

PRE
LEFT
WAYS

The paleo movement that Rothbard was describing was the coalition between paleoconservatives and paleolibertarians. Paleolibertarianism was a branch of libertarianism that enjoyed some popularity in the early 1990s thanks to its endorsement by respected figures like Rothbard and Lew Rockwell. Paleolibertarians differed from other libertarians primarily in tone and strategy rather than in policy preferences. Rockwell explained the logic of paleolibertarianism in a 1990 article in *Liberty*.[55]

Rockwell argued that the conservative coalition was on the verge of breaking up now that the cold war no longer held the various factions together. Many of these conservatives could be persuaded to align themselves with the libertarian movement, but Rockwell argued that this could not occur "until libertarianism is deloused."[56] The great problem for libertarianism as a political philosophy was libertarian individuals as they actually existed. Too many libertarians happily conformed to the stereotype of unkempt libertines. They rejected not just government authority but all authority. They attacked religion, cultural tradition, and the family almost as aggressively as they attacked the state. As a result, libertarians were repulsive to Middle Americans who continued to support conservative Republicans by default.

Rockwell contended that there was no part of libertarian political philosophy that implied an association with the counterculture. Instead, libertarians should recognize that a free society requires other forms of hierarchy besides the state. On this point he echoed conservative thinkers such as Robert Nisbet who argued that intermediate forms of authority are necessary to prevent a further expansion of centralized government. According to Rockwell, many libertarians had fundamentally incorrect attitudes toward authority: "Authority will always be necessary in society. Natural authority arises from voluntary social structures; unnatural authority is imposed by the State."[57]

The paleolibertarians were also generally amenable to the restrictionist immigration policies supported by the paleoconservatives. Because immigrants tended to support left-wing politics, open immigration represented a threat to liberty. Further, paleolibertarians were, compared to other libertarians, more hospitable to arguments about the need for cultural cohesion and homogeneity. Generally speaking, libertarians within the paleo camp were more willing to use racially charged language than the more mainstream libertarians, such as those affiliated with *Reason* and the Cato Institute.

Rockwell took libertarians to task for accepting the progressive position on egalitarianism. It was on this subject that paleolibertarians were at their most controversial. Rockwell directly attacked the 1964 Civil Rights Act, and he condemned fellow libertarians who refused to do the same. Beyond decrying civil rights legislation as an attack on property rights, he also defended the rights of individuals to discriminate, arguing that it was not immoral to do so.[58] Rockwell was of course not the only libertarian to embrace the paleo strategy. Murray Rothbard was arguably the most important unifying intellectual within the paleoconservative–paleolibertarian network. The most important public figure was Pat Buchanan, who was briefly able to secure the support of both groups on the paleo right.

Reflecting on the paleo movement nearly a decade later, Lew Rockwell noted that the paleoconservatives and the paleolibertarians always recognized their crucial differences. However, the issues on which they both agreed trumped those on which they differed: "Mostly, we would focus on the issue that had brought us together in the first place: crushing the US domestic and international empire."[59] According to Rockwell, however, this alliance became untenable when Buchanan chose not to focus on those areas on which there was widespread agreement and instead focused all of his energy on his positions that most aggravated the libertarians, particularly free trade. The alliance did not break down entirely at the end of the Republican presidential primaries in 1992. Rothbard was optimistic about Buchanan's second presidential run's prospects, for example.

There were many reasons the alliance between paleoconservatives and paleolibertarians proved untenable. Buchanan's defeat in 1996, for one, demonstrated that there was insufficient popular support for his particular brand of populist, noninterventionist conservatism, and if paleoconservatives were not their ticket to political power, then libertarians had little reason for making common cause with them. Murray Rothbard's death in 1995 also played a major role in the end of the paleo strategy. Rothbard had been one of the more enthusiastic promoters of the strategy and viewed the alliance as a resurgence of his beloved old right. Without Rothbard, the divide between the two groups became unbridgeable. At the 1996 meeting of the John Randolph Club, Hans-Hermann Hoppe delivered a scathing attack on the economic policies of paleoconservatives such as Buchanan and Francis.[60]

The paleolibertarian movement is now clearly defunct. Not even Rockwell uses the term anymore. When Ron Paul ran for president again in 2008, he jettisoned the paleo rhetoric that was pervasive in his newsletters from the 1980s and 1990s. Instead he ran a campaign that was generally mainstream on issues of race; Ron Paul's successors, such as Rand Paul, are even more cautious when it comes to staying within the bounds of acceptability.

One issue remains unclear: how sincere was the paleolibertarian movement? I noted in this section, and in the earlier discussion of Murray Rothbard's thinking, that the figures associated with paleolibertarianism were willing to cross certain boundaries when it comes to discourse on race. Did these instances of racially charged rhetoric about immigrants and African Americans represent real convictions, or were they trying to harness the same energies that propelled David Duke to national prominence and use those energies to fuel the antistate movement? Were the leading figures associated with paleolibertarianism just feigning outrage about minority behavior and policies such as affirmative action in order to benefit from white racial insecurities in the early 90s? I cannot claim to know the answer to this question.

Similarly, was there ever anything really libertarian about the paleoconservative movement? This, of course, varies according to which figure we are considering, but for the most part, the answer is clearly no. Sam Francis in particular was never really an antistatist. His problem was not the state per se. Rather, he viewed the current elite as hostile to the interests of white, middle-class Americans. Rather than overthrow the state, or even abolish the welfare state, he simply wanted to replace the present elite with an elite more hospitable to Middle America. He was, in fact, openly hostile to libertarian economics.[61] Other paleoconservatives were more economically conservative than Francis, but many did not support free trade, which is not an issue libertarians will easily concede.

There are now few formal ties between paleoconservatives and libertarians. One organization that fosters continued communication between these ideological camps is the Property and Freedom Society, founded by Hans-Hermann Hoppe, who remains president of the organization. The organization hosts an invitation-only annual meeting in Bodrum, Turkey, and while these meetings are predominantly libertarian in orientation, they host speakers from across the political right. Past speakers have included paleoconservatives such as Paul Gottfried, libertarians such as Thomas DiLorenzo, and even figures associated with white nationalism, such as Richard Spencer and Jared Taylor.

Paul Gottfried

Paul Gottfried was a crucial player within the paleoconservative movement throughout its existence. He claims to have personally coined the term, and in 2008 he declared the movement officially dead.[62] Like Francis, Gottfried had a long relationship with many mainstream conservative institutions—such as the Intercollegiate Studies Institute, for example—but has also been a vocal critic of the mainstream American right for many decades. Although he is not unusual among paleoconservatives for having a PhD, Gottfried is one of the few prominent paleoconservatives who spent an entire career working in academia (Clyde Wilson is another).

Gottfried has long been one of the most acrimonious right-wing critics of the mainstream conservative movement, particularly the neoconservative faction. Besides breaking with the neoconservatives on issues such as foreign policy and immigration, Gottfried differs from the conservative movement in his appreciation for European political theory, particularly German political theory. An observer of the conservative intellectual movement will likely note that American conservatives have generally had little use for continental political philosophy. In *The Conservative Mind*, every figure that Kirk examined was British or American, with the sole exception of Tocqueville, who was primarily worth noting because of his astute observations of the United States. Most of the twentieth-century Europeans that contemporary American conservatives respect and recognize as influences on their own thinking were Jewish, emigrated to America, or both. In contrast, Gottfried has conducted scholarship on several important European political thinkers generally ignored or disparaged by the American conservative movement.

Gottfried's second book, *The Search for Historical Meaning* (1986), argued that the postwar conservative movement was more influenced by Georg

Wilhelm Friedrich Hegel than is generally acknowledged. In spite of many conservatives' proclaimed opposition to historicism,[63] Hegelian, dialectical thinking is apparent in the work of such conservative luminaries as Frank Meyer, James Burnham, and even Russell Kirk.[64] Gottfried has also written a book on Carl Schmitt, a German legal theorist associated with the Revolutionary Conservative movement in Weimar Germany (a subject that will be dealt with in greater detail in the next chapter). Although Schmitt is still of interest to scholars in the United States, he has generally been ignored by mainstream conservative intellectuals. In *Carl Schmitt: Politics and Theory* (1990), Gottfried argued that Schmitt's work is too trenchant and important to be ignored despite Schmitt's skepticism of pluralistic democracy.[65]

Gottfried has also written multiple books on the left and the American right. In *The Strange Death of Marxism* (2005), Gottfried analyzed trends in the European left in the post–cold war era. He noted that the left, even the extreme left, has largely abandoned the project of nationalizing major industries and redistributing wealth; instead it is primarily focused on interest group politics: feminism, gay rights, and the rights of racial minorities and immigrants.[66] To Gottfried, the only thing the contemporary left shares with the older, Marxist–Leninist left is an antipathy toward bourgeois Christian culture. *ESP. TRUE IN USA*

One of Gottfried's key arguments is that the post-Marxist left may be classified as a political religion. It views politics in clear good-versus-evil terms. It possesses a blind faith in ideals such as multiculturalism, and it is ruthless in its treatment of heretics and infidels who reject the leftist worldview: *WHY THE RIGHT IS INEPT*

> While the Marxist agenda of the European Left has changed, what has not is the ill will vented on those who resist its interests. Whether fighting to allow unrestricted Third World immigration into Europe, gay marriage, the lowering of the legal age for male homosexual prostitution, the building of mosques at the expense of European taxpayers, this Left is implacably hostile to those who think differently and trace this deviation to fascist sympathies.[67]

Gottfried made similar arguments in *Multiculturalism and the Politics of Guilt* (2002). In this book, he attempted to explain Western governments' enthusiasm for multiculturalism. Like Francis, Gottfried flatly rejects the notion that this trend is solely in the interest of morality; instead, he insists that multiculturalism helps the ruling elite maintain a grip on power. By declaring that the state's primary function is to protect the interests of an ever-expanding group of designated victims, "the expanding central state is authorized to make constant interventions, directly or indirectly, in a wide range of human and commercial relations."[68] The ruling elite further consolidate their power with the establishment and maintenance of an ideological doctrine—now largely accepted by the mainstream right as well as the left—that elevates pluralism, tolerance, and diversity to supreme moral goals.

Although Gottfried argued that the reigning ideological orthodoxies serve the interests of the powerful rather than further an abstract morality, he does not dismiss the role that religion has played in current trends. Instead, he argues that liberalism has replaced Christianity as the dominant religion in much of the West, while still possessing many hallmarks of Christian thought: "Religious myth is not something to be replaced in the secularizing process by scientific materialism or some variant thereof. Transpositions take place as well—for example, the substitution of designated victims for the older adoration of religious martyrs or that of successive utopian visions for the biblical final age."[69] Gottfried argued that secular cultures with a strong Protestant tradition are particularly likely to embrace multicultural liberalism because of the cultural residue of their religious past. Protestantism fosters a culture of guilt and redemption, and this culture endured even as pews emptied. People steeped in such a culture are more willing to accept their collective guilt for sins committed against minorities today and in the distant past, and thus are more willing to acquiesce to policies that elevate minority concerns above their own group interests.

As a paleoconservative, Gottfried has long been critical of the mainstream conservative movement. From his writings, it is clear that he feels more bitterness toward conservatives, particularly neoconservatives, than toward the left. He has long been known to quarrel with conservative journalists, and he blames neoconservatives for torpedoing his academic appointment at Catholic University of America. According to Gottfried, his opponents blocked this appointment because he was "not reliable on Israel."[70] If his recounting of events is true,[71] this charge is rather odd, as Gottfried is both Jewish and, from what I can tell from his writings, generally supportive of Israel. He spent most of his academic career at Elizabethtown College in Pennsylvania.

Was Russell Kirk a Paleoconservative?

As an aside, it is worth considering whether we can properly classify Russell Kirk as a paleoconservative. Many paleos would certainly like to claim him as one of their own, though others have been critical of Kirk.[72] Toward the end of his life, Kirk was a supporter of Pat Buchanan's presidential run. We should remember, however, that *National Review* (half-heartedly) endorsed Buchanan in 1992, and no one would accuse that publication of having paleoconservative leanings. Kirk certainly had his share of run-ins with leading neoconservatives, and there was definitely a mutual hostility between Kirk and prominent neoconservatives such as Midge Dector.

Although these are all true statements, Russell Kirk should not be considered part of the paleoconservative intellectual movement.[73] For one, he never claimed to be part of the paleoconservative faction of the right. More importantly, I would argue that most paleoconservatives were and are quite ideological in their orientation; most certainly did not share Kirk's distaste for radicalism. Unlike Kirk, the paleoconservatives do not see present-day America as a continuation of a conservative tradition that can be traced back to Edmund Burke. To paleoconservatives, contemporary Americans are completely cut off from a healthy traditional society, and thus it is necessary to take a revolutionary stance that attacks the entire governing regime.[74] Kirk's emphasis on slow, organic change would certainly be rejected by paleoconservatives.

Conclusion

This chapter did not provide an exhaustive list of all the figures associated with paleoconservative thought. The late Joseph Sobran, for example, may be appropriately considered part of the paleoconservative milieu, despite his long affiliation with *National Review*, though toward the end of his life he was more of a libertarian or even an anarchist than a paleoconservative. The political philosopher Claes Ryn, who has emerged as one of the more incisive critics of the conservative movement on the right, may also be labeled a paleoconservative, though his work is less racially charged and controversial than that of many of the intellectuals and journalists considered in this chapter.

Paul Gottfried was correct when he stated that paleoconservatism is no longer a meaningful ideological force in the United States. Most of the key figures of that movement are now either deceased, elderly, or have changed their views on major issues. There is no well-known and prominent journal of paleoconservative thought. In its early years, it may have been accurate to describe the *American Conservative* as a paleoconservative magazine, but I do not believe that moniker remains appropriate. In its first issues, it published many essays by figures long associated with the paleoconservative movement, such as Chilton Williamson, Joe Scotchie, and Sam Francis. More recently, the publication has been dominated by figures from elsewhere on the right—Rod Dreher now blogs for the magazine, for example—or even from the left—another recently added blogger, Noah Millman, cannot really be described as right wing in any sense of the word.[75] The Rockford Institute and *Chronicles* still exist, but their influence remains limited.

A lack of funding has always been a critical problem for the paleoconservative movement. Indeed, it is remarkable that the movement made so many waves during the 1980s and 1990s, given its lack of resources. Neoconservatives are certainly the most lavishly funded element of the conservative coalition, though the religious right and libertarians have impressive war chests as well. The paleoconservative movement has always operated on a shoestring budget, and the Rockford Institute has never had the kind of clout enjoyed by the Heritage Foundation, the Cato Institute, or the Manhattan Institute, and *Chronicles* never came close to enjoying *National Review* or *Reason* levels of circulation. To the limited extent that paleoconservative arguments ever received a hearing on a national scale, the movement can predominantly thank Pat Buchanan.

Although it never achieved real power, and probably never will, what remains of the paleoconservative movement can take some consolation in the fact that time has proven them correct on many points, at least when it comes to foreign policy. As W. James Antle III pointed out in the *Daily Caller*, now that we have the benefit of more than a decade of hindsight, it is clear that Pat Buchanan and other paleoconservatives dubbed "unpatriotic conservatives" by David Frum in 2003 were often quite accurate in their predictions regarding the Iraq invasion. The reality of that war was certainly more congruent with Buchanan's dour predictions than the sanguine forecasts provided by prowar conservatives such as Donald Rumsfeld and Dick Cheney.[76] Similarly, the paleoconservative argument that mass immigration would ultimately doom the Republican Party to permanent minority status is also beginning to appear prescient, though it is too early to definitively declare that the paleoconservatives were correct on that point.

A problem for paleoconservatism is that it is defined almost entirely by what it opposes: neoconservatism. When paleos and neos were both competing factions within the broader right-wing coalition, the paleoconservatives possessed a degree of relevance. However, by the time George W. Bush was inaugurated, the neoconservatives were not just one more faction within the conservative movement. In terms of influencing GOP policy makers, and seeing their preferred policies enacted, the neoconservatives were clearly the dominant faction of the conservative movement. All other groups on the right had to toe the neoconservative line on several critical issues if they wanted a seat at the conservative table. With no money of its own, no outlets on the right, and hostility from the left, paleoconservatism withered away.

This does not mean that paleoconservative arguments have been completely forgotten, but they are now being advanced by groups in other ideological camps. Libertarians are now the most powerful force on the right lobbying for noninterventionism. A number of Republicans in Congress are now vocal immigration restrictionists, though not affiliated with the paleoconservatives. The religious right, though now considerably weaker than it was even a decade ago, continues to fight the culture war. Economic protectionism is the only major paleoconservative argument that has not been embraced by any other significant element of the American right.

The end of paleoconservatism demonstrates the limits to the right-wing maxim "ideas have consequences." Although few today would say that they agree with every aspect of paleoconservatism—indeed, the paleos often disagreed with each other on important issues—the paleos were an intellectually serious bloc on the right. Leading paleoconservatives were no less likely than leading neoconservatives to possess PhDs from prestigious institutions. Even if they were fundamentally wrong in many ways, and temperamentally they often lived up to their reputations as angry curmudgeons, their understanding of American history and political science was based on real scholarship. They were defeated so completely because they were outgunned in the political arena. They had little money and few institutions and publications, were less adept at partisan politics, and were generally less media savvy. Paleoconservatives have, on average, shown less of an interest in applied politics as a vocation, and as a result they ultimately became little more than a footnote in American ideological history.

Against Capitalism, Christianity, and America

THE EUROPEAN NEW RIGHT

This book is focused predominantly on the right as it exists in the United States and has generally ignored conservative and right-wing thought elsewhere. One may therefore question whether this chapter belongs in this volume. Indeed, if I was writing this book even a few years ago, I would not have included a chapter on the European New Right. In fact, it would have been very difficult for me to do so; the most important works by these ideologues were not available in English until recently. However, it appears that dissident right-wing thinkers in the United States—particularly those with an explicitly racial or tribalist ideological orientation—have taken an increasing interest in the ideas of Alain de Benoist and others associated with the New Right in Europe. An ever-growing number of books from this tradition are now available in English. It remains to be seen whether the ideas associated with the fringe right in Europe will ever take root in the United States, but at least now it appears possible, if still unlikely. For that reason, a brief discussion of the European right is timely and appropriate.

When the far right in Europe is discussed today, the media tends to focus on right-wing political parties, especially the National Front in France. There is sound logic to this emphasis, as these parties are presently the only possible means for the far right to exercise power in the near future and are presently enjoying high levels of support. Like the New Right think-

INC,
DL
(ONLY
BACK IN
1970's)

ers discussed in this chapter, these parties are particularly concerned with non-European immigration. However, I should clarify that the European New Right is both more extreme and more intellectually serious than the major right-wing political parties presently disrupting partisan politics throughout Europe. As political parties hoping to achieve elected office, right-wing political parties rationally emphasize their ideas that resonate with the electorate and downplay those that are unpopular and highly controversial. The intellectual leaders of the New Right have, for the most part, eschewed such moderation and have held political parties—even those that are often classified as radical right—at arm's length.

It is not difficult to see why the ideas of the European New Right have received little interest from Americans. Besides being marginalized in the countries where these ideas originated, this right-wing vision is anathema to American conservatives for many reasons: it is openly antibourgeois and anticapitalist; it is anti-Christian and pro-pagan or atheist; it is openly skeptical of modern liberal democracy; it is intensely anti-American and largely blames the United States for the decline of European culture. Since the postwar era, if not before, the mainstream American right has been founded on precisely the opposite principles. Additionally, while the New Right has struggled to distance itself from its fascist antecedents, many of its arguments are based on the same premises as fascism and National Socialism.

Because of its openly anti-American stance and exclusively European orientation, the leading figures of the European New Right have, until recently, shown no interest in proselytizing in the United States, leaving even those Americans who might be open to their ideas ignorant of their arguments. Given that the best-known figures of the European New Right are French and that Francophobia is a common attribute of American conservatives (a tendency that reached absurd new heights at the start of the Iraq invasion of 2003), it is not surprising that the American right has shown virtually no interest in the European New Right.

Right-wing thinking on continental Europe has long been decidedly different from that which developed in the United States. The United States is commonly and understandably viewed as a pure child of the Enlightenment, with no throne-and-altar reactionary tradition. There was never a formal aristocracy or established clergy to fight the rise of the bourgeoisie, and both political parties have long positioned themselves as champions of the middle class. It is true that the South once possessed an aristocratic, even feudal, social order. But that social order was destroyed permanently in 1865. Modernity took hold in the United States largely unopposed. We should not downplay the significant struggles between the American left and right, but if we look at the broader political spectrum, I believe it fair to say that these ideological disputes within the United States took place within the family, so to speak. Although doctrinaire socialists and libertarians may view themselves as at opposite ends of the ideological continuum, in truth their views are built on a similar economic, materialistic foundation. For both, the end goal is a materially prosperous and peaceful world, in which people are able to self-actualize free from established social hierarchies. From the far right's perspective, both are, to borrow Nietzsche's phrase, fighting to make the *TRUE* world safe for the Last Man. They simply disagree on how to bring that world about. *DEMS. & REPS*

In Europe, liberal democracy developed more slowly and fitfully, and there was a stronger intellectual tradition in opposition to modernity and the Enlightenment. This tradition believed in a premodern social order out of principle and rejected the idea that all modern trends represented encouraging progress. In comparison to the rootlessness and apparent social chaos that reigned in North America, it celebrated rootedness, identity, order, and *YES* tradition. This ideological orientation was threatened by the French Revolution and the subsequent Napoleonic wars, as well as the revolutions of 1848, but it remained dominant in Europe until the social upheavals after World War I. One might view the right-wing movements in Europe that gained power in the 1920s and 1930s as a haphazard, reactionary attempt to reassert traditional norms and stave off the threats to those traditions posed by both Soviet communism in the east and American and British capitalism in the west.

After 1945, this right-wing vision was completely discredited and marginalized. Openly promoting these ideals was criminalized in many countries. The social orders and political principles dominant in the United States and the Soviet Union thus represented the new bounds of acceptable ideological discourse. Despite the impressive ideological chasm between the two, both empires embraced ideologies that were essentially modern, materialistic, egalitarian, and cosmopolitan, in theory if not in practice. To the extent that anti-Americanism was present in Europe, many of the popular criticisms of the United States were founded on the premise that the United States was insufficiently modern and egalitarian. Right-wing anti-Americanism was largely dormant.

European political history since 1945 indicates that most Western Europeans have been relatively content with this state of affairs. Most successful right-wing parties in Europe may be described as softer versions of the Republican Party in the United States, though a number of parties that might be justifiably described as far-right and nationalist, such as the Freedom Party of Austria and the National Front in France, have enjoyed impressive electoral success, raising concerns among some observers about a rising right-wing tide in Europe. Among European intellectuals, however, individuals on the extreme right have long been a small minority.

Since World War II, a new right-wing school of thought—decidedly different from the mainstream right in America—has developed in Europe. Although its proponents are still relatively small in number, it seeks to offer an alternative to the dominant ideologies in the West, borrowing ideas from the prewar right while emphasizing its distinctiveness from fascism and Nazism. This New Right, as it has been called, is the subject of this chapter.

It is worth noting that the use of the term New Right may be confusing to some readers because in the English-speaking world, there is another ideological and political movement that bears this name, though the term is now used infrequently in the United States. The New Right in the United States, which Richard Viguerie declared "ready to lead" in 1981,[1] was best represented by President Ronald Reagan. It was pro-capitalist, populist, motivated by middle-class concerns, and closely tied to the growing Christian religious right. As we have already noted, the New Right in Europe possesses none of these attributes, and it may be fairly said that the European New Right is as ideologically distant from American Republicans as it is from the egalitarian left. RIGHTLY SO

NO ENR U.S. NEW RIGHT OF 80's AXIS I AM WITH THE ENR HERE (OL)

To add further confusion, some of the figures associated with the European New Right—most notably Alain de Benoist—dispute that the movement should be properly classified as right wing, instead arguing that it stands outside of the traditional left–right dichotomy.[2] On the basis of my own broad classification scheme, the European New Right can be treated as properly right wing, given its utter rejection of egalitarianism.

MINE ALSO

The Conservative Revolution

The ideas that animated the New Right in Europe were not entirely new, and much of the New Right's thought is derivative of an older right-wing tradition. Of particular importance were those thinkers on the right who were prominent during the interwar period. Some of these figures are well known by scholars and frequently cited and discussed, such as Carl Schmitt and Martin Heidegger. Others are now little remembered or remarked upon, such as Oswald Spengler and Arthur Moeller van den Bruck. All of these authors possessed a Nietzschean skepticism of democratic values and wished to halt and reverse societal trends in Europe, though it would be inaccurate to state that they formulated a single, coherent ideology that they all more or less agreed on. The Conservative Revolutionaries, as they came to be called, were dissimilar from Marxists in that they did not settle on a single unified theory of history, and thus I must use the term "movement" somewhat loosely. All of the figures discussed in this section have a long literary record and deserve a greater discussion than I am able to provide here; in no case am I able to deliver a comprehensive survey of their work. I therefore will focus as well as I can on those elements of their thought that are most relevant to my larger discussion of the New Right.

After World War I—the war presumably fought to make the world safe for democracy—a new social order was imposed on Germany and the war's other defeated powers. The Kaiser was gone, and a new democratic system took his place. Not all German intellectuals were content with the effort to remake their nation in the image of the United States and Britain. Many of these antiliberals took inspiration from Marxism and the new Soviet Union, embracing the far left. Others, however, adopted an entirely different political worldview, one that was decidedly antimodern in its orientation. They rejected the rationalism and the individualism that had dominated much of the West since the Enlightenment. They believed that the modern view of the world was fundamentally mistaken in its conception of human beings and that a social order built on these modern views would be chaotic and alienating.

CARL SCHMITT

Carl Schmitt is one of the best-known figures of the Conservative Revolutionary movement, though one can question whether his thought properly belongs within that intellectual category. His legal theories remain widely discussed—if rarely endorsed—by contemporary scholars. Schmitt argued that the world was increasingly retreating from politics as he defined the term. To Schmitt, politics is fundamentally about conflict and friend–enemy distinctions. Although we may try to escape politics in this sense through economic ties and parliamentary procedures, politics will always return. A nation that unilaterally embraces a postpolitical view will be preyed on by other nations. The friend–enemy dichotomy can never truly be escaped and must therefore be embraced:

> It would be ludicrous to believe that a defenseless people has nothing but friends, and it would be a deranged calculation to suppose that the

enemy could perhaps be touched by the absence of a resistance. No one thinks it possible that the world could, for example, be transformed into a condition of pure morality by the renunciation of every aesthetic or economic productivity. Even less can a people hope to bring about a purely moral or purely economic condition of humanity by evading every political decision. If a people no longer possesses the energy or the will to maintain itself in the sphere of politics, the latter will not thereby vanish from the world. Only a weak people will disappear.[3]

To Schmitt, the enemy was an outsider who threatened a group's collective existence. Enemy was a collective concept, and threatened the existence of a group; thus it should be distinguished from private hostilities between individuals. The existence of enemies does not imply a perpetual state of war, but it does suggest that war is always a possibility.

Schmitt opposed liberalism precisely because it negated the political and held depoliticization as its final goal. Liberals deny that the stakes of politics are literally life and death and prefer to view conflict as stemming from mere differences of opinion or economic competition. Liberals further inject morality into their political thinking. To Schmitt, an enemy was not necessarily morally deficient. Relatedly, "the morally evil, aesthetically ugly or economically damaging need not necessarily be the enemy."[4] The moral virtues or vices of a competing group are irrelevant. Schmitt possessed a Hobbesian realism when it comes to human interactions. He viewed the nation-state as an important development because it helped to civilize warfare, as the states possessed a monopoly on justified violence. Wars between states were limited in their aims and scope, and subject to international law.

Liberalism denies that the existence of enemies is natural and that conflict is inevitable. Liberal states prefer the use of economic tools to achieve dominance, but to Schmitt, this does not make them inherently peaceful or non-imperial. When a liberal regime is confronted by an enemy, it tends to frame the conflict in moral terms: "The adversary is thus no longer an enemy but a disturber of the peace and is thereby designated to be an outlaw of humanity. A war waged to expand or protect economic power must, with the aid of propaganda, turn into a crusade and into the last war of humanity."[5] Like many New Right thinkers who followed, Schmitt argued that politics founded on high-minded ideals could lead to far worse outcomes than a political order based on realism.

Like the leaders of the later New Right, Schmitt utterly rejected the utopian romanticism of liberalism. He further insisted on the importance of group identities—opposed to "the other; the stranger"[6]—with clear geographic boundaries, possessing a unified way of life, and under the banner of a single state. Such thinking clearly implies the necessity of culturally coherent ethnostates. Also like the New Right, he rejected the possibility of a universal brotherhood of all humanity; those who speak in such utopian terms are, he believed, often concealing a more insidious agenda.

Schmitt is also similar to the later New Rightists in that his views on democracy diverged from the dominant liberal view. He argued that liberalism had to be distinguished from democracy and that the two were actually incompatible: "Every actual democracy rests on the principle that not only are equals equal but unequals will not be treated equally. Democracy requires, therefore, first homogeneity and second—if the need arises—elimination or eradication of heterogeneity."[7]

Although still cited and discussed with some frequency, Schmitt remains a controversial figure because of his affiliation with National Socialism. Schmitt joined the Nazi Party in 1933, and he defended Nazi excesses— such as the Night of the Long Knives incident—as being justified. His allegiance to Nazi doctrine remains uncertain, however. Before Hitler's rise, Schmitt had opposed the Nazis. Regardless of whether he was a sincere Nazi or a mere opportunist, Schmitt's personal politics in the 1930s and 1940s have not cost him his status as an important legal theorist, and most of his important works have been translated into English.

OSWALD SPENGLER

Conservatives in the United States have long accused their opponents on the left of cultural or moral relativism. That is, conservatives claim to affirm permanent, universal principles that are applicable in all contexts, and they accuse the left of denying the existence of transcendent values. Conservatives are not always clear as to which universal values they affirm; their own worldview is often a mix of classical liberalism and Protestant Christian morality. Nonetheless, the American right has long claimed it stands in opposition to the relativistic left and instead defends the "permanent things." This is decidedly not the case for the European New Right, which is perhaps more openly in favor of cultural relativism than both the mainstream left and the mainstream right. The New Right's view of human cultures recognizes crucial differences and champions the right of cultures to remain distinct from one another. In its embrace of relativism, the New Right echoes the thought of Oswald Spenger, who declared, "Truths are truths only in relation to a particular mankind. Thus, my own philosophy is able to express and reflect *only* the Western (as distinct from the Classical, Indian or other) soul, and that soul only in its present civilized phase by which its conception of the world, its practical range and its sphere of effect are specified."[8]

Many readers will be at least somewhat familiar with Oswald Spengler, though contemporary scholars have shown considerably less interest in his work than in Schmitt. Spengler is best known for positing a cyclical theory of history, in which cultures have a natural cycle of life and death analogous to plants and animals. He developed his theory in his best-known work, *The Decline of the West.* This lengthy treatise was first published in Germany at the close of World War I in 1918. In spite of his lack of formal training as a historian, the work was a commercial success and widely discussed in postwar Germany and elsewhere. Like other thinkers on the right, Spengler rejected the notion that history represented an unrelenting march of progress, in which the present is superior to the past and the future will be superior to the present. Instead, all cultures must inevitably decline and eventually self-destruct. The history of the world must be viewed as the history of various discrete cultures that followed their own independent path but nonetheless exhibited the same general patterns. Like earlier thinkers such as Joseph de Maistre, Spengler rejected the idea of a universal mankind in which all people are essentially interchangeable.[9]

Spengler used the analogy of seasons to describe the rise and fall of cultures; each experiences a period of growth, maturity, and eventual stagnation and death. He also introduced a novel distinction between culture and civilization. To Spengler, civilization was the final phase of a culture:

> A Culture is born in the moment when a great soul awakens out of the proto-spirituality of ever-childish humanity, and detaches itself, a form from the formless, a bounded and mortal thing from the boundless and enduring. It blooms on the soil of an exact definable landscape, to which plant-wise it remains bound. It dies when the soul has actualized the full sum of its possibilities in the shape of peoples, languages, dogmas, arts, states, sciences, and reverts into the proto-soul. . . . Each Culture stands in a deeply symbolic, almost mystical relation to the Extended, the space, in which and through which it strives to actualize itself. The aim once attained—the idea, the entire content of inner possibilities, fulfilled and made externally actual—the Culture suddenly hardens, it mortifies, its blood congeals, its force breaks down, and it becomes *Civilization,* the thing which we feel and understand in the words Egyptism, Byzantism, Mandarism. As such it may, like a worn-out giant of a primeval forest,

thrust decaying branches towards the sky for hundreds or thousands of years, as we see in China, in India, in the Islamic world.[10]

Spengler argued that the "Faustian" West had already begun its transition from a culture to a civilization, and as part of this transition we see the rise of cosmopolitan, mob-ruled cities ("megalopolises") that drain a region of its vitality, a new obsession with money, and a drive toward imperialism. The end result in the west will be a transition to "Caesarism" and the end of democracy.[11] The decadent age of a culture can continue for many decades or even centuries, but its final demise is inevitable. Spengler argued that a culture could survive for approximately one thousand years before entering its terminal phase.

Like many other figures on the right, Spengler had no use for utopian views of mankind; he saw human beings as natural "beasts of prey."[12] Although he viewed the decline of the West as inevitable, Spengler was hopeful that Germany would lead the Western world during this final stage. However, his views diverged from the National Socialists in a number of ways. When Spengler spoke of race, his emphasis was always on culture rather than biology. Although he emphasized differences, he did not posit that his own race was superior on the grounds of a universal, objective measure. He also believed Hitler and his followers were too narrowly focused on Germany and its struggle with other European powers, and they failed to understand the threat that other non-European groups posed to the West. Spengler argued that Western civilization made a mistake by not jealously guarding its technological innovations. According to Spengler, it is inevitable that competing cultures will appropriate Western technology and use them as weapons in their struggle against the West; he cited the rapid industrialization of Japan, and its great success in the Russo-Japanese war, as an example of this.[13] Spengler's 1934 book, *The Hour of Decision*, was ultimately banned in Hitler's Germany as a result of its criticism of the regime. Shortly before his death in 1936, Spengler predicted that the German Reich would fall within a decade.

Given his deserved reputation as a pessimist who viewed civilizational decline as inevitable and irreversible, it seems odd that a new ideological movement would view Spengler's work as a useful resource. However, although the death of a culture is no more avoidable than the death of an individual, Spengler argued that this did not justify apathy or a withdrawal from world affairs. Spengler's remarks at the conclusion of *Man and Technics* remains frequently cited by his admirers on the right:

Faced as we are with this destiny, there is only one world outlook that is worthy of us, that which has already been mentioned as the Choice of Achilles—better a short life, full of deeds and glory, than a long life without contentment. Already the danger is so great, for every individual, every class, every people, that to cherish any illusion whatever is deplorable. Time does not suffer itself to be halted; there is no question of prudent retreat or wise renunciation. Only dreamers believe that there is a way out. Optimism is cowardice.

We are born into this time and must bravely follow the path to the destined end. There is no other way out. Our duty is to hold onto the lost position, without hope, without rescue, like that Roman soldier whose bones were found in front of a door in Pompeii, who, during the eruption of Vesuvius, died at his post because they forgot to relieve him. That is greatness. That is what it means to be a thoroughbred. The honourable end is the one thing that cannot be taken from a man.[14]

ERNST JÜNGER

If someone claims to be influenced by Ernst Jünger, they should subsequently clarify which aspect of Jünger's thought they found useful. Over the course of his exceptionally long life and literary career, Jünger made a number of novel and interesting arguments, not always in agreement with each other. Jünger the war diarist was different from Jünger the Conservative Revolutionary, who was far different from Jünger the "anarch."

Jünger first achieved notoriety for his reflections on World War I. During that war, he earned a reputation as a brave soldier, receiving several wounds and serving in some of the most gruesome battles—the front lines at the horrific Battle of the Somme, for example. Throughout his service, he maintained a journal, which became the nucleus of his best-known work, *Storm of Steel*, published in 1920. Jünger's reflections are decidedly different from those of other well-known German authors who wrote on the war, such as Erich Maria Remarque (who published *All Quiet on the Western Front* in 1929 but who had personally experienced little direct combat). Jünger did not emphasize the futility or horror of trench warfare; instead, he made it clear that he found the war an electrifying experience. Even his recollections of serious wounds were presented without any indication that he felt fear or resentment.[15] *Storm of Steel* is similarly remarkable for its complete lack of a greater context; Jünger says nothing about the reasons for the war or the strategies of the generals. Nor is there any chauvinism or hostility toward his French and English opponents in the work. Before the war, Jünger had actually served in the French Foreign Legion, and throughout *Storm of Steel* he remarks on the courage of his enemies and the sorrow, but not remorse, he felt when he killed them. It has been remarked that modern technology removed all chivalry from war. Jünger clearly disagreed; he felt that it was precisely the brutality and inhuman nature of the Great War that gave it an epic quality and uplifted the men who experienced it.

Having achieved fame as a memoirist, Jünger became known as a nationalist, and like other figures of the Conservative Revolutionary movement, he had contempt for the bourgeoisie, their values, and their liberal democracy. However, while he rejected modern values, he embraced modern technology. He believed it would usher in a world of harder men. By being incorporated into the machinery of the modern world, mankind would develop a sense of discipline and detachment. In his 1934 work, *On Pain*, Jünger actually predicted the development of suicide bombers as a weapon of war.[16]

It is not difficult to see why Jünger's writings were admired by the National Socialists, but he remained aloof from the Nazis, even when they were at the height of their power, and he never joined the party (which cannot be said of many other figures associated with the Conservative Revolution). Before the outbreak of World War II, Jünger declined to reenter the military voluntarily, though he did serve in the Wehrmacht during the war, primarily in Paris. His disgust with violent mass movements and totalitarianism was made clear in his allegorical novel, *On the Marble Cliffs*, published in 1939.[17] Jünger had earlier described the path of "inner emigration," in which one remains within a despised regime and does not personally engage in active dissent, instead simply withdrawing from politics and focusing on solitary contemplation.

There was a decisive change in Jünger's tone in his postwar writings. While remaining indisputably on the right, his later works lacked any militant nationalism and had a decidedly anarchistic and elitist quality. Several of his works dealt with the proper stance of a person who wishes to maintain a degree of inner freedom in a totalitarian world that demands conformity. These ideas were introduced in his short book, *The Forest Passage* (1951). Jünger introduced the character of the Forest Rebel, who exercises self-directed freedom, well aware that he cannot personally change the world in a meaningful way. He engages in minor acts of rebellion, such as being the one person out of a hundred who votes "no" on a ballot in a rigged election. Although the Forest Rebel recognizes the difficulties associated with challenging the oppressive state, backed by the acquiescent masses, he nonetheless feels compelled to resist whenever possible: "Indeed, we see that even in these states with their overpowering police forces not all movement has died out. The armor of the new Leviathans has its own weak points, which must continually be felt out, and this assumes both caution and daring of a previously unknown quality."[18]

Jünger continued to develop these themes in his dystopian science fiction novel *Eumeswil* (1977). In this work, Jünger's protagonist describes himself as an "anarch." Jünger's anarch borrows much from the individualist anarchism of the German philosopher Max Stirner, though the anarch is not an anarchist. The anarch does not fight the existing state; he treats the existing social structure as a given and understands that he can no more effectively fight its laws than he can fight the law of gravity: "Any man who swears allegiance to a political change is a fool, a *facchino* for services that are not his business. The most rudimentary step toward freedom is to free oneself from all that. Basically each person senses it, and yet he keeps voting."[19] Jünger also distinguished the figure of the anarch from the Forest Rebel, noting that the Forest Rebel has "been expelled from society, while the anarch has expelled society from himself."[20]

The protagonist in *Eumeswil* actually serves as the night steward of the local dictator. However, while he accepts the prevailing social order, he does not grant it any moral authority. To the anarch, maintaining his personal strength and autonomy is the overriding concern. He remains unaffected by the prevailing spirit of the times. This perfect detachment is the source of the anarch's freedom:

> The positive counterpart of the anarchist is the anarch. The latter is not the adversary of the monarch but his antipode, untouched by him, though also dangerous. He is not the opponent of the monarch, but his pendant.
>
> After all, the monarch wants to rule many, nay, all people; the anarch, only himself. This gives him an attitude both objective and skeptical toward the powers that be; he has their figures go past him—and he is untouched, no doubt, yet inwardly not unmoved, not without historical passion.[21]

Jünger died at the age of 102 in 1998. His influence on the New Right is indisputable, but he received numerous accolades from mainstream figures as well. In spite of the accusation that he was a fascist, he earned several prestigious literary awards in his later years, including the Goethe Prize of Frankfurt.

ARTHUR MOELLER VAN DEN BRUCK

A final figure worth discussing in some detail had a much shorter literary career and died at a relatively young age in 1925. Arthur Moeller van den Bruck was one of the more influential figures associated with the Conservative Revolutionary movement, and he later influenced many New Right thinkers. Moeller has received less attention from contemporary scholars than the other figures discussed in this section, however. This is partly because of the degree to which Moeller's thinking has become inextricably associated with Nazism. Moeller's most influential work, published in 1923, was actually titled *Das dritte Reich* (The Third Reich), and Hitler was clearly influenced by his work. His thoughts on population and geography also clearly presaged the Nazi's idea of lebensraum.[22] He further called for an empire that would encompass all German people, including Austria. There is little in his translated writings that indicate Moeller shared Hitler's vicious anti-Semitism; he did, however, argue that Jews viewed the world differently than other Europeans, and that Marx's prophesies were mistaken because his Jewish heritage left him unable to understand the degree to which people, including the proletariat, are wedded to their national identities.[23] Although Moeller may be clearly seen as an intellectual precursor to Hitler's regime, we cannot know how Moeller would have felt about the Third Reich had he lived to see its rise.

Like all other figures presented in this chapter, Moeller despised liberalism, which he called "the death of nations." Like later figures associated with the New Right, Moeller argued that liberal individualism breaks the bond between people and their nations, and liberalism ultimately seeks a homogenous world free from any distinctions:

> The liberal professes to do all he does for the sake of the people; but he destroys the sense of community that should bind outstanding men to the people from which they spring. The people should naturally regard the outstanding man, not as an enemy but as a representative sample of themselves.
>
> Liberalism is the party of upstarts who have insinuated themselves between the people and its big men. Liberals feel themselves as isolated individuals, responsible to nobody. They do not share the nation's traditions, they are indifferent to its past and have no ambition for its future. They seek only their own personal advantage in the present. Their dream is the great International, in which the differences of peoples and languages, races and cultures will be obliterated.[24]

AKIN TO THE LIBERALS — THE SOCIALIST LEFT

Moeller provided his own definition of conservatism and explained how the true conservative differed from the reactionary. The reactionary simply wants to turn back the clock, undoing history back to a specific point in time when society remained in good order: "He believes that if only he had the political power it would be perfectly simple to reorganize the world according to the admirable scheme of older days."[25] Moeller argued that the reactionary stance comes from a superficial reading of history and fails to recognize that time cannot be reversed. In contrast, Moeller's conservatism looks to the future while remaining firmly attached to eternal principles that remain valid in spite of ephemeral political developments and even revolution. Conservatives will never win a total victory or expect that the creation of well-ordered institutions will maintain a conservative social order in perpetuity. Instead, conservatives must recognize that they must win and re-win their battles every generation. In spite of the necessity of a permanent struggle, Moeller argued that conservatism had the advantage of being congruent with nature, whereas "revolutions have eternity against them."[26]

Like the later thinkers on the New Right, Moeller argued that democracy had to be disassociated from parliamentarism. It is not merely the existence of universal suffrage and democratic institutions that make a democracy. Instead, democracy is the result of a common heritage and customs, expressed by the state: "Democracy is the political self-consciousness of a people: and its self-assertion as a nation."[27] On the basis of this definition, a state may be a monarchy and still democratic, provided the monarchy is an expression of the people's will. Similarly, for some people, in particular the Germans, an elected parliament may be an inappropriate system of government:

> The memory of the German Reichstag is associated with no great events in which it bore a part; but the memory of its blunders is inexhaustible. It is impotent because it is despised. Our friend the socialist . . . asked: "May not the day be coming when the people will have lost faith in parliaments?" The day has long since come. There is not a man in the country who does not call parliament "the chatter house." The feeling is universal that no help is to be found there. Our socialist opined that "every people has the parliamentary system it deserves." True. But our conclusion differs from his. We believe that the day of parliaments is over. We believe that Germany will lead the way in thought and deed. The parliamentary system has failed more gravely in Germany than in any other country; we have therefore greater reason than any other country to cast it from us and to create a new, worthier,

more suitable form of government representative of the people. Let us rejoice that Germany has proved too good for parliaments.[28]

As Moeller and many other Conservative Revolutionaries desired, parliamentary democracy did come to an end in Germany. Whatever misgivings the leading ideologues of this intellectual movement may have had with Hitler's Germany, it is not possible to totally disassociate antiliberal thinkers of the interwar period from the Third Reich. The defeat of the Axis powers, combined with the Nazi atrocities committed during the war, led to the near-total discrediting of all prewar right-wing European thought. This is understandable, given the devastation unleashed by regimes founded on these right-wing premises.

On the other hand, this may not be entirely fair. Proponents of liberal democracy can justifiably reject the ultranationalist and intolerant ideas promoted by the Conservative Revolutionaries. It is also fair to argue that this type of thinking is dangerous and would represent a destabilizing force if it ever again enjoyed mainstream popularity. However, to directly link the entire Conservative Revolutionary intellectual movement to the Holocaust and other wartime atrocities may be a step too far. To apply such logic consistently, one would have to similarly assign blame for the Holodomor and the Killing Fields to all Marxists and far leftists. Although ideas certainly have consequences, intellectuals cannot know beforehand precisely what those consequences will be or how their views will be twisted or misunderstood by those wielding power.

The European New Right represents one of the few postwar intellectual movements to respectfully engage with the ideas associated with the Conservative Revolution, borrowing ideas that can be rehabilitated and discarding those that cannot. Both movements reject modern notions of egalitarianism and multicultural democracy, as well as bourgeois materialist values.

OBSESSED WITH MONEY + PHYSICAL POSSESS-IONS

I chose to focus on the above figures affiliated with the Conservative Revolution because of their influence on later right-wing political thought. In the interest of space, I am not able to provide a comprehensive survey of all the prominent figures associated with this intellectual movement. The reader may question one conspicuous omission, however. By far, the philosopher Martin Heidegger had a greater influence on contemporary thought than any other figure associated with the Conservative Revolution in Germany. Although Heidegger was indisputably a man of the right, he also had an important influence on left-wing existentialists such as Jean-Paul Sartre. His stature as one of the greatest philosophers of the twentieth century endured despite his controversial affiliation with Nazism.[29] I chose not to discuss Heidegger in detail here because, while there are certainly political implications to Heidegger's major writings, he was far more interested in the deepest philosophical questions than in the minutiae of contemporary politics. Attempting to build a coherent and practical political platform on Heideggerian principles would be a major challenge, as Heidegger's writing can be frustratingly vague. Alexander Dugin, a figure who is (loosely) connected to the European New Right, and whose ideas I will discuss shortly, enthusiastically promotes the idea that Heidegger can provide the framework for a political philosophy. In my estimation, even Dugin—at least in his translated work—has failed to show what that political philosophy entails, in practical terms.[30]

[handwritten margin note: TOO LOOSELY]

The European New Right also drew on the ideas of thinkers not directly associated with the Conservative Revolution. The Italian economist and sociologist Vilfredo Pareto, for example, has inspired a great deal of New Right thought.[31] They have also incorporated the ideas of certain left-wing and even Marxist theorists into their own ideological framework. The Italian Marxist Antonio Gramsci's theories of cultural power have largely been appropriated by the New Right, as have Georges Sorel's ideas about the power of myth.[32]

René Guénon, Julius Evola, and the World of Tradition

The European New Right has been highly critical of Christianity from the outset. This does not mean that they did not directly engage with the ideas of deeply religious thinkers. Two such writers, whose ideas will appear especially strange to an American audience, were René Guénon and Julius Evola. Given the Eurocentric thinking of most of the figures discussed in this chapter, these figures possessed another curious attribute: they were particularly interested in religious thought outside the West, particularly Hinduism, Taoism, and Buddhism. Like other thinkers who influenced New Right thinking, both also expressed utter contempt for the modern world and its underlying metaphysical premises. In place of modernity, they advocated a return to Tradition (always capitalized).

René Guénon, born in 1886, shared many ideas with the religious viewpoint known as perennialism. Guénon believed there was a unity of all the world's great religious traditions, all stemming from the same transcendent source. Guénon became interested in Eastern religions and the occult at an early age, and became an expert on many religious traditions. He wrote numerous books on these traditions, introducing many Westerners to Eastern religious thought for the first time. He initially hoped for a reinvigoration of Catholic traditions in Europe, but he ultimately determined that such an effort was futile. This led to his move to Cairo and conversion to Sufi Islam. Though formally a Muslim, he maintained his belief in the transcendent unity of religions. This belief was of course at odds with Islamic—and Christian—theology, as these monotheistic religions maintain that they have a monopoly on religious truths.

Like secular thinkers such as Spengler, Guénon rejected the very notion of progress. He viewed history in cyclical terms, though his own understanding was decidedly religious in nature. To Guénon, modernity represented the absolute low point of human history, as it cut mankind off from true spirituality. Unlike other conservative and reactionary thinkers, however, Guénon did not trace the origins of the present degenerate age to events of the relatively recent past, instead positing that man has lived in a state of disarray for most of recorded history:

> The Hindu doctrine teaches that a human cycle, to which it gives the name of Manvantara, is divided into four periods marking so many stages during which the primordial spirituality becomes more and more obscured; these are the same periods that the ancient traditions of the West called the Golden, Silver, Bronze and Iron Ages. We are now in the fourth age, the Kali-Yuga or "dark age," and have been so already, it is said, for more than six thousand years, that is to say since an epoch far earlier than any known to "classical history." Since that time, the truths which were formerly within reach of all men have become more hidden and inaccessible; those who possess them grow gradually less and less numerous, and although the treasure of "non-human" wisdom that was before the ages can never be lost, it becomes enveloped in ever more impenetrable veils, which hide it from men's sight and make it extremely difficult to discover.[33]

Given his tendency to think in extraordinarily long time frames, Guénon showed little interest in ephemeral political developments. He did, however, view the development of democracy as yet another sign of societal degeneration: "The most decisive argument against democracy can be summed up in a few words: the higher cannot emanate from the lower, because the greater cannot come out of the less; this is an absolute mathematical certainty that nothing can gainsay."[34] He further denounced the contemporary

West for being materialistic in multiple senses of the word. First, it is materialistic in the sense that it recognizes nothing but the material world, ignoring all things that cannot be quantified or have no obvious practical use.[35] He further denounced the West for viewing history in exclusively materialistic terms—that historical events were all the result of economic conditions.[36] He also rejected the notion that the West could, in any meaningful sense, still be described as Christian.

In contrast to the modern West, Guénon praised various Eastern civilizations for maintaining their connection to ancient traditions. He was concerned, however, that even ancient civilizations such as India would eventually be seduced by the Western mind-set, and he saw some evidence that this was beginning to occur, though he was hopeful that the traditional mind-set still prevalent farther east would be able to resist Western materialism.

As noted, Guénon wrote relatively little about the contemporary political situation. Thus, despite his popularity among many later right-wing thinkers, it is difficult to classify Guénon as a member of the radical right. The same cannot be said of Julius Evola, who was described by the right-wing orator and author Jonathan Bowden as "one of the world's most right-wing—certainly the most elitist—thinkers."[37] Although for the most part I have avoided dwelling on the biographical details of the figures presented in this text, Evola's life was so unusual that it is worth discussing. Indeed, I suspect it is the unusual nature of Evola's biography that attracts contemporary right-wingers to his writings. Evola was born to an aristocratic family in Sicily in 1898. From an early age he developed a fervent hatred of the bourgeoisie and its values, which is why, despite studying engineering, he ultimately rejected the profession. This contempt for bourgeois values extended to other elements of his life, such as his complete lack of interest in marriage or having children. He conspicuously lacked material possessions. This antibourgeois sentiment was so great that in his later years Evola—a man on the most radical fringes of the radical right—experimented with drugs and offered some tepid praise for beatniks and hippies, but chastised them for being insufficiently radical.[38]

Evola served in World War I as an artillery officer. After the war, he became a dadaist painter of some renown. Despite being a decidedly modern form of art, Evola was attracted to dadaism because of its inherent radicalism: "Dadaism is not merely conceived as a new avant-garde artistic tendency; rather, it stood for an outlook on life which expressed a tendency towards total liberation, combined with the upsetting of all logic, ethic and aesthetic categories, in the most paradoxical and baffling ways."[39] He eventually abandoned his artistic endeavors to devote himself to the study of religious and traditional thought.

Evola was well known by the fascists and later the National Socialists, and he had a personal relationship with Mussolini, though he was sharply critical of fascism. However, throughout all of his writings, he critiqued fascism from the right. That is, he viewed both fascism and Nazism as insufficiently hierarchical and radical, though he admired many elements of Hitler's regime, particularly the SS, for its elitism and traditionalistic focus on initiation.[40]

During World War II, Evola hoped to again serve as an officer, ideally on the Eastern Front. His hopes never materialized, however. He spent much of the later years of the war in Vienna. During bombing raids of the city, Evola refused to join others in shelters, preferring to continue his work or simply wander the empty streets in order to contemplate human fate as the bombs fell around him. During one of these raids, he was grievously injured, suffering wounds that left him paralyzed below the waist for the rest of his life. He later claimed that the injury had little impact on his life, and he did not lament his paralysis because he had "always thoroughly subscribed to the traditional doctrine . . . which teaches that we have wished all relevant events in our life before our birth."[41]

In 1951, Evola was arrested and imprisoned by the new democratic government in Italy, charged with glorifying fascism. When defending himself from these charges, he did not disavow any of his earlier writings. He readily admitted that he supported ideological currents within Mussolini's regime, but also pointed to his criticisms. However, even during his trial, he emphasized that his criticisms of fascism were always traditional and counter-revolutionary: "I have defended, and I still defend, 'fascist ideas,' not inasmuch as they are 'fascist' but in the measure that they revive ideas superior and anterior to Fascism. As such they belong to the heritage of hierarchical, aristocratic, and traditional conceptions of the State, a conception having a universal character and maintained in Europe up to the French Revolution."[42] Evola was ultimately found not guilty on all charges.

Evola's best-known book on politics, *Revolt Against the Modern World*, was first published in 1934. The book discusses both his religious ideas and his radical critique of modernity. Like the New Right thinkers who followed many years later, Evola argued in this book that the United States and the Soviet Union were not really ideological adversaries but rather represented variations of the same disordered thinking. Thus Europeans should not view one system as inherently superior to the other. In fact, America may be an even more pernicious force in the world:

> It would be easy to produce more evidence concerning the similarities between the two countries that would allow us to see in communist Russia and America two faces of the same coin, or two movements whose destructive paths converge. The former is a reality unfolding under the iron fist of a dictatorship and through a radical nationalization and rationalization. The latter is a spontaneous realization (therefore more worrisome) of a mankind that accepts and even *wants* to be what it is, that feels healthy, free, and strong and that implements the same tendencies as communism but without the fanatical and fatalistic dedication of the communist Slav. And yet, behind both "civilizations" those who have eyes to see can detect the warning signs of the advent of the "Nameless Beast."[43]

Evola would certainly be considered a racist by the contemporary definition, and he wrote on race extensively, but his views on race differed from those of the Nazis. Congruent with his rejection of modern thinking, Evola opposed merely biological views on race. To Evola, race was both spiritual and biological—and an individual's spiritual race may not be congruent with that person's biological race. The obsession with race among right-wing movements in the 1930s was, to Evola, evidence of their fundamentally modern mind-set: "As for the racism of the German state, it merged a sort of pan-Germanic nationalism with the ideas of biological science. With respect to the latter, I believe that Trotsky was not far off the mark when he described racism as a kind of zoological materialism. The German state embraced biology, eugenics, and the theory of heredity, accepting all the materialist assumptions behind such doctrines."[44] Evola criticized Mussolini's embrace of German doctrines on race in the late 1930s.

Evola may also be properly classified as an anti-Semite, and many of his writings include attacks on Jews, but on this issue Evola's views also diverged from those of the Nazis. He did not seem to have many problems with the Jewish religion per se, and had favorable things to say about Kabbalah. In fact, Evola seems to have had a higher estimation of Orthodox Judaism than Christianity. Nor does he seem to have believed that there was something biologically inferior about Jews. However, he was certainly critical of secular Jews in Europe, and he even wrote an introduction to *The Protocols of the Elders of Zion*, a fraudulent text that claimed to lay out a plan for Jewish global domination. Given the prevailing attitudes in Europe during the interwar period, Evola does not appear to be a uniquely vicious anti-Semite, and he criticized the National Socialists for their obsession with Jews while ignoring other causes of subversion.[45] Evola's writings on Jews are certainly outside the bounds of acceptable discourse today, and these writings are a reason he remains so controversial. However, before the war, he was condemned by at least one contemporary for being a "Jew lover."[46]

Although right-wing thinkers, Christian or otherwise, do not typically embrace egalitarianism in practical politics, most at least acknowledge a degree of spiritual equality among human beings. According to Christians, we are all precious to God; according to atheists, we are all destined to face the same total annihilation of our personality upon our deaths. Even this brand of egalitarianism was anathema to Evola's thinking. For Evola, even the notion that people are equal in the eyes of God is preposterous. Even in his view of death, Evola was an elitist. Evola argued that most people's personalities will fade away after death. Only the best have any hope of true immortality:

> Thus, as far as the destiny of the soul after death is concerned, there are two opposite paths. The first is the "path of the gods," also known as the "solar path" or Zeus's path, which leads to the bright dwelling of the immortals. This dwelling was variously represented as a height, heaven, or an island, from the Nordic Valhalla and Asgard to the Aztec–Inca "House of the Sun" that was reserved for kings, heroes, and nobles. The other path is that trodden by those who do not survive in a real way, and who slowly yet inexorably dissolve back into their original stocks, into the "totems" that unlike single individuals, never die; this is the life of Hades, of the "infernals," of Niflheim, of the chthonic deities.[47]

Evola's thinking was similar to Guénon's in many important ways, and the two men influenced each other strongly. Both figures seem totally out of place in the twentieth century, taking ideas such as magic completely seriously.[48] When reading ancient religious texts, both men took it for granted that these texts described the world as it actually existed—that gods once roamed the earth in a golden age now forgotten and unremarked upon by conventional historians. They did disagree with one another on a number of points, however. Notably, Guénon did not approve of Evola's direct engagement with politics. Evola was critical of anyone, including Guénon, who thought that he or she could escape modernity by fleeing to another civilization that had not yet reached the West's level of degeneration.[49] Evola had a much lower opinion of Christianity than Guénon; Evola viewed Christianity as a fundamentally chthonic and feminine religion, and that it was thus inferior to the pagan religions that dominated pre-Christian Europe. Because of his hostility toward Christianity and the Catholic Church, Evola disapproved of Mussolini's Lataran Treaty with the Vatican.

In his postwar writings, Evola made it clear that engaging directly with politics was futile. The Allied victory made it utterly impossible for Traditionalist sentiments to be made manifest in practical politics. Although he was never an uncritical admirer of fascism or National Socialism, he held out hopes that these movements could be cleansed of their modern influences and channeled in a more traditional direction. The total defeat of the Axis powers by the United States and the Soviet Union ended the possibility of a state governed by a traditional framework. There was no chance that the new governments established in the postwar period could become vehicles for his ideas. Thus, Evola needed to formulate a new attitude for proponents of Tradition. Seeing no hope in political action, Evola advocated the principle of *apoliteia*—a complete disinterest toward and detachment from mainstream politics. This does not necessarily imply that one should withdraw entirely from the world and become a monk or a hermit; Evola's discussions on this subject are somewhat analogous to Jünger's thoughts on the anarch. Although one may engage with politics as an act of personal development or simply an interest in acting for its own sake, it is important to recognize that no higher value can be realized through politics. At such a late stage in the historical cycle, proponents of Tradition must recognize that the trends of modernity will have to reach their logical, disastrous conclusion. Only then will the possibilities of a new golden age be within reach:

> We shall now examine the principle of "riding the tiger" as applied
> to the external world and the total environment. Its significance
> can be stated as follows: When a cycle of civilization is reaching its
> end, it is difficult to achieve anything by resisting it and by directly
> opposing the forces in motion. The current is too strong; one would
> be overwhelmed. The essential thing is to not let oneself be impressed
> by the omnipotence and apparent triumph of the forces of the epoch.
> These forces, devoid of any connection with any higher principle, are in
> fact on a short chain. One should not become fixated on the present and
> on things at hand, but keep in view the conditions that may come about
> in the future. Thus the principle to follow could be that of letting the

forces and processes take their own course, while keeping oneself firm and ready to intervene when "the tiger, which cannot leap on the person riding it, is tired of running."[50]

The New Right cannot be properly considered an offshoot of Evola or Guénon's Traditionalism, though it borrows many of their ideas. In particular, this intentional detachment from mainstream politics is echoed in the New Right's focus on metapolitics.

Alain de Benoist and GRECE

The New Right in France was born when the revolutionary left in that country was at an apogee. In 1968 France experienced extraordinary civil unrest, including general strikes and the occupation of universities and factories. The protests were sufficiently strong to raise the possibility of civil war or revolution. The government was in real danger of collapsing completely. Although 1968 was a watershed year for the European left, it was also the year in which a new right-wing movement was created—though with considerably less notice or fanfare.

The Groupement de recherche et d'études pour la civilisation européenne (GRECE), translated as the Research and Study Group for European Civilization, was founded by a young journalist named Alain de Benoist in early 1968. This right-wing think tank was decidedly different in its orientation than prominent American conservative think tanks in that it os- *NOTE* tentatiously neglected engagement with mainstream partisan politics. Like its intellectual predecessors, it was critical of both communism and liberalism. Although it clearly shared many ideas with the Conservative Revolutionaries, and to a lesser extent Traditionalists like Evola, and discussed these figures and their thought frequently in their main publications, they also deviated from older right-wing thinking in a number of ways. Their anticolonial and anticapitalist rhetoric often mirrored that of the postwar New Left. The leading thinkers of GRECE expressed interest in subjects such as ecology, and they were emphatic in their rejection of racism—though they also were unreserved critics of egalitarian multiculturalism. GRECE also rejected nationalism as it is generally understood in the modern context, preferring a broader European identity that nonetheless acknowledges and accepts regional cultural and linguistic differences. In 1969, Benoist created the first New Right journal, *Nouvelle École*.

GRECE and its leading thinkers deliberately neglected partisan politics because it gave them greater freedom to develop their ideas and because their singular focus on philosophy and culture would presumably allow them greater influence in the long run. Had the New Right rushed into parliamentary politics, it would have been immediately bogged down with the issue of coalition building rather than formulating a coherent alternative to modernity; partisan politics would have required entering coalitions with traditional Catholics, for example, or explaining how their policies will assist the middle class with its material concerns. The New Right's ambitions were ultimately much more radical, and to ever see them realized, they first needed to fundamentally change the culture. Thus, they focused primarily on so-called metapolitics. Like Gramsci, the New Right believed that the power of the state was ultimately reliant on acceptance by the culture. To effectively create a radically different regime, the road to power must first be paved by capturing and changing the major cultural institutions—the media, the major religious organizations, the education system, and so on. A revolution, even one that successfully gains control of the state, will ultimately fail if the revolution's opponents maintained control of the culture and if the revolutionary ideas did not already have widespread acceptance within the broader population. In contrast, if the war of ideas is won first, political power will be inevitable.

Although Benoist and other figures of the New Right are critical of parliamentary democracy as it is practiced in the West, they claim to support democracy—at least as they define it. To Benoist, a people is an organic organism, rather than an aggregation of isolated and atomized individuals. The problem with democracy as it is presently practiced is that it is rooted in rationalism and individualism, and presumably does not require a sense of cultural unity. He contrasts this with democracy as it existed in Ancient Greece, which he considers a superior model:

> Ancient democracy defined citizenship by one's origins, and gave citizens the opportunity to participate in the life of the city. Modern democracy organizes atomized individuals into citizens, primarily viewing them through the lens of abstract egalitarianism. Ancient democracy was based on the idea of organic community; modern democracy, as an heir to Christianity and the philosophy of the Enlightenment, on the individual. The meaning of the words "city," "people," "nation," and "liberty" radically changes from one model to the other.[51]

As already noted, GRECE was entirely open in its hostility toward Christianity. Benoist's first book translated into English, originally published in

1981, was actually titled *On Being a Pagan.*[52] Although Christianity has long been assaulted from the radical left, the New Right's opposition to Christianity is qualitatively different. The far left typically opposes Christianity for its supposed intolerance—toward gays, feminists, and other groups—and its generally reactionary stance on a host of other issues. The New Right, in contrast, opposes Christianity precisely because it is so individualistic and universalistic. Like Nietzsche before it, the New Right blames Christianity for the rise of egalitarian values. Further, as Christianity began in the Middle East as an offshoot of Judaism, they reject the religion as being fundamentally alien to European civilization.

Benoist has argued that Christianity and all other monotheistic religions are inherently totalitarian because they claim to possess a monopoly on universal truth. This was of course put into practice in European history when Constantine converted the Roman empire to Christianity and all other religious practices and beliefs were subsequently outlawed. It was further evident throughout the medieval period when Christians systematically converted, by force when necessary, the entire continent to the faith. Benoist went further, however, and argued that modern totalitarian regimes, even those that were formally atheist, had Christian roots and demonstrated that they still had a Christian outlook: "Modern forms of totalitarianism have only secularized and transformed into a profane theodicy the system of the unique truth and one model to which all diversity must be boiled down."[53] The utopianism of modern secular ideologies such as Marxism similarly has roots in the messianic elements of monotheistic religions. In contrast to Christian monotheism, Benoist lauded the polytheistic cults of pre-Christian Europe for their tolerance; in these societies, it was understood that different peoples worshiped different gods, and no religion had a monopoly on universal truth. These religions also lacked any belief in a future universal utopia.

This open attack on Christianity clearly limited the popular appeal of the New Right. As is the case in the United States, religious traditionalists in Europe were always the leading opponents of the left. In the absence of its hostility to Christianity, conservative Catholics in France may have been more receptive to New Right thinking. To Benoist, however, this was not a major problem, as building a powerful electoral coalition was never his primary objective, at least in the short term. Just as Marx and the first communists were initially focused on developing a coherent theory, the New Right emphasized ideas and building their ideological framework. It therefore would not soften any of its stances in the interests of ephemeral political gains. If Christianity was part of the problem, and they believed it was, then Christianity needed to be attacked in no uncertain terms.

The New Right was also intensely hostile to the United States and the ideas it represented; it was perhaps even more anti-American than anti-Soviet. To the New Right, Americans represented universalism, materialism, and egalitarianism even more consistently than the Soviet Union, and they were troubled by the degree to which Western Europe was exhibiting signs of Americanization. America was the primary engine of economic globalization, and globalization is a pernicious force because it undermines cultural differences. According to New Right thinkers, organizations like the World Bank and the World Trade Organization are not innocuous. They represent a new form of imperialism. Economic globalization destroys regional and local identities, and replaces them with American pop music and fast food. They further argued that NATO existed not just to protect Western Europe from Soviet aggression. It also ensured European submission to the United States.[54]

In opposition to the United States, Benoist argued that Europeans should make common cause with people in the third world. Although it was always against immigration, the New Right was supportive of populist anti-American movements in the Middle East, Asia, Africa, and Latin America. These other regions of the world were no less threatened by Americanization than Europe, and therefore their efforts to resist American dominance were worthy of support. These movements, combined with their own efforts, represented a possibility for a new multipolar world and an end to American hegemony.[55]

Despite adamantly denying that the New Right is racist or xenophobic, its proponents continue to face such charges. These accusations are not entirely without merit. The New Right rejects the cosmopolitan and multicultural vision of the mainstream left and much of the procapitalist right; the latter, focused entirely on economic growth, sees immigration as a blessing. Although the New Right does not typically argue that any culture or race is inherently superior to another, it does emphasize the right to difference. Although this phrase seems innocuous and almost xenophilic, it is important to remember the implications of such a stand. The right for cultures to maintain their autonomy and homogeneity necessarily implies a right to exclude. Within such a framework, a community could justifiably expel or deny entrance to immigrants who threaten the dominant cultural norms—though Benoist claimed to oppose the idea of uprooting and expelling all non-

Europeans from the continent.[56] Critics argue that the New Right is simply trying to advance a more politically palatable form of racism, whose practical effect would be identical to that of more explicit racists and xenophobes.

[handwritten: WHO CARES ABOUT THE ENEMY CRITICS]

The term New Right (*nouvelle droite*) was not applied to GRECE and its leading intellectuals until more than a decade after its inception. Benoist and his colleagues have received harsh criticism from mainstream journalists and scholars in Europe and elsewhere, and their efforts to build bridges to groups on other parts of the political spectrum—such as elements of the far left that expressed similar social critiques—have thus far yielded few dividends. Christian conservatives have similarly rejected or ignored the arguments put forward by the New Right, with a few exceptions. Benoist has also been criticized from the far right. In spite of his rejection of modernity and history of radical stances, thinkers to the right of Benoist have argued that his vigorous antiracism is a politically correct pose designed to insulate him from criticism from the egalitarian left. They argue that this is both dishonest and completely ineffective. They also argue that the insistence on metapolitics, rather than concrete political action in the real world, makes the New Right nothing more than an intellectual curiosity, one that does nothing to face the existential threat faced by contemporary Europe.

[handwritten: A POINT HERE. WORK WITH FN OK TO MB]

Guillaume Faye and Archeofuturism

One of Benoist's most vocal critics on the right, Guillaume Faye, was initially an important figure within the European New Right. However, he ended his affiliation with GRECE in the late 1980s in order to focus on journalism and other interests, taking a thirteen-year break from polemical writing. Faye came to reject the softer positions of Benoist, as well as the exclusive focus on metapolitics. Whereas Benoist attempts to make his arguments as universal as possible—in the sense that he asserts all societies have a right to difference—Faye does not feign to care about anyone but Europeans:

[handwritten: AND EUROPEANS ABROAD]

Why do we fight? We don't fight for "the cause of peoples," because the identity of every people is its own concern, not ours, and because history is a cemetery of peoples and civilizations. We fight only for the cause of our own people's destiny. Our political activities—the most quotidian cultural or metapolitical, the most down-to-earth, the most humble activities, even in the formulation of our practical programs—are guided by the imperative of all Grand Politics: that is, by the struggle for the heritage of our ancestors and the future of our children.[57]

Similarly, Faye also rejects the xenophilia embraced by some elements of the New Right and the Traditionalists; the latter in particular had a propensity to favor non-Western cultures over their own. Although opposition to immigration and multicultural societies is a common theme in New Right thought, Faye is much more radical in his opposition to immigration, and he is more willing to engage with radical, populist right-wing movements. He is forthright in his declarations that immigration from the Muslim world threatens to destroy European civilization, and that reversing this tide must be the primary goal of his movement. For this reason, he is frustrated with other elements of the New Right that focus all of their attention on the United States and its deleterious impact on the world, even to the point of making common cause with Islamists. Faye is no less critical of the United States than other figures associated with the New Right, but he views American dominance of the world as less of an existential threat to Europe than Islamic immigration, though he suggests that the two are related. In fact, he believes that America is deliberately promoting immigration into Europe in order to ensure that the continent never reemerges as a competitor: "In the spirit of 'the Islamo-American pact,' the US seeks to weaken Europe by favouring her Islamization and her transformation into a multi-racial, Africanized society."[58]

As noted, Faye is less enamored with Traditionalists like Evola and Guénon than other figures associated with the New Right. Although he rejects modern and postmodern morality, he does not reject technology or modern science. He is particularly interested in issues such as ecology and in how modern technology such as nuclear power can both protect the environment and ameliorate the economic collapse that will follow the decline in oil reserves. Although a promoter of scientific discovery and innovation, Faye also argues that it is simply impossible for the entire world to enjoy a first world standard of living without creating massive ecological devastation. Much of Faye's recent work has a decidedly apocalyptic tone.

Faye argues that the modern world will be brought down by a "convergence of catastrophes."[59] Beyond his concerns about the demographic displacement of native Europeans, Faye points to a number of additional ominous trends. The rapidly aging populations in developed countries will put insurmountable stress on social services and will only increase calls for more immigration. Social unrest and religious fanaticism is growing in developing countries, and this unrest will have consequences across the world. Widespread pollution may eventually make the world uninhabitable for humans. The spread of nuclear weapons and the possibility of new epidemics remain terrible threats.[60] Although Faye clearly thinks a catastrophe is inevitable, he does not engage exclusively in critique, and he has sought to formulate a sustainable alternative to the modern world.

Faye calls his vision for the post–catastrophic era archeofuturism. It is archaic in the sense that it is founded on traditionalist values such as hierarchy and distinction, and it rejects the egalitarianism that dominates modern thought. It is futuristic in the sense that it embraces technological advancement. Unlike traditionalist conservatives, or Traditionalists like Evola, archeofuturism is not backward looking or seeking to turn back the clock to a previous golden age. It says that this is both impossible and undesirable. However, even with tremendous technological innovation, there are ecological limits to economic growth, and this must be recognized.

Instead of allowing natural limits of growth to drag all of humanity back to the level of subsistence farmers, Faye argues for the development of a two-tiered world economy. Because of natural boundaries to perpetual growth, the majority of mankind will need to revert to traditional agrarian societies, and global GDP will necessarily contract dramatically. This will even be true of large portions of the presently developed world, including in Europe. Some percentage of the globe, perhaps 10 to 20 percent of humanity, will enjoy continued technological progress. These advanced centers across the world will remain linked to each other commercially via high-speed transportation. Faye gave a fictionalized account of this world order at the end of his book *Archeofuturism*.[61]

In Faye's vision of the future, the world experiences a massive economic and ecological collapse in the early twenty-first century. After the chaos, a new order is established in Europe and Russia—a "Eurosiberian Federation" is created, in which regions have large amounts of individual autonomy, but each sends representatives to an imperial senate. Within this federation, large cities remain, but even the largest are much smaller than the sprawling metropolises that developed in the twentieth century, and the vast majority of the population is engaged in traditional agriculture and craftsmanship. Traditional Christianity makes a major comeback outside the small technological enclaves. Different civilizations across the globe react in a similar manner, though Faye says that North America suffers the most damage and is the slowest to recover.

Alexander Dugin and the Fourth Political Theory

In Western Europe, the New Right's ideas have never truly penetrated the mainstream. In Eastern Europe, and Russia in particular, the bounds of acceptable political discourse are different, though I hesitate to say wider. Though Soviet-style communism was discredited, liberal reforms implemented during the Yeltsin years failed to achieve widespread prosperity for ordinary Russians. Within the political vacuum, space was opened for alternatives to liberal democracy and free-market capitalism, as forcefully demonstrated by the political success of Vladimir Putin's quasi-authoritarian regime. In post-Soviet Russia, a political theorist heavily influenced by New Right ideas has achieved preeminence and is even said to directly influence state policy. For decades, Alexander Dugin has sought to formulate a new political theory that will challenge the liberal ideology that has dominated the world since 1991.

Dugin argues that there have been three prominent political theories in the modern era. The first, and most successful, is liberalism, which emerged in the eighteenth century and has both left-wing and right-wing varieties. Liberalism's first great challenge came from the second political theory: communism, and its less radical variants, socialism and social democracy. Fascism, which includes National Socialism, was the third political theory. The third political theory largely vanished from the earth in 1945 and cannot be revived. The second political theory died of natural decay at the end of the cold war. This left just one political theory dominant across the globe: liberalism. In his analysis, Dugin is not entirely dissimilar from Francis Fukuyama, who argued that the collapse of the Soviet Union ushered in a postideological age and "the end of history."[62] Unlike Fukuyama, however, Dugin opposes the global dominance of liberalism and global capitalism.

To defeat liberalism, a new political theory must be developed. Neither communism nor fascism can be revived, nor should we want them to be revived—though Dugin is clearly more sympathetic to fascism than the two existing alternatives.[63] This new political theory must be forceful in its repudiation of liberalism and can borrow the useful elements of both communism and fascism while discarding the wrong-headed elements of those failed ideologies. Dugin admits that his Fourth Political Theory is not fully developed at this time, but he has borrowed heavily from the Traditionalists and the New Right, as well as the philosophy of Martin Heidegger (particularly Heidegger's concept of *Dasein*, which Dugin believes can help orient the Fourth Political Theory). Like the other figures discussed in this chapter, Dugin blames the United States and its imperial ambitions for much of the disorder in the world, and he seeks the creation of a coalition that can effectively check American power and create a new multipolar world. He envisions a global alliance between traditionalists from all civilizations against the United States and the values it represents:

> Another question is the structure of a possible anti-globalist and anti-imperialist front and its participants. I think we should include in it all forces that struggle against the West, the United States, against liberal democracy, and against modernity and post-modernity. The common enemy is the necessary instance for all kinds of political alliances. This means Muslims and Christians, Russians and Chinese, both Leftists and Rightists, the Hindus and Jews who challenge the present state of affairs, globalization and American imperialism. They are thus all virtually friends and allies. Let our ideals be different, but we have in common one very strong feature: hatred of the present social reality. Our ideals that differ are potential ones (*in potential*). But the challenge we are dealing with is actual (*in actu*). That is the basis for a new alliance. All who share a negative analysis of globalization, Westernization and postmodernization should coordinate their effort in the creation of a new strategy of resistance to the omnipresent evil. And we can find common allies even within the United States as well, among those who choose the path of Tradition over the present decadence.[64]

Dugin argued that pluralism should stand against the universalist ideology that dominates in the modern world. Although such thoughts may seem initially appealing to antiglobalists on the left, it is important to remember that Dugin also rejects the premise that ideas like human rights and democracy are universal values that must be respected in all places. Dugin believes a political alliance between Orthodox Christian and Islamic civilizations could be a particularly effective traditionalist opposition to the West and its materialist values. He is considered a leading thinker of the Eurasia movement, and he is especially hopeful about the prospects of an alliance between Russia and Iran.[65]

Dugin envisioned a special role for Russia in the struggle against the United States and the forces of modernity and postmodernity. He argued that Russia was never fully part of the West and has its own special destiny. He also notes that Russia has always been a hindrance to the dream of a world state, and the liberal hope that Russia would be seamlessly incorporated into the new world order after the cold war was never realized. According to Dugin, liberalism has never really taken root in Russia: "In Russia, irrespective of the whole period of the 1990s, liberalism did not penetrate deeply and did not spawn a political generation of authentic, convinced liberals."[66] Because they are opposed to liberalism by nature, and because Russia remains a powerful and important nation, Russians are in an ideal position to lead the crusade against the West.

As noted, Dugin is an important public intellectual in Russia and is said to have the ear of important policy makers. He has been associated with a number of political movements. He was, for example, an early member of the (now banned) National Bolshevik Party. It is becoming a fairly common refrain, especially among Americans hostile to Putin, that Dugin is providing the intellectual framework for the current expansionist tendencies of the Russian government. From the outside, it is difficult to estimate the degree to which he actually influences the direction of Russian foreign policy, however.[67] Although relations between the United States and Russia have certainly deteriorated in recent years—reaching new lows with the recent crisis in Ukraine—it is difficult to blame Dugin and his ideas specifically for present disputes.

The American Right's Reaction to the European New Right

For the most part, the American conservative movement has shown little interest in the European New Right. There has certainly not been any major cooperation, or even much in the way of respectful dialogue. This does not mean that American conservatives have been completely ignorant of right-wing intellectual currents across the Atlantic or have shown no interest in the figures and ideas associated with the New Right.

The New Right has received some attention from American paleoconservatives. This should not be surprising, as the two movements often reach similar conclusions about policy, although they are based on different metaphysical foundations. Some from the paleoconservative intellectual tradition have written on the New Right in generally positive terms. Paul Gottfried, for example, disagrees with Benoist's insistence that Christianity is a primary cause of the West's current cultural crisis, but he nonetheless has praised Benoist as an intellectual.[68] *Chronicles* has published many essays by Tomislav Sunić—who is clearly part of the New Right's intellectual milieu—including essays praising the New Right.[69] Other paleoconservatives, however, such as Thomas Fleming, have openly rejected the New Right, largely because of its anti-Christian stance.[70]

Thomas Molnar, a Hungarian-born Catholic philosopher and political theorist who wrote frequently for prominent American conservative pub-

A GOOFY REASON

lications, was the only American conservative of any significance who had any meaningful collaborative relationship with Benoist.[71] The two actually coauthored a book. Although he acknowledged the many ways that Benoist's movement differed from American conservatism in fundamental ways, he nonetheless praised the New Right in the pages of *National Review* in 1978.[72] He was even more effusive when writing about the New Right in *Chronicles* in 1981:

> What does [the New Right] offer to people in general? It offers some of the best and most courageous analyses in the French press and book market. Since they have been semi-officially ostracized, [New Right] intellectuals can afford to call the emperor naked, to call the bluffs of the left-liberal orthodoxy. [The New Right] offers an *alternative* in content, approach and style, which, far from being primitive and negative, is sophisticated, original and usually (when religion is not involved) balanced.[73]

Molnar aside, the mainstream conservative movement has largely responded to the New Right with silence, offering neither praise nor critique. The reality is there has been little reason for American conservatives to take notice of the New Right. As long as the New Right was focused on metapolitics, rather than practical electoral politics, and its metapolitical endeavors were focused entirely on Europe, there was no significant chance the New Right would have any meaningful influence on the United States. Given that the European New Right did not pose a serious threat to American dominance internationally, nor was it seeking in any serious way to gain American acolytes, there has been little reason for American conservatives to translate New Right manifestos into English or discuss New Right ideas in their publications.

Although the figures associated with the New Right in Western Europe have, for the most part, been ignored by the mainstream conservative movement, the same cannot be said of Alexander Dugin. In fact, Dugin has also become something of a boogeyman to conservatives opposed to Putin's Russia; conservative radio and television personality Glenn Beck described Dugin as "truly terrifying."[74] Indeed, Dugin is sometimes treated by American conservatives like a crazed Rasputin, secretly controlling Russian foreign policy. It is not surprising that Dugin is receiving more notice from Americans than the Western European thinkers who influenced his thinking. Unlike France, Russia does have the potential to rival the United States as a global power. Also unlike France, there is the possibility that thinkers influenced by New Right ideas in Russia could play an important role in developing foreign policy. Further, one looking through Dugin's writings over the course of his long career will find no shortage of quotes indicating that he is a lunatic—and many conservatives have been eager to share these quotes. His ideology was described in an article in *National Review Online*, for example, as a "satanic cult."[75] This same article implied that American failure to stand up to Putin's Russia on the issue of Ukraine would lead to a new cold war, or perhaps even the end of the world:

> Without Ukraine, Dugin's fascist Eurasian Union project is impossible, and sooner or later Russia itself will have to join the West and become free, leaving only a few despised and doomed islands of tyranny around the globe. But with Ukraine underfoot, the Eurasianists' program can and will proceed, and a new Iron Curtain will fall into place imprisoning a large fraction of humanity in the grip of a monstrous totalitarian power that will become the arsenal of evil around the world for decades to come. That means another Cold War, trillions of dollars wasted on arms, accelerated growth of the national-security state at home, repeated proxy conflicts costing millions of lives abroad, and civilization itself placed at risk should a single misstep in the endless insane great-power game precipitate the locked and loaded confrontation into a thermonuclear exchange.

Again, I am not in a position to tell the degree to which Dugin actually influences Russian policy—though there is no doubt that his ideas are well known in that country. I should note that others have expressed skepticism toward the idea that Dugin is the leading ideologue of Russia. Anton Shekhovtsov, an expert on right-wing movements in Europe and elsewhere, made the point that similarities between Putin's policies and Dugin's preferences does not mean Dugin is in charge: "There are obvious similarities between Dugin's and Putin's narratives: anti-Westernism, expansionism, rejection of liberal democracy, etc. However, it would be wrong to suggest that any of these or similar ideological elements are exclusive to either Putin or Dugin, as they have been embedded in Russian politics for more than a century."[76]

Conclusion

As noted at the outset, the ideas associated with the New Right are relatively unknown in the United States. In fact, the major writings associated with this movement have not been accessible in English. This is increasingly no longer the case. The small publisher Arktos, in particular, has been working to translate the major works of figures such as Benoist, Faye, and Dugin, and thus introduce their ideas to American readers. The degree to which these newly translated works will find a major audience in English-speaking countries remains to be seen.

In the interest of space, this chapter was only able to focus on a small number of figures associated with the New Right. Although the most important thinkers on the New Right were French, they have collaborators in other European countries, such as Italy and Germany—though these other intellectuals and journalists are even less known in English-speaking countries than Benoist and Faye.

There is also a dearth of book-length secondary sources on the New Right available in English. For those interested in reading more on this ideological current, however, I can recommend a few relevant works. Tomislav Sunić's *Against Equality and Democracy* (first published in 1990) and Michael O'Meara's *New Culture, New Right* (2004) both provide a useful history of the European New Right. I should note that both authors are sympathetic to the New Right's primary ideas; they may even be considered more right-wing and radical than the figures they analyze. This does not diminish their work's usefulness for scholars and general readers, however. For a much more critical examination of the European New Right, I recommend two books by Tamir Bar-On: *Rethinking the French New Right* (2013) and *Where Have All the Fascists Gone?* (2007).[77]

On the subject of Bar-On's work, many critics of the New Right question the degree that it is new. Opponents such as Bar-On charge that the New Right is simply reviving earlier fascistic thinking and repackaging it in a politically palatable rhetoric. Although the New Right may borrow a few ideas from the New Left, it remains a transparently right-wing intellectual movement:

> De Benoist's continued anti-egalitarianism, rejection of the Rights of Man and representative democracy, and valorization of pagan elite rule makes him more primordially a man of the right than the left. Right and left might be categories that are not useful in an age of "communism in ruins," but the fact that the [New Right] leader still

rejects administratively imposed equality based on the model of the 1789 French Revolution separates him definitively from pro-egalitarian liberal, centre, centre-right, and left-wing political movements and parties. Moreover, in rejecting the allegedly "abstract" Rights of Man, de Benoist unambiguously ties himself to radical right-wing traditions that have a long historical lineage dating back to the eighteenth century: counter-revolutionary monarchists, integral nationalists, Vichyites, "non-conformists," [Conservative Revolutionary] thinkers, fascists, and contemporary radical right-wing populist parties.[78]

At present, the most active groups in Western Europe that are influenced by New Right thinking are those calling themselves Identitarians, a term sometimes used interchangeably with the term New Right. This movement is best organized in France, where groups like Bloc Identitaire and Généra-tion Identitaire have held a number of large demonstrations, such as a pro-test against a proposed mosque in Poitiers. The Identitarian movement is clearly based on many of the same principles as the New Right, but its ac-tions show that it no longer considers metapolitics sufficient and that it be-lieves the time for direct political engagement has arrived.

As noted above, the American right has shown little interest in New Right ideas. American patriotism remains a common denominator across most right-wing movements in the United States. Thus, a right-wing intellec-tual movement that forthrightly blames the United States for most of the ills of the modern world will find few American supporters. The American right—whether conservative, libertarian, or paleoconservative—continues to drape itself in the flag; for the most part, it believes that the nation's foun-dational principles were sound. That being said, there is no guarantee that the right in the United States will maintain its patriotism in the years ahead. As I will explain in the concluding chapter, the American conservative move-ment faces extraordinary challenges in the years ahead. If conservatism is not able to cope with these challenges, and if the mainstream right continues to weaken as a force in American politics, will right-wing Americans begin to lose faith in American ideals? If so, will they be more inclined to accept anti-American arguments? At present, there is little evidence that this is oc-curring. For the time being, the American ideologues most willing to seri-ously engage with the European New Right are on the farthest right-wing fringes of the political spectrum: white nationalists. This ideological cate-gory is the subject of the next chapter.

Voices of the Radical Right

WHITE NATIONALISM IN THE UNITED STATES

I embarked on this chapter with some hesitation for a number of reasons. Racism is now generally treated as nothing more than a reactionary opposition to the loss of privilege, or even as a psychiatric disorder, rather than the source of a logical and coherent ideology. Across the spectrum of acceptable opinion in the United States, practically every commentator agrees that explicit racism is unacceptable and has no place in public discourse. We saw in chapter 2 that accusations of racism were often catalysts for purges within the conservative movement. Although voices on the left accuse various movements on the right of being too cozy with certain racist ideas and the Republican Party of deliberately activating white racial anxieties in pursuit of electoral gains, the indisputable reality is that the mainstream right (and most of the libertarian movement and localist movement) officially rejects racism and wants no affiliation with any groups or individuals who promote explicitly racist objectives. Even most paleoconservatives accept the reality of racial pluralism in the United States.

When racists are portrayed in the media, they are usually treated as ignorant, regressive, and violent. The generally accepted image of a white nationalist is a hood-wearing Klansman or a poor, bitter skinhead. Few commercial or academic book publishers would provide a platform for authors advocating a white supremacist or white nationalist viewpoint. That being

[handwritten marginalia: THE ME TOO RIGHT (INC. FOX NEWS); OPPORTUNISM]

the case, one could justifiably argue that white nationalists have little to say that is worthy of scholarly examination. Carol Swain is one academic who disagrees with this position, and her books *The New White Nationalism in America* (2002) and *Contemporary Voices of White Nationalism in America* (2003) argue that racial egalitarians need to pay close attention to what white nationalists are saying.[1] This position contends that in order to refute white nationalists, progressives and racially egalitarian conservatives need to know their specific arguments. I present the ideas and individuals in this chapter in a similar spirit and will maintain the dispassionate tone of the previous chapters.

Writing on white nationalism presents an additional difficulty, however. For all the previous chapters (with the exception of localism), it was relatively easy to determine the major leaders and intellectuals driving particular movements. Most other ideological categories discussed in this volume have their own think tanks, major publishing houses, and a pantheon of respected scholars and journalists. At the very least, each can claim writers who have access to major mainstream publications and who express ideas that are taken seriously, even by their ideological opponents. Identifying the most influential figures in American white nationalism is more difficult. When it comes to mainstream media access, the most polite and erudite white racist is no more welcome than the most vulgar and ignorant. Thus, identifying the most respected and influential figures within this movement was not an easy task.

The pervasiveness of the Internet has created an additional difficulty. Although the Internet has certainly been a boon to the radical right in that it allows marginalized voices to reach a larger audience than ever, it has not been a completely unmixed blessing for the white nationalist movement. Although the number of explicitly racist websites and blogs has exploded, there has also been an apparent decline in the number of offline membership organizations that engage in public demonstrations and activism. The National Alliance did not long survive the death of its founder, William Luther Pierce. Aryan Nations was sued into oblivion. David Duke has long been out of the public eye and appears to have no further political ambitions. I see little evidence that the racist World Church of the Creator has many current followers. The Ku Klux Klan is a shadow of its former self. White nationalist organizations certainly still exist, but they are all small and atomized. This makes it more difficult to tell which individuals are actually influential and who is simply a lone blogger, broadcasting his or her ideas to no one.

For this reason, the choices I made in this chapter regarding who is influential were based largely on my own subjective judgment.

There is near-universal agreement that racism is immoral, and political movements—such as white nationalism—grounded in racism are generally condemned. However, it may seem curious that white racism is considered a unique evil in the world. Although there is certainly a long historical record of atrocities committed by European peoples, it is difficult to argue that Europeans are unique in this regard. Slavery, exploitation, and even genocide have been an unfortunate element of the human condition from the beginning, and such acts have been committed by people of all races—and it is not true that these atrocities were always justified by racial hatred. Why, then, is the hostility toward white nationalists generally greater than the hostility toward other racial, ethnic, and religious nationalists that seek to control a specific geographic unit and exclude others? Why, for example, is Zionism generally considered an acceptable political position, but an individual who wanted to create a republic restricted to white Christians would be barred from mainstream debates?

Bryan Caplan, a libertarian economist who opposes all forms of nationalism, has attempted to discern why white nationalists are considered worse than other nationalists. He pointed out that the track record of white nationalists is not qualitatively worse than Japanese nationalists, yet there is no similar outcry against racist exclusionary policies that exist in Japan or the people who support these policies.[2] Caplan argues that we can identify white nationalists as being especially dangerous precisely because white nationalism is so unpopular; the fact that they embrace these political views in spite of their unpopularity tells us something about their character:

> Consider a world where 80% of people are Conformists, 10% of people are Righteous, and 10% are Reprobates. The Conformists are epistemically and morally neutral, so they believe and support whatever is popular. The Righteous are epistemically and morally virtuous, so they believe and support whatever is true and right. The Reprobates are epistemically and morally vicious, so they believe and support the *opposite* of what the Righteous believe and support. . . .
>
> On the plausible assumption that most real-world people are basically conformists, you can't accurately assess virtue by studying people's views in isolation. You have to look at their *unpopular views*. Believing true&right things despite their unpopularity is a sign of genuine

virtue. Believing false&wrong things despite their unpopularity is a sign of genuine vice.

Consider, for example, the fact that almost all Americans now oppose Jim Crow laws. Is this a strong sign that they're more virtuous than Southerners in 1960? Not really. After all, how many modern Americans would still oppose Jim Crow if they grew up in a Jim Crow society? Only unpopular positions on Jim Crow reveal much about your character. Opposing Jim Crow in 1960 shows great virtue, especially if you live in the South. Supporting Jim Crow in 2013, similarly, shows great vice: You're willing to become a social pariah rather than betray the cause of evil.[3]

Throughout this chapter, I use the term white nationalist as narrowly as possible. To be included in this category, I consider it insufficient to have made racist remarks or supported racist policies. I consider a person a white nationalist if he or she advocates the creation of a nation-state whose membership is restricted to people of pure European descent. Such a person has a decidedly different stance from one who accepts the reality of a multiracial society but who wishes to maintain the supremacy of white culture and a superior social standing for whites. Although white nationalists are the focus of this chapter, I will discuss a number of figures who influence contemporary white nationalists, even if they do not use that term to describe themselves or even share white nationalist ideals.

The term white nationalism is often treated as synonymous with the term white supremacism; critics of white racial ideologies tend to view them all as some variety of white supremacy. In my readings, however, I have encountered very few white nationalists who actually describe themselves as white supremacists. White nationalists may eschew the term white supremacy because they are concerned with public relations—though white nationalism and white separatism are hardly neutral terms likely to garner positive media coverage. However, there is also a real distinction between white nationalism and white supremacy, at least theoretically. A white supremacist wants the social and legal domination of whites in a multiracial society, as was the case in South Africa during apartheid or in the South during the Jim Crow era. A white nationalist believes that races should not live together in the same country at all, even if the prevailing social structure benefits whites.[4]

Although racial nationalist sentiments can be found all over the globe, white nationalists in the United States are in a somewhat unique position. On the one hand, it could be persuasively argued that the United States embraced de facto white supremacist and white nationalist domestic policies until the 1960s, when steps were finally taken to incorporate nonwhites into the political process and immigration restrictions on nonwhites were loosened. However, such racialist policies were always at odds with the founding creeds of the nation; a nation ostensibly based on the proposition that all men are created equal has a harder time justifying exclusionary policies than a nation based on a more traditional foundation such as a shared history or language. White nationalists in the United States must therefore admit that their views diverge from many widely accepted political principles in America, which is a problem for an ideology that hopes to make inroads among patriotic conservatives. Further, whites in the United States cannot rely on the argument that they are the continent's indigenous population and thus have special rights to exclude others.

A problem for white nationalists is how white should be defined. There is no unanimity on this question, but white nationalists certainly do not use the US Census Bureau definition, which presently classifies most Hispanics and Arabs as white. American white nationalists certainly view the growing Hispanic population as a threat, and they consider Arabs and Hispanics—particularly those Hispanics with Native American or African ancestry—as nonwhite. Neo-Nazis of course follow a tradition that holds Slavs to be an inferior race, though anti-Slavic sentiments do not appear common among contemporary American white nationalists. The question as to whether European Jews should be classified as white also remains a debate among white racialists. *HPL SAID THAT THEY ARE*

Although it certainly faces many challenges, in some respects racial nationalism may actually have an easier time developing in the United States than in Europe. Although there is a long history of tension between different white ethnic groups in the United States, to a significant degree, these differences faded in the twentieth century as the white versus nonwhite political divide became more divisive than the divide between WASPs and other European ethnic groups.[5] In Europe, of course, ethnicity remains important. Despite the relative peace on the continent since 1945 and the development of the European Union, many Europeans still identify strongly with their individual countries rather than their shared sense of whiteness. A white Norwegian and a white Croatian may not consider their shared skin color and continent as a strong source of shared identity. In other words, explicitly racial solidarity may be more likely to develop among whites in the United States than among whites in Europe, though there are hurdles to such solidarity in both contexts. *INTERESTING THOUGHTS*

Although all of the groups discussed in this volume are critical of conservatism and the Republican Party that advances the conservative agenda, white nationalists are some of the most bitterly anti-Republican ideologues I have come across. The left often accuses the mainstream right of appealing to so-called dog-whistle racism to activate white racial anxieties and encourage white support for conservatism even when it is against their economic self-interest. It is interesting to note that white nationalists often agree with this assessment. They note that the GOP relies almost entirely on white voters for its electoral support, and part of this support must stem from the implicit whiteness of the GOP. However, once racial anxieties have been effectively manipulated to ensure electoral victory, the Republican Party does nothing to actually advance white interests; in spite of a supposed mandate to do so, Republicans have not rolled back affirmative action or ended mass immigration, for example. An article in a leading white nationalist website argued that "the fact that Republican voters may be motivated by implicit racial consciousness does not mean that Republican politicians will serve white interests. Quite the contrary, they would be the first to deny any hint of racism. They would deny it *strenuously*."[6] The article noted that this is not just a problem for white nationalists who put hope in the GOP; the pro-life movement has long been an integral element of the Republican coalition yet has enjoyed few policy dividends as a result of Republican victories at the national level.

Racialism in the Progressive Era

For many years, conservative journalists have relied heavily on a clever rhetorical trick. They point out, again and again, that the Democratic Party was once the party of white Southerners and segregation. Over the Democratic Party's long history, it was only in the most recent decades that the Democrats became the party of racial integration and equality. On the other hand, Republicans began as the party of abolition. The supposed implication of this historical fact is that the Democrats are the real racists. Similarly, mainstream conservatives also point out that many leading figures of the early twentieth-century progressive movement favored eugenics or believed that certain races were inherently superior to others.[7] This was even true of many progressives who remain admired by the contemporary left, such as Margaret Sanger, a birth control advocate and founder of Planned Parenthood. There is little evidence that many people have been persuaded by these arguments from mainstream conservative commentators, however;

few voters seem to care where the respective parties stood on racial issues decades or even a century ago.

I am not accusing contemporary liberals of secretly harboring racist or eugenic ideas. Despite efforts to identify today's left with the some of the more disreputable ideas embraced progressives of a previous generation, it is clear that the contemporary left rejects all eugenic and white supremacist thought. That being said, it is worth discussing some of these older ideas and the people who promoted them because they remain influential on the radical right. The fact that these ideas were once a key element of progressive thinking is no longer particularly relevant to mainstream debates.

In contrast to the far right that existed in Europe in the early twentieth century, the progressive movement in the United States was never uncomfortable with modernity or the modern worldview. They viewed reason and technical expertise as the most valuable tools of social progress. The ideas of Charles Darwin and Francis Galton, which had by then been accepted by leading American intellectuals, provided a framework for improving humanity. With this knowledge in hand, it was presumably possible to improve mankind by encouraging higher birthrates from some parts of the population and discouraging high birthrates, or even promoting sterilizing, among other groups.

At present, when the subject of eugenics is discussed, the conversation quickly turns to Nazi Germany. It is therefore important to remind readers that Germany's eugenics policies in the 1930s were not particularly remarkable at the time, and many of the eugenic policies implemented by the Nazis were actually imports from the United States. In particular, Hitler himself was strongly influenced by the work of Madison Grant, a Progressive-era figure in the United States who promoted a doctrine of scientific racism.[8] Grant was one of the most notable promoters of scientific racism in an era when such attitudes were common. He was also one of the most important conservationists in early twentieth-century America. To Grant, there was no contradiction between the two positions; protecting the genetic inheritance of white Americans was no different from protecting natural wonders like the California redwoods.

Like other figures of the era, Madison Grant argued that racial differences explained trends in different societies. Grant's most influential book on these subjects was *The Passing of the Great Race*, first published in 1916.[9] This book argued that much of history can only be understood by looking at events from a racialist perspective, and it makes the case for scientific racism. In Grant's view, the rise and decline of empires can be explained by the degree to which conquering groups maintained their racial purity. For example, he argued that the Macedonian empire did not long survive the death of Alexander because "pure Macedonian blood was impaired by intermixture with Asiatics."[10]

While clearly a white supremacist, Grant did not believe that all European groups were equal to each other. In his taxonomy, Europeans should be disaggregated into Alpines, Mediterraneans, and Nordics. Grant described the physical and social characteristics of these different racial groups and argued that Nordics are objectively superior to other Europeans. Although the scope of *The Passing of the Great Race* is enormous and covers a vast portion of world history, he was clearly making the case that his racial outlook had consequences for the United States. Grant believed that the founding stock of the United States was Nordic, that racial mixing was relatively inconsequential for most of US history,[11] and that policies should be implemented that maintain the Nordic population in North America in the future. Although such arguments today receive no serious attention, Grant was extraordinarily influential by the early 1920s, and his disciples played a critical role in passing restrictive immigration policies in 1924.[12] Grant was also a founder of the American Eugenics Society.

Although Grant was the most renowned scientific racist of his era, he was not a unique figure. Lothrop Stoddard was his best-known protégé. Like Grant, Stoddard was concerned that demographic trends threatened to swamp the Nordic race around the world, and he published books with provocative titles such as *The Rising Tide of Color against White World-Supremacy* (1920) and *The Revolt Against Civilization: The Menace of the Under-Man* (1922).[13] Although whites still dominated the globe politically at the time Stoddard was writing, he argued that the demographic writing was on the wall and that a revolt against the white world was inevitable in the absence of a new sense of white solidarity:

> "Finally perish!" That is the exact alternative which confronts the white race. For white civilization is today conterminous with the white race. The civilizations of the past were local. They were confined to a particular people or a particular group of peoples. If they failed, there were always some unspoiled, well-endowed barbarians to step forward and "carry on." But today *there are no more white barbarians.* The earth has grown small, and men are everywhere in close touch. If white civilization goes down, the white race is irretrievable ruined. It will be

swamped by the triumphant colored races, who will obliterate the white man by elimination or absorption.[14]

After the horrors of World War II, the ideas of figures like Grant and Stoddard were emphatically rejected by most American and European intellectuals—seemingly permanently. In the social sciences particularly, disparities between racial groups are now typically explained by discrimination or other economic dynamics. After the successes of the civil rights movement, this type of explicitly racial thinking largely disappeared from mainstream political discourse, and a public figure expressing such thoughts in such explicit language would now be denied access to mainstream venues. Within the marginalized radical right, however, this type of thinking survived World War II and can still be found today. Wilmot Robertson's *The Dispossessed Majority* (1976) is an example of a postwar book from this genre that received a fair amount of attention and praise from the radical right.[15] This book cited much of the older racial literature, discussing such issues as the skull shapes of various racial groups, as well as their various personality and cognitive attributes.

(margin note: LEFTIST MANTRA *)*
(margin note: ANTI-FREE SPEECH PC. *)*

Science and Race Today

In contemporary mainstream science, we see little public discussion of how various racial groups possess nonsuperficial physical differences or differences in intellect and behavior. This does not mean that works making such arguments are not published. Although no credible scientist or science journalist working today would write anything analogous to the sensationalistic and polemical works of Grant and Stoddard, mainstream presses continue to publish books that argue that race possesses a real biological significance, and different racial groups possess, on average, different social characteristics.

(margin note: NOTE ✗ *)*

A point must be emphasized here. A scientist or public intellectual who seriously considers the notion that different human population groups developed consequential differences resulting from different evolutionary pressures will likely be praised by racist ideologues; such research is, after all, congruent with their worldview. This is not necessarily evidence that such a figure is personally racist. I am justified in discussing a few of the prominent people who discuss these issues because their work clearly conforms to the prejudices of the radical right and often receives praise from white nationalists, but I am not implying any kind of guilt by association. Although their work may be flawed or mistaken, we cannot automatically infer that

HBD

they are motivated by racial animus. I should also note that in this section
I refrain from discussing the more technical works of scientists working in
this field; instead, I focus entirely on those books written for nonexperts. I
do so because as a political scientist I am not qualified to judge which technical works are most important, methodologically sound, and influential,
and also because only books marketed to a wide audience have much potential to shape public debate.

Although a number of scholars and nonscholars have written works in
the last several decades arguing that biological racial differences exist and
have important real-world consequences, most received little popular attention.[16] *The Bell Curve*, by Charles Murray and Richard Herrnstein, was
by far the most controversial and widely discussed book from this genre in
recent memory. Published in 1994, the book argued that IQ was an important predictor of social success in the United States. Although there remain
skeptics regarding the validity of IQ tests as a measure of intelligence, the
general thesis of the book was relatively uncontroversial: cognitive ability is
an important predictor of life outcomes, and cognitive ability is at least partially determined by genetics. The book wandered into contentious issues
when it broached the subject of race, ethnicity, and intelligence in two of its
later chapters. These chapters note that blacks and Hispanics, on average,
perform less well on tests of intellectual ability than whites and Asian Americans, and at least some of this can be explained by genetics.[17]

The discussion of race and IQ made up only a small percentage of *The
Bell Curve*, and Herrnstein and Murray were careful to argue that their hypotheses, if true, did not warrant racial discrimination.[18] The book nonetheless received a great deal of criticism. Much the 1996 second edition of
Stephen Jay Gould's *The Mismeasure of Man* was dedicated to challenging the
claims made in *The Bell Curve*.[19] Several other books were written by other
authors attempting to debunk *The Bell Curve*.[20] Herrnstein and Murray's
book does not appear to have led to any obvious changes in social policy in
the United States, but neither did the book's critics successfully convince all
readers that many of its hypotheses were not at least partially correct.

The Bell Curve is considered a classic among advocates of what has been
called human biodiversity (HBD), a term popularized online by the blogger
and online columnist Steve Sailer. In the last decade, the number of blogs
and websites dedicated to popularizing the notion that racial differences are
genetic and meaningful has exploded. Unsurprisingly, many of these websites contain ostentatiously racist and right-wing sentiments—though there
are exceptions.[21] Some of these writers appear to have the requisite aca-

demic credentials to speak with some authority on these subjects,[22] although a much larger number clearly do not. Although there are many websites dedicated this this topic, and obviously a larger number of readers for these sites, the ideas they promote are not generally accepted or even acknowledged within mainstream discourse.

Since *The Bell Curve*, a few additional books on related topics were published by mainstream commercial presses that garnered a significant amount of popular attention. In 2009, Gregory Cochrane and Henry Harpending published *The 10,000 Year Explosion: How Civilization Accelerated Human Evolution*. Although this book says relatively little about race per se, it seeks to undermine the generally accepted notion that there was relatively little human evolution over the last several thousand years. Specifically, the book argued that the creation of agriculture and the establishment of permanent cities led to a natural selection for behavioral traits different from the traits associated with hunter-gatherer cultures. Although the book generally sidesteps the issue, the implication is that human groups that developed advanced civilizations in the more distant past are qualitatively different from those that did not, and these differences are genetic. The book also introduces a theory that the above-average IQ scores recorded for Ashkenazi Jews are the result of genetic differences and can be explained by the social structure that prevailed in medieval Europe.[23]

In 2014, a book in this genre was written by Nicholas Wade, a former writer for the science section of the *New York Times*. His book, *A Troublesome Inheritance: Genes, Race, and Human History*, argued that recent scientific advances such as the Human Genome Project have irrefutably demonstrated that human evolution is a continuing process and that different population groups have evolved in different directions over the past several thousand years. Specifically, he stated that human evolution has been "recent, copious, and regional."[24] In the latter sections of the book, Wade speculated how genes might be leading to different average behaviors of different racial groups. Not surprisingly, Wade's book was immediately denounced by many reviewers[25]—though some mainstream reviewers had positive things to say about the work.[26] Although Wade spent much of the book denouncing racist policies such as discrimination and eugenics,[27] his book was warmly received by many racialists who viewed the work as a validation of their views.[28]

The relationship between white nationalism and books and websites in the HBD genre is not entirely straightforward. Few of the best-known proponents of this view can be accurately described as white nationalists; Charles Murray is a libertarian and Steve Sailer, though an immigration restrictionist, calls his ideology "citizenism." Although anything that validates the idea that race is a legitimate biological category will be welcomed by racialist circles, the major works advocating HBD are not entirely congruent with a white supremacist worldview. For example, such works generally note that East Asians have a higher average IQ than European whites and Ashkenazi Jews have a higher average IQ than any other group on earth—a particularly troublesome conclusion for any who embrace anti-Semitism on the grounds that Jews are an inferior race.

The Decline and Endurance of the White Racial Organizations

The most famous and notorious white racial organization in US history is the Ku Klux Klan, first founded in the Reconstruction era. This history of the Klan is well known, and it is now an insignificant and marginalized organization, even by the standards of white nationalist groups. For both of these reasons, it requires only a brief discussion in these pages. At the time of its founding, the KKK was dedicated the restoring white supremacy in the South after its defeat in the Civil War, often using the most brutal methods. The group was quickly declared a terrorist organization, and many of its members were arrested. The organization began to disintegrate as early as the late 1860s.[29]

The KKK experienced a resurgence in the early twentieth century, largely thanks to the release of *The Birth of a Nation*, a 1915 film that glorified the Klan's exploits. The revived Klan remained hostile to blacks, but it was also opposed to the rising Catholic and Jewish populations in America, and it was intensely anticommunist. It became a powerful force both within the South and elsewhere, becoming especially influential in the Midwest. The revived KKK also eventually faded from prominence. Part of this decline was due to high-profile scandals involving prominent Klansmen; the murder conviction of the Indiana grand dragon David Stevenson in 1926 was particularly devastating to the KKK.[30] The Klan experienced a new, smaller revival during the civil rights era, and their resistance to social changes was often violent; Klansmen were responsible for a number of bombings and assassinations in the South in the 1950s and 1960s. After the victories of the civil rights movement, the Klan again experienced a precipitous decline.

Although the Klan remain perhaps the best-known white supremacist organization, surely as a result of the group's outlandish costumes and grandiose titles as well as for its history of violence, its long-term decline shows no signs of abating, even as other white supremacist and white nationalist organizations have experienced growth. There remain scattered groups calling themselves the KKK, but the organization has no real national or even regional leadership. Although it is impossible to know exact numbers, fewer (perhaps far fewer) than five thousand people in the United States consider themselves part of the KKK.[31]

Other explicitly racial organizations also experienced a period of substantial growth in the years after World War II, though they are generally less remembered or commented upon. The American Nazi Party, founded by George Lincoln Rockwell in 1959, received considerable attention during the civil rights era. Rockwell had previously enjoyed a successful career in the navy, earning the rank of commander. Many of his early political interests were fairly conventional. He was a supporter of Senator Joseph McCarthy, and he backed General Douglas MacArthur's failed presidential bid. Over time, his views became more radical as he was drawn to Holocaust denial and neo-Nazism. He formed the American Nazi Party in 1959.

Not surprisingly, Rockwell was denounced in the pages of *National Review*, yet Rockwell continued to hope that the conservative movement would realize that they shared common goals with his organization.[32] He remained committed to many conservative causes, such as the war in Vietnam. Rockwell quickly moved to engage directly with electoral politics; he ran for governor of Virginia in 1965 as an independent. He lost badly, earning barely 1 percent of the vote.[33] Undeterred, Rockwell declared his confidence that he would be president of the United States after the 1972 election.[34] Although there is virtually no chance that Rockwell's prediction could have come true, we can never know for sure because Rockwell was murdered by a disgruntled colleague in 1967, and his party lost what little momentum it possessed. It soon changed its name to the National Socialist White People's Party, then became a religious organization calling itself the New Order. Although the American Nazi Party was clearly a failure, other individuals and groups continued Rockwell's efforts, though not usually in the arena of electoral politics.

The National Alliance, led by William Luther Pierce, was another white nationalist organization that enjoyed a long history. Pierce had a PhD in physics, and for a time he was a professor in that field at Oregon State University. He abandoned his academic career in the mid-1960s in order to focus on his political activities. He was affiliated with the American Nazi Party and later with the National Socialist White People's Party. Pierce founded the National Alliance in 1974, and it became his primary means of spreading his message for the rest of his life. He maintained an office in Arlington, Virginia, for many years, before moving the National Alliance headquarters to the mountains of West Virginia.

In order to expand his organization's reach to young whites, the National Alliance purchased Resistance Records, which produced heavy metal and punk rock albums with racist and anti-Semitic lyrics. As has often been the case for the white nationalist movement, Pierce had to choose between quality and quantity when it came to the National Alliance's membership. In terms of sheer numbers, the best source for growth was in the skinhead movement and other lowbrow social groups. The problem with creating a welcoming atmosphere for people from this milieu, however, is that that it makes an organization completely unappealing to white Americans living a more conventional bourgeois life. Pierce apparently decided quantity was the more important concern for the National Alliance, and it provided a welcome mat for skinheads and other more antisocial white nationalists.[35] At its peak, the group had several thousand members.

Pierce is best known as the author of *The Turner Diaries* (1978), a fictional account of a race war in the United States taking place sometime in the near future, though he originally published the book under the pen name Andrew Macdonald.[36] In this book, the narrator, Earl Turner, explains his role in this race war. *The Turner Diaries* revealed that Pierce possessed a genocidal bloodlust that was unusual even for a racial nationalist. Gruesome murders of both nonwhites and white "race traitors" occur throughout the book. The journal ends moments before Turner engages in an aerial suicide bombing mission against the Pentagon. In the epilogue, it is explained that the race war concluded with the complete extermination of all nonwhites in America, and it is implied that nonwhites worldwide suffer a similar fate. All of East Asia suffers a mass genocide using weapons of mass destruction that make that entire region of the globe uninhabitable. *The Turner Diaries* was largely brought to public attention because of some of the high-profile crimes it inspired. Most significantly, the Oklahoma City bombing appears to have been inspired by *The Turner Diaries*. The book also inspired a white nationalist terrorist organization called the Order, which carried out a series of robberies, a counterfeiting operation, and murder before being brought down by law enforcement.[37] Pierce's other, less well-known novel, *Hunter* (1989), follows a white nationalist who engages in a series of assassinations, beginning with low-profile targets, such as interracial couples, and eventually moving onto more high-profile victims.[38] Pierce died in 2002, and his successors apparently lacked his leadership and organizational abilities; the National Alliance has not to my knowledge held any kind of public event in several years.

Aryan Nations was another well-known group that vied with the National Alliance for the distinction of being the most notorious white racial organization in America in the late twentieth century. Founded in the 1970s by Richard Butler, Aryan Nations maintained a compound in northern Idaho. Aryan Nations was ultimately brought down by a lawsuit after a shooting, which cost the group its compound. Butler's death in 2004 led to a leadership vacuum within the organization that was never filled. Butler's most significant long-term contribution to white nationalist thought was his identification of the Pacific Northwest as the ideal location to establish a homeland for whites in North America.

Butler's idea of creating an all-white nation in the Northwest has since been promoted by Harold Covington, another figure with a long history in the white nationalist movement in the United States. Covington specifically argues that Washington, Oregon, Idaho, and western Montana will form the geographic basis for a new white republic. With his blogs and weekly Internet radio show, *Radio Free Northwest,*[39] Covington tries to recruit white nationalists from across the country to move to the Northwest. He is best known for his self-published novels about a revolutionary struggle to create the Northwest Republic at some point in the near future. Although Covington denies that he advocates his readers and listeners to engage in violent acts, his novels, like Pierce's, contain many scenes of vicious violence against Jews, gays, and nonwhites. Unlike Pierce's books, however, Covington's novels do not end with worldwide genocide of nonwhites.

Although some white racial nationalists in America embrace a more flamboyant aesthetic—either modeled on the KKK or the Third Reich—others have deliberately embraced a more scholarly and reasonable tone. Groups and individuals that meet this description tend to avoid hateful slurs; instead, they use the language of fairness or discuss the natural instinct of most people to favor their own kind over others. American Renaissance, founded by Jared Taylor in the early 1990s, has long been the standard-bearer for this variety of highbrow white racial advocacy. Taylor does not use the term white nationalist to describe his views, and he also rejects the use of the term racist:

> Well, "racist" is inappropriate because it's pejorative, and I think that my views on race are perfectly natural, normal, and healthy, and I wish everyone had them. So it's not acceptable to me that my views be labeled with this emotional and morally charged term. Unfortunately, having rejected that and just about any other label that you'd propose, I don't

have one to offer in its place, because the way I view race is something
that has been the way Americans viewed race up until just a few decades
ago, and so there was never really any term to describe it. I think
my views on race are by and large quite similar to those of Thomas
Jefferson or Abraham Lincoln, to those of practically every American
president clear up until John Kennedy, and because those were the views
that were taken for granted by virtually every American, there's no word
to describe them.[40]

The American Renaissance website includes a mix of commentary as well
as links to news stories dealing with race, often stories about minority corruption or crimes committed against whites. Taylor's first book on race,
Paved with Good Intentions, published in 1992, argued that all efforts to end
minority poverty not only failed but made American society demonstrably
worse.[41] American Renaissance used to publish a print magazine as well, but
they transitioned to an exclusively online format in 2012. American Renaissance is also known for hosting conferences, which it has attempted to do every other year since 1994. At these conferences, white racial activists gather
to hear speeches from prominent figures associated with the movement. Although the content is decidedly different, videos of these events indicate that
they have a similar tone to academic conferences. In contrast to Klan rallies
or skinhead gatherings, the speakers and attendees at American Renaissance
conferences are generally well-dressed and well-spoken, and they avoid the
more inflammatory rhetoric generally associated with this movement. In
2010 and 2011, Taylor was forced to cancel the American Renaissance conferences when antiracist activists threatened the hotels in which the events
were scheduled. To avoid this problem in subsequent years, American Renaissance began hosting its conference at a public space in Tennessee; by
utilizing public property, the organizers are guaranteed their First Amendment protections.

The National Policy Institute (NPI), founded in 2005, is a relatively
young organization on the white nationalist right that maintains a more
academic tone similar to that of American Renaissance. It presents itself
more as a think tank than as a grassroots advocacy organization. The institute's current director, Richard Spencer, was once affiliated with more mainstream right-wing venues such as *American Conservative* and *Taki's Magazine*.
His work subsequently became more radical and right wing. NPI also runs
Washington Summit Publishers, which has published books by a number of
authors associated with the European New Right and with the HBD move-

ment.[42] The organization also publishes a print journal and runs a website featuring daily commentary about current events. Both the journal and the site have the title *Radix*. RADICAL

White Nationalism Online

Not surprisingly, marginalized ideologies—such as radical libertarians, Maoists, and white nationalists—were some of the first political groups to see the potential of the Internet for effectively reaching a new audience by simply bypassing the traditional media gatekeepers. It costs extraordinary sums of money to create attractive print media or purchase substantive airtime on television or radio. In the absence of a large pool of wealthy donors, these ideologues were for many years reliant on cheap pamphleteering. The Internet opened up new opportunities for both coordination between groups across the country and outreach to new individuals. White nationalists were among the first to recognize this potential; for instance, the leader of White Aryan Resistance, Tom Metzger, created a computer bulletin board as early as the 1980s, before most people had even heard of the Internet.[43] There are now thousands of white racist websites. *UNLIKE MARXISTS*

Many of these sites contain the conventional images of white supremacism—swastikas, Confederate flags, and so on—but a large number do not. Many downplay their hateful rhetoric, eschew racial slurs, and take a decidedly bookish tone. An unsuspecting reader may not even initially realize that they are reading racist material, as such sites may emphasize ordinary conservative concerns such undocumented immigration, crime, and affirmative action. However, even sites that are not particularly vitriolic in tone will often contain links to other sites that are more explicitly racist and radical.

Stormfront, founded by Don Black in the early 1990s, was one of the first white racist websites to enjoy high levels of success. The site enjoys as many as 400,000 visitors per month.[44] Stormfront is really just a forum for different varieties of white racists to discuss ideas—ideas not always directly related to race. Although the stereotype of American white nationalists suggests that such people are typically older, less educated men out of touch with the more progressive contemporary mind-set, a *New York Times* study of Stormfront members suggests that this is not always the case. This study found that nineteen is the most common age at which people join Stormfront, and a majority of its members are under thirty. A significant minority of Stormfront users are female (about 30 percent). The demographic profile of Stormfront members, as well their often-conventional interests, clearly surprised and disturbed the study's author: "Perhaps it was my own naïveté, but I would have imagined white nationalists' inhabiting a different universe from that of my friends and me. Instead, they have long threads praising 'Breaking Bad' and discussing the comparative merits of online dating sites, like Plenty of Fish and OkCupid."[45]

LEFTIST

The Southern Poverty Law Center, which is the leading organization tracking hate groups in the United States, argues that Stormfront users are responsible for a large number of murders and other acts of terrorism. The group attributes nearly 100 hate-based homicides to Stormfront users since 2009.[46] Some commentators on the right have criticized these numbers, however, noting that the overwhelming majority of these murders were perpetrated by one man, Anders Breivik, a Norwegian who murdered sixty-nine people in 2011.[47] Although Breivik did post to Stormfront a number of times before his rampage, his own political views were somewhat idiosyncratic. His lengthy manifesto contained many concerns shared by the racist right, such as Muslim immigration into Europe, but many of his thoughts were clearly at odds with white nationalism or white supremacism as they are normally understood.[48] Even if we discount Breivik, however, there is no doubt the many people who read and contribute to racist websites have and continue to engage in real-world violence. Stormfront is not the only white nationalist online forum with a large number of active members. Vanguard News Network is another large, active forum. Although the bulletin board website Reddit does not officially espouse an ideology, it does not censor its users or close communities unless they actively promote criminal activity. It has thus also become a major center of online racism, though the vast majority of Reddit posts and forums are not racist.[49]

Racism online is not isolated to expressly racist websites. Such sentiments often find their way into mainstream news and commentary via open comments sections. Much of this is spontaneous, but there is also a larger campaign to hijack these discussions and push them in a more racial direction. Robert Whitaker, a prominent white nationalist writer and activist, wrote what has been called the mantra, and some variation of it can often be found posted in the comments section of major news articles that deal, even tangentially, with the subject of race. The full mantra is as follows:

ASIA FOR THE ASIANS, AFRICA FOR THE AFRICANS, WHITE COUNTRIES FOR EVERYBODY!

Everybody says there is this RACE problem. Everybody says this RACE problem will be solved when the third world pours into EVERY white country and ONLY into white countries.

"NEWS" ORGANIZATIONS LIKE CNN (COUNTERFEIT NEWS NETWORK)

The Netherlands and Belgium are just as crowded as Japan or Taiwan, but nobody says Japan or Taiwan will solve this RACE problem by bringing in millions of third worlders and quote assimilating unquote with them.

Everybody says the final solution to this RACE problem is for EVERY white country and ONLY white countries to "assimilate," i.e., intermarry, with all those non-whites.

What if I said there was this RACE problem and this RACE problem would be solved only if hundreds of millions of non-blacks were brought into EVERY black country and ONLY into black countries?

How long would it take anyone to realize I'm not talking about a RACE problem. I am talking about the final solution to the BLACK problem?

And how long would it take any sane black man to notice this and what kind of psycho black man wouldn't object to this?

But if I tell that obvious truth about the ongoing program of genocide against my race, the white race, Liberals and respectable + PHONEY conservatives agree that I am a naziwhowantstokillsixmillionjews.

They say they are anti-racist. What they are is anti-white.

Anti-racist is a code word for anti-white.[50] SOME TRUTH HERE

As noted previously, while the Internet has certainly been a boon to the white nationalist movement in the sense that is allows its proponents to spread their ideas far wider and faster than previously possible, it may not have been completely beneficial for this ideology. The rise of white racism online has not apparently coincided with a great deal of real-world organizing and activism. The stigma against open racists remains, and many people who feel comfortable leaving anonymous comments on the Internet would never dare express such sentiments publicly. The existence of these websites may simply offer a way for racially frustrated whites to vent in a relatively harmless manner and then return to their otherwise normal lives. This is a common complaint among white nationalists who want to move their activism from the Internet to the real world, and it has also been noted by the movement's most vigorous opponents. As Mark Potok of the Southern Poverty Law Center noted, "Some analysts have suggested that posting extremist material actually lessens violence, serving as a kind of safety valve for people who might otherwise engage in terrorism or, at least, real-world movement-building activity. And there is probably some truth in that—most 'keyboard commandos' don't accomplish much."[51]

ANTIFA + BLM
REAL TERRORISTS

Questions about the role of the Internet in mobilizing white nationalists and spurring them to violence have a new urgency, given the 2015 attack on a church in Charleston, South Carolina, that left nine people dead. The apparent killer, Dylann Roof, was a white supremacist who was apparently radicalized by various racist websites, although at the time of this writing it does not appear that any specific group or individual encouraged the attack or knew it was coming. Whether sincere or not, most prominent white racist websites formally discourage violence and other criminal activity.

Whether the online white nationalist community will remain scattered, disorganized, and uninvolved in real-world activism remains to be seen. Like many radical ideologies, a significant number of white nationalists yearn for a societal collapse that will leave much of the public more amenable to extreme ideas. In such an event, extremists will certainly benefit greatly from the organizing power of the Internet—assuming the Internet survives such a cataclysm, of course.

Kevin MacDonald on the Jews

Traditionally, white racism and anti-Semitism are generally assumed to go hand in hand: a white racist who dislikes blacks, Hispanics, and Asians is assumed to also dislike Jews. There is certainly historical justification for this view. However, the attitudes of racists toward Jews is not always this straightforward. Although the Confederate States of America was certainly a white supremacist state, it was not apparently an anti-Semitic state—the Confederacy's secretary of state, Judah P. Benjamin, was Jewish. Fascist Italy, in its early years, did not exhibit a great deal of anti-Semitism. Although contemporary racists who view themselves as neo-Nazis certainly share the Third Reich's antipathy toward Jews, other white racists are neutral on the so-called Jewish question, or even favorably disposed toward Jews; Jared Taylor's American Renaissance conference has invited a number of Jewish speakers, for example. HBD enthusiasts often have favorable things to say about the Jews because of their high levels of academic achievement and high average performance on intelligence tests. That being said, antipathy toward Jews is certainly higher, on average, among racists than others. Of all the major anti-Semites on the racialist right, none in recent decades has garnered more attention or created more controversy than Kevin MacDonald.

Kevin MacDonald is a somewhat unusual figure on the white nationalist right. He earned his PhD in behavioral sciences from the University of Connecticut. Possessing an advanced degree is not particularly uncommon among leading white nationalists—a number of the people discussed in this chapter earned PhDs. However, MacDonald is certainly an outlier in that he continued to work in academia after he began publicizing his views on race. He only recently retired from California State University, Long Beach, where he had taught psychology for three decades.[52] Much of MacDonald's research had nothing to do with race, ethnicity, or religion, and his work was published in many leading peer-reviewed journals. However, MacDonald is best known for a series of books in which he examined the history of the Jews from an evolutionary psychology perspective.

In his books, *A People That Shall Dwell Alone* (1994), *Separation and Its Discontents* (1998), and *The Culture of Critique* (1998),[53] MacDonald described Judaism as not just a religion but as a group evolutionary strategy. MacDonald does not endorse the idea that Jews are engaged in a global conspiracy analogous to that described in *The Protocols of the Elders of Zion*. Instead, he argues that Jews are predisposed to support radical egalitarian and universalist ideologies because they weaken the ethnic identities of other groups and hence they ameliorate the danger of anti-Semitism—though their proclaimed support for these universalist ideologies does not correspond to a weakening of their own ethnocentrism or their concern about their specific group interests. According to MacDonald, "Multiculturalist ideology was invented by Jewish intellectuals to rationalize the continuation of separatism and minority-group ethnocentrism in a modern Western state."[54] Like many figures on the far right, MacDonald notes that Jews are generally overrepresented in ideological movements that seek to weaken white identity and solidarity. He points to the overrepresentation of Jews in such movement as Boasian anthropology and the Frankfurt School as recent examples of this. He similarly points out that Jews played a prominent role in the movement to loosen immigration restrictions to the United States.

MacDonald is certainly not the first to note the overrepresentation of Jews within the neoconservative movement; this has been noted by many neoconservatives themselves. However, MacDonald has argued that neoconservatism is specifically intended to increase Jewish power and advance Jewish interests: "Neoconservatism has also provided a Jewish influence on the American conservative movement to counterbalance the strong tendency for Jews to support liberal and leftist political candidates. Jewish ethnic interests are best served by influencing both major parties toward a consensus on Jewish issues, and . . . neoconservatism has served to define the limits of conservative legitimacy in a manner that conforms to Jewish interests."[55]

MacDonald now serves as the editor of the *Occidental Observer,* an online magazine dedicated to presenting "original content touching on the themes of white identity, white interests, and the culture of the West."[56]

The European New Right and White Nationalism in America

The right in the United States has never existed in a vacuum, and the radical right in America has certainly been influenced by European ideas. As obvious examples, we can point to pro-Nazi Americans before World War II and neo-Nazi organizations that have existed in the United States since that time. However, the racist right in the United States has always been distinct from the far right in Europe. Although most of the postwar European right was eager to reject the legacy of the Third Reich—even while it borrowed ideas from figures associated with that regime—American neo-Nazi organizations have freely flown swastika flags and praised Hitler. Part of this may be the result of the different legal climate in Europe and the United States. Although some of the New Right's rejection of fascism and National Socialism was surely due to principled criticisms of those governing systems, the reality is that openly glorifying Nazism has long been illegal in much of Western Europe. In the United States, where all forms of political speech are protected by the First Amendment, this has not been an issue.

I have found little evidence that American rightists—even those who could be called neo-Nazis—were particularly inspired by the intellectuals associated with the conservative revolution in Germany. Nor, until recently, has there apparently been much coordination between the European New Right and the far right in the United States. The European New Right generally condemns racism in principle, making it an awkward partner for white racial advocates in the United States, though the policies the New Right advocates (such as an end to non-European immigration into Europe) have been criticized for being racist in practice.

Prominent neo-Nazis like George Lincoln Rockwell furthermore did not share the European New Right's skepticism of capitalism; on economics, Rockwell was a fairly conventional American conservative. The same was true of David Duke during his political campaigns. Indeed, many of the leading racists in twentieth-century America will appear to be fairly typical conservatives if their views on race are ignored. Nonetheless, some of the ideas advocated by the European New Right have received increasing attention from white nationalists in the United States, though these ideas take a slightly different shape on this side of the Atlantic.

The American racialist right in the mid-twentieth century was not entirely ignorant of the intellectual currents that inspired National Socialism. Francis Parker Yockey, generally considered one of the most important figures of the racial right in the United States in the postwar years, was clearly well familiar with the main thinkers associated with the conservative revolution. He considered his best-known work, *Imperium,*[57] to be something of a sequel to Spengler's *Decline of the West.* This book also included large sections that were completely plagiarized from Carl Schmitt.[58] Yockey's extensive engagement with European ideas made him something of an outlier, however.

In recent years, elements of the radical right in the United States have exhibited greater interest in right-wing ideas from continental Europe. In 2010, the North American New Right was founded by Greg Johnson, the former editor of the *Occidental Quarterly.* While clearly focused on promoting white nationalism in the United States, the North American New Right is heavily influenced by both Traditionalism and the European New Right, and its website (http://www.counter-currents.com/) regularly includes translations from many European New Right intellectuals. The site also embraces the New Right's idea of metapolitics, noting that the time will not be right for white nationalists to engage in more conventional political activities until a critical number of intellectuals have been persuaded that their ideas are morally and intellectually correct.

In recent years, we have seen figures from the European New Right share the stage with American white nationalists at conferences. Guillaume Faye has spoken at American Renaissance conferences. Alain de Benoist was a speaker at the 2013 National Policy Institute Conference in Washington, DC, and in 2014 the National Policy Institute attempted to hold a conference in Budapest, and would have included speakers such as Alexander Dugin and Tomislav Sunić. This event, titled "The European Congress," was to argue for worldwide solidarity among Europeans: "The European Congress holds that European peoples, cultures, and communities around the world compose a unique identity, one that we seek to guard, awaken, and renew."[59] Hungary probably seemed like a logical choice for this conference, as that country presently has perhaps the most right-wing government in Europe and its current prime minister, Viktor Orbán, has vigorously denounced immigration and multiculturalism.[60] This conference never came to pass. Shortly before it was to occur, the Hungarian government banned the event.[61] The government even arrested and briefly detained Richard Spencer, the conference's organizer.

There remain some ways in which white nationalists in the United States remain decidedly different from the European New Right. Alexander Dugin, who admits he was strongly influenced by the New Right, claims to reject biological theories of race. While Benoist is clearly willing to engage with elements of the racial right in America, he does not hesitate to share his criticisms of the white nationalist right's single-minded focus on race. As he said in an interview with American Renaissance: "If I compare you and me, the first difference is that I am aware of race and of the importance of race, but I do not give to it the excessive importance that you do. For me it is a factor, but only one among others."[62]

DE BENOIST

EUROPE DOESN'T HAVE NUMBER OF NON-WHITES THAT

Conclusion *THE USA DOES*

White nationalism remains well outside the mainstream political discussion in America, and that is likely to remain the case for the foreseeable future. The question is whether the media blackout and mainstream condemnation will prove to be an insurmountable obstacle for the white nationalist movement. The Internet, for example, allows marginalized ideologies to bypass traditional media and take its message directly to interested readers, listeners, and viewers. However, while the amount of racist material on the Internet is immense and always growing, this has not apparently translated into greater white nationalist influence on real-world events. Many extreme ideologues contend that they will not be vindicated until there is a major cataclysm that demonstrates the inherent instabilities and contradictions of the present social order. This is likewise the case for many white nationalists. The social stigma suffered by open white nationalists is sufficiently great that it will likely remain on the fringes even if a significant percentage of white Americans come to embrace its basic premises.

That being said, the degree to which Americans will go out of their way to avoid being called racist makes it difficult to gauge just how many white Americans secretly harbor white nationalist or white supremacist views. We cannot infer that all white Americans who tell pollsters that they emphatically reject racism are telling the truth; many certainly know the "correct" answers to questions about racial attitudes and answer such questions accordingly. I am not suggesting that white racial attitudes have not evolved since the civil rights movement—they clearly have—but given the degree to which tribal and exclusionist thinking has been a common attribute throughout most of human history, one cannot assume that racial nationalism has been permanently defeated, in the United States or anywhere else.

Conclusion

THE CRISIS OF CONSERVATISM

Though it is relatively short, I hoped to accomplish a number of ambitious goals in this text. I aimed to develop a workable definition of the right—a definition sufficiently broad to capture a wide variety of ideological movements but not so broad as to be completely meaningless. I sought to provide a new interpretation of the conservative movement in America—one that differs both from the narrative the movement provides itself, and the narrative promoted by its progressive critics. Finally, the bulk of this text was dedicated to providing an overview of right-wing ideologies that fundamentally break with one or more of the fundamental principles of American conservatism.

Today, the right can only be understood in terms of its relation to the left. I argue that the left is defined by its concern for universal equality, and that this is the ultimate goal of all major left-wing movements and intellectuals. Although leftists disagree with each other, sometimes vigorously and violently, broadly speaking, they all share this goal. I further argue that the left-wing vision for equality has dominated political and intellectual discourse in the Western world for several decades. One can name few prominent public figures who ostentatiously reject equality as goal to which mankind should aspire. Even the most vocal and extreme figures associated with the American conservative movement will express reverence for the ideals ex-

NO SUCH POSSIBILITY OR DESIRE.

pressed in the Declaration of Independence, and in their rhetoric they often emphasize that their preferred policies will ultimately lead to a more equitable society. They may argue that their interest is in equality of opportunity rather than equality of results, but in either case, they are careful not to reject equality as an ideal.

There is not a single ideological principle that unifies the right. To be on the right, according to my definition, one simply needs to hold some other social value in greater esteem than equality. This does not mean that all right-wing movements are opposed to equality—though some are, as we saw in this volume. In America, liberty is the value that competes with equality for ideological dominance. To many conservatives and most libertarians, liberty is the most important political value, and they argue that it should not be sacrificed in the name of equality. They often also note that this is ultimately a false choice anyway; a free society may actually be more equitable than a society that vigorously pursues equality through state intervention. Furthermore, the costs of greater equality may not be worth the benefits. A society of paupers may be equal, but surely everyone is better off in a society that is unequal but prosperous.

Conservatives often criticize the American left for being little more than a collection of aggrieved interest groups, with little interest in engaging with political theory and ideas in general. As Ramesh Ponnuru said in *National Review*, "Conservatives tend to place a lot of emphasis, maybe too much, on the idea that ideas have consequences. They hoist their ideas on flagpoles and see who salutes."[1] Given the origins of the conservative movement, it may seem odd that conservatives claim a high level of intellectual sophistication for their political philosophy. Conservatism in America, as we now understand the term, generally implies three basic principles: a strong national defense, free-market capitalism, and moral traditionalism. I am not the first to note that these three principles do not necessarily need to be connected with each other, and may at times be at odds. In fact, before the postwar period, there was not a general consensus that these three principles were connected or even necessarily right wing.

A cynic may persuasively argue that the conservative movement was an ideological wedding of convenience. After World War II, there were three broad groups that opposed the New Deal liberalism that dominated the United States: hawks who thought the Democrats were weak on defense, economic libertarians who rejected the welfare state and onerous government regulation, and Christian traditionalists who bristled at the rising hedonism and secularism that was becoming associated with the New Left.

(AMER.) AN N TYPE OF CONS. REJECTS 2 + 3

Alone, none of these groups represented a winning political platform. Together, they were a coalition capable of becoming a majority.

It is not my contention that Frank Meyer, William F. Buckley, and other
"fusionists" who sought to unify these divergent tendencies into a single
ideology were insincere opportunists. I do not actually think this was the
case. However, it is clear that the practical need to create a large political
coalition was at least as important as defining an internally coherent ideological framework. When the basic principles of conservatism were being
established, the prominent theoreticians were not simply running ideas up
the flagpole. Their eye was always on gaining real political power.

Given these intellectual origins, it is interesting that American conservatism rapidly became remarkably calcified. Once the basic tenets of conservatism were established, and once conservatives effectively captured the Republican Party, relatively few mainstream conservative voices deviated from
these basic principles. No one who emphatically rejected one or more of
the conservative stool's three legs was welcome in the big conservative tent.
Disagreements occurred at the margins and were often focused on the degree to which conservatives should compromise with the left for pragmatic
reasons. Even today, the conservative movement remains largely similar to
the conservative movement that existed in Barry Goldwater's day—at least
in terms of rhetoric.

DL NOT ACCEPTED

Only on the issue of race have we seen a dramatic change in the mainstream conservative movement since the 1960s, at least when it comes to
public statements. Few prominent conservative voices today reject the
legacy of the civil rights movement or openly oppose racial equality as a
goal. Some of this evolution may be attributed to the influence of the neoconservatives, but given the major societal changes that have occurred over
the last fifty years, this development would likely have occurred anyway.
Conservatism's opponents on the left may convincingly argue that Republican leaders and the conservative movement still attempt to activate white
racial anxiety to garner support, and that they are simply now better at mask-
ing their racial animus, but the mainstream right's change in tone on racial
issues is nonetheless undeniable.

NEO CONS. DOMINATE AT FOX NEWS

The question is whether or not the conservative movement as we understand it will long survive. As we shall see, conservatism faces several existential challenges that will not likely be surmounted by minor reforms. The
United States of today is not the United States of 1950 or even 1980, and the
previous generation's conservatism may appear increasingly anachronistic
and out of touch in the years ahead.

TRUE ✗

U.S.A BECOMING ANOTHER BRAZIL

Conservatism's Challenges

THE BUSH YEARS

It was not long ago that the future of the conservative movement in America looked bright. The GOP was the dominant political party in the United States throughout most of George W. Bush's presidency, and his re-election was evidence that Americans supported his conservative vision. Conservative confidence after the 2004 presidential election proved unwarranted. To begin with, Bush had prevailed in 2004 by the smallest margin, in terms of the popular vote, of any reelected president in living memory. Bush further began his second term with a comparatively low approval rating for a newly reelected president. According to Gallup, only 51 percent of Americans approved of how Bush was handling his job as president as of January 2005.[2]

Bush's second term in office yielded few conservative policy victories and badly damaged the Republican Party's brand. In 2005, Bush made a serious legislative push to partially privatize Social Security, spending considerable political capital on this effort. Bush failed to recognize the widespread popularity of a program that has provided considerable peace of mind to American seniors since the Roosevelt administration. Even if much of the electorate recognized problems with program's solvency in the long term, most Americans did not desire a radical alteration to the program.[3] Bush was completely unsuccessful in this effort.

The failure to stem the violence in Iraq further undermined Republican credibility on the issue of foreign policy—a subject that was once a source of considerable strength for Republicans. Faced with a mounting death toll, and little in the way of tangible benefits for the United States, Americans became increasingly skeptical of Republican belligerence abroad.

The Republicans made several other political missteps during this period, including the political battle over whether to allow the removal of Terry Schiavo's feeding tube; Schiavo had been in a persistent vegetative state for years up to that point. This event turned into a political fiasco when Congress passed a bill that moved Schiavo's case to a federal court. The conservative Republicans who fought to keep Schiavo alive were at odds with public opinion, and to make matters worse, a large majority of the public (74 percent) believed Congress and President Bush were motivated more by politics than by concern for Schiavo.[4]

During this period, the Republican Party was rocked by a series of scandals that led to several prominent resignations. In 2005, Representative Duke Cunningham resigned from his position in the House after pleading guilty to charges of conspiracy to commit bribery; in that same year, Representative Tom DeLay resigned amidst charges that he had violated election laws; and Representative Mark Foley resigned from the House in 2006 over allegations that he had sent sexually explicit messages to teenage boys. By the 2006 midterm elections, the Republican Party was increasingly tainted with corruption, and they were punished accordingly by voters. According to national polls, corruption was a key source of the resounding Republican defeat in 2006.[5]

It was not just political miscalculations and personal foibles that ended the Republican dominance of American politics, however. Several scholars who studied demographics and voting patterns recognized that the long-term prospects of the Republican Party were in jeopardy, and they noticed this well before the 2006 midterms. In 2002, John B. Judis and Ruy Teixeira published *The Emerging Democratic Majority*. In this work, they argued that all of the major demographic trends favored the Democratic Party. They noted that racial minorities remained, on average, committed to the Democrats, and their numbers were growing quickly. Women voters had also been increasingly likely to vote Democratic. The Democrats were also enjoying new strength among professionals such as teachers, engineers, and nurses.[6] These trends, if not reversed, would soon make it difficult for the GOP to win a majority of the popular vote at the national level. By 2008, Judis and Teixeira appeared remarkable prescient.

THE DECLINE OF RELIGION

The Republican Party has also suffered as a result of the declining political clout of the religious right. Conservative Christians felt the political winds were with them as recently as 2004. George W. Bush was an outspoken evangelical Christian, and the religious right could correctly claim him as one of their own. Conservative Christians furthermore could take credit for securing Bush's narrow victory over John Kerry. Evangelical leaders like James Dobson could be accurately described as kingmakers in American politics. The religious right further enjoyed a string of victories at the state level in the form of bans on gay marriage.

Since 2004, the political muscles of the religious right have clearly atrophied. Some of this can be attributed to death or retirement of prominent figures in this political movement. Jerry Falwell died in 2007, as did D. James Kennedy. Ted Haggard, a famous evangelical, retreated from the public eye when it was revealed that he had paid for homosexual sex and methamphetamines. The lack of young new figures with similar esteem has left a leadership vacuum on the religious right.

20% NON-RELIGIOUS

The power of the religious right is surely also on the wane because of a decline in religious affiliation among Americans. According to a recent Pew survey, the fastest growing religious category in the United States is "none."[7] Specifically, just under 20 percent of Americans, as of late 2012, described themselves as atheist, agnostic, or "nothing in particular" when it comes to religion. This was a significant increase from just five years before. This is not a new trend. During the 1990s, the percentage of Americans who identified with no religion more than doubled.[8] According to the same Pew survey mentioned above, a large majority of the religiously unaffiliated identify as Democrats or lean toward the Democratic Party, and only 26 percent identified as Republican or leaned toward the Republican Party.

SECULAR RELIGION OF DEMS, LIKE THE SOCIALISTS AND REDS

It is well established that religious affiliation is an important predictor of vote choice and party identification, although this relationship has evolved over time. The primary religious schism in the United States was once Protestant versus Catholic; Protestants were, on average, more Republican, and a majority of Catholics supported the Democratic Party. This gap is no longer as strong as it once was. Latinos, now a large percentage of American Catholics, and also typically more Democratic than non-Hispanic whites, are part of the reason this gap remains at all. Even if we consider non-Hispanic whites alone, however, a modest Catholic–Protestant gap in party identification remains.[9]

In twenty-first-century America, one of the most important religious schisms is between those who regularly attend a worship service and those who do so rarely or never—what Laura Olson and John Green called "the worship-attendance gap."[10] This political gap is relatively new and did not really appear on the scene until 1992.[11]

Given the tremendous growth among the religiously unaffiliated, it is surprising that the GOP has not suffered more at the ballot box than has actually been the case. One reason the electoral consequences of greater secularism have been somewhat muted is that the growth of secularism has been largely at the expense of religious groups that are less likely to support Republicans, on average. The decline in religious identification has hit liberal, mainline Protestant churches the hardest—denominations such as the Evangelical Lutheran Church of America, the United Methodist Church, and the Episcopal Church. Members of these denominations were not as overwhelmingly Republican as members of evangelical denominations (such as the Southern Baptists) that have not experienced such a precipitous decline.

THE DECLINE OF MARRIAGE

Perhaps related to the decline of traditional religious affiliation is the decline of marriage in the United States. At present, marriage is a powerful predictor of vote choice and party identification in the United States. Married Americans are much more likely to vote Republican than unmarried Americans. This is true even after controlling for a number of additional variables that are correlated with both marriage and vote choice—race, age, income, and education. The cause of the marriage gap in politics is not entirely clear. It may be that marriage leads to a change in peoples' order of preferences; the unmarried may be more concerned with gender equity and access to abortion, for example, but the married may be more concerned with things like property values and taxes. According to the Quinnipiac University Polling Institute, "Married voters are more likely to focus on the economy and health care, while single voters are more focused on issues such as gay rights and reproductive issues."[12] It may also be that the Republican Party's message of family values does not resonate with people until they have spouses and children of their own. The causal arrow may also point the other direction. That is, getting married does not change one's political attitudes, but people who are more conservative and religious (and thus more likely to vote Republican) are also more likely to get married and to do so at a younger age.

Regardless of the cause of the marriage gap in politics (and there may be many different causes), marriage is a strong predictor of individual vote choice, and aggregate marriage rates are strong predictors of aggregate vote choice at the county and state level.[13] States with a younger median age at first marriage give, on average, much more support to Republican presidential candidates than states with a higher median age at first marriage. This represents a problem for the American right because marriage is on the decline. Americans are getting married later in life, and a growing number are not getting married at all.

Various scholars have attempted to understand what accounts for the declining marriage and fertility rates in the United States and the rest of the developed world. Ron Lesthaeghe and his colleagues have written many works discussing the second demographic transition that has occurred in most economically developed countries.[14] Social trends associated with the second demographic transition include higher rates of cohabitation, average marriages later in life, higher rates of divorce, higher rates of out-of-wedlock birth, and lower levels of fertility. We see these trends throughout

Europe and northeast Asia. Of the most developed economies, only in the United States has this transition been less pronounced. However, marriage and fertility trends are not consistent throughout the United States.[15] Particularly interesting is the degree to which family formation patterns in the United States geographically mirror political patterns. That is, in parts of the country that are heavily Democratic (the Northeast, the West Coast), the family formation patterns are similar to those of Western Europe. In strongly Republican regions of the country (the South, the Great Plains), patterns of family formation remain more traditional.[16]

This strong relationship between family formation patterns and voting at both the individual and the aggregate level is relatively new. As recently as the 1980s, the evidence for a marriage gap was weak, or it disappeared entirely after controlling for additional variables like income.[17] As stated above, the reason for this new, strong relationship is not entirely clear. One possibility is that as the social stigma associated with cohabitation and delayed marriage has weakened, only those with a strong desire to get married actually do so, and the people with such a desire also, on average, possess characteristics associated with Republican voting.

Part of the growing marriage gap is related to other gaps in American politics, particularly racial/ethnic gaps and the generation gap: younger Americans, African Americans, and Latinos are all less likely to vote Republican and less likely to be married.[18] However, the marriage gap is not spurious. Even after controlling for a myriad of additional variables, marriage is an important predictor of political attitudes and behavior.[19] The marriage gap is slightly larger for women than for men; according to exit polls, only about 31 percent of single women voted for Romney in the 2012 presidential election, but Romney actually won among married women, capturing about 55 percent of the married female vote.[20] However, when I examined whether relationship between marriage and vote choice is different for men and women,[21] I could find little evidence suggesting that marriage has a systematically different effect on men than women, after controlling for other variables.

The emergence of a marriage gap did not necessarily represent a problem for the GOP. After all, throughout US history, a majority of Americans, at some point in their lives, got married. The Republican problem stems from the temporal congruence of the political marriage gap's emergence and the decline of marriage. If the average age at first marriage in the United States continues to increase, the political fortunes of the Republican Party will likely wane further. It is worth noting that although the Republican

Party still performs very well among non-Hispanic white voters and has steadily been increasing its share of this demographic group in recent decades, GOP presidential candidates perform very poorly among unmarried white women; exit polls indicate that Romney only won 44 percent of the vote among unmarried white women. Unless the decline of marriage can be halted, or even reversed, or if the Republican Party and the conservative movement can become more appealing to the unmarried, it will have a difficult time rebuilding a majority coalition.

THE GROWING NONWHITE POPULATION

Another demographic trend is perhaps even more problematic for the Republican Party and the conservative movement: the increasing nonwhite population in the US electorate. Although the organized conservative movement has recently endeavored to shed its image as the natural political home of racist reactionaries uncomfortable with the nation's sweeping demographic changes, the reality remains that the overwhelming majority of the Republican Party's support comes from non-Hispanic whites. The party has furthermore had little success among nonwhites. In recent presidential elections, the Republican share of the African American vote was in the single digits. Although Republicans perform better among Latinos and Asian Americans, they still lose among these demographic groups by wide margins; according to exit polls, Mitt Romney won only 26 percent of the Asian American vote and only 27 percent of the Latino vote.[22] Beyond party identification, it is also well established that African Americans, Asian Americans, and Latinos are much more liberal, on average, than non-Hispanic whites across a wide variety of policy issues. Asian Americans, Latinos, and African Americans[23] are all much more likely to describe themselves as liberal than non-Hispanic whites.

The need for conservatism to appeal to nonwhites was simply not on anyone's mind in the early years of the movement. We should recall that during the 1940s, 1950s, and 1960s, the electorate of the United States was overwhelmingly white. Although there was a large African American population in many US states, much of that population was effectively barred from voting. Poll taxes, literacy tests, grandfather clauses, white-only primaries, residency requirements, and other roadblocks to voting—which were only selectively enforced—ensured white dominance of the political system. The Voting Rights Act of 1965 outlawed all of these forms of overt voter discrimination. *ANOTHER TOTALITARIAN MEASURE LIKE THE IMMIGRATION ACT OF 1965*

Although the extension of the franchise to blacks should, on its face, have benefited the Democratic Party, given that African Americans are majority Democrat, the reality was more complicated. As noted, by embracing the cause of civil rights, the Democratic Party alienated a large percentage of Southern whites who subsequently began voting for the Republican Party. White Southerners ultimately became some of the most consistent GOP voters. As the demographic profile of the United States has continued to change, however, Republican strength among Southern whites has become less politically important than Republican weakness among nonwhites across the nation.

The conservative movement was born during a period of little immigration to the United States, and most foreign-born Americans at the time were from Europe. Although immigration rates during the late nineteenth and early twentieth century were high, Congress passed a series of restrictive immigration laws in the 1920s that effectively ended large-scale immigration. The Immigration Restriction Act of 1921, also known as the Emergency Quota Act, restricted the number of immigrants that could be admitted from any given country, with a strong bias in favor of Northern European countries. This act was followed by the even more restrictive Immigration Act of 1924, also known as the National Origins Act. Southern and Eastern Europeans, who represented the main source of new immigrants in the years leading up to these acts, were the primary targets of this legislation. This system of quotas remained in place during the formative years of the conservative movement, and thus immigration was not initially a salient issue to American conservatives.

Nonwhites and immigrants did not remain a small fraction of the American electorate. The Immigration and Nationality Act of 1965 was surely the most important catalyst for the high levels of racial and ethnic diversity across the United States. More than any other legislative act, this bill helped assure that the United States would one day become a nation without a single ethnic/racial majority. It removed the National Origins Formula that had been in place since the 1920s, ending the bias in favor of Northern European immigrants. This ultimately opened the door to large-scale immigration from Latin America, Asia, and Africa. From this point on, the foreign-born population in the United States steadily grew, and relatively few of the new foreign-born Americans were from Western Europe. It was not just legal immigration that led to a steady growth in the nonwhite population in the United States. The increasing undocumented immigration to the country also played an important role in this trend. Undocumented immigrants are overwhelmingly from Latin America, predominantly from Mexico.

All political efforts to curtail or reverse undocumented immigration to the United States have been unsuccessful. Congress passed the Immigration Reform and Control Act (IRCA) in 1986. This bill both provided amnesty to a portion of the undocumented population in the United States and included provisions designed to punish employers who hire undocumented workers. This bill was supposed to provide the solution to the contentious issue of undocumented immigration. It failed. While the amnesty was applied, the employer-enforcement provisions were not implemented. As a result, IRCA did not stem the number of undocumented immigrants entering the United States.[24]   *A CRIME!*

In recent decades, the immigration restrictionist movement was able to successfully lobby for the creation of a strong border fence in parts of California. This certainly reduced the flow of undocumented immigrants into certain cities, such as San Diego. However, this may have been a victory that did more harm than good for immigration restrictionists. Douglas Massey has suggested that strong border security actually increased the number of undocumented immigrants in the United States.[25] Although border fences effectively discourage border crossings where they are in place, migrants simply look for other places to cross. However, the new routes followed by undocumented immigrants tended to be in much more difficult and dangerous areas, such as the Arizona desert. Whereas many migrant workers once preferred to enter the United States for a single season and then return home to Mexico for the remainder of the year, the difficulties and dangers associated with crossing the United States–Mexico border now discourages them from making repeated trips. According to this theory, undocumented immigrants are now more likely to cross the United States–Mexico border only once; they then remain in the United States and bring in their families. Although there is no way to precisely determine the number of undocumented immigrants in the United States, demographers usually estimate the total at somewhere around 12 million.[26] *— 20 MIL, NOW (2020)*   *TRUMP'S WALL MOST IMPORTANT!*

The demographic impact of undocumented immigration on the United States is amplified by the Fourteenth Amendment to the US Constitution. Although this amendment was specifically intended to ensure the fair treatment of former slaves in the aftermath of the Civil War, its language had unintended consequences. Specifically, the amendment states: "All persons born or naturalized in the United States, and subject to the jurisdiction thereof, are citizens of the United States and of the State wherein they reside." As a result of this unambiguous language, all children born in the United States, whether or not their parents are in the country legally, are citizens and entitled to the rights associated with citizenship—including voting. The children of these immigrants lean heavily toward the Democratic Party. Although in the United States birthright citizenship is generally taken for granted, and there have been few major efforts to end this practice, most countries are much less liberal in this regard. As of 2010, only 30 of the 194 recognized nations in the world granted birthright citizenship, and only one other nation with an advanced economy has a similar policy (Canada).[27]

[handwritten: DUMB USA]

It has been suggested that one reason why immigrants are so opposed to the Republican Party, and the conservative movement more generally, is that the GOP and the major conservative institutions are anti-immigrant. This narrative suggests that anti-immigrant rhetoric and policy proposals drive Latinos away from the GOP and conservatism more generally. This is not an implausible hypothesis. When pundits and scholars explain how immigration restrictionism has driven Latinos to the Democratic Party and done irreparable damage to the GOP, they frequently discuss the case of California.[28] In the 1990s, Proposition 187,[29] a highly restrictive immigration initiative, was placed on the ballot in California and was endorsed by prominent California Republicans such as Governor Pete Wilson. This initiative passed, but in the process, the GOP may have alienated Latino voters in the state who had once been swing voters and amenable to the Republican Party. This ballot initiative furthermore failed to achieve any of its goals, as the most restrictive elements of the bills were struck down by the courts.

[handwritten: MARXIST COURTS]

Similarly, Republican efforts to enact restrictive immigration bills at the national level may have hurt the party among immigrants and Latinos more generally. Commentators on the left and the right have opined that anti-immigration posturing has permanently cost the GOP support from non-whites, and as a result it will soon be unable to be competitive at the national level; it will be permanently locked out of the White House and soon lose its ability to win majorities in Congress.[30] These commentators have a point. It is true that non-Hispanic whites are more in favor of immigration restrictions than other racial and ethnic groups, and it is almost certainly true that many nonwhites will not consider supporting the GOP because they believe the party and its supporters are racist or nativist.

If the Republican Party's reputation for nativism and its willingness to endorse strong immigration restrictionists really is the only thing keeping large percentages of Latinos and Asians from embracing the GOP and conservative ideology, then there may be no real crisis for American conservatism; a change to a single element of their policy platform will be sufficient to overcome this apparent demographic challenge. However, as I have said in other venues,[31] I am skeptical that changing its views on immigration will prove an electoral panacea for the Republican Party. A problem with this hypothesis is that it ignores the fact that Latinos and Asian Americans are more progressive than non-Hispanic whites on many policy areas, not just immigration. Gun control, taxes, federal spending on social services—on all these topics, nonwhites are considerably more progressive, on average, than whites.[32] This will remain true even if immigration is completely removed from the table. Furthermore, even if a drastic move to the left on immigration did lead to an electoral windfall among Latinos and Asian Americans for the Republican Party, such a move may cost them support from restrictionist whites. Indeed, it may cost them more than they gain. For all of these reasons, I argue that the demographic challenge faced by the Republican Party and the organized conservative movement will not be fixed by a marginal change to a single policy area. Barring either a major move to the political right among a substantial percentage of the nonwhite US population or a major boost in the GOP's share of the non-Hispanic white vote, the number of states in the solid blue category will only increase as this century progresses. *HASN'T HAPPENED*

DIMINISHING RETURNS FOR CONSERVATIVE POLICIES

In many ways, the conservative movement, and the Republican Party with which it is inextricably linked, is a victim of its own success. Chapter 1 noted that the cold war was the only common element strong enough to bind together the disparate elements of the nascent conservative movement in the years after World War II. Foreign policy hawks, economic libertarians, and Christian social conservatives may not have much else in common, but they agreed that the Soviet Union represented an existential threat. As the Democratic Party increasingly became the political home of the antiwar movement during and after the Vietnam war, the GOP became progressively more attractive to those who wanted to end the cold war via total American victory. Polls in the latter half of the twentieth century consistently demonstrated that Americans trusted the Republican Party on foreign policy more than the Democratic Party. As Daniel W. Drexner noted in *Foreign Affairs*:

> Republican presidents from the 1950s through the early 1990s had variegated records, but they had one thing in common: they left behind favorable legacies on foreign policy. Eisenhower stabilized the rivalry with the Soviet Union, preventing it from escalating into a violent

conflagration. He dramatically improved the US foreign-policy-making process, strengthened domestic infrastructure, extricated the United States from the Korean War, and limited US involvement in Vietnam. Nixon improved relations with the Soviet Union, opened relations with China, and extricated the United States from Vietnam. Reagan spoke truth to power by railing against the Soviet Union as an "evil empire," but when faced with a genuine negotiating partner in Mikhail Gorbachev, he did not hesitate to sign numerous treaties, reduce Cold War tensions, and cut nuclear stockpiles. George H. W. Bush adroitly seized the opportunities afforded by the end of the Cold War to expand the West's liberal order to the world at large, as well as overseeing German reunification, rebuffing Iraq's invasion of Kuwait, and locking in Mexico's path toward economic liberalization.[33]

This reputation for strength and seriousness when it comes to foreign policy is certainly one of the primary reasons why the Republicans were able to dominate the presidency in the latter half of the twentieth century, despite a considerable Democratic advantage nationwide when it came to party identification. However, after the sudden and unexpected demise of the Soviet Union, the American conservative movement found itself without one of its primary reasons for being. With the existential threat of communism gone and no new comparable threats on the horizon, the Republican advantage in foreign policy was apparently less of a boon in presidential elections than was once the case. After all, who but a few wonks really care about foreign policy at—to use Fukuyama's phrase—the end of history?

Further, the end of the cold war led to a schism within the American conservative movement. There was an element of the American right that had never been fully comfortable with the expansion of the American empire. Although they may have tolerated what William F. Buckley called the "totalitarian bureaucracy within our shores"[34] for the sake of winning the cold war, they were now ready to bring our troops home and once again enjoy living in a normal country rather than a superpower. The story of this internal struggle—seen most dramatically in the presidential campaigns of Pat Buchanan—was explored in greater detail in chapter 2. The important thing to note for our present purposes is that the mainstream conservative movement did not abandon its commitment to maintaining the United States as the world's dominant military power even after the cold war concluded.

Although foreign policy was not a particularly salient political issue throughout most of the 1990s—the most significant event in American foreign policy during the Clinton administration was the bombing of Serbia—the relative tranquility of the post–cold war era ended shortly into the first term of President George W. Bush when terrorists crashed hijacked airplanes into the World Trade Center, the Pentagon, and rural Pennsylvania. The new focus on foreign affairs and international terrorism led inevitably to the attack on Afghanistan and the Taliban regime—this surely would have occurred regardless of which party controlled the White House. The 9/11 attacks were more significant in that they provided an opportunity for an invasion of Iraq, a policy many members of the Bush administration publicly supported long before 9/11. For example, the Project for a New American Century was founded in 1997. This group urged the Clinton administration to support a regime change in Iraq as early as the late 1990s.[35] This is significant because a substantial number of high-ranking members of the Bush administration were signatories or members of the Project for a New American Century, including Dick Cheney, Donald Rumsfeld, and Paul Wolfowitz.

The threat of weapons of mass destruction was the justification for the 2003 invasion of Iraq, though it is clear that regime change in that country was the desired policy of many prominent Bush administration officials regardless of the presence of such weapons. Although it is difficult to prove that there was any willful deception on the part of those agitating for war against Iraq, the failure to uncover any evidence of such a weapons program proved politically problematic for conservatives. To make matters worse, while Saddam Hussein was removed from power after less than a month of fighting, pacifying Iraq proved much more difficult than many Americans anticipated. The rising death toll soured Americans on the war. At the start of the war, 72 percent of Americans believed the invasion was the right decision, but by early 2008, that number had dropped below 40 percent.[36] By losing its edge over Democrats on the foreign policy issue, the GOP did considerable damage to its brand. It is possible that enough time has passed that the Iraq war will no longer be an albatross for Republican presidential candidates, but we have certainly not yet reached the point where the GOP can again count on foreign policy to be an asset.

If the political problems associated with the Iraq war were due to failures by the GOP and the conservative movement that provides the party much of its intellectual energy, other political problems can be attributed to conservatism's victories. For example, while it is true that conservatives continue to focus heavily on the issue of tax cuts, the reality is that they have already achieved major successes on this front—successes that, for the most part, were not overturned by subsequent Democratic administrations. Compared to the 1960s, 1970s, and early 1980s, tax rates in the United States are extraordinarily low.[37] President Reagan slashed the top marginal tax rate. Presidents George H. W. Bush and Bill Clinton both oversaw a slight increase in this rate, but it remained far lower than was the case several decades prior. President George W. Bush again cut taxes, including taxes on capital gains and dividends.

Whether or not tax rates in the United States are presently at the "correct" level is certainly beyond the scope of this project. Members of the Tea Party and other conservatives may genuinely feel that they shoulder an unfair tax burden. However, it is likely also true that the Republican Party has reached a ceiling when it comes to how much they can cut taxes without also cutting spending on popular programs. Although some savings can certainly be found in discretionary spending, a dramatic spending cut would require major reductions in spending on the military, Medicare, or Social Security—or, failing that, a new explosion in the national debt. Furthermore, the American public appears rather amenable to higher taxes on at least some percentage of the population. An examination of the 2012 American National Election Study survey shows that nearly 60 percent of Americans approve of higher taxes on corporations in order to reduce the deficit; this same survey shows that more than 75 percent of Americans approve of higher taxes on millionaires.[38]

This leads to an additional problem. It is increasingly apparent that most Americans have little interest in removing, or even significantly reforming, entitlement programs such as Social Security or Medicare. As noted previously, Bush's 2005 push to partially privatize Social Security ended disastrously, and the idea has not been enthusiastically embraced by Republican presidential candidates since that time. It is true that the Republican Party was able to harness discontent over the Affordable Care Act in order to raise money and bring conservatives to the polls, but it has not aggressively promoted a genuine free-market alternative.

Having achieved significant tax cuts, as well as other conservative goals such as welfare reform in the 1990s, conservatives may have accomplished as much as they can when it comes to conservative economic policies, given the policy preferences of the electorate. This does not mean that the electorate necessarily wants to see major new progressive economic policies, and the GOP can benefit at the ballot box when the Democratic Party overreaches on these issues. But Republicans may have difficulty formulating new, groundbreaking, and popular economic policies of their own.

Similarly, the issue of crime and social disorder, which was once a winning issue for conservative Republicans, is not as salient as was once the case. Crime rates in the United States have dropped substantially since peaking in the early 1990s.[39] This trend has been ascribed to many different causes, including higher incarceration rates, innovative policing strategies, a higher median age of the population, and even the legalization of abortion in the 1970s.[40] Whether specific public policies actually led to a reduction of crime is beside the point for our purposes. What matters is that violent crime is down, and as a result voters have one fewer reason to be skeptical of progressives—after all, the accusation that a candidate is weak on crime will be less compelling to a voter without a serious fear of crime.

THE INTELLECTUAL CRISIS

As a political philosophy dedicated to preserving what Russell Kirk called the permanent things, one should not expect conservatism to constantly evolve and reverse itself. However, conservatives in the Burkean sense also recognize the inevitability, and even desirability, of organic change. As American society evolves, conservatives must also evolve in order to remain relevant. This occurs to a certain extent, and it would be unfair to the conservative movement to claim otherwise. For example, if we consider how conservative discourse on race has changed since the 1960s, there can be little doubt that conservatives are much less tolerant of open racists than was once the case—though some have argued that the conservative movement must do more work on that front.

In another sense, one could fairly argue that American conservatism has become calcified and lacks intellectual energy. Conservative talking points remain virtually unchanged since the 1980s. Nor has there been much acknowledgment that any of the ideas conservatives promoted vigorously were mistaken, or that the Republican Party is to blame for any of the problems facing contemporary America. Author and journalist Sam Tanenhaus attended a prominent conservative magazine's luncheon and subsequently remarked on the degree to which contemporary conservative rhetoric had become vacuous:

> What these conservative intellectuals said wasn't just mistaken. It was meaningless, the clatter of a bygone period, with its "culture wars" and attacks on sinister "elites." There was no hint of a new argument being formulated or even an old one being reformulated. More disturbing still, not one of the three panelists acknowledged that the Republican Party and its ideology might bear any responsibility for the nation's

current plight. None urged its best thinkers and writers to reexamine their ideas and methods. Each offered only the din of ever-loudening distraction, gratingly ill attuned to the conditions of present-day America.[41]

Some conservatives have also lambasted the GOP for its rigidity. In their 2008 book *Grand New Party*, Ross Douthat and Reiham Salam argued that the Republican Party's insistence on "libertarian purity" on economic matters robs it of the ability to make further inroads among working-class Americans. They argued that "by confusing being pro-market with being pro-business, by failing to distinguish between spending that fosters dependence from spending that fosters independence and upward mobility, and by shrinking from the admittedly difficult task of reforming the welfare state so that it serves the interests of the working class rather than the affluent," the GOP may be denying itself the votes of many working-class people.[42]

Although one can justifiably make the case that liberal pundits and talking heads are pushing an equally stale package of talking points, one must also acknowledge the rather lowbrow tone of discourse on Fox News and most conservative talk radio. The existence of political media aimed at a large, mainstream audience is not itself problematic. More troublesome is the dearth of recent conservative books and other media on a higher intellectual plane. In recent decades, dozens of nonacademic conservative books have been tremendous best sellers. *The Way Things Ought to Be* by Rush Limbaugh, published in 1992, was number one on the *New York Times* bestseller list for 54 weeks, selling millions of copies. Since that time, bookstores have been perennially stocked with books with a conservative radio or television show host's face on the cover. Some publishers, like Regnery, only release conservative books. Other major publishers have conservative imprints. Many conservatives have enjoyed great commercial success as authors and other media figures, but these conservatives are universally populist in their tone; Glenn Beck, Bill O'Reilly, Sean Hannity, Michael Savage, Ann Coulter, and others are examples of this trend. The number of highbrow and intellectually rigorous books by conservative authors remains small.

The organized conservative movement has also been openly hostile to academia. One could argue that this goes all the way back to Buckley's first book, *God and Man at Yale* (1951). To some extent this is understandable, as there probably is a liberal bias in most academic departments. There can be no doubt that conservatives are underrepresented in most academic fields.

In a study of political diversity within the social sciences and the humanities, it was determined that Democrats outnumber Republicans in anthropology departments by more than thirty to one. The ratio is only slightly less skewed in sociology. Political science is slightly more balanced, but among political scientists, the ratio is still more than six to one in favor of Democrats.[43] The skewed political ratio at major universities is apparently taken by some conservatives as prima facie evidence that conservatives are discriminated against. Horror stories about the mistreatment of conservatives in academia are common in conservative media.

Although I do not question the honesty of those conservatives who claim to have suffered mistreatment at the hands of liberal colleagues, there is some evidence that the underrepresentation of right-wing intellectuals at major universities is driven by other factors. Recent research indicates that there is an ideological divide regarding interest in a doctoral degree among undergraduate students in their first year of college.[44] Before they could be subjected to a liberal bias in the classroom, on average, conservatives were more likely to express interest in majors such as business or criminal justice, whereas liberals were more likely to be interested in liberal arts majors. This same research project found little evidence that conservative professors feel discriminated against.[45]

Regardless of the reasons, it is problematic for conservatives—who still claim that ideas have consequences—to ostentatiously embrace an anti-intellectual tone. Although a populism that pits ordinary folks against out-of-touch intellectuals is politically useful, it will make it more difficult to advance a conservative political theory capable of solving twenty-first-century problems. Further, the failure to update conservative rhetoric that is now several decades old will only solidify the movement's reputation for being out of touch and merely reactionary.

Those who wish to write conservatism's eulogy, or even declare American conservatism in a state of long-term decline, would be wise to exercise a degree of humility. Conservatism, and the Republican Party, have been declared down for the count before, only to come roaring back. The present disarray of the conservative movement and the Republican Party is not comparable to that of the mid-1960s after Goldwater's humiliating defeat. In fact, at the time of this writing, the GOP seems quite strong.

As R. Emett Tyrell has noted, the obituary of the conservative movement has been written again and again, making it America's "longest dying political movement."[46] Every setback for conservatives is declared evidence that conservatives are doomed to years in the wilderness, if not permanent irrelevance. Goldwater's defeat in 1964, Nixon's resignation in 1974, Bill Clinton's 1992 election, the Democratic congressional victories in 2006, and President Obama's 2008 election all led to confident declarations that liberalism had finally triumphed in the United States. Each time, conservative Republicans struck back shortly thereafter, winning important victories.

Further, one could argue that the Republican Party's political problems are overstated, at least in the short term. Republicans have a number of electoral advantages at present. Because of the Republican Party's disproportionate strength in small rural states—such as those in the South and the Great Plains—and the Constitution's guarantee of equal representation in the US Senate for each state, the GOP can capture a Senate majority even if it receives a minority of the vote in all Senate races combined. In the House of Representatives, the geographic distribution of partisan voters also favors the Republicans. Because Democratic voters tend to be clustered together in metropolitan areas, a great number of Democratic districts are overwhelmingly Democratic. Given this geographic concentration, it is more difficult to gerrymander these districts in such a way as to disperse some of these superfluous Democratic voters into more competitive districts. Although there are fewer congressional seats won by Republicans by landslide margins, there are more districts won by Republicans by small or merely comfortable margins.

Finally, while it is not the focus of this chapter, it is important to note that the progressive movement has problems of its own. Although all elements of the left presumably stand for universal equality, there are certainly major schisms among progressives. The perceived interests of labor unions, the poor, immigrants, environmentalists, ethnic lobbies, LGBT activists, and feminists are not always congruent. There are also disagreements regarding the degree to which the Democratic Party should embrace moderate positions in order to maintain electability. Many progressives are frustrated by the Democratic Party's refusal to seriously take on Wall Street and big business. Others worry that an emphasis on minority concerns will alienate members of the white working class—a demographic the Democrats still need to secure the presidency and majorities in Congress. Infighting within the progressive movement and Democratic Party may win the GOP a reprieve.

The left in America also has a demographic challenge of its own: on average, and controlling for all other variables, Republicans tend to have more children than Democrats.[47] As party identification tends to run in families, this suggests that future generations will be more Republican than the present generation. This should not be overstated, however; while intergenerational transmission of party preference is a real, nontrivial occurrence, there is not a perfect correlation between the politics of parents and their children.[48] The effect of higher birthrates among Republicans is furthermore not as politically significant as the high rates of immigration to the United States.

In spite of the above caveats, the challenges conservatives face are real. The demographic challenges in particular cannot be easily dismissed or ignored. All indicators suggest that as the century progresses, Americans will become, on average, less conservative, at least as we define the term today. Furthermore, if the Republican Party's electoral fortunes wane in the decades ahead—and most commentators who examine demographics and voting patterns believe they will—where will that leave the conservative movement? The conservative movement has long put the overwhelming majority of its energy toward electing Republicans. Some conservatives have argued that this was a mistake, and not a mistake made by progressives. Writing in the *Washington Times*, Donald Lambro argued that conservatives find themselves at a huge disadvantage as a result of their refusal to engage with pop culture: "What the Republican Party needs to do now is figure out how to make up for 40 years of ignoring the net effect of film, television and music, and the youth culture that goes along with it. When will the people who make the big decisions and write the big checks realize the AM radio band is not enough?"[49] This line of argument suggests that although progressives have not ignored electoral politics, they have also endeavored—successfully—to dominate the institutions that shape American culture, such as the entertainment industry and education. Conservatives, on the other hand, have largely considered it sufficient to campaign for Republicans. If the Republican Party finds itself permanently marginalized, conservatives may find themselves with no significant influence on American life whatsoever.

American elites and the electorate in general have become ideologically sorted in recent decades. That is, most conservative voters belong to the Republican Party and most progressive voters belong to the Democratic Party. In Congress, this partisan ideological divide is even starker. The days of conservative Blue Dog Democrats and of liberal and moderate Republicans appears to be behind us. This being the case, the success of conservative public policies appears entirely dependent on the electoral fortunes of the GOP. If there were still conservative elected representatives in the Democratic Party, or even if conservative think tanks had good working relationships with Democrats, conservative public policies could potentially still be implemented. At present, it seems unlikely that new conservative Democrats will emerge on the political scene, or that the Democrats in Congress will exhibit much interest in policy papers written by the American Enterprise Institute.

Looking Ahead

Many on the left have long awaited the demise of conservatism as a force in America and will cheer its departure from the scene—should such a departure ever occur. However, progressives who seek the downfall of the conservative movement should be cautious in this regard. They are not the only ideologues who desperately wish to see American conservatism sent to the dustbin of history. As this volume demonstrates, there are multiple right-wing movements that have been denied access to the mainstream political debate, largely as a result of the conservative movement's aggressive enforcement of the boundaries of acceptable right-wing thought. It is possible that a rapid implosion of mainstream conservatism will usher in a new progressive consensus in American politics. It is also possible that such an implosion will offer crucial breathing space for one or more of these alternative right-wing ideologies. In a postconservative America, one or more of the ideologies discussed in this volume may find new followers and gain new wealthy benefactors who previously backed the mainstream conservative movement. Although progressives may view some of these alternatives as superior to traditional conservatism—or at least not any worse—they will surely also view others as much more dangerous and threatening to their values. If conservatism breaks down, many of its present constituents may embrace a more radical right-wing ideology, making American politics far more unstable.

As I stated previously, it is too early to declare the conservative movement terminally ill. At the time of this writing, the Republican Party majority in the House of Representatives is unlikely to be threatened in the immediate future. Some Republicans furthermore remain optimistic that effective outreach can lead to new inroads among minority voters—though at present there is little evidence that this will occur anytime soon. Although I hesitate to speculate when the conservative movement will collapse—or even claim with any confidence that such a collapse will occur—I can comment on which of the competing ideologies discussed in this volume are most likely to experience substantial growth in the years ahead.

Of all the groups discussed in this volume, I argue that moderate and mainstream libertarianism is the right-wing ideology most likely to enjoy greater influence in the coming decades. This group already exercises influence within the Republican Party, and it has elected several of its own to Congress, such as Justin Amash and Rand Paul. This is true of no other ideological category examined in this volume. If Rand Paul secures the GOP presidential nomination in 2016, or even performs well in the presidential primaries, prospects for this variety of libertarianism will reach an all-time high. It is of course not coincidental that the ideology most likely to make inroads in conventional politics is also the ideology most similar to conventional conservatism. Although Rand Paul is certainly less hawkish than most other Republicans in Congress, he is also a less consistent noninterventionist than his father. He is careful to assure voters of his devotion to the state of Israel, for example.[50]

Libertarians of this type are also clearly hopeful that they can successfully appeal to a large percentage of America's minority population. They point out that many of the policies that they oppose—such as the war on drugs—disproportionately affect African Americans. After the fatal shooting of Michael Brown, an African American, in Ferguson, Missouri, by a white police officer, Rand Paul was one of the first voices to denounce the increasing militarization of American police forces.[51] Whether this brand of libertarianism will ultimately be appealing to minority voters remains to be seen, and there are reasons for skepticism.[52] However, if a Republican running on such a platform does manage to win a large percentage of the minority vote without simultaneously alienating the GOP's traditional white voting base, we could see a major change in the Republican Party's platform and in the ideals espoused by the mainstream American right.

The other ideologies discussed in this volume have a greater challenge ahead of them. Although many people surely find localism fairly benign and unthreatening, current demographic trends indicate that Americans are not seeking a greater degree of rootedness. Nor is there much evidence that either major political party is committed to weakening the power of big business. Millions of Americans have abandoned the small towns in which they grew up in favor of cosmopolitan metropolitan areas or their surrounding suburbs. Americans remain a highly mobile people, and there are no signs that this trend is abating. Nor are there any major think tanks or high-profile political figures advocating substantive policies that would reverse these trends. Although politicians may rhetorically declare their love for Main Street and hometown values, it is not always clear what this means from a policy standpoint.

Secularists on the right may enjoy greater success in steering the conservative movement in a less overtly religious direction. If the number of voters who find staunch religious conservatives such as Rick Santorum and Mike Huckabee appealing continues to dwindle, we may see fewer such candidates in the future. That being said, the religious right remains a powerful constituency within the Republican Party, and such people remain important donors to the conservative movement. We are unlikely to see a Republican presidential candidate in the near future who does not ostentatiously declare and defend his or her religious faith.

Radical libertarians at this time appear politically hopeless. Their radical rhetoric, the degree to which they loathe both progressives and mainstream conservatives, and their distaste for electoral politics will surely keep them marginalized for the foreseeable future. Like many radical ideologies—on both the right and the left—they view a total collapse of the existing state as their best bet for creating their ideal society. Libertarians usually argue that a currency collapse will be the catalyst for such a crisis. Although they may view such a collapse as inevitable, if it never occurs, there is little chance that radical libertarians will find a large number of new followers who want to dismantle all welfare programs, close down all military bases, and perhaps even abolish government entirely.

The demise of paleoconservatism is somewhat curious, as twenty years ago one could have plausibly named it as the greatest threat on the right to mainstream conservatism. In Pat Buchanan's presidential campaigns, the proponents of this anachronistic brand of conservatism threatened to capture the Republican Party. However, the prospects for paleoconservatism largely died at the end of the 1990s. Many of its prominent theoreticians have died or are now elderly, and a new generation has not taken up their banner. The number of Americans who can even remember the supposedly idyllic America of the 1950s continues to shrink, and fewer Americans express a desire to turn back to the clock. Although many Americans may continue to support the ideal of a noninterventionist foreign policy, most of those sentiments are now expressed on the right by libertarians.

Not surprisingly, the views expressed by the European New Right have little chance of attaining influence in the United States. This cannot even be called a failure on the part of the New Right; as an explicitly European movement, it has had little interest in gaining American adherents. Even if it had aggressively courted Americans, it faced considerable barriers. For one, its view of the United States as the main source of the world's problems would certainly not appeal to patriotic Americans with right-wing sympathies. Its antipathy to Christianity would similarly have represented a barrier to growth in a country in which right-wing politics and the Christian religion are intimately intertwined. Although Americans can now at least access the foundational texts of the New Right thanks to new translations, most of the New Right's attention on this side of the Atlantic has come from the racialist right, which is also highly marginalized. There is certainly a possibility that New Right and Identitarian thinking will dramatically shake up European politics in the years ahead. If that is the case, Americans will likely become more aware of this movement and learn about it simply out of curiosity.

Explicit white nationalism is surely the most aggressively marginalized ideology discussed here. As we have seen, advocating racism is perhaps the fastest way for a politician, pundit, or public intellectual to find himself or herself a social pariah. That being the case, there is little chance that transparent white racism will again become a major political force in the United States in the immediate future. However, the fact that antiracists on the right and left are extraordinarily vigilant in their effort to drive racists from public discourse can be viewed as evidence that they believe such views could once again have a large constituency, should racists ever again be allowed to reenter the mainstream public debate. Whether their fears in this regard are justified is impossible to determine at this time. What we should remember, however, is that the marginalization of the racist right in America was largely possible thanks to cooperation from the mainstream conservative movement, which has frequently jettisoned people from its ranks for openly expressing racist views. If the mainstream conservative movement loses its status as the gatekeeper on the right, white nationalism may be among the greatest beneficiaries, though even in this case it will face serious challenges.

This has not been a fully comprehensive examination of all existing dissident right-wing ideologies. Such an examination would probably not be possible, as the political spectrum is littered with tiny groups advocating strange things. The reader may think I neglected to mention a number of groups and individuals who deserve greater attention, however. Do conspiracy theorists such as Alex Jones warrant their own unique chapter? Jones, for example, has millions of listeners and readers, who eagerly await his new theories about 9/11, vaccinations, the new world order, and a global eugenics conspiracy.[53] In my estimation, however, Jones and those with similar attitudes do not constitute a unique ideological category. Jones, like many who embrace more far-fetched conspiracy theories, can be described as a libertarian. Others inclined to that type of thinking tend to occupy a space on the far left. In any event, this is not a separate and distinct ideology.

While I was in the middle of this project, a series of breathless articles were published in fairly mainstream venues about a new ideological movement called the Dark Enlightenment.[54] As I read through the first exposés on this ideology, I thought that this new movement might be a good candidate for its own chapter in this book. Reading these articles also prompted a degree of frustration on my part, as by then I thought I had become well familiar with all major varieties of contemporary right-wing thought. I therefore began to read much of the work associated with the Dark Enlightenment, which has also been called neoreaction. This is a movement that is generally characterized by skepticism toward democracy, a belief in biological racial and ethnic differences (though not support for white nationalism), and a general rejection of egalitarianism. The best-known figure associated with this movement is a blogger who uses the pen name Mencius Moldbug.[55] The philosopher Nick Land is also influential within this movement. The major bloggers associated with this ideological movement are not always easy to read and understand. The Dark Enlightenment bloggers have their own terminology, and they generally assume that readers understand their many neologisms.[56] These writers are not generally known for pithiness. Moldbug in particular has a habit of writing exceptionally long blog posts—far longer than the norm for that medium.

I ultimately decided that the Dark Enlightenment did not warrant a separate investigation. There are two reasons for this. At present, this movement exists exclusively on the Internet, and I suspect its ability to grow further is decidedly limited. It is more a loose association of likeminded bloggers than a true ideological movement. More importantly, having invested much time reading the figures associated with the brand of reactionary thought, I concluded that there is relatively little about this movement that is genuinely new and innovative. It is clearly interested in the subject of genetic racial differences, but it has not made much of a contribution of its own to that issue. Skepticism about democracy and equality are certainly radical positions, but they are shared by the several ideologies of the far right. It rejects white nationalism despite sharing many of its premises, but the same could be said for the European New Right. At this point, the Dark Enlightenment is predominantly interesting because of its unique style and lingo, but it adds relatively little to the political debate that is truly inventive. It is possible that I am dismissing this movement too easily. If I am proven wrong on this over time, perhaps an updated version of this book will include a deeper exploration of this movement.

Another movement that I initially considered as a possible addition to this volume is also predominantly found on the Internet. The so-called Manosphere has apparently enjoyed impressive growth recently. This corner of the Internet is perhaps even more loosely united ideologically, as it includes pickup artists (writers who provide advice to men interested in meeting and seducing women), bodybuilders and other advocates of self-improvement, and different variations of the men's rights movement. The only thing that truly unites all of the disparate websites and writers is a support for traditional masculinity and opposition to feminism—though they often vary even in this. Much of this movement is apolitical. It also lacks internal agreement on more than a handful of issues. Both of these traits make it unlikely that this movement will break out of its Internet isolation and into the broader political conversation in the near future. Again, I may be mistaken on this, and I will revisit these writers and their ideas if future events warrant.

Although the future of the conservative movement cannot be predicted with any certainty, this volume should make it clear that mainstream conservatives are not the only critics of progressive egalitarianism. The preceding pages also argued that progressives are not the only ideologues with trenchant criticisms of the conservative movement. I strongly believe that scholars and others with an interest in ideology should, at least on occasion, venture outside the mainstream debate and listen to outside voices. Today, the mainstream right and left are so used to debating each other—and only each other—that they have no real tool kit for rhetorically engaging opponents with a fundamentally different political weltanschauung. In fact, they often act as if such ideologues do not exist, or that those outside the mainstream are simply cranks, fools, or monsters unworthy of serious engagement. This negative assessment of marginalized ideologies may be correct in many cases. Nonetheless, the day may be approaching when one or more of these other right-wing movements is given the opportunity to make its case, and it is therefore important to know what that case will be, even if such knowledge is used only to refute their arguments.

Chapter 1. The Twilight of the Old Right

1. John Micklethwait and Adrian Wooldridge, *The Right Nation: Conservative Power in America* (New York: Penguin Press, 2004), 13.

2. In Hayek's words: "As has often been acknowledged by conservative writers, one of the fundamental traits of the conservative attitude is a fear of change, a timid distrust of the new as such, while the liberal position is based on courage and confidence, on a preparedness to let change run its course even if we cannot predict where it will lead. There would not be much to object to if the conservatives merely disliked too rapid change in institutions and public policy; here the case for caution and slow process is indeed strong. But the conservatives are inclined to use the powers of government to prevent change or to limit its rate to whatever appeals to the more timid mind. In looking forward, they lack the faith in the spontaneous forces of adjustment which makes the liberal accept changes without apprehension, even though he does not know how the necessary adaptations will be brought about. It is, indeed, part of the liberal attitude to assume that, especially in the economic field, the self-regulating forces of the market will somehow bring about the required adjustments to new conditions, although no one can foretell how they will do this in a particular instance. There is perhaps no single factor contributing so much to people's frequent reluctance to let the market work as their inability to conceive how some necessary balance, between demand and supply, between exports and imports, or the like, will be brought about without deliberate control. The conservative feels safe and content only if he is assured that some higher wisdom watches and supervises change, only if he knows that some authority is charged with keeping the change 'orderly.'" F. A. Hayek, *The Constitution of Liberty* (Chicago: University of Chicago Press, 1960), 525.

3. Ibid., 530.

4. James Davison Hunter, *Culture War: The Struggle to Control the Family, Art, Education, Law, and Politics in America* (New York: Basic Books, 1992), 42.

5. Thomas Sowell, *A Conflict of Visions: Ideological Origins of Political Struggles* (New York: Basic Books, 2002).

6. Ibid., 75–76.

7. Ibid., 111–115.

8. Jonah Goldberg, *Liberal Fascism: The Secret History of the American Left, From Mussolini to the Politics of Change* (New York: Doubleday, 2007).

9. "What Is Left, What Is Right?" *American Conservative*, August 28, 2006, http://www.theamericanconservative.com/.

10. The full list of ten principles is as follows: "First, the conservative believes

that there exists an enduring moral order"; "Second, the conservative adheres to custom, convention, and continuity"; "Third, conservatives believe in what may be called the principle of prescription"; "Fourth, conservatives are guided by their principle of prudence"; "Fifth, conservatives pay attention to the principle of variety"; "Sixth, conservatives are chastened by their principle of imperfectability"; "Seventh, conservatives are persuaded that freedom and property are closely linked"; "Eighth, conservatives uphold voluntary community, quite as they oppose involuntary collectivism"; "Ninth, the conservative perceives the need for prudent restraints upon power and upon human passions"; "Tenth, the thinking conservative understands that permanence and change must be recognized and reconciled in a vigorous society." Russell Kirk, *The Politics of Prudence*, 2nd ed. (Wilmington, DE: Intercollegiate Studies Institute, 2004), 17–25.

11. Robert Nisbet, *Prejudices: A Philosophical Dictionary* (Cambridge, MA: Harvard University Press, 1982), 59.

12. William F. Buckley, introduction to *Did You Ever See a Dream Walking: American Conservative Thought in the Twentieth Century*, ed. William F. Buckley (Indianapolis, IN: Bobbs-Merrill, 1970), xvii.

13. Specifically, Weaver defined a conservative as follows: "It is my contention that a conservative is a realist, who believes that there is a structure of reality independent of his own will and desire. He believes that there is a creation which was there before him, which exists now not by just his sufferance, and which will be there after he's gone. This structure consists not merely of the great physical world but also of many laws, principles, and regulations which control human behavior. Though this reality is independent of the individual, it is not hostile to him. It is in fact amenable by him in many ways, but it cannot be changed radically and arbitrarily. This is the cardinal point. The conservative holds that man in this world cannot make his will his law without regard to limits and the fixed nature of things." Richard Weaver, "Conservatism and Libertarianism: The Common Ground," in *In Defense of Tradition: Collected Shorter Writings of Richard Weaver*, ed. Ted Smith (Indianapolis, IN: Liberty Fund, 2000), 447.

14. Willmoore Kendall and George W. Carey, "Towards a Definition of 'Conservatism,'" *Journal of Politics* 26 (1964): 410.

15. Paul Gottfried, "Reflections on the Political Right and Left," *Nomocracy in Politics*, December 6, 2013, http://nomocracyinpolitics.com/.

16. It is worth pointing out that many of the left's critics on the right question the degree to which leftists are sincere in their devotion to equality. This line of critique goes as least as far back as Pareto, who made the following argument, which has since been echoed by many conservatives: "The sentiment that is very inappropriately named equality is fresh, strong, alert, precisely because it is not, in fact, a sentiment of equality and is not related to any abstraction, as a few native 'intellectuals' still believe; but because it is related to direct interests of individuals who are bent on escaping certain inequalities not in their favour, and setting up new inequalities that will be in their favour, this latter being their chief concern." Vilfredo Pareto, *The Mind and Society*, ed. Arthur Livingston, trans. Andrew Bongiorno, Arthur Livingston, and James Harvey Rogers, 4 vols. (New York: Harcourt, Brace, 1935), 2:735–736.

ON SO-CALLED EQUALITY

17. Noberto Bobbio, *Left and Right: The Significance of Political Distinction*, trans. Allan Cameron (Chicago: University of Chicago Press, 1996), 71.

18. George H. Nash, *The Conservative Intellectual Movement in America Since 1945* (1976), 30th anniversary ed. (Wilmington, DE: ISI Books, 2006).

19. Morton Blackwell, "Read to Lead," Leadership Institute, 2010, http://www .leadershipinstitute.org/resources/files/read-to-lead.pdf.

20. Lionel Trilling, *The Liberal Imagination* (New York: New York Review of Books Classics, 2008), xv.

21. Robert Crunden, ed., *Superfluous Men: Conservative Critics of American Culture, 1900–1945*, 2nd ed. (Wilmington, DE: ISI Books, 1999).

22. For an introduction to the radical anti-Semitic right that was prominent in the United States during the 1930s, I recommend Leo P. Ribbuffo, *The Old Christian Right: The Protestant Far-Right from the Great Depression to the Cold War* (Philadelphia: Temple University Press, 1983). Although I do not entirely agree with Ribbuffo's conclusions—I am especially skeptical of his view that there is anything more than a superficial continuity between the prewar Christian right, embodied by figures such as William Dudley Pelley, Gerald B. Winrod, and Gerald L. K. Smith, and the postwar religious right, led by fundamentalists such as Jerry Falwell—the book does provide an excellent summary of the prewar American far right.

23. Nock said the following in response to the suggestion that he was a conservative: "It seems that the reason for so amiably labeling me a conservative in this instance was that I am indisposed to the present Administration. This also appears to be one reason why Mr. Sokolsky labels himself a conservative, as he did in the very able and cogent paper which he published in the August issue of the *Atlantic*. But really, in my case this is no reason at all, for my objections to the Administration's behavior rest no more logically on the grounds of either conservatism or radicalism than on those of atheism or homoeopathy. They rest on the grounds of common sense and, I regret to say, common honesty. I resent the works and ways of the Administration because in my opinion such of them as are not peculiarly and dangerously silly are peculiarly and dangerously dishonest, and most of them are both. No doubt a person who wears the conservative label may hold this opinion and speak his mind accordingly, but so may a radical, so may anyone; the expression of it does not place him in either category, or in any category of the kind. They mark him merely as a person who is interested in having public affairs conducted wisely and honestly, and who resents their being conducted foolishly and dishonestly." Albert Jay Nock, "A Little Conserva-tive," *Atlantic Monthly*, October 1936, 481–489.

24. Albert Jay Nock, *Our Enemy, the State* (Caldwell, ID: Caxton Printers, 1950).

25. Nash, *Conservative Intellectual Movement*, 18–19.

26. Albert Jay Nock, "Isaiah's Job," in Buckley, *Did You Ever See a Dream Walking*, 509–522.

27. Ibid., 518.

28. H. L. Mencken, *On Politics: A Carnival of Buncombe* (Baltimore, MD: Johns Hopkins University Press, 2006), 21.

29. H. L. Mencken, *A Mencken Chrestomathy* (New York: Knopf, 1949), 145–146.

30. Ralph Adams Cram, "Why We Do Not Behave Like Human Beings," in Crunden, *Superfluous Men*, 121.

31. Ibid., 134.

HAVE 32. Ortega y Gasset, *The Revolt of the Masses* (1929; reprint, New York: Norton, 1994), 18.

33. Richard Weaver, *Ideas Have Consequences* (Chicago: University of Chicago Press, 1948), 33.

34. Albert Jay Nock, "The Amazing Liberal Mind," *American Mercury* 44 (1938): 467–472.

35. John T. Flynn, *As We Go Marching* (Garden City, NY: Doubleday, Doran, 1944), 212.

36. Robert Nisbet, *Twilight of Authority* (Indianapolis, IN: Liberty Fund, 2000), 174.

37. Russell Kirk, "Conscription Ad Infinitum," *South Atlantic Quarterly* 45 (1946): 313–319.

38. Russell Kirk, "A Conscript on Education," *South Atlantic Quarterly* 44 (1945): 82–99.

39. Specifically, Weaver argued the following: "It was William of Occam who propounded the fateful doctrine of nominalism, which denies that universals have a real existence. His triumph tended to leave universal terms mere names serving our convenience. The issue ultimately involved is whether there is a truth higher than, and independent of, man; and the answer to the question is decisive for one's view of the nature and destiny of humankind." Weaver, *Ideas Have Consequences*, 3.

40. Richard Weaver, *The Southern Tradition at Bay: A History of Postbellum Thought*, ed. George Core and M. E. Bradford (New Rochelle, NY: Arlington House, 1968), 391.

41. Ibid., 31.

42. Weaver, *Ideas Have Consequences*, 42.

43. Ibid., 48.

44. Ibid., 129.

45. Russell Kirk, *The Conservative Mind* (Chicago: Regnery, 1953), 5.

46. Ibid., 42.

47. Richard Weaver, *The Ethics of Rhetoric* (1953; reprint, Davis, CA: Hermagoras Press, 1985), 57.

48. Russell Kirk, *The American Cause* (Wilmington, DE: ISI Press, 2002), 2.

49. Murray Rothbard, "The Transformation of the American Right," *Continuum* 2 (1964): 220–231.

50. Whittaker Chambers, *Witness* (1952), 50th anniversary ed. (Washington, DC: Regnery, 2001).

51. James Burnham, *The Managerial Revolution* (New York: John Day, 1941).

52. James Burnham, *Suicide of the West* (1964; reprint, Chicago: Regnery, 1986), 297.

53. Nash, *Conservative Intellectual Movement*, 134.

54. Chambers, *Witness*, 25.

55. Nash, *Conservative Intellectual Movement*, 156.

56. James Burnham, *The Struggle for the World* (New York: John Day, 1947), 247.

57. William F. Buckley Jr., *God and Man at Yale: The Superstitions of "Academic Freedom"* (Chicago: Regnery, 1951).

58. Nash, *Conservative Intellectual Movement*, 212.

59. William F. Buckley, "Mission Statement," *National Review*, November 19, 1955.

60. Nash, *Conservative Intellectual Movement*, 228.

61. Frank S. Meyer, *In Defense of Freedom: A Conservative Credo* (Chicago: Regnery, 1962).

62. Ibid., 49.

63. Nash, *Conservative Intellectual Movement*, 229.

64. Murray Rothbard, "Frank Chodorov, RIP," *Left and Right* 3, no. 1 (Winter 1967): 5.

65. Buckley, introduction to *Did You Ever See a Dream Walking*, xviii.

66. Weaver, "Conservatism and Libertarianism," 482.

67. Heritage Foundation, "Sharon Statement," September 11, 1960, http://www.heritage.org/.

68. William F. Buckley, "The Party and the Deep Blue Sea," *Commonweal*, January 1952, 391–392.

69. David Horowitz, "Neo-Communists Out of the Closet," *Front Page Magazine*, January 17, 2013, http://www.frontpagemag.com/.

70. Irving Kristol, *Neo-Conservatism: The Autobiography of an Idea—Selected Essays, 1949–1995* (New York: Free Press, 1995), x.

71. James Atlas, "A Classicist's Legacy: New Empire Builders," *New York Times*, May 4, 2003, http://www.nytimes.com/.

72. Shadia B. Drury, *Leo Strauss and the American Right* (New York: St. Martin's Press, 1997), 4.

73. Steven B. Smith, *Reading Leo Strauss: Politics, Philosophy, Judaism* (Chicago: University of Chicago Press, 2007), ix.

74. For one of Strauss's more approachable critiques of historicism, see Leo Strauss, "Natural Right and the Historical Approach," *Review of Politics* 12 (1950): 422–442.

75. Grant Havers, *Leo Strauss and Anglo-American Democracy: A Conservative Critique* (DeKalb: Northern Illinois University Press, 2013).

76. Allan Bloom, *The Closing of the American Mind* (New York: Simon & Schuster, 1987).

77. Leo Strauss, *Persecution and the Art of Writing* (Glencoe, IL: Free Press, 1952), 32.

78. For examples of this, see Jim Lobe, "Leo Strauss' Philosophy of Deception," *AlterNet*, May 18, 2003, http://www.alternet.org; and Adam Kirsch, "Jonathan Franzen, the Iraq War, and Leo Strauss," *New Republic*, September 22, 2010, http://www.newrepublic.com/.

79. Harry Jaffa, *How to Think about the American Revolution* (Durham, NC: Carolina Academic Press, 1978), 41.

80. Paul Greenberg, "Martin Luther King: The Radical as Conservative," *Town Hall*, January 21, 2008, http://townhall.com/.

81. Willmoore Kendall and George W. Carey, *The Basic Symbols of the American Political Tradition* (1970; reprint, Baton Rouge: Louisiana State University Press, 1995), 9.

82. Nash, *Conservative Intellectual Movement*, 459–460.

83. Ibid., 319.

84. Niel Bjerre-Poulsen, *Right Face: Organizing the American Conservative Movement, 1945–65* (Copenhagen: Museum Tusculanum Press, 2002), 182.

85. Bart Barnes, "Barry Goldwater, GOP Hero, Dies," *Washington Post*, May 30, 1998, http://www.washingtonpost.com/.

86. Barry Goldwater, July 16, 1964, acceptance speech for nomination for president, 1964 Republican National Convention, San Francisco, CA, http://www.washingtonpost.com/.

87. Richard A. Viguerie, *The New Right: We're Ready to Lead* (Falls Church, VA: Viguerie, 1980), 26–28.

88. Ibid., 34.

89. Robert D. Novak, *The Prince of Darkness: 50 Years Reporting in Washington* (New York: Three Rivers, 2008), 225.

90. Kevin P. Phillips, *The Emerging Republican Majority* (New Rochelle, NY: Arlington House, 1969), 25.

91. Ibid., 37.

92. Nash, *Conservative Intellectual Movement*, 87.

93. The Republican majority in the Senate was short lived, as the defection of Jim Jeffords of Vermont once again led to a Democratic majority in the Senate. However, in 2002, the Republicans again won sufficient Senate seats to have a majority in both chambers.

94. The Project for a New American Century, for example, had called for regime change in Iraq during Bill Clinton's presidency.

95. Hugh Hewitt, *Painting the Map Red: The Fight to Create a Permanent Republican Majority* (Washington, DC: Regnery, 2006).

Chapter 2. Defining Conservatism's Boundaries

1. Jason Zengerle, "Grover's Best Trick," *New York Magazine*, November 30, 2012, http://nymag.com/.

2. According to Norquist, American politics is largely the competition between two competing camps: the Leave Us Alone Coalition and the Takings Coalition. The former camp, which aligns with Republicans, is primarily motivated by a desire for government to leave them alone on one or more crucial issue—gun owners, antitax crusaders, home schoolers, and the like. The latter coalition, which aligns with Democrats, is primarily motivated by a desire for government to provide them with greater resources or to put in place more regulations—labor unions, ethnic lobbies, environmentalists, and so on. Grover Norquist, *Leave Us Alone: Getting the Government's Hands off Our Money, Our Guns, Our Lives* (New York, Harper Collins, 2008).

3. Specifically, there has been a trend toward greater party-line voting within Congress, and the days of liberal Republicans and conservative Democrats playing important roles in US politics appear to be permanently behind us. For an excellent overview of this phenomenon, I recommend Nolan McCarty, Keith T. Poole, and Howard Rosenthal, *Polarized America: The Dance of Ideology and Unequal Riches* (Cambridge, MA: MIT Press, 2006).

4. For an excellent summary of the trends toward "correct" voting according to ideology in the US electorate—correct in the sense that conservatives vote for Republicans and liberals vote for Democrats—I recommend Matthew Levendusky,

The Partisan Sort: How Liberals Became Democrats and Conservatives Became Republican (Chicago: University of Chicago Press, 2009).

5. Samuel T. Francis, *Beautiful Losers: Essays on the Failure of American Conservatism* (Columbia: University of Missouri Press, 1993), 222–223.

6. David Frum, *Dead Right* (New York: Basic Books, 1994), 124.

7. Jonathan M. Schoenwald, *A Time for Choosing: The Rise of Modern American Conservatism* (New York: Oxford University Press, 2001), 78.

8. Bjerre-Poulsen, *Right Face*, 191.

9. Barbara S. Stone, "The John Birch Society: A Profile," *Journal of Politics* 36 (1974): 187.

10. Schoenwald, *Time for Choosing*, 81.

11. Ibid.

12. Robert Welch, *The Blue Book* (Belmont, MA: Western Islands, 1959), 37.

13. Ibid.

14. Schoenwald, *Time for Choosing*, 75.

15. William F. Buckley, *Getting It Right* (Washington, DC: Regnery, 2003).

16. William F. Buckley, "Goldwater, the John Birch Society, and Me," *Commentary*, March 3, 2008, http://www.commentarymagazine.com/.

17. Ibid.

18. William F. Buckley Jr., "The Question of Robert Welch," *National Review*, February 13, 1962, 83–88.

19. Bjerre-Poulsen, *Right Face*, 206–207.

20. Ibid.

21. James Burnham, "Get US Out," *National Review*, October 19, 1965, 927.

22. "Frequently Asked Questions," John Birch Society, http://www.jbs.org/.

23. John F. McManus, *William F. Buckley: Pied Piper for the Establishment* (Appleton, WI: John Birch Society, 2002).

24. William F. Buckley and L. Brent Bozell, *McCarthy and His Enemies: The Record and Its Meaning* (Chicago: Regnery, 1954).

25. Jennifer Burns, *Goddess of the Market: Ayn Rand and the American Right* (New York: Oxford University Press, 2009), 9–19.

26. "*Playboy* Interview: Ayn Rand," *Playboy* 11 (March 1964): 36.

27. Ayn Rand, *The Letters of Ayn Rand*, ed. Michael S. Berliner (New York: Plume, 1997), 13.

28. Burns, *Goddess of the Market*, 106.

29. Ibid., 144.

30. Ayn Rand, *Atlas Shrugged* (1957; reprint, New York: Signet, 1996), 951.

31. Whereas many radical libertarians are openly hostile to the American military, Rand was not antiwar per se, though she did defend the draft. When it comes to the actual practice of war against a totalitarian state, Rand stated her belief that there should be no distinction between civilians and the military, as civilians all bear responsibility for the establishment of such a state. Thus, Rand had no moral objection to events like the bombing of Hiroshima or Dresden, and she did not oppose such tactics in a hypothetical war with the Soviet Union: "If we go to war with Russia, I hope the *innocent* are destroyed along with the guilty. There aren't many innocent people there; those who do exist are not in the big cities, but mainly in concentration camps. Nobody has to put up with aggression, and surrender his right

to self-defense, for fear of hurting anyone else, innocent or guilty. When someone comes at you with a gun, if you have an ounce of self-esteem, you answer with force, never mind who he is or who is standing behind him. If he's out to destroy you, you owe it to your life to defend yourself." Ayn Rand, *Ayn Rand Answers: The Best of Her Q&A*, ed. Robert Mayhew (New York: Penguin Books, 2005), 94–95.

32. Whittaker Chambers, "Big Sister is Watching You," *National Review*, December 28, 1957, 594–596.

33. Whittaker Chambers, *Cold Friday* (New York: Random House, 1964), 69.

34. Chambers, "Big Sister is Watching You," 594.

35. Russell Kirk, "To the Editor," *National Review*, February 1, 1958, 118.

36. Burns, *Goddess of the Market*, 176–177.

37. David Kelley, "Rand versus Hayek on Abstraction," *Reason Papers* 33 (2011): 12–30.

38. Nash, *Conservative Intellectual Movement*, 241–242.

39. In his obituary for Murray Rothbard, for example, Buckley said Rothbard "had defective judgment," that he "couldn't handle moral priorities," and that he was a victim of "deranging scrupulosity." William F. Buckley, "Murray Rothbard: RIP," *National Review*, February 6, 1995, 19.

40. William F. Buckley Jr., "Ayn Rand: RIP," *National Review*, April 2, 1982, 380.

41. Jane Mayer, "Ayn Rand Joins the Ticket," *New Yorker*, August 11, 2012, http://www.newyorker.com/.

42. Mark Gerson, *The Neoconservative Vision: From the Cold War Years to the Culture Wars* (New York: Madison Books, 1996), 312.

43. Michael M. Jordan, "Bradford, M. E.," *First Principles*, November 17, 2010, http://www.firstprinciplesjournal.com/.

44. Paul V. Murphy, *The Rebuke of History: The Southern Agrarians and American Conservative Thought* (Chapel Hill: University of North Carolina Press, 2001), 246.

45. George F. Will, "A Shrill Assault on Mr. Lincoln," *Washington Post*, November 29, 1981, http://www.washingtonpost.com/.

46. Gerson, *Neoconservative Vision*, 313.

47. Stephen J. Tonsor, "Why I Too Am Not a Neoconservative," *National Review*, June 20, 1986, 54.

48. Gerson, *Neoconservative Vision*, 315.

49. Frum, *Dead Right*, 130.

50. Alexander P. Lamis, *The Two-Party South* (New York: Oxford University Press, 1990), 26.

51. Lance Hill, "Nazi Race Doctrine in the Political Thought of David Duke," in *The Emergence of David Duke and the Politics of Race*, ed. Douglas D. Rose (Chapel Hill: University of North Carolina Press, 1992), 94–112.

52. William V. Moore, "David Duke: The White Knight," in Rose, *Emergence of David Duke*, 41–58.

53. Peter Applebome, "Ex-Klansman Puts New Racial Politics to the Test," *New York Times*, June 18, 1990, http://www.nytimes.com/.

54. Moore, "David Duke," 55.

55. Robert Shogan, "GOP Facing a 'Nightmare' after Duke Makes Runoff: Politics: Republicans Can Back Ex-Klansman or a Partisan Democrat. Party's Status in the South Is at Stake," *Los Angeles Times*, October 21, 1991, http://latimes.com/.

56. Ibid.

57. Roberto Suro, "The 1991 Election: Louisiana; Bush Denounces Duke as Racist and Charlatan," *New York Times*, November 7, 1991, http://www.nytimes.com/.

58. Ben C. Toledano, "The Lull within the Lull," *National Review*, October 21, 1991, 21–22.

59. William F. Buckley, "The David Duke Problem," *National Review*, December 2, 1991, 62–63.

60. Kristol, *Neo-Conservatism*, 346.

61. Nash, *Conservative Intellectual Movement*, 591.

62. George H. W. Bush, August 18, 1988, acceptance speech for nomination for president, 1988 Republican National Convention, New Orleans, LA, http://www.presidency.ucsb.edu/.

63. Patrick J. Buchanan, "America First—and Second, and Third," *National Interest*, March 1990, 77–82.

64. Timothy Stanley, *The Crusader: The Tumultuous Times of Pat Buchanan* (New York: St. Martin's Press, 2012), 129.

65. George H. W. Bush, "Address before a Joint Session of Congress (September 11, 1990)," Miller Center, University of Virginia, http://millercenter.org/.

66. "Pat Buchanan's Small World," *New York Times*, January 13, 1992, http://www.nytimes.com/.

67. Stanley, *Crusader*, 138.

68. Charles Krauthammer, a prominent neoconservative, stated in 1992 that "the real problem with Buchanan (as Jacob Weisberg suggested two years ago in the *New Republic*) is not that his instincts are antisemitic but that they are, in various and distinct ways, fascistic." Charles Krauthammer, "Buchanan Explained," *Washington Post*, March 1, 1992, http://www.washingtonpost.com/.

69. Joshua Muravchik, "Patrick J. Buchanan and the Jews," *Commentary*, January 1991, 31.

70. William F. Buckley Jr., "In Search of Anti-Semitism," *National Review*, December 31, 1991, 56.

71. Gerson, *Neoconservative Vision*, 319–320.

72. Stanley, *Crusader*, 211.

73. Buckley, "In Search of Anti-Semitism," 23.

74. Ibid.

75. Unfortunately, Gerson did not provide a citation for this, so I am unable to independently verify whether he actually wrote this statement. Gerson, *Neoconservative Vision*, 307.

76. Ibid.

77. John Judis, "The Conservative Wars," *New Republic*, August 11 and 18, 1986.

78. Jeffrey Hart, *The Making of the American Conservative Mind: National Review and Its Times* (Wilmington, DE: Intercollegiate Studies Institute, 2005), 322.

79. Ibid., 323.

80. Ibid.

81. Joseph Sobran, "'Getting to Know WFB': Joe Sobran's Last Testament," VDARE.com, October 3, 2010, https://www.vdare.com/.

82. Samuel T. Francis, *Power and History: The Political Thought of James Burnham* (Lanham, MD: University Press of America, 1984).

83. Francis, *Beautiful Losers*, 227.

84. Samuel T. Francis, *Illegal Immigration: A Threat to US Security* (Washington, DC: Institute for Security and Conflict Studies, 1986).

85. Murphy, *Rebuke of History*, 242.

86. Dinesh D'Souza, "Racism: It's a White (and Black) Thing," *Washington Post*, September 24, 1995, http://www.washingtonpost.com/.

87. Samuel T. Francis. "Morality Not the Only Target on Monday Night Football," VDARE.com, November 26, 2004, https://www.vdare.com/.

88. "Presidential Debate Excerpts: Gov. George W. Bush vs. Vice President Al Gore," *PBS Newshour*, October 12, 2000, http://www.pbs.org/.

89. David Frum, "Unpatriotic Conservatives: A War against America," *National Review*, April 7, 2003, 32–40, quotation at 32.

90. Damon Linker, "Richard John Neuhaus and the Perils of Theologically Motivated Hyper-Partisanship," *The Week*, March 13, 2015, http://theweek.com/.

91. Hart, *Making of the American Conservative Mind*, 356.

✓ 92. John Derbyshire, "The Talk: The Non-Black Version," *Taki's Magazine*, April 5, 2012, http://takimag.com/.

93. Rich Lowry, "Parting Ways," *National Review Online*, April 7, 2012, http://www.nationalreview.com/.

94. Rich Lowry, "Regarding Robert Weissberg," *National Review Online*, April 10, 2012, http://www.nationalreview.com/.

 95. For example, the essay stated the following: "The president knows that if it is true that African-American males are viewed suspiciously, it is probably because statistically they commit a disproportionate amount of violent crime." Victor Davis Hanson, "Facing the Facts about Race," *National Review Online*, July 23, 2013, http://www.nationalreview.com/.

96. Camille Dodero, "Just How Racist Do You Have To Be for *National Review* to Fire You?" *Gawker*, July 24, 2013, http://gawker.com/.

97. Aaron Blake, "Jason Richwine Resigns from Heritage," *Washington Post*, May 10, 2013, http://www.washingtonpost.com/.

98. Greg Pollowitz, "L'Affaire Richwine," *National Review Online*, May 10, 2013, http://www.nationalreview.com/.

99. Jason Richwine, "About That Dissertation," *National Review Online*, May 20, 2013, http://www.nationalreview.com/.

100. Katie Glueck, "Rand Paul Aide Slammed after Report," *Politico*, July 9, 2013, http://www.politico.com/.

101. W. James Antle III, "Southern Avenger No More: Rand Paul Aide Jack Hunter Leaves Staff, Returns to Punditry," *Daily Caller*, July 21, 2013, http://dailycaller.com/.

102. Ibid.

103. Kirk, *Politics of Prudence*, 180.

104. David Welch, "Where Have You Gone, Bill Buckley?" *New York Times*, December 3, 2012, http://www.nytimes.com/.

105. Geoffrey Kabaservice, "What William F. Buckley Would Think of Today's GOP," *New Republic*, April 2, 2012, http://www.newrepublic.com/.

106. Jeremy Lott, "Like William F. Buckley, the Tea Party Is Taking the Long View," *American Spectator*, September 17, 2010, http://spectator.org/.

107. Rick Perlstein, "Why Conservatives Are Still Crazy After All These Years," *Rolling Stone*, March 1, 2012, http://www.rollingstone.com/.

108. Valerie Richardson, "Stop the Presses! *Human Events* to Shutter Newspaper after 70 Years," *Washington Times*, February 27, 2013, http://www.washingtontimes.com/.

109. Damon Linker, "Is *National Review* Doomed?" *The Week*, January 30, 2014, http://theweek.com/.

110. Jonah Goldberg, "L'Affaire Coulter," *National Review Online*, October 2, 2001, http://www.nationalreview.com/.

Chapter 3. Small Is Beautiful

1. Murphy, *Rebuke of History*, 12–13.

2. Twelve Southerners, *I'll Take My Stand: The South and the Agrarian Tradition*, 75th anniversary ed. (Baton Rouge: Louisiana State University Press, 2006), xlii.

3. Ibid.

4. Ibid., li.

5. For example, in one of the first essays, we find remarks such as the following: "Slavery, as we shall see, was part of the agrarian system, but only one element and not an essential one. To say that the irrepressible conflict was between slavery and freedom is either to fail to grasp the nature and magnitude of the conflict, or else to make use of deliberate deception by employing a shibboleth to win the uninformed and unthinking to the support of a sinister undertaking." Frank Lawrence Owsley, "The Irrepressible Conflict," in Twelve Southerners, *I'll Take My Stand*, 73.

6. Ibid., 77.

7. Andrew Nelson Lytle, "The Hind Tilt," in Twelve Southerners, *I'll Take My Stand*, 203.

8. Murphy, *Rebuke of History*, 137–138.

9. Peter Viereck, "The Rootless 'Roots': Defects in the New Conservatism," *Antioch Review* 15 (1955): 218.

10. Murphy, *Rebuke of History*, 168.

11. Willmoore Kendall, "How to Read Richard Weaver," *Intercollegiate Review* 2 (1965): 78.

12. Richard Weaver, "Integration Is Communization," *National Review*, July 13, 1957, 67–68.

13. Wendell Berry, *Jayber Crow* (Washington, DC: Counterpoint, 2000), 351.

14. Wendell Berry, "A Citizen's Response to 'The National Security Strategy of the United States of America,'" *Orion*, March/April 2003, http://www.orionmagazine.org/.

15. Wendell Berry, *The Art of the Commonplace: The Agrarian Essays of Wendell Berry* (Berkeley, CA: Counterpoint, 2002), 178.

16. Ibid., 179.

17. Ibid., 167.

18. Wendell Berry, "Faustian Economics," *Harper's*, May 2008, 35–42.

19. Allan Carlson, "Wendell Berry and the Twentieth-Century Agrarian 'Se-

ries,'" in *Wendell Berry: Life and Work*, ed. Jason Peters (Lexington: University Press of Kentucky, 2007), 96.

20. Berry, *Art of the Commonplace*, 47.

21. Ibid., 52.

22. Ibid., 61.

23. Ibid., 63.

24. Ibid., 63–64.

25. Robert Nisbet, *The Sociological Tradition*, 6th ed. (New Brunswick, NJ: Transaction, 2004), 47.

26. Robert Nisbet, *The Quest for Community*, background ed. (Wilmington, DE: Intercollegiate Studies Institute, 2010), 259.

27. Ibid., 233.

28. Ibid., 234.

29. Ibid., 247.

30. Ross Douthat, "The Age of Individualism," *New York Times*, March 15, 2004, http://www.nytimes.com/.

31. Ross Douthat, introduction to Nisbet, *Quest for Community*, viii.

32. Robert Nisbet, *Conservatism: Dream and Reality*, 4th ed. (New Brunswick, NJ: Transaction, 2008), 111.

33. Nisbet, *Quest for Community*, 221.

34. Ibid.

35. Christopher Lasch, *The Revolt of the Elites and the Betrayal of Democracy* (New York: Norton, 1995), 109–110.

36. Paul Gottfried, *Encounters: My Life with Nixon, Marcuse, and Other Friends and Teachers* (Wilmington, DE: Intercollegiate Studies Institute, 2009), 181.

37. Christopher Lasch, *The Culture of Narcissism: American Life in an Age of Diminishing Expectations* (New York: Warner Books, 1979), 22.

38. Ibid., 267–268.

39. Ibid., 308.

40. Ibid., 370.

41. Ibid., 387–395.

42. Lasch, *Revolt of the Elites*, 44.

43. Ibid., 4.

44. Ibid., 46.

45. Christopher Lasch, *The True and Only Heaven: Progress and Its Critics* (New York: Norton, 1991), 17.

46. Ibid.

47. Lasch, *Revolt of the Elites*, 9.

48. Ibid., 215.

49. Christopher Lasch, "What's Wrong With the Right?" *Tikkun* 1 (1987): 29.

50. Lasch, *Revolt of the Elites*, 96.

51. Ibid., 106.

52. Ibid., 22.

53. Lillian Rubin, "A Feminist Response to Lasch," *Tikkun* 1 (1987): 89–91.

54. Richard Florida, *The Rise of the Creative Class* (New York: Basic Books, 2002).

55. John Zmirak, *Wilhelm Röpke: Swiss Localist, Global Economist* (Wilmington, DE: Intercollegiate Studies Institute, 2001), 45.

56. Wilhelm Röpke, *The Social Crisis of Our Time*, trans. E. W. Dickes (1942; reprint, New York: G. P. Putnam's Sons, 1947), 25.

57. Zmirak, *Wilhelm Röpke*, 148.

58. Wilhelm Röpke, *A Humane Economy*, trans. Elizabeth Henderson (1958; reprint, Chicago: Regnery, 1960), 36.

59. Ibid., 41.

60. Röpke, *Social Crisis*, 45.

61. Röpke, *Humane Economy*, 229.

62. Wilhelm Röpke, *Civitas Humana: The Moral Foundations of Civil Society*, trans. Cyril Spencer Fox (1944; reprint, New Brunswick, NJ: Transaction, 1996), 154.

63. Zmirak, *Wilhelm Röpke*, 179.

64. Röpke, *Humane Economy*, 8.

65. E. F. Schumacher, *Small Is Beautiful: A Study of Economics as if People Mattered* (London: Blond and Briggs, 1973), 54.

66. Ibid., 62.

67. Ibid., 64.

68. Ibid., 59.

69. Ibid.

70. Schumacher noted that Buddhism is not the only religious system that was congruent with his economic thinking: "The choice of Buddhism for this purpose is purely incidental; the teachings of Christianity, Islam, or Judaism could have been used just as well as those of any other of the great Eastern traditions." Ibid., 47.

71. Ibid., 49.

72. Ibid., 52.

73. For an example, see Jay Nordlinger, "The New Colossus," *National Review Online*, April 5, 2004, http://www.nationalreview.com/.

74. Betsy Woodruff, "Palin Takes a Big Gulp," *National Review Online*, March 16, 2013, http://www.nationalreview.com/.

75. Rod Dreher, *Crunchy Cons: How Birkenstocked Burkeans, Gun-Loving Organic Gardeners, Evangelical Free-Range Farmers, Hip Homeschooling Mamas, Right-Wing Nature Lovers, and Their Diverse Tribe of Countercultural Conservatives Plan to Save America (Or at Least the Republican Party)* (New York: Crown Forum, 2006).

76. Ibid., 10.

77. Ibid., 1–2.

78. Ibid., 31.

79. Ibid., 25.

80. Jonah Goldberg, "Crunchy Conservatism, Reconsidered," *National Review Online*, October 8, 2002, http://www.nationalreview.com/.

81. Florence King, "Sing-Song Conservatism," *American Spectator*, July/August 2006, 73–75.

82. Rod Dreher, "Benedict Option," *American Conservative*, December 12, 2013, http://www.theamericanconservative.com/.

83. Bill Kauffman, "My Pen Pal Gore Vidal," *American Conservative*, September 14, 2012, http://www.theamericanconservative.com/.

84. Bill Kauffman, *Look Homeward, America: In Search of Reactionary Radicals and Front-Porch Anarchists* (Wilmington, DE: Intercollegiate Studies Institute, 2006), xii.

85. Bill Kauffman, *Dispatches from the Muckdog Gazette: A Mostly Affectionate Account of Small Town's Fight to Survive* (New York: Henry Holt, 2002).

86. Ibid., 199.

87. Kauffman, *Look Homeward, America,* 172.

88. Bill Kauffman, *Ain't My America: The Long, Noble History of Anti-War Conservatism and Middle American Anti-Imperialism* (New York: Metropolitan Books, 2008).

89. Ibid., 32.

90. Ibid., 47–52.

91. Allan Carlson, *The New Agrarian Mind: The Movement Toward Decentralist Thought in Twentieth-Century America* (New Brunswick, NJ: Transaction, 2000).

92. David Riesman, Nathan Glazer, and Reuel Denney, *The Lonely Crowd* (New Haven, CT: Yale University Press, 1961), 26.

93. William H. Frey, "The Great American Migration Slowdown: Regional and Metropolitan Dimensions" (Washington, DC: Brookings Institution, 2009).

94. Patrick J. Carr and Maria J. Kefalas, *Hollowing Out the Middle: The Rural Brain Drain and What It Means for America* (Boston, MA: Boston Press, 2009).

Chapter 4. Godless Conservatism

1. Chambers, *Witness,* 9.

2. Kirk, *Politics of Prudence,* 17.

3. Ibid., 199.

4. F. A. Hayek, *The Fatal Conceit: The Errors of Socialism* (Chicago: University of Chicago Press, 1988), 137.

5. William F. Buckley, introduction to *Have You Ever Seen a Dream Walking?,* ed. William F. Buckley (Indianapolis, IN: Bobbs-Merrill, 1970), xxix.

6. Ibid.

7. Laura R. Olson and John C. Green, "The Worship-Attendance Gap," in *Beyond Red State, Blue State: Electoral Gaps in the Twenty-First Century American Electorate,* ed. Laura R. Olson and John C. Green (Upper Saddle River, NJ: Pearson Prentice Hall), 41.

8. Robert D. Putnam and David E. Campbell, *American Grace: How Religion Divides and Unites Us* (New York: Simon & Schuster, 2010), 384–388.

9. Kendall and Carey, *Basic Symbols,* 138.

10. Brooke Allen, *Moral Minority: Our Skeptical Founding Fathers* (Chicago, IL: Ivan R. Dee, 2006).

11. Ibid., 32–33.

12. Ibid., 59.

13. Allen C. Guelzo, *Abraham Lincoln: Redeemer President* (Grand Rapids, MI: William B. Eerdmans, 1999), 447.

14. For a thorough discussion of how human behavior is largely biologically determined, and therefore the doctrine that the human mind possesses no intrinsic characteristics is wrong, I recommend Steven Pinker's *The Blank Slate: The Modern Denial of Human Nature* (New York: Penguin Books, 2002).

15. Theodore Dalrymple, "Curing the Soul," *City Journal,* July 15, 2004, http://www.city-journal.org/.

16. James Madison, "Federalist 10," in *The Federalist Papers* (1887; reprint, New York: Barnes and Noble Classics, 2006), 53.

GEORGE

17. In this interview, Will first described himself as a "heathen" but declared, "I'm not decisive enough to be an atheist." He settled on being described as an agnostic. *Colbert Report*, June 3, 2008.

18. Will actually brought up the subject in the context of discussing the 2005 film *The March of the Penguins:* "'March of the Penguins' raises this question: If an Intelligent Designer designed nature, why did it decide to make breeding so tedious for those penguins? The movie documents the 70-mile march of thousands of Antarctic penguins from the sea to an icy breeding place barren of nutrition. These perhaps intelligently but certainly oddly designed birds march because they cannot fly. They cannot even march well, being most at home in the sea." "Penguins, People and a Grisly Bear Tale," *Washington Post*, August 28, 2005, http://www.washington post.com/.

19. Here is the full quotation: "I am a member of a cohort that the Pew public-opinion surveys call the 'nones.' Today, when Americans are asked their religious affiliation, 20%—a large and growing portion—say 'none.'" George F. Will, "Religion and the American Republic," *National Affairs* 16 (Summer 2013), http://www .nationalaffairs.com/.

20. Ibid.

21. For an example, see Charles C. W. Cook, "Stand with . . . Death," *National Review Online*, June 27, 2013, http://www.nationalreview.com/.

22. Charles Krauthammer, "How to Debunk the 'War on Women,'" *National Review Online*, January 30, 2014, http://www.nationalreview.com/.

23. John Derbyshire, "God and Me," *National Review Online*, October 30, 2006, http://www.nationalreview.com/.

24. John Derbyshire, "A Frigid and Pitiless Dogma," *New English Review*, June 2006, http://www.newenglishreview.org/; review of Ramesh Ponnuru, *Party of Death: The Democrats, the Media, the Courts, and the Disregard for Human Life* (Washington, DC: Regnery, 2006).

25. Craig Bannister, "Bozell Denounces CPAC: 'No Conservative Should Have Anything to Do with This,'" CNSNews.com, February 25, 2014, http://cnsnews .com/.

26. Charles C. W. Cook, "Yes, Atheism and Conservatism Are Compatible," *National Review Online*, February 26, 2014, http://www.nationalreview.com/.

27. Razib Khan, "Ten Questions for Heather Mac Donald," *Gene Expression*, January 2, 2007, http://www.gnxp.com/.

28. S. E. Cupp, *Losing Our Religion: Why the Liberal Media Want to Tell You What to Think, Where to Pray, and How to Live* (New York: Threshold Editions, 2010).

29. For example, she has noted that the seemingly arbitrary degree to which some prayers are clearly answered and others are ignored is evidence that the practice has no real value: "I take it that believers do not ascribe such inconsistent results to capriciousness on God's part, but rather to their own limited capacities to understand God's ways: 'Thy Will be done.' But why continue directing any psychic energy to a being so lacking in sympathetic correspondence to human needs and values. It will not do to say: 'God does respond to our prayers, but in ways that we cannot fathom.' Saving a child from cancer and letting a child die from cancer cannot both be a sympathetic response to prayer; if we had wanted a stricken child to die in order to secure an earlier entry to heaven, we would have said so. And if pre-

ATHEIST

mature death from cancer is such a boon, why doesn't a loving God provide it to one and all?" Heather Mac Donald, "The Conundrum of Prayer," *Secular Right*, June 5, 2009, http://secularright.org/.

30. "President: Full Results," *CNN Politics*, December 10, 2012, https://web archive.org/web/20140715213318/http://www.cnn.com/election/2012/results/race /president.

31. Theodore Dalrymple, "Why Religion is Good for Us," *New Statesman*, April 21, 2003, http://www.newstatesman.com/.

32. Theodore Dalrymple, "What the New Atheists Don't See," *City Journal*, Autumn 2007, http://www.city-journal.org/.

33. Razib Khan, *"The God Delusion*—Amongst the Unbelievers," *Gene Expression*, October 4, 2006, http://blogs.discovermagazine.com/.

34. "What Is Secular Right?" *Secular Right*, November 2008, http://secularright .org/.

35. Kathleen Parker, "Giving Up on God," *Washington Post*, November 19, 2008, http://www.washingtonpost.com/.

36. For example, Amy Sullivan wrote the following in the *Washington Monthly:* "[Romney's] obstacle is the evangelical base—a voting bloc that now makes up 30 percent of the Republican electorate and that wields particular influence in primary states like South Carolina and Virginia. Just as it is hard to overestimate the importance of evangelicalism in the modern Republican Party, it is nearly impossible to overemphasize the problem evangelicals have with Mormonism. Evangelicals don't have the same vague anti-LDS prejudice that some Americans do. For them it's a doctrinal thing, based on very specific theological disputes that can't be overcome by personality or charm or even shared positions on social issues. Romney's journalistic boosters either don't understand these doctrinal issues or try to sidestep them. But ignoring them won't make them go away. To evangelicals, Mormonism isn't just another religion. It's a cult." "Mitt Romney's Evangelical Problem," *Washington Monthly*, September 25, 2005, http://www.washingtonmonthly.com/.

37. George Hawley, "Attitudes toward Mormons and Voting Behavior in the 2012 Presidential Election," *Politics and Religion* 8 (2015): 60–85.

38. Jim Wallis, "The Religious Right's Era Is Over," *Time*, February 16, 2007, http://time.com/.

Chapter 5. Ready for Prime Time?

1. Brian Doherty, *Radicals for Capitalism: A Freewheeling History of the Modern American Libertarian Movement* (New York: Public Affairs, 2007), 21.

2. Murray Rothbard, *For a New Liberty* (1973; reprint, Auburn, AL: Ludwig von Mises Institute, 2006), 27.

3. Ibid., 33–34.

4. John Locke, "An Essay Concerning the True Original Extent and End of Civil Government" (1690), in *Social Contract*, ed. E. Barker (New York: Oxford University Press, 1948), 17–18.

5. Ludvig von Mises, *Liberalism* (1929; reprint, New York: Foundation for Economic Education, 1985), 19.

6. Bryan Caplan, "The Austrian Search for Realistic Foundations," *Southern Economic Journal* 65 (1999): 823–838.

7. Robert Nozick, *Anarchy, State, and Utopia* (1974; reprint, New York: Basic Books, 1999), ix.

8. Ibid., 169.

9. I should note that it is not always easy to distinguish libertarian from conservative think tanks, particularly if a think tank is focused exclusively on domestic economic issues, which is frequently the case. Because conservatives and libertarians are typically in agreement on economic policies, a think tank that only focused on these matters and ignored foreign policy and social issues could be accurately described as libertarian or economically conservative.

10. Caplan makes this argument in the following way: "My question: How is mandatory discrimination against foreigners less wrong than mandatory discrimination against blacks, women, or Jews? The leading rationale is that 'we should take care of our own first.' That might be a good argument against sending foreigners welfare checks. But it's an Orwellian argument for stopping immigrants from working or renting here. Minding your own business when two strangers trade with each other is not a form of charity." Bryan Caplan, "America Should Open Its Borders: My Opening Statement for the *Reason* Immigration Debate," *Library of Economics and Liberty*, April 23, 2014, http://econlog.econlib.org/.

11. Manuel Klausner, "Inside Ronald Reagan: A *Reason* Interview," *Reason*, July 1975, http://reason.com/.

12. Kirk, *Politics of Prudence*, 165–166.

13. Nick Gillespie, "D'Souza on Libertarians: Gay or Drugged-out or Loose or All Three," *Reason*, December 21, 2007, http://reason.com/.

14. Jonah Goldberg, "Libertarians, in Theory," *National Review Online*, August 6, 1999, http://www.nationalreview.com/.

15. Doherty, *Radicals for Capitalism*, 17.

16. Ibid., 301.

17. George Nash refers to the book as "one of the most significant works of conservative scholarship of the 1960s." Nash, *Conservative Intellectual Movement*, 447.

18. Milton Friedman, *Capitalism and Freedom*, 40th anniversary ed. (Chicago: University of Chicago Press, 2002).

19. Ibid., 110.

20. Milton Friedman and Rose Friedman, *Two Lucky People* (Chicago: University of Chicago Press, 1998), 381.

21. For example, the 2012 Republican platform included the following language: "The Republican Party is the party of fresh and innovative ideas in education. We support options for learning, including home schooling and local innovations like single-sex classes, full-day school hours, and year-round schools. School choice—whether through charter schools, open enrollment requests, college lab schools, virtual schools, career and technical education programs, vouchers, or tax credits—is important for all children, especially for families with children trapped in failing schools. Getting those youngsters into decent learning environments and helping them to realize their full potential is the greatest civil rights challenge of our time. We support the promotion of local career and technical educational programs and entrepreneurial programs that have been supported by leaders in industry and will retrain and retool the American workforce, which is the best in the world. A young person's ability to achieve in school must be based on his or her God-given

talent and motivation, not an address, zip code, or economic status." GOP, https://www.gop.com/.

22. Brian Doherty, "The Economist and the Dictator," *Reason*, December 15, 2006, http://reason.com/.

23. For example, see Paul Krugman, "Fantasies of the Chicago Boys," *New York Times*, March 3, 2010, http://www.nytimes.com/.

24. "America's Largest Private Companies, 2013," *Forbes*, December 18, 2013, http://www.forbes.com/.

25. Doherty, *Radicals for Capitalism*, 414.

26. Ibid., 410.

27. Jane Mayer, "Covert Operations: The Billionaire Brothers Who Are Waging a War against Obama," *New Yorker*, August 30, 2010, http://www.newyorker.com/.

28. Americans for Prosperity, "About Americans for Prosperity," http://americansforprosperity.org/.

29. Tom Hamburger, Kathleen Hennessey, and Neela Banerjee, "Koch Brothers Now at Heart of GOP Power," *Los Angeles Times*, February 6, 2011, http://latimes.com/.

30. George Monboit defines AstroTurf campaigns as follows: "An Astroturf campaign is a fake grassroots movement: it purports to be a spontaneous uprising of concerned citizens, but in reality it is founded and funded by elite interests. Some Astroturf campaigns have no grassroots component at all. Others catalyse and direct real mobilisations." "The Tea Party Movement: Deluded and Inspired by Billionaires," *Guardian*, October 25, 2010, http://www.theguardian.com/.

31. Ibid.

32. Washington Free Beacon Staff, "DWS: Liar," *Washington Free Beacon*, June 20, 2012, http://freebeacon.com/.

33. Lawrence V. Cott, "Cato and the Invisible Finger," *National Review*, June 8, 1979, 740–742.

34. David Gordon, "The Kochtopus vs. Murray Rothbard," LewRockwell.com, April 22, 2008, http://archive.lewrockwell.com/.

35. Doherty, *Radicals for Capitalism*, 412.

36. David Gordon, "Why the Koch Brothers Went After Murray Rothbard," LewRockwell.com, March 10, 2011, http://www.lewrockwell.com/.

37. Nina J. Easton, "Making America Work: RED WHITE AND SMALL: Ed Crane's Cato Institute Is a Think Tank That Believes the Country Would Work Better if There Was Less Government," *Los Angeles Times*, July 9, 1995, http://latimes.com/.

38. Doherty, *Radicals for Capitalism*, 454.

39. Brink Lindsey, "Terrorism's Fellow Travelers," *Cato Policy Report*, November/December 2001, 13.

40. Tom Palmer, "Building a Free Society in Iraq," *Cato's Letter*, 3 (2005), 6.

41. Allen McDuffy, "Koch Brothers Sue Cato Institute, President," *Washington Post*, March 1, 2012, http://www.washingtonpost.com/.

42. Justin Logan, "What a Koch Takeover of Cato Would Mean for the Foreign Policy Debate," *American Conservative*, March 6, 2012, http://www.theamericanconservative.com/.

43. David Weigel, "Cato at Peace," *Slate*, June 25, 2012, http://www.slate.com/.

44. Margalit Fox, "Lanny Friedlander, Founder of *Reason* Magazine, Dies at 63," *New York Times*, May 6, 2011, http://www.nytimes.com/.

45. Ibid.

46. Nick Gillespie and Matt Welch, "The Libertarian Moment," *Reason* 40 (December 2008): 62.

47. "35 Heroes of Freedom: Celebrating the People Who Have Made the World Groovier and Groovier since 1968," *Reason* 37 (December 2003): 64–69.

48. Kevin Michael Grace, "Burke versus Reason," *DoubleThink Online*, January 18, 2004, http://americasfuture.org/.

49. Mia L. Sobin, "Millennials Harbor Distrust toward Government, IOP Reports," *Harvard Crimson*, May 2, 2013, http://www.thecrimson.com/.

50. Ron Paul, *Mises and Austrian Economics: A Personal View* (Auburn, AL: Ludwig von Mises Institute, 2004), 4.

51. Ibid., 3.

52. Howard LaFrinchi, "In Former Congressman, Libertarians Think Party Has Best Candidate Ever," *Christian Science Monitor*, September 29, 1987, 3.

53. Eric Dondero, "Ron Paul on the Verge of Going Third Party?" *National Ledger*, January 7, 2008, http://www.nationalledger.com/.

54. S. C. Gwynne, "Dr. No," *Texas Monthly*, October 2001, http://www.texasmonthly.com/.

55. Katherine Q. Seelye, "Web Takes Ron Paul for a Ride," *New York Times*, November 11, 2007, http://www.nytimes.com/.

56. Ron Paul, "Get Out of the WTO," LewRockwell.com, November 17, 2005, http://archive.lewrockwell.com/.

57. Brian Doherty, "Is He Good for the Libertarians?" *Reason*, July 27, 2007, http://reason.com/.

58. James Kirchik, "Angry White Man," *New Republic*, January 8, 2008, http://www.newrepublic.com/.

59. Julian Sanchez and David Weigel, "Who Wrote Ron Paul's Newsletters?" *Reason*, January 16, 2008, http://reason.com/.

60. Rand Paul, "Sen. Paul: My Filibuster Was Just the Beginning," *Washington Post*, March 8, 2013, http://www.washingtonpost.com/.

61. Deborah Solomon, "Tea Time," *New York Times*, March 31, 2010, http://www.nytimes.com/.

62. James Hohman, "Ron Paul Movement Not Ready to Pass the Torch to Rand Paul," *Politico*, August 28, 2012, http://www.politico.com/.

63. Nicholas Confessore, "Rand Paul and Wealthy Libertarians Connect as He Weighs Running," *New York Times*, April 24, 2014, http://www.nytimes.com/.

64. Jerome Tuccille, *Radical Libertarianism: A Right Wing Alternative* (Indianapolis, IN: Bobs-Merrill, 1970).

65. Ibid., 99.

66. Ibid., 103.

67. Ibid., 109.

68. Young Americans for Liberty, "About Young Americans for Liberty," http://www.yaliberty.org/.

69. Young Americans for Liberty, "YAL Statement of Principles," http://www.yaliberty.org/.

70. Fred Roeder, "Alexander McCobin: 'Gay Marriage Is the Civil Rights Issue of 21st Century,'" *Students for Liberty*, March 8, 2014, http://studentsforliberty.org/.

71. Alexander McCobin, "Why Ann Coulter Doesn't Understand Libertarianism," *Daily Caller*, March 19, 2013, http://dailycaller.com/.

72. Ronald P. Formisano, *The Tea Party: A Brief History* (Baltimore, MD: Johns Hopkins University Press, 2012), 8.

73. Juan Williams, "The Surprising Rise of Rep. Ron Paul," FoxNews.com, May 10, 2011, http://www.foxnews.com/.

74. Kate Zernike, "Tea Party Avoids Divisive Social Issues," *New York Times*, March 12, 2010, http://www.nytimes.com/.

75. Seung Min Kim, "Tea Party Leader Backs Immigration Reform," *Politico*, May 14, 2014, http://www.politico.com/.

76. "An Open Letter to RNC Chair Reince Priebus," *Tea Party Immigration Coalition*, http://teapartyimmigrationcoalition.org/.

77. Vanessa Williamson, Theda Skocpol, and John Coggin, "The Tea Party and the Remaking of Republican Conservatism," *Perspectives on Politics* 9 (2011): 27.

Chapter 6. Enemies of the State

1. Rothbard, *For a New Liberty*, 16.

2. Ibid.

3. Randolph Bourne, "The State" (1918), http://fair-use.org/randolph-bourne/the-state/.

4. Randy E. Barnett, "Libertarians on the War," *Wall Street Journal*, July 17, 2007, http://www.wsj.com/.

5. Walter Block, "Randy Barnett: Pro War Libertarian?" LewRockwell.com, July 23, 2007, http://archive.lewrockwell.com/.

6. Justin Raimondo, "Bizarro 'Libertarianism,'" AntiWar.com, July 19, 2007, http://original.antiwar.com/.

7. Caplan has written extensively on this subject, but a good introduction to his thought can be found in "Why Should We Restrict Immigration?" *Cato Journal* 32 (2012): 5–24.

8. Tyler Cowen, "How Immigrants Create More Jobs," *New York Times*, October 30, 2010, http://www.nytimes.com/.

9. Stephen Moore, "What Would Milton Friedman Say?" *Wall Street Journal*, May 29, 2013, http://www.wsj.com/.

10. Stephen Cox, "The Fallacy of Open Immigration," *Liberty*, October 2006, 26–31.

11. Hans-Hermann Hoppe, "Secession, the State, and the Immigration Problem," LewRockwell.com, May 16, 2001, http://www.lewrockwell.com/.

12. David Weigel, "Rand Paul, Telling the Truth," *Washington Post*, May 20, 2010, http://www.washingtonpost.com/.

13. David Bernstein of the Cato Institute noted, "My own view is that the basic federal laws banning discrimination in employment, housing, and public accommodations, as originally conceived in 1964—before the courts and civil rights bureaucracies devised problematic doctrines like 'disparate impact' liability—were relatively benign." Bernstein, "Context Matters: A Better Libertarian Approach to

Antidiscrimination Law," *Cato Unbound*, June 16, 2010, http://www.cato-unbound
.org/. It is worth pointing out, however, that not everyone associated with Cato
agreed with this position. David Miron, also affiliated with Cato, argued against the
aspects of the Civil Rights Act that related to discrimination by private businesses:
"Should libertarians support Title II of the 1964 Civil Rights Act? David Bernstein
believes they should. David's position is understandable, and his arguments are well
crafted. But libertarians should not only oppose Title II; they should shout that opposition from the highest roof tops." Miron went on, "To begin, Title II is a bald-
faced assault on a principle that libertarians hold dear: that private property is private. This means libertarians should be incredibly suspicious of Title II and insist on
an overwhelming case before violating this principle. No such case exists." Miron,
"What Matters Are Consequences, Not Context," *Cato Unbound*, June 23, 2010,
http://www.cato-unbound.org/.

14. As an example, Cathy Young, a contributing editor at *Reason*, wrote the following:

> Most likely, over the long haul, overt discrimination against blacks in the
> private sector would have become socially unacceptable and mostly extinct.
> But could American society have afforded to wait? To answer "yes" is to
> underestimate the urgency of the issue, the evil of Jim Crow. Segregation
> was not merely an inconvenience or a violation of abstract principle but the
> systematic degradation of American citizens who were black. When African-
> American singer Dorothy Dandridge sang in all-white nightclubs, she often had
> to urinate into a cup because she wasn't allowed to use the bathroom.
>
> It's fine to discuss the intellectual merits of free-market and free-association
> arguments against the ban on private discrimination. But the reminder that fifty
> years ago, such obscene practices were not only condoned but socially approved
> in large parts of this country should shock our conscience as Americans. A
> dispassionate or glib attitude on the subject is not a good way to win people
> over. One cannot talk about anti-discrimination law as an infringement on
> liberty and forget that for the first two centuries of America's existence, its
> treatment of blacks was a grotesque stain on its libertarian ideals.

Cathy Young, "Racism, Civil Rights and Libertarianism," *Real Clear Politics*, June 11,
2010, http://www.realclearpolitics.com/.
15. Doherty, *Radicals for Capitalism*, 39.
16. Warren made the following argument, for example: "From the study of this
Individuality, together with our natural instinct for self-preservation, I draw the
conclusion, that each individual should be at all times free to differ from every other
in thought, feeling, word, and deed; and free to differ from himself, or to change
from time to time; in other words, that every one is constituted by nature to be at
all times SOVEREIGN OF HIMSELF OR HERSELF, and every thing that constitutes a part
of his or her Individuality. That society to be harmonious and successful, must be so
constituted that there shall be no demand for an outward show of conformity or uniformity—that no person must have any power over the persons or interests of others; but that every one shall be at all times, the SUPREME LAW UNTO HIMSELF." Josiah

Warren, *Equitable Commerce: A New Development of Principles for the Harmonious Adjustment and Regulation of the Pecuniary, Intellectual, and Moral Intercourse of Mankind, Proposed as Elements of New Society,* 2nd ed. (Utopia, OH: Amos E. Senter, 1849), 8.

17. Ibid., 11.

18. Lysander Spooner, *The Unconstitutionality of Slavery* (1845, 1860), http://lysanderspooner.org/.

19. For example, Spooner declared, "The pretense that the 'abolition of slavery' was either a motive or justification for the war, is a fraud of the same character with that of 'maintaining the national honor.' Who, but such usurpers, robbers, and murderers as they, ever established slavery? Or what government, except one resting upon the sword, like the one we now have, was ever capable of maintaining slavery? And why did these men abolish slavery? Not from any love of liberty in general—not as an act of justice to the black man himself, but only 'as a war measure,' and because they wanted his assistance, and that of his friends, in carrying on the war they had undertaken for maintaining and intensifying that political, commercial, and industrial slavery, to which they have subjected the great body of the people, both black and white. And yet these impostors now cry out that they have abolished the chattel slavery of the black man—although that was not the motive of the war—as if they thought they could thereby conceal, atone for, or justify that other slavery which they were fighting to perpetuate, and to render more rigorous and inexorable than it ever was before. There was no difference of principle—but only of degree—between the slavery they boast they have abolished, and the slavery they were fighting to preserve; for all restraints upon men's natural liberty, not necessary for the simple maintenance of justice, are of the nature of slavery, and differ from each other only in degree." Lysander Spooner, *No Treason: The Constitution of No Authority* (1870), http://lysanderspooner.org/.

20. Spooner wrote (ibid.),

> If it be said that the consent of the *most numerous party*, in a nation, is sufficient to justify the establishment of their power over the less numerous party, it may be answered:
>
> First. That two men have no more natural right to exercise any kind of authority over one, than one has the right to exercise the same authority over two. A man's natural rights are his own, against the whole world; and any infringement on them is a crime, whether committed by one man, calling himself a robber, (or by any other name indicating his true character,) or by millions, calling themselves a government.

21. Wendy McElroy, "Benjamin Tucker, *Liberty*, and Individualist Anarchism," *Independent Review* 2 (1998): 424–425.

22. Ibid., 426.

23. Ibid., 432.

24. Doherty, *Radicals for Capitalism*, 45.

25. Murray Rothbard, "The Spooner–Tucker Doctrine: An Economist's View," *Journal of Libertarian Studies* 20 (2006): 5–15.

26. Ibid., 5.

27. Thomas C. Taylor, *An Introduction to Austrian Economics* (Washington, DC: Cato Institute, 1980), 10.

28. For a short introduction to the Austrian theory of the trade cycle, I recommend Murray Rothbard, "Economic Depressions: Their Cause and Cure," in *The Austrian Theory of the Trade Cycle and Other Essays*, ed. Richard M. Ebeling (Auburn, AL: Ludwig von Mises Institute, 1996), 65–92.

29. Mises argued that this was the key problem with socialism, and one that would be impossible to ever resolve, thus the entire socialist enterprise was doomed to fail: "To prove that economic calculation would be impossible in the socialist community is to prove also that Socialism is impracticable. Everything brought forward in favour of Socialism during the last hundred years, in thousands of writings and speeches, all the blood which has been spilt by the supporters of Socialism, cannot make Socialism workable. The masses may long for it so ardently, innumerable revolutions and wars may be fought over it, still it will never be realized. Every attempt to carry it out will lead to syndicalism or, by some other route, to chaos, which will quickly dissolve the society, based upon division of labour, into tiny autarkous groups." Ludwig von Mises, *Socialism: An Economic and Sociological Analysis* (1922; reprint, New Haven, CT: Yale University Press, 1962), 135.

30. Friedrich Hayek, *The Road to Serfdom* (1944; reprint, New York: Routledge, 2006), 59–60.

31. Ibid., 32.

32. Murray Rothbard, *Rothbard vs. the Philosophers: Unpublished Writings on Hayek, Mises, Strauss, and Polanyi* (Auburn, AL: Ludwig von Mises Institute, 2009), 75–79.

33. Walter Block, "Hayek's *Road to Serfdom*," *Journal of Libertarian Studies* 12 (1996): 365.

34. Specifically, Hayek noted the following: "[To] avoid giving the impression that I generally reject the mathematical method in economics. I regard it as indeed the great advantage of the mathematical technique that it allows us to describe, by algebraic equations, the general character of a pattern even where we are ignorant of the numerical values determining its particular manifestation. Without this algebraic technique we could scarcely have achieved that comprehensive picture of the mutual interdependencies of the different events in the market." F. A. Hayek, "The Pretense of Knowledge," in *Unemployment and Monetary Policy* (Washington, DC: Cato Institute, 1979), 28.

35. Bryan Caplan, "Why I Am Not an Austrian Economist," unpublished, 1997, http://scholar.google.com/scholar?cluster=9583767989805721665&hl=en&as_sdt=0,1.

36. Gary North, for example, wrote the following in 2005:

There is a life cycle to personal investing. There is a life cycle in the capital structure. People grow old and die. They must be replaced. Businesses and churches must plan for the retirement of today's leaders.
How will tomorrow's leaders be able to move through the cycle if they are locked out of the housing market?
I asked the audience this question: "With the median price of a home this

high, how will all those kids at the check-in desk ever become home owners?" I gave the answer in one word: "Later." The price of houses will fall.

There is another answer: "They will move."

In either case, today's home owner in San Andreas fault country will see the bubble burst. I think the mortgage market will do the job. But if I am wrong, then greener pastures will. California has lost 100,000 residents over the past year.

The American economy as never before rests on the housing boom. Yet this boom cannot be sustained much longer in the bubble regions. A recession looms. Even without a recession, the boom will falter because of ARMs: adjustable rate mortgages. These time bombs are about to blow, contract by contract.

Gary North, "Surreal Estate on the San Andreas Fault," LewRockwell.com, November 25, 2005, http://archive.lewrockwell.com/.

37. Justin Raimondo, *An Enemy of the State: The Life of Murray Rothbard* (New York: Prometheus Books, 2000), 23.

38. Ibid., 35.

39. Indeed, many years later, Rothbard remarked, "It was, in fact, McCarthy and 'McCarthyism' that provided the main catalyst for transforming the mass base of the right wing from isolationism and quasi-libertarianism to simple anti-Communism. Before McCarthy launched his famous crusade in February 1950, he had not been particularly associated with the right wing of the Republican Party; on the contrary, his record was more liberal and centrist, statist rather than libertarian." Murray Rothbard, *The Betrayal of the American Right* (1991; reprint, Auburn, AL: Ludwig von Mises Institute, 2007), 151.

40. Ibid., 154–155.

41. Raimondo, *Enemy of the State*, 99.

42. Ibid., 100–105.

43. Rothbard's feelings about the postwar conservative movement are nicely summed up in the following passage: "Of course the New Rightists of *National Review* would never quite dare to admit this crazed goal in public, but the objective would always be slyly implied. At right-wing rallies no one cheered a single iota for the free market, if this minor item were ever so much as mentioned; what really stirred up the animals were demagogic appeals by *National Review* leaders for total victory, total destruction of the Communist world. It was that which brought the right-wing masses out of their seats. It was *National Review* editor Brent Bozell who trumpeted, at a right-wing rally: 'I would favor destroying not only the whole world, but the entire universe out to the furthermost star, rather than suffer Communism to live.' It was *National Review* editor Frank Meyer who once told me: 'I have a vision, a great vision of the future: a totally devastated Soviet Union.'" Rothbard, *Betrayal of the American Right*, 169.

44. Raimondo, *Enemy of the State*, 110–112.

45. Ibid., 118.

46. Murray Rothbard, "Confessions of a Right-Wing Liberal," *Ramparts*, June 15, 1968.

47. Hess said the following about the New Left student movement: "Student

dissenters today seem to feel that somehow they have crashed through to new truths and new politics in their demands that universities and communities be made responsive to their students or inhabitants. But most of them are only playing with old politics. When the dissenters recognize this, and when their assault becomes one against political power and authority rather than a fight to gain such power, then this movement may release the bright potential latent in the intelligence of so many of its participants. Incidentally, to the extent that student activists the world over are actually fighting the existence of political power, rather than trying to grab some of it for themselves, they should not be criticized for failing to offer alternative programs; i.e., for not spelling out just what sort of political system will follow their revolution. What ought to follow their revolution is just what they've implicitly proposed: no political system at all." Karl Hess, "The Death of Politics," *Mises Daily*, October 16, 2009, http://mises.org/ (originally published in *Playboy*, March 1969).

48. Raimondo, *Enemy of the State*, 188.

49. Ibid., 186–187.

50. Murray Rothbard, "My New Year's Wish for the Movement," *Libertarian Forum*, December 1975, 5.

51. In Rothbard's words:

But what, philosophically, is "equality"? The term must not be left unanalyzed and accepted at face value. Let us take three entities: A, B, and C. A, B, and C are said to be "equal" to each other (that is, A = B = C) if a particular characteristic is found in which the three entities are uniform or identical. In short, here are three individual men: A, B, and C. Each may be similar in some respects but different in others. If each of them is precisely 5 feet 10 inches in height, they are then equal to each other in height. It follows from our discussion of the concept of equality that A, B, and C can be completely "equal" to each other only if they are identical or uniform in all characteristics— in short, if all of them are, like the same size of nut or bolt, completely interchangeable. We see, then, that the ideal of human equality can only imply total uniformity and the utter stamping out of individuality.
It is high time, then, for those who cherish freedom, individuality, the division of labor, and economic prosperity and survival, to stop conceding the supposed nobility of the ideal of equality. Too often have "conservatives" conceded the ideal of equality only to cavil at its "impracticality." Philosophically, there can be no divorce between theory and practice. Egalitarian measures do not "work" because they violate the basic nature of man, of what it means for the individual man to be truly human. The call of "equality" is a siren song that can only mean the destruction of all that we cherish as being human.

Murray Rothbard, "Freedom, Inequality, Primitivism, and the Division of Labor," *Modern Age*, September 1971, 238.

52. Murray Rothbard, "Egalitarianism as a Revolt Against Nature," *Modern Age*, December 1973, 350.

53. Murray Rothbard, *The Irrepressible Rothbard* (Burlingame, CA: Center for Libertarian Studies, 2000), 39.

54. Ibid., 41.

55. Ibid., 391.

56. Hans-Hermann Hoppe, *Democracy: The God That Failed* (New Brunswick, NJ: Transaction, 2001).

57. Ibid., 18–19.

58. Ibid., 24.

59. Ibid., 25–27.

60. Ibid., 34.

61. Ibid., 36–37.

62. Unlike many libertarians, Hoppe rejects that even a minimal state is necessary for defense, and he further argues that no state actually defends its citizens: "The state does not defend *us*; rather, the state aggresses against us and it uses *our* confiscated property to defend *itself*." Hans-Hermann Hoppe, "The Mind of Hans-Hermann Hoppe," *Daily Bell*, March 27, 2011, http://mises.org/.

63. Ibid., 206.

64. Ibid., 208.

65. Hoppe contrasted his position from that of more mainstream and well-known libertarians: "Contrary to the left libertarians assembled around such institutions as the Cato Institute and the Institute for Justice, for instance, who seek the assistance of the central government in the enforcement of various policies of nondiscrimination and call for a nondiscriminatory or 'free' immigration policy, true libertarians must embrace discrimination, be it internal (domestic) or external (foreign). Indeed, private property means discrimination. I, not you, own such and such. I am entitled to exclude you from my property. I may attach conditions to your using my property, and I may expel you from my property. Moreover, You and I, private property owners, may enter and put our property into a restrictive (or protective) covenant. We and others may, if we both deem it beneficial, impose limitations on the future use that each of us is permitted to make with our property." Ibid., 208–209.

66. Hans-Hermann Hoppe, "My Battle with the Thought Police," Mises.org, April 12, 2005, http://mises.org/.

67. In Rockwell's own words: "I cannot remember the day that I finally came around to the position that the state is unnecessary and destructive by its nature—that it cannot improve on, and indeed only destroys, the social and economic system that grows out of property rights, exchange, and natural social authority—but I do know that it was Rothbard who finally convinced me to take this last step." Lew Rockwell, "Libertarianism and the Old Right," Mises.org, August 5, 2006, http://mises.org/.

68. Ibid.

69. More specifically, Rockwell said, "A scam was perfected in the early 1980s among leading politicians and the think-tanks. A group celebrates a politician's supposed achievements in exchange for which the politician pretends to be influenced by the group. It's all a public relations game. This is a major reason why Murray was never able to work within that system. He had an irrepressible urge to tell the truth regardless of the consequences. Sure, he was a loose cannon, as any cannon should be on the ship of an imperial state." Ibid.

70. Ibid.

71. A 2006 article in *Wall Street Journal* explained the logic of the institute's location:

But a nagging question remains: How does a world-class think tank end up in east Alabama?.

Mr. [Jeffrey] Tucker notes that, back in 1982, Auburn University had one of the few Austrian-tolerant economics departments. (The Mises Institute might not be affiliated with the university, but its founders most likely anticipated a healthy intellectual exchange. A hostile nearby faculty wasn't desirable.) Mr. Tucker also observes that the city of Auburn has many redeeming qualities: a charming downtown, low prices for room and board, easy access to Atlanta's international airport, good ol' Southern hospitality (and cooking) and few distractions.

All true. But allow me to make an additional point. At the heart of Austrian economics is a skepticism of powerful, central authority. And Southerners have always been distrustful of government. Our libertarian streak—which flares up from time to time, for reasons both good and bad—makes us natural allies for the Austrian tradition.

Kyle Wingfield, "Von Mises finds a Sweet Home in Alabama," *Wall Street Journal*, August 11, 2006, http://www.wsj.com/.

72. Sam Tanenhaus and Jim Rutenberg, "Rand Paul's Mixed Inheritance," *New York Times*, January 25, 2014, http://www.nytimes.com/.

73. Doherty, *Radicals for Capitalism*, 390–391.

74. Murray Rothbard, "The Party," *Libertarian Forum* 4 (1972): 1.

75. Les Antman, "The Dallas Accord Is Dead," LewRockwell.com, May 12, 2008, http://archive.lewrockwell.com/.

76. Doherty, *Radicals for Capitalism*, 397.

77. Ibid., 415.

78. Raimondo, *Enemy of the State*, 241.

79. Ibid., 248.

80. "2008 Official Presidential General Election Results," Federal Election Commission, January 22, 2009, http://www.fec.gov/.

81. "2012 Official Presidential General Election Results," Federal Election Commission, January 17, 2013, http://www.fec.gov/.

82. Jack Donovan, "Anarcho-Fascism," JackDonovan.com, March 3, 2013, http://www.jack-donovan.com/.

83. Jack Donovan, *The Way of Men* (Milwaukie, OR: Dissident Hum, 2012), 158.

84. Gary North, "The Bible Mandates Free Market Capitalism. It Is Anti-Socialist," *Gary North's Specific Answers*, n.d., http://www.garynorth.com/.

85. Gary North and Gary DeMar, *Christian Reconstruction: What It Is, What It Isn't* (Tyler, TX: Institute for Christian Economics, 1991), 81.

86. Ibid., 82.

87. Brink Lindsey, "Liberaltarians," *New Republic*, December 11, 2006, 14–16.

88. As Lindsey put it, "Furthermore, it has become increasingly clear that capitalism's relentless dynamism and wealth-creation—the institutional safeguarding of which lies at the heart of libertarian concerns—have been pushing US society in a decidedly progressive direction. The civil rights movement was made possible by the mechanization of agriculture, which pushed blacks off the farm and out of

the South with immense consequences. Likewise, feminism was encouraged by the mechanization of housework. Greater sexual openness, as well as heightened interest in the natural environment, are among the luxury goods that mass affluence has purchased. So, too, are secularization and the general decline in reverence for authority, as rising education levels (prompted by the economy's growing demand for knowledge workers) have promoted increasing independence of mind." Ibid., 16.

89. Will Wilkinson, "Liberaltarianism: Back to the Future," WillWilkinson .net, May 30, 2008, http://www.willwilkinson.net/.

Chapter 7. Nostalgia as a Political Platform

1. Joseph Scotchie, *The Paleoconservatives: New Voices for the Old Right* (New Brunswick, NJ: Transaction, 1999), 1.

2. Joseph Scotchie, *Revolt from the Heartland: The Struggle for Authentic Conservatism* (New Brunswick, NJ: 2002), vii.

3. Nash, *Conservative Intellectual Movement*, 568.

4. Justin Raimondo, "Dialoguing with Douthat," *Chronicles*, July 1, 2010, https://www.chroniclesmagazine.org/.

5. Chris Woltermann, "What Is Paleoconservatism?" *Telos* 97 (1993): 9.

6. Ibid., 12.

7. Ibid.

8. In Flynn's words: "If you would know, therefore, who are the fascists in America, you must ask yourselves not who are the men and women most vocal in their denunciations of Hitler and Mussolini. The most ardent enemies of those two leaders were some of their rival fascist dictators in Europe. The test of fascism is not one's rage against the Italian and German war lords. The test is—how many of the essential principles of fascism do you accept and to what extent are you prepared to apply those fascist ideas to American social and economic life? When you can put your finger on the men or the groups that urge for America the debt-supported state, the autarchial corporative state, the state bent on the socialization of investment and the bureaucratic government of industry and society, the establishment of the institution of militarism as the great glamorous public-works project of the nation and the institution of imperialism under which it proposes to regulate and rule the world and, along with this, proposes to alter the forms of our government to approach as closely as possible the unrestrained, absolute government—then you will know you have located the authentic fascist." John T. Flynn, *As We Go Marching* (1944; reprint, New York: Free Life Editions, 1973), 252.

9. Garet Garrett, *The People's Pottage* (Caldwell, ID: Caxton Printers, 1953), 15.

10. Ibid., 18.

11. M. E. Bradford, *Remembering Who We Are: Observations of a Southern Conservative* (Athens: University of Georgia Press, 1985), 87.

12. M. E. Bradford, "The Heresy of Equality: Bradford Replies to Jaffa," *Modern Age* 20 (1976): 63.

13. Ibid., 69.

14. M. E. Bradford. "On Remembering Who We Are: A Political Credo," *Modern Age* 26 (1982): 149.

15. M. E. Bradford, "On Being Conservative in a Post-Liberal Era," *Intercollegiate Review* 21 (1986): 15.

16. Ibid.

17. Patrick J. Buchanan, *A Republic, Not an Empire* (Washington, DC: Regnery, 1999), 285–287.

18. Patrick J. Buchanan, *Churchill, Hitler, and the Unnecessary War: How Britain Lost an Empire and the West Lost the World* (New York: Three Rivers Press, 2008), 265.

19. Patrick J. Buchanan, "On Treating Putin as a Pariah," Buchanan.org, April 25, 2014, http://buchanan.org/.

20. Patrick Buchanan, "The Isolationist Myth," Buchanan.org, December 3, 1994, http://buchanan.org/.

21. Patrick J. Buchanan, *The Death of the West: How Dying Populations and Immigrant Invasions Imperil Our Country and Civilization* (New York: St. Martin's Press, 2002), 135.

22. Peter Brimelow, "Peter Brimelow on 'Electing a New People in America and Britain,'" VDARE.com, February 16, 2014, https://www.vdare.com/.

23. A quick scan shows that this quote has been referenced dozens of times on VDARE.com/. For an additional recent example, see Anthony Boehm, "July 17, 1953: Sixty Years of 'Electing a New People,'" VDARE.com, June 17, 2013, https://www.vdare.com/.

24. Peter Brimelow, "Time to Rethink Immigration?" *National Review*, June 22, 1992, 30–46.

25. Samuel Huntington, *Who Are We? The Challenges to America's National Identity* (New York: Simon & Schuster, 2004).

26. Buchanan, *Death of the West*, 125.

27. Patrick J. Buchanan, *Suicide of a Superpower: Will America Survive Until 2025?* (New York: St. Martin's Press, 2011), 68–69.

28. Ibid., 63.

29. Buchanan, *Suicide of a Superpower*, 410–428.

30. Ibid., 148.

31. Tim Mak, "MSNBC Drops Pat Buchanan," *Politico*, February 17, 2012, http://www.politico.com/.

32. Patrick J. Buchanan, "The New Blacklist," Buchanan.org, February 17, 2012, http://buchanan.org/.

33. Scotchie, *Revolt from the Heartland*, 51.

34. Thomas Fleming, "Old Rights and the New Right," in *The New Right Papers*, ed. Robert W. Whitaker (New York: St. Martin's Press, 1982), 182.

35. Ibid., 184.

36. Thomas Fleming, "Back to the Stone Age, B," *Chronicles*, September 27, 2012, https://www.chroniclesmagazine.org/.

37. Scotchie, *Revolt from the Heartland*, 69.

38. For one exception to this, I can point out Mark Krikorian's *Case against Immigration: Both Legal and Illegal* (New York: Sentinel, 2008). However, most conservative critics of immigration focus primarily on the undocumented variety.

39. Chilton Williamson Jr., *The Immigration Mystique: America's False Conscience* (New York: Basic Books, 1996).

40. According to Fleming, "I always enjoyed our chats about the failure of the conservative movement. Paul's bête noire—one he shared with our friend Peter Stanlis—was the perfidious neoconservatives. I shared his distaste for most of them,

but my view came closer to contempt than hostility. Of the movement's two most prominent leaders, one was a bright man and clever operator, whose education was at best rudimentary and range of intellectual interests pedestrian if not primitive, while the other was a student of 20th century literature, a subject that is not exactly a solid intellectual formation. The lesser lights of the movement were, for the most part, not worth the effort it takes to hate someone." Thomas Fleming, "Back to the Stone Age: A Primer for Paleoconservatives," *Chronicles*, September 26, 2012, https://www.chroniclesmagazine.org/.

41. Paul Gottfried, *The Conservative Movement*, rev. ed. (New York: Twayne, 1993), 144.

42. Samuel T. Francis, *Shots Fired: Sam Francis on America's Culture War* (Vienna, VA: Fitzgerald Griffin Foundation, 2006), 203–204.

43. In Francis's words, "The ideology or formula of liberalism grows out of the structural interest of the elite that espouses it. Liberalism barely exists as an independent set of ideas and values. Virtually no significant thinker of this century has endorsed it, and many have explicitly rejected, criticized, or ridiculed it. Internally, the doctrines of liberalism are so contrary to established fact, inconsistent with each other, and immersed in sentimentalism, resentment, and egoism that they cannot be taken seriously as a body of ideas. Liberalism flourishes almost entirely because it reflects the material and psychological interests of a privileged, power-holding, and power-seeking sector of American society." Samuel T. Francis, "Message from MARS," in *The New Right Papers*, ed. Robert W. Whitaker (New York: St. Martin's Press, 1982), 69.

44. Francis, *Shots Fired*, 217.

45. Ibid.

46. Francis on Duke: "Mr. Duke has gained and kept a political following because he understands something most contemporary conservatives have forgotten or never knew: What attracts voters to a candidacy of the right is not what the candidate thinks or says about the gold standard, creating democracy in Afghanistan, expanding economic opportunities, or being kinder and gentler, but what he will say and do to preserve and protect what used to be called the American Way of Life, the normative patterns and institutions that define and distinguish what Americans believe and do from what other people believe and so—in short, the American culture." Samuel T. Francis, *Revolution from the Middle* (Raleigh, NC: Middle America Press, 1997), 59–60.

47. Ibid., 136.

48. According to Paul Gottfried's autobiography, Samuel T. Francis and Russell Kirk argued over whether their movement should be properly labeled conservative or right wing in the 1990s. Unsurprisingly, Kirk preferred to be called a conservative. Francis, in contrast, declared, "I am not a conservative but a man of the Right, perhaps of the far Right." Gottfried, *Encounters*, 150.

49. Samuel T. Francis, "Anarcho-Tyranny—Where Multiculturalism Leads," VDARE.com, December 30, 2004, https://www.vdare.com/.

50. Samuel T. Francis, "An Infantile Disorder," VDARE.com, February 2, 1998, https://www.vdare.com/.

51. The Southern Poverty Law Center, for example, called Francis a white nationalist; "Sam Francis," http://www.splcenter.org/.

52. Paul Gottfried explained the logic of paleoconservative support for a strong stand against the Soviet Union: "Most paleoconservatives backed an active American role in combating communism and the Soviet Union as its most menacing armed advocate, but had little patience for big government and nonmilitary foreign aid. They advocated victory over communism for two reasons: because they viewed the communists as irreconcilably hostile to both traditional Western order and political liberty, and because they saw the communists as the extension of a violent revolutionary impetus going back to the French Revolution and now threatening the United States and the rest of the Western world." Paul Gottfried, "Paleoconservatism," *First Principles*, May 18, 2012, http://www.firstprinciplesjournal.com/.

53. Gottfried, *Conservative Movement*, 146–147.

54. Murray Rothbard, "A Strategy for the Right," speech given to the John Randolph Club, January 18, 1992.

55. Lew Rockwell, "The Case for Paleo-Libertarianism," *Liberty* 3 (1990): 34–38.

56. Ibid., 34.

57. Ibid., 36.

58. As Rockwell put it, "Wishing to associate with members of one's own race, nationality, religion, class, sex, or even political party is a natural and human impulse. A voluntary society will therefore have male organizations, Polish neighborhoods, black churches, Jewish country clubs, and white fraternities." Ibid., 37.

59. Lew Rockwell, "What I Learned from Paleoism," LewRockwell.com, May 2, 2002, http://www.lewrockwell.com/.

60. Scotchie, *Revolt from the Heartland*, 95.

61. Francis further argued that Middle Americans agreed with him on economic issues, and would have continued to support the left if the left had not embraced cultural radicalism: "Middle American Forces, emerging from the ruins of the old independent middle and working classes, found conservative, libertarian, and pro-business Republican ideology and rhetoric irrelevant, distasteful, and even threatening to their own economic interests. The post-World War II middle class was in reality an affluent proletariat, economically dependent on the federal government through labor codes, housing loans, educational programs, defense contracts, and health and unemployment benefits. All variations of conservative doctrine rejected these as illegitimate extensions of the state and not infrequently boasted of plans to abolish them, and Middle American allegiance to political parties and candidates espousing such doctrine could never become firm." Francis, *Revolution from the Middle*, 234.

62. Paul Gottfried, "A Paleo Epitaph," *Taki's Magazine*, April 7, 2008, http://takimag.com/.

63. Many prominent right-wing intellectuals, including Leo Strauss, Eric Voegelin, and F. A. Hayek, have attacked the Hegelian interpretation of history.

64. Paul Gottfried, *The Search for Historical Meaning: Hegel and the Postwar American Right* (DeKalb: Northern Illinois University Press, 1986).

65. Paul Gottfried, *Carl Schmitt: Politics and Theory* (New York: Greenwood Press, 1990).

66. Paul Gottfried, *The Strange Death of Marxism: The European Left in the New Millennium* (Columbia: University of Missouri Press, 2005).

67. Ibid., 127.

68. Paul Gottfried, *Multiculturalism and the Politics of Guilt: Toward a Secular Theocracy* (Columbia: University of Missouri Press, 2002), 88.

69. Ibid., 134.

70. Gottfried, *Encounters*, 34.

71. Although Gottfried tells this story in his autobiography and in many of his columns, I have not been able to find any other sources that confirm his version of events.

72. For an example of a paleoconservative critique of Russell Kirk, see Paul Gottfried, "How Russell Kirk (and the Right) Went Wrong," VDARE.com, November 4, 2004, https://www.vdare.com/.

73. I am not alone in this estimation. For example, Gerald Russello, one of Kirk's biographers, shares this assessment. Gerald Russello, *The Post-Modern Imagination of Russell Kirk* (Columbia: University of Missouri Press, 2007), 18.

74. On this point, I am in agreement with the neoconservative critic of paleoconservatives, Adam Wolfson: "Commonly thought to be the heirs of Russell Kirk and the traditionalists, paleoconservatives in fact dissent from what conservatives considered true conservative principles. They are not conservatives so much as reactionaries or pseudo-radicals. The paleos can be said to despise much of contemporary America life and would like somehow to move beyond the modern American political debate." Adam Wolfson, "Conservatives and Neoconservatives," in *The Neocon Reader*, ed. Irwin Stelzer (New York: Grove Press, 2004), 219.

75. Millman admits as much himself:

> In 2002 and 2003, I was a full-throated supporter of the Iraq War. In 2000, I supported John McCain for President. In 2008, I supported Barack Obama. I expect to support him again.
>
> I support gay marriage. I'm not an immigration restrictionist. I think the Affordable Care Act was largely a good piece of legislation, should not be repealed, and is plainly constitutional. I don't think the Federal Reserve should be abolished or that we should return to the gold standard.

Noah Millman, "What's a Nice Jewish Boy Like You Doing at a Website Like This?" *American Conservative*, January 16, 2012, http://www.theamericanconservative.com/.

76. W. James Antle III, "Pat Buchanan Was Right," *Daily Caller*, June 26, 2014, http://dailycaller.com/.

Chapter 8. Against Capitalism, Christianity, and America

1. Richard A. Viguerie, *The New Right: We're Ready to Lead* (n.p.: Viguerie, 1981).

2. Benoist discussed how the school of thought he helped found came to be called the New Right, as well as his misgivings with the term, in his preface to Tomislav Sunić's book on the subject: "It should be recalled that, when it [the expression New Right] was first coined, was never used as a self-description. In fact, the label was invented by the media in 1979 to depict a school of thought and an intellectual and cultural current, born eleven years earlier and which, until then, had never described itself using this label. However, in view of the fact that this expres-

sion had become so widespread, it had to be more or less adopted thereafter. But it was never used without apprehensions, for several reasons: first, it suggested that the ENR was essentially a political organization—which has never been the case. It also positioned our school of thought within a denomination (the 'Right') which our school of thought has always opposed." Alain de Benoist, "The New Right: Forty Years After," preface to *Against Equality and Democracy: The European New Right*, by Tomislav Sunić, 3rd ed. (London: Arktos Media, 2011), 23.

3. Carl Schmitt, "The Concept of the Political" (1927), trans. George Schwab (Chicago: University of Chicago Press, 2007), 53.

4. Ibid., 27.

5. Ibid., 79.

6. Ibid., 27.

7. Carl Schmitt, *The Crisis of Parliamentary Democracy* (1985), trans. Ellen Kennedy (Cambridge, MA: MIT Press, 1988), 9.

8. Oswald Spengler, *The Decline of the West: An Abridged Edition* (1918), trans. Charles Francis Atkinson (New York: Vintage Books, 2006), 36–37.

9. Spengler makes this argument early in *Decline of the West:* "Mankind, however, has no aim, no idea, no plan, any more than the family of butterflies or orchids. 'Mankind' is a zoological expression, or an empty word. But conjure away the phantom, break the magic circle, and at once there emerges an astonishing wealth of *actual* forms—the Living with all its immense fullness, depth and movement—hitherto veiled by a catchword, a dry-as-dust scheme and a set of personal 'ideals.' I see, in place of that empty figment of *one* linear history which can be kept only by shutting one's eyes to the overwhelming multitude of the facts, the drama of *a number* of mighty Cultures, each springing with primitive strength from the soil of the mother region to which it remains firmly bound throughout its whole life cycle; each having *its own* idea, *its own* passions, *its own* life, will and feeling, *its own* death." Spengler, *Decline of the West,* 17.

10. Ibid., 73–74.

11. Ibid., 25–30.

12. Oswald Spengler, *Man and Technics* (1931), trans. Charles Francis Atkinson (New York: Greenwood Press, 1976), 13.

13. Ibid., 51.

14. Ibid., 52.

15. As an example of this, I point to Jünger's remarks about his final combat experience: "It had me at last. At the same time as feeling I had been his, I felt the bullet taking away my life. I had felt Death's hand once before, on the road at Mory—but this time his grip was firmer and more determined. As I came down heavily on the bottom of the trench, I was convinced it was all over. Strangely, that moment is one of the very few in my life of which I am able to say they were utterly happy. I understood, as in a flash of lightning, the true inner purpose and form of my life. I felt surprise and disbelief that it was to end there and then, but this surprise had something untroubled and almost merry about it. Then I heard the firing grow less, as if I were a stone sinking under the surface of some turbulent water. Where I was going, there was neither war nor enmity." Ernst Jünger, *Storm of Steel* (1920), trans. Michael Hoffmann (New York: Penguin Books, 2003), 281–282.

16. The exact passage reads:

Recently, a story circulated in the newspapers about a new torpedo that the Japanese navy is apparently developing. This weapon has an astounding feature. It is no longer guided mechanically but by a human device—to be precise, by a human being at the helm, who is locked into a tiny compartment and regarded as a technical component of the torpedo as well as its actual intelligence.

The idea behind this organic construction drives the logic of the technical world a small step forward by transforming man in an unprecedented way into one its component parts. If one enlarges upon this thought, one soon realizes that it is no longer considered a curiosity once achieved on a larger social scale, i.e., when one disposes over a breed of resolute men obedient to authority. Manned planes can be constructed as airborne missiles, which from great heights can dive down to strike with lethal accuracy the nerve centers of enemy resistance.

Ernst Jünger, *On Pain* (1934), trans. David C. Durst (New York: Telos, 2008), 18.

17. Ernst Jünger, *On the Marble Cliffs* (1939), trans. Stuart Hood (New York: New Directions, 1947).

18. Ernst Jünger, *The Forest Passage* (1951), trans. Thomas Friese (Candor, NY: Telos Press, 2013), 23.

19. Ernst Jünger, *Eumeswil* (1977), trans. Joachim Neogroschel (New York: Marsilio Library, 1993), 340.

20. Ibid., 147.

21. Ibid., 43.

22. For example, Moeller wrote: "The population problem lifts its head where there is a people which has not living room proportioned to its numbers and lacks the opportunity for its people to earn their living outside, wherever a growing population is forced to draw from abroad its food supplies and the raw or half-raw materials for its industry. The population problem cannot be isolated; it develops into an economic and then a political problem: the problem of all blockaded states." Arthur Moeller van den Bruck, *Germany's Third Empire* (1923), trans. E. O. Lorimer (London: Arktos Media, 2012), 63.

23. Ibid., 45.

24. Ibid., 82.

25. Ibid., 153.

26. Ibid., 188.

27. Ibid., 116.

28. Ibid., 115.

29. For perhaps the most critical view of Heidegger's political affiliations, see Emmanuel Faye, *Heidegger: The Introduction of Nazism into Philosophy in Light of the Unpublished Seminars of 1933–1935* (2005), trans. Michael B. Smith (New Haven, CT: Yale University Press, 2009).

30. Dugin admits as much in his book on Heidegger: "But Heidegger neither gives us answers, nor points the way. His philosophy is something opposite of a system, teaching, or theory. Instead, it is the life-giving flesh of thoughts that excludes any closed and irreversible trajectories, any fixation, or any construction." Alexander Dugin, *Martin Heidegger: The Philosophy of Another Beginning*, trans. Nina Kouprianova (Arlington, VA: Radix/Washington Summit, 2014), 387.

31. In his book on the European New Right, Tomislav Sunić dedicates an entire chapter to Vilfredo Pareto. Sunić, *Against Equality and Democracy*, 99–106.

32. Georges Sorel was a French revolutionary syndicalist who emphasized the importance of myth and violence for revolutionary movements. He opposed parliamentary democracy, and he believed that workers should withdraw from democratic political activity in favor of more radical action. His work has inspired elements of both the radical right and the radical left.

33. René Guénon, *The Crisis of the Modern World* (1927), trans. Arthur Osborne (Delhi, India: First Impression, 1999), 15.

34. Ibid., 92.

35. Ibid., 107.

36. Ibid., 109.

37. Jonathan Bowden, "Julius Evola: The World's Most Right-Wing Thinker," speech delivered in London, YouTube.com, n.d., https://www.youtube.com/watch?v=4YqKf3v2aPs.

38. Julius Evola, *The Path of Cinnabar* (1963, 1972), trans. Sergio Knipe (London: Integral Tradition, 2009), 237–238.

39. Ibid., 19.

40. H. T. Hansen, "Julius Evola's Political Endeavors," introduction to *Men Among the Ruins* (1953), by Julius Evola, trans. Guido Stucco (Rochester, VT: Inner Traditions, 2002), 61–62.

41. Ibid., 183.

42. Evola, *Men Among the Ruins*, 293.

43. Julius Evola, *Revolt Against the Modern World* (1934), trans. Guido Stucco (Rochester, VT: Inner Traditions, 1995), 356.

44. Evola, *Path of Cinnabar*, 165.

45. Evola's feelings on the Jews were summarized in his autobiography: "The influence of Judaism on modern culture and society, by means of both international capitalism and by revolutionary, corrosive political agitation, cannot be denied. In my work, I sought to prove that this influence has chiefly come from the secular side of Judaism, which abandoned the ancient Jewish tradition. Certain aspects of this ancient tradition were distorted and materialized by secular Judaism, allowing for the kind of instinctual outbreaks of a given human type that had previously been held in check. In fact, I held little against the Jewish tradition as such: in my studies of esotericism, I had frequently quoted the Kabbalah, ancient Hebrew texts and Jewish authors (not to mention my praise of Michelstaedter, himself a Jew, and my interest in the work of another Jew, Weininger, whose most important book I endeavored to publish in a new Italian edition)." Evola, *Path of Cinnabar*, 177.

46. Hansen, "Julius Evola's Political Endeavors," 79.

47. Evola, *Revolt Against the Modern World*, 50–51.

48. In Evola's biography, he recounts a correspondence with Guénon in which the two speculated as to whether Evola's injury during the bombing of Vienna may have been the result of some enemy using occult magic as a weapon against him. Evola decided against this interpretation, as it would have required an extraordinarily powerful magic spell to set such a course of events in motion. However, both were in agreement that a debilitating illness that struck Guénon for a period was the result of such an occult attack. Evola, *Path of Cinnabar*, 183–184.

49. Julius Evola, *Ride the Tiger: A Survival Manual for the Aristocrats of the Soul* (1961), trans. Joscelyn Godwin and Constance Fontana (Rochester, VT: Inner Traditions, 2003), 12.

50. Ibid., 10.

51. Alain de Benoist, *The Problem of Democracy* (1985), trans. Sergio Knipe (London: Arktos Media, 2011), 28.

52. Alain de Benoist, *On Being a Pagan* (1981), trans. Jon Graham (Atlanta, GA: Ultra, 2004).

53. Ibid., 120.

54. Michael O'Meara, *New Culture, New Right: Anti-Liberalism in Postmodern Europe*, 2nd ed. (London: Arktos Media, 2013), 214–215.

55. Ibid., 217–218.

56. Benoist says this in his "Manifesto for a European Renaissance" (1999), co-authored with Charles Champetier: "As regards the immigrant population which resides today in France, it would be illusory to expect their departure *en masse.*" This manifesto is included in the appendix of Sunić's *Against Equality and Democracy,* 231.

57. Guillaume Faye, *Why We Fight: Manifesto of the European Resistance* (2001), trans. Michael O'Meara (London: Arktos Media, 2011), 39.

58. Ibid., 66.

59. Guillaume Faye, *Convergence of Catastrophes* (2004), trans. E. Christian Kopff (London: Arktos Media, 2012).

60. For a summary of the threats Faye perceives, see *Archeofuturism: European Visions of the Post-Catastrophic Age,* trans. Sergio Knipe (London: Arktos Media, 2010), 59–68.

61. Ibid., 195–249.

62. Francis Fukuyama, *The End of History and the Last Man* (New York: Free Press, 1992).

63. Dugin credits fascism for at least acknowledging the importance of traditional society and appropriating some of its symbols. However, he emphatically rejected the racism and totalitarianism of fascism, and he even argued that racism was precisely the reason National Socialism collapsed. Alexander Dugin, *The Fourth Political Theory* (2009), trans. Mark Sleboda and Michael Millerman (London: Arktos Media, 2012), 89–90.

64. Ibid., 194.

65. In an interview with an American journalist, Dugin remarked, "With Iranians we have common interests . . . because I consider that to stop American unipolarity is the most important thing, the absolute thing. . . . These parties, these pro-Westerners here in the Russian government, they insisted that Iran, being fundamentalist, could at some time aggress us. But . . . that was a kind of propaganda against Iranians made by pro-American, pro-Western forces in Moscow." Megan Stack, "Russian Nationalist Advocates Eurasian Alliance Against the US," *Los Angeles Times,* September 4, 2008, http://latimes.com/.

66. Ibid., 153.

67. Writing in *National Review,* Robert Zubrin argued that Dugin is directly shaping Russia's relationship with its neighbors, and Putin is creating a "Fascist Eurasian Union project" that threatens freedom throughout the globe. Robert Zubrin,

"The Eurasionist Threat," *National Review Online*, March 3, 2014, http://www.nationalreview.com/.

68. Paul Gottfried, "The Western Front: Inhuman Rights," *Chronicles*, April 2004, 13.

69. Tomislav Sunić, "The New Right of the Old World," *Chronicles*, February 1993, 19–21.

70. Thomas Fleming, "Athens and Jerusalem," *Chronicles*, April 1996, 8–10.

71. Sunić, *Against Equality and Democracy*, 65.

72. Thomas Molnar, "A Cultural Coup d'Etat," *National Review*, November 24, 1978, 1481–1482.

73. Thomas Molnar, "Letters from Paris: The French 'New Right,'" *Chronicles*, January/February 1981, 35.

74. Erica Ritz, "'Truly Terrifying': Beck Introduces Viewers to the Man He Believes Is the 'Architect' of Russia's Geopolitical Strategy," *The Blaze*, January 13, 2015, http://www.theblaze.com/.

75. Robert Zubrin, "Dugin's Evil Theology," *National Review Online*, June 18, 2014, http://www.nationalreview.com/.

76. Anton Shekhovtsov, "Putin's Brain?" *New Eastern Europe* 4 (2014): 78.

77. Tamir Bar-On, *Rethinking the French New Right: Alternatives to Modernity* (New York: Routledge, 2013); Tamir Bar-On, *Where Have All the Fascists Gone?* (Burlington, VT: Ashgate, 2007).

78. Bar-On, *Rethinking the French New Right*, 162.

Chapter 9. Voices of the Radical Right

1. Carol M. Swain, *The New White Nationalism in America: Its Challenge to Integration* (New York: Cambridge University Press, 2002); Carol M. Swain and Russ Nieli, eds., *Contemporary Voices of White Nationalism in America* (New York: Cambridge University Press, 2003).

2. As Caplan stated, "Even if you only count Nazism and European colonialism, white nationalism has a massive body count. But several non-European nationalisms—especially Chinese and Japanese—are in the same bloody ballpark." Bryan Caplan, "How Bad Is White Nationalism?" *Library of Economics and Liberty*, December 30, 2013, http://econlog.econlib.org/.

3. Bryan Caplan, "You Will Know Them by Their Unpopular Views," *Library of Economics and Liberty*, May 15, 2013, http://econlog.econlib.org/.

4. For a more thorough discussion of this issue, see Betty A. Dobratz and Stephanie L. Shanks-Meilem, *"White Power, White Pride": The White Separatist Movement in the United States* (New York: Twayne, 1997), 9–12.

5. I discuss the degree to which ethnicity remains a dividing line among whites in the United States in my book *White Voters in 21st Century America* (New York: Routledge, 2014), 50–84.

6. Greg Johnson, "Implicit Whiteness and Republicans," *Counter-Currents*, November 12, 2010, http://www.counter-currents.com/.

7. For a recent example of this form of argumentation, see Wesley J. Smith, "Human Exceptionalism," *National Review Online*, April 5, 2014, http://www.nationalreview.com/.

8. Jonathan Peter Spiro, *Conservation, Eugenics, and the Legacy of Madison Grant* (Lebanon, NH: University Press of New England, 2009), xii.

9. Madison Grant, *The Passing of the Great Race, or The Racial Basis of European History*, 4th ed. (New York: Charles Scribner's Sons, 1932).

10. Ibid., 161–162.

11. Grant acknowledged that miscegenation was fairly common in the Americas, but he was not concerned about it because the children of such pairings were simply considered part of the minority group. For example, a child born to a white man and a black woman was simply considered black and was not incorporated into the white mainstream: "There was plenty of mixture with Negroes as the light color of many Negroes abundantly testifies, but these mulattoes, quadroons or octoroons were then and now universally regarded as Negroes." Ibid., 85.

12. Spiro, *Conservation, Eugenics*, 167.

13. Lothrop Stoddard, *The Rising Tide of Color against White World-Supremacy* (New York: Charles Scribner's Sons, 1920); Lothrop Stoddard, *The Revolt Against Civilization: The Menace of the Under-Man* (New York: Charles Scribner's Sons, 1922).

14. Stoddard, *Rising Tide of Color*, 303.

15. Wilmot Robertson, *The Dispossessed Majority* (Cape Canaveral, FL: Howard Allen, 1976).

16. For a few examples of these, see Christopher Brand, *The g Factor* (New York: Wiley, 1996); Michael E. Levin, *Why Race Matters* (Westport, CT: Praeger, 1997); and Richard Lynn, *Race Differences in Intelligence: An Evolutionary Analysis* (Washington, DC: Washington Summit, 2006).

17. Richard J. Herrnstein and Charles Murray, *The Bell Curve: Intelligence and Class Structure in American Life* (New York: Simon & Schuster, 1994), 269–340.

18. They specifically argue that their findings should not influence how we treat individuals on a daily basis: "We cannot think of a legitimate argument for why any encounter between individual whites and blacks need be affected by the knowledge that an aggregate ethnic difference in measured intelligence is genetic instead of environmental." Ibid., 313.

19. Stephen Jay Gould, *The Mismeasure of Man*, rev. and expanded ed. (New York: Norton, 1996), 367–390.

20. Steven Fraser, ed., *The Bell Curve Wars: Race, Intelligence, and the Future of America* (New York: Basic Books, 1995); Claude S. Fischer, Michael Hout, Martín Sánchez Jankowski, Samuel R. Lucas, Ann Swidler, and Kim Voss, *Inequality by Design: Cracking the Bell Curve Myth* (Princeton, NJ: Princeton University Press, 1996); Russell Jacoby and Naomi Glauberman, eds., *The Bell Curve Debate* (New York: Times Books, 1995).

21. For example, the blogger using the pen name JayMan accepts the basic premises of human biodiversity but is also part African American and a political liberal. He blogs at http://jaymans.wordpress.com/.

22. For example, Gregory Cochrane and Henry Harpending both have PhDs and presently work in academia. They blog at http://westhunt.wordpress.com/.

23. Gregory Cochrane and Henry Harpending, *The 10,000 Year Explosion: How Civilization Accelerated Human Evolution* (New York: Basic Books, 2009), 187–224.

24. Nicholas Wade, *A Troublesome Inheritance: Genes, Race, and Human History* (New York: Penguin Books, 2014), 2.

25. For example, an open letter denouncing the book, signed by more than 100 working scientists, was published in the *New York Times:* "A Troublesome Inheritance," *New York Times,* August 8, 2014, http://www.nytimes.com/.

26. For example, *New York Times* columnist Ross Douthat had generally positive things to say about the book. "What I've been Reading," *New York Times,* May 8, 2014, http://www.nytimes.com/.

27. Wade, *Troublesome Inheritance,* 16–38.

28. For example, the book received a positive review from American Renaissance. Jared Taylor, "A Troublesome Inheritance," *American Renaissance,* May 6, 2014, http://www.amren.com/.

29. Stanley F. Horn, *Invisible Empire: The Story of the Ku Klux Klan, 1866–1871* (Boston: Houghton-Mifflin, 1939), 356–380.

30. "The Various Shady Lives of the KKK," *Time,* April 9, 1965, 32–33.

31. Brian Palmer, "Ku Klux Kontraction: How Did the KKK Lose Nearly One-Third of Its Chapters in a Single Year?" *Slate,* March 8, 2012, http://www.slate.com/.

32. William H. Schmaltz, *Hate: George Lincoln Rockwell and the American Nazi Party* (Washington, DC: Brassey's, 1999), 209–210.

33. Ibid., 264.

34. Frederick James Simonelli, *American Fuehrer: George Lincoln Rockwell and the American Nazi Party* (Champaign: University of Illinois Press, 1999), 33.

35. For a critical discussion of Pierce's outreach to the more unhinged and violent aspects of the racial right from the perspective of a movement supporter, see Kevin Alfred Strom, "I Remember Dr. Pierce," *Counter-Currents,* July 30, 2012, http://www.counter-currents.com/.

36. William Luther Pierce (as Andrew Macdonald), *The Turner Diaries* (Hillsboro, WV: National Vanguard Books, 1978).

37. "Death List Names Given to Jury," *New York Times,* September 17, 1985, http://www.nytimes.com/.

38. William Luther Pierce, *Hunter* (Hillsboro, WV: National Vanguard Books, 1989).

39. All episodes of *Radio Free Northwest* can be found at http://northwestfront.org/media/radio-free-northwest/.

40. Interview with Jared Taylor, December 21, 1999, in Swain and Nieli, *Contemporary Voices,* 105.

41. Jared Taylor, *Paved with Good Intentions: The Failure of Race Relations in Contemporary America* (New York: Carroll & Graf, 1992).

42. A list of NPI's available books can be found on its website at http://www.washsummit.com/.

43. Phyllis B. Gerstenfeld, Diana R. Grant, and Chau-Pu Chiang, "Hate Online: A Content Analysis of Extremist Internet Sites," *Analyses of Social Issues and Public Policy* 3 (2003): 29.

44. Seth Stephens-Davidowitz, "The Data of Hate," *New York Times,* July 12, 2014, http://www.nytimes.com/.

45. Ibid.

46. Heidi Beirich, "White Homicide Worldwide," *Southern Poverty Law Center Intelligence Report* 154 (2014): 2.

47. Richard Spencer, "Big Hate," *Radix*, July 15, 2014, http://www.radixjournal .com/.

48. Breivik seemed more concerned with the intolerant elements of Islam as a religion and did not express dislike of the racial groups often associated with Islam. One of his chief complaints against Muslims was that they are generally anti-Semitic, and in this they are supposedly similar to the Nazis—whom he also claimed to despise. He also claimed to support Israel. Of course, as a political document, we cannot know for sure the degree to which Breivik's manifesto represented his own views, or if he was trying to make his political agenda more palatable to a wider audience. Anders Breivik, "2083: A European Declaration of Independence," July 28, 2011, https://publicintelligence.net/.

49. For a thorough discussion of the most viciously racist Reddit communities and Reddit's reaction to these communities, see Bridget Todd, "Does Anything Go? The Rise and Fall of a Racist Corner of Reddit," *Atlantic*, July 16, 2013, http://www .theatlantic.com/.

50. "The Mantra," *B.U.G.S.: Fighting White Genocide*, n.d., http://www.whita keronline.org/.

51. Mark Potok, "The Year in Hate and Extremism," Southern Poverty Law Center, 2015, http://www.splcenter.org/.

52. Joann Row, "Controversial Psychology Professor to Retire in the Fall," *Daily 49er*, April 14, 2014, http://www.daily49er.com/.

53. Kevin MacDonald, *A People That Shall Dwell Alone: Judaism as a Group Evolutionary Strategy, with Diaspora Peoples* (Westport, CT: Praeger, 1994); Kevin Mac-Donald, *Separation and Its Discontents: Toward an Evolutionary Theory of Anti-Semitism* (Westport, CT: Praeger, 1998); Kevin MacDonald, *The Culture of Critique: An Evolutionary Analysis of Jewish Involvement in Twentieth-Century Intellectual and Political Movements* (Westport, CT: Praeger, 1998).

54. MacDonald, *Culture of Critique*, 313.

55. Ibid., 315.

56. Kevin MacDonald, "Mission Statement," *Occidental Observer*, February 20, 2010, http://www.theoccidentalobserver.net/.

57. Francis Parker Yokey (as Ulick Varange), *Imperium: The Philosophy of History and Politics* (1948; reprint, annotated ed., Abergele, Wales, UK: Palingenesis Project, 2013).

58. Sebastian Linderhof, "Concealed Influence: Francis Parker Yockey's Plagiarism of Carl Schmitt," *Occidental Quarterly* 10 (Winter 2010): 19–62.

59. "Who We Are," European Congress, http://www.europeancongress.org/.

60. Krisztina Than, "Hungary PM Orban Says Immigration a Threat, Must Be Stopped," *Reuters*, January 12, 2015, http://www.reuters.com/.

61. James Kirchick, "American Racist Richard Spencer Gets to Play the Martyr in Hungary," *Daily Beast*, October 7, 2014, http://www.thedailybeast.com/.

62. Alain de Benoist, "We Are at the End of Something," *American Renaissance*, November 22, 2013, http://www.amren.com/.

Chapter 10. Conclusion

1. Ramesh Ponnuru, "A Conservative No More," *National Review*, October 11, 1999, 36.

2. "Presidential Approval Ratings—George W. Bush," *Gallup*, http://www.gallup.com/.

3. For a detailed discussion of why Bush's 2005 efforts to reform Social Security failed, I recommend William A. Galston, "Why President Bush's 2005 Social Security Initiative Failed, and What It Means for the Future of the Program," *Research Brief 1* (Washington, DC: Brookings Institution, 2007).

4. Dotty Lynch, "Schiavo Politics, Up Close," *CBS News*, March 25, 2005, http://www.cbsnews.com/.

5. "Corruption Named as Key Issue by Voters in Exit Polls," CNN.com, November 8, 2006, http://www.cnn.com/.

6. John B. Judis and Ruy Teixeira, *The Emerging Democratic Majority* (New York: Scribner, 2002).

7. Cary Funk and Greg Smith, "'Nones' on the Rise: One in Five Adults Have No Religious Affiliation," Pew Research Center, October 9, 2012, http://www.pew-forum.org/files/2012/10/NonesOnTheRise-full.pdf.

8. Michael Hout and Claude S. Fischer, "Why More Americans Have No Religious Preference: Politics and Generations," *American Sociological Review* 67 (2002): 165.

9. Hawley, *White Voters in 21st Century America*, 148.

10. Olson and Green, "Worship-Attendance Gap," 41.

11. Ibid., 44–45.

12. Quinnipiac University Polling Institute, "Big Marriage Gap Keeps Obama Ahead by a Nose, Quinnipiac University National Poll Finds; American Voters Give Supreme Court Best Scores in DC," media release, July 11, 2012, http://www.quinnipiac.edu/.

13. George Hawley, "Home Affordability, Female Marriage Rates, and Vote Choice in the 2000 US Presidential Election: Evidence from US Counties," *Party Politics* 18 (2012): 771–789.

14. Ron J. Lesthaeghe and Christopher Wilson, "Modes of Production, Secularization, and the Pace of the Fertility Decline in Western Europe, 1870–1930," in *The Decline of Fertility in Europe*, ed. A. J. Coale and S. C. Watkins (Princeton, NJ: Princeton University Press, 1986); Ron J. Lesthaeghe and K. Neels, "From the First to a Second Demographic Transition: An Interpretation of the Spatial Continuity of Demographic Innovation in France, Belgium, and Switzerland," *European Journal of Population* 18 (2002): 325–360.

15. Ron J. Lesthaeghe and Lisa Neidert, "The 'Second Demographic Transition' in the US: Spatial Patterns and Correlates," PSC Research Report 06-592, March 2006.

16. Lauren Sandler, "Tell Me a State's Fertility Rate, and I'll Tell You How It Voted," *The Cut*, November 19, 2012, http://nymag.com/thecut/.

17. A 1987 study showed that although there was a marriage gap, it disappeared after controlling for other variables: Herbert F. Weisberg, "The Demographics of a New Voting Gap: Marital Differences in American Voting," *Public Opinion Quarterly* 51 (1987): 342. A different 1987 study provided little evidence that marriage directly influenced political attitudes and behavior after controlling for other characteristics: Paul William Kingston and Stephen E. Finkel, "Is There a Marriage Gap in Politics?" *Journal of Marriage and the Family* 49 (1987): 60–62. A 1991 study also found

little evidence for a strong marriage gap in most presidential elections: Eric Plutzer and Michael McBurnett, "Family Life and American Politics: The 'Marriage Gap' Reconsidered," *Public Opinion Quarterly* 55 (1991): 126.

18. Diana B. Elliott, Kristy Krivickas, Matthew W. Brault, and Rose M. Kreider, "Historical Marriage Trends from 1890–2010: A Focus on Race Differences," paper presented at the annual meeting of the Population Association of America, San Francisco, CA, SEHSD Working Paper 2012-12, https://www.census.gov/hhes /socdemo/marriage/data/acs/ElliottetalPAA2012paper.pdf.

19. Hawley, *White Voters in 21st Century America*, 138.

20. The Reuters/Ipsos poll is an excellent resource for anyone examining the 2012 presidential election, as it provides a user-friendly means to generate cross tabs for various demographic and geographic groups in the electorate (http://elections .reuters.com/).

21. I tested this by running a logistic regression model in which vote choice was the dependent variable and marriage and gender were included separately and as interactions.

22. CNN exit polls, December 10, 2012, https://web.archive.org/web/20140309 105421/http://www.cnn.com/election/2012/results/race/president.

23. Jeffrey M. Jones, "Asian-Americans Lean Left Politically," *Gallup*, February 3, 2010, http://www.gallup.com/; Mackenzie Weinger, "Poll: Latinos Say They're More Liberal," *Politico*, April 4, 2012, http://www.politico.com/; "Partisan Polarization Surges in Bush, Obama Years," Pew Research Center, June 4, 2012, http://www .people-press.org/files/legacy-pdf/06-04-12%20Values%20Release.pdf.

24. Pia M. Orrenius and Madeline Zavodny, "Do Amnesty Programs Reduce Undocumented Immigration? Evidence from IRCA," *Demography* 40 (2003): 437–450.

25. Douglas S. Massey, "Borderline Madness: America's Counterproductive Immigration Policy," in *Debating Immigration*, ed. Carol M. Swain (New York: Cambridge University Press, 2007), 129–138.

26. Jeffrey S. Passes, "The Size and Characteristics of the Unauthorized Migrant Population in the US: Estimates Based on the March 2005 Current Population Survey," Pew Hispanic Center, March 7, 2006, http://www.pewhispanic.org/.

27. Jon Feere, "Birthright Citizenship in the United States: A Global Comparison," *Center for Immigration Studies, Backgrounder*, August 2010, http://www.cis .org/.

29. Shaun Bowler, Stephen P. Nicholson, and Gary M. Segura, "Earthquakes and After-shocks: Race, Direct Democracy, and Partisan Change," *American Journal of Political Science* 50 (2006): 146–159.

29. This initiative would have prohibited undocumented immigrants from accessing social services such as health care and education.

30. Conservative strategist Grover Norquist, for example, has repeatedly argued that Republican efforts to stir up anti-immigrant sentiments have backfired, costing them Latino and Asian support while failing to win any new support from other racial and ethnic groups: "The best lesson of the 2006 congressional election is that anti-immigrant rhetoric and votes in favor of walling off the southern border did not win votes for Republicans. What seemed so exciting when bandied about on right-wing talk radio was not a winner on Election Day. Not only was there

no 'upside' with the white or African American vote for focusing on immigration, there was a downside as the Republican vote among Hispanics fell to 30 percent." Norquist, *Leave Us Alone*, 189.

31. George Hawley, "Liberalizing Immigration Will Liberalize the US," *Real Clear Policy*, October 24, 2013, http://www.realclearpolicy.com/.

32. Hawley, *White Voters in 21st Century America*, 10.

33. Daniel W. Drexler, "Rebooting Republican Foreign Policy: Needed: Less Fox, More Foxes," *Foreign Affairs*, January/February 2013, retrieved March 19, 2014, http://www.foreignaffairs.com/articles/138461/daniel-w-drezner/rebooting-republican-foreign-policy.

34. Buckley, "The Party and the Deep Blue Sea," 392.

35. A memo from the Project for a New American Century written shortly after the President Clinton's 1998 bombing campaign said the following:

Now that the dust has settled from the 70-hour aerial attack on Iraq, it has become clear that the only solution for the threat Iraq poses is to remove Saddam.

That truth has prompted questions about the viability of the Iraqi democratic opposition, which the United States has embarked on supporting with the Iraq Liberation Act. Assisting that opposition is essential to bringing a decent government to Iraq. Recent critiques of this approach (Byman, Pollack, and Rose, "The Rollback Fantasy," *Foreign Affairs*, Jan./Feb. 1999) have raised questions about such a policy. But if backed by American military power, both from the air and on the ground, support for the Iraqi opposition can work. Support for the opposition should be only a part of a broader political-military strategy, one which must include a willingness to send US ground forces into Iraq to complete the unfinished business of the Gulf War.

"Mark Lagon to OPINION LEADERS," *Project for a New American Century*, January 7, 1999, http://web.archive.org/web/20030212225110/www.newamericancentury.org/iraqjan0799.htm.

36. Pew Research Center, "Public Attitudes toward the War in Iraq: 2003–2008," March 19, 2008, http://www.pewresearch.org/.

37. Henry Blodget, "The Truth about Taxes: Here's How High Today's Rates Really Are," *Business Insider*, July 12, 2011, http://www.businessinsider.com/.

38. American National Election Studies, 2012 survey election data, http://www.electionstudies.org/.

39. Steven Levitt, "Understanding Why Crime Fell in the 1990s: Four Factors that Explain the Decline and Six that Do Not," *Journal of Economic Perspectives* 18 (2004): 163.

40. Steven Levitt and Stephen Dubner, *Freakonomics: A Rogue Economist Explores the Hidden Side of Everything* (New York: William Morrow, 2005), 117–146.

41. Sam Tanenhaus, *The Death of Conservatism* (New York: Random House, 2009), 6.

42. Ross Douthat and Reiham Salam, *Grand New Party: How Republicans Can Win the Working Class and Save the American Dream* (New York: Doubleday, 2008), 11.

43. Daniel B. Klein and Charlotta Stern, "How Politically Diverse Are the Social Sciences and Humanities?" *Academic Questions* 18 (2005): 40–52.

44. Matthew Woessner, "Rethinking the Plight of Conservatives in Higher Education," *Academe* 98 (2012), http://www.aaup.org/.

45. Ibid.

46. R. Emmett Tyrell Jr., *After the Hangover: The Conservatives' Road to Recovery* (Nashville, TN: Thomas Nelson, 2010), 2–27.

47. Arthur C. Brooks, "The Fertility Gap," *Wall Street Journal*, August 22, 2006, http://www.wsj.com/.

48. Donald Green, Bradley Palmquist, and Eric Schickler, *Partisan Hearts and Minds: Political Parties and the Social Identities of Voters* (New Haven, CT: Yale University Press, 2002), 78–80.

49. Donald Lambro, "Breitbart: No Magic Internet Button for GOP," *Washington Times*, January 18, 2009, http://www.washingtontimes.com/.

50. Shane Goldmacher, "Inside Rand Paul's Jewish Charm Offensive," *National Journal*, July 20, 2014, http://www.nationaljournal.com/.

51. Rand Paul, "We Must Demilitarize the Police," *Time*, August 14, 2014, http://time.com/.

52. There have been many times when Republicans believed they would experience a new surge in minority support by appealing to issues on which minority voters disagree, on average, with the Democratic Party platform. African Americans and Latinos, for example, have been generally more antiabortion and anti–gay marriage than other Democrats. Emphasizing these issues, however, has not apparently led to a greater Republican vote share among these groups. Perhaps a new emphasis on ending the war on drugs will succeed where emphasis on these other issues failed, but we cannot predict this with any confidence.

53. Nate Blakeslee, "Alex Jones Is About to Explode," *Texas Monthly*, March 2010, http://www.texasmonthly.com/.

54. Jamie Bartlett, "Meet the Dark Enlightenment: Sophisticated Neo-Fascism that's Spreading Fast on the Internet," *Telegraph*, January 20, 2014, http://telegraph.co.uk/; Klint Finley, "Geeks for Monarchy: The Rise of the Neo-Reactionaries," *Tech Crunch*, November 22, 2013, http://techcrunch.com/; Matt Sigl, "The Dark Enlightenment: The Creepy Internet Movement You'd Better Take Seriously!" *Vocativ*, December 12, 2013, http://www.vocativ.com/.

55. Moldbug's real name is Curtis Yarvin. He blogs at http://unqualified-reservations.blogspot.com/.

56. There are two examples of this that are most obvious. These writers refer to "The Cathedral," which refers to the institutions that enforce ideological orthodoxy in the United States; these institutions include the media, universities, and federal bureaucracies. Another term that is used with some frequency is the "red pill," which is a reference to the 1999 film *The Matrix*. People who take the red pill are ostensibly awakened to the true nature of reality and the insidious elements of the modern world.

TRUE *

INDEX

Abolitionism, 115, 152, 153
Abortion, 33, 61, 100, 106, 112, 134, 137, 142
   conservatism and, 2
   legalization of, 34, 283
   opposition to, 110, 338n52
   right to, 185
ACA, Republican Party and, 282
ACLU, 41
Activism, 127, 261, 262
   conservative, 13–14
   libertarian, 122
ACU. *See* American Conservative Union
ADA, 41
Adams, John, 21, 107, 108
Adorno, Theodor, 100
Affirmative action, 30, 51, 54, 55, 166, 200, 259
Affordable Care Act, 127, 282, 326n75
African Americans, 1, 338n52
   economic status of, 81
   vote by, 274, 275–276
Against Equality and Democracy (Sunić), 241
Agnosticism, 17, 110, 111
Agrarianism, 20, 74, 76–80, 82, 100
   conservative movement and, 79
   criticism of, 78–79
   localism and, 80
Agriculture, 76, 77–78, 191, 235
   local, 80, 101
   mechanization of, 321–322n88
Ain't My America (Kauffman), 99
Alexander the Great, 250
Allen, Brooke, conservatives/Christianity and, 107
All Quiet on the Western Front (Remarque), 216

Amash, Justin, 137, 289
America First Committee, 181
American Atheists, 111
American Conservative, The, 10, 11, 66, 97, 204, 258
American Conservative Union (ACU), 43, 111
American Enterprise Institute, 38, 43, 64, 66, 288
American Eugenics Society, 250
American Mercury, 25, 69, 72
American National Election Study, survey by, 112, 282
American Nazi Party, 255
American Renaissance, 64, 66, 258, 262, 266
   founding of, 257
American Revolution, 6, 29, 107, 117, 152, 184
Americans for Prosperity, 127, 128, 130, 142
Americans for Tax Reform, 38
American Spectator, 72, 97
Anarchism, 97–99, 129, 145, 147, 158
   individualist, 152, 154–155
   libertarianism and, 139, 143, 152, 166, 175–176
   minarchists and, 173
   nineteenth-century, 152–155
   radical, 154
   right-wing, 139, 145, 146, 159, 167, 175
Anarchocapitalism, 145, 154, 172
Anarchy, State, and Utopia (Nozick), 119
Anticapitalism, 195, 208
Anticommunism, 24, 26, 40–44, 159
Anti-Defamation League, 60, 190
Anti-Imperialist League, 99

Bloom, Alan, 28, 29
Boaz, David, on Paul, 137
Bobbio, Norberto, political taxonomy
of, 12
Booth, John Wilkes, 69
Bourne, Randolph, on war, 148
Bowden, Jonathan, on Evola, 224
Bowling Alone (Putnam), 85, 100
Bozell, L. Brent, III, 31, 104, 111,
218n43
Bradford, M. E. "Mel," 48–51, 60, 80,
183–185
conservative movement and, 185
equality and, 183–184
hostility for, 50
NEH and, 49, 50
Brecht, Bertolt, 188
Brennan, John, 137
Brevik, Anders, 260, 334n48
Brimelow, Peter, 188
Bromfield, Louis, 99
Brooks, David, 2, 38
Brooks, Garth, 64
Brown, Michael, 289
Bryan, William Jennings, 103, 115
Buchanan, James, 120
Buchanan, Patrick J., 10, 13, 19, 51, 64,
164, 166, 181, 186–190, 197, 198,
200, 303n68
anti-Semitism and, 59–60
campaigns of, 59, 280, 290
cold war and, 58
"culture war" speech and, 60
defeat of, 199
denunciation of, 66
foreign policy and, 58, 187
Francis and, 195
free trade and, 186, 187
immigration and, 187, 189
insurgence of, 56–61
Kirk and, 204
Lasch and, 85
nativism and, 59
neoconservatives and, 40, 57–58, 60
paleoconservatism and, 60–61, 187–
188, 205
Paul and, 134
political philosophy of, 186
populism of, 60

Republican Party and, 61
Rockwell and, 199
Rothbard and, 199
support for, 59, 61, 70
on tribal politics, 190
Buckley, William F., Jr., 1, 30, 49, 104,
138, 284
anti-Semitism and, 60
conservative movement and, 24, 40,
70
criticism of, 44
description of, 71–72
on Duke, 55
Eastman and, 105
fusionism and, 269
goals of, 72
Goldwater and, 43
influence of, 15, 44, 70–71
Iraq war and, 67
JBS and, 42, 43
on *National Review*, 25
purge by, 40
Rand and, 48
religion and, 105
Rothbard and, 160
Sobran and, 61, 62
speech by, 138–139
on survival, 27
Tea Party and, 71
totalitarian bureaucracy and, 280
on Weaver/conservatism, 10–11
Welch and, 42
on *Witness*, 24
YAF and, 26, 138
Buddhism, 222, 307n70
Burke, Edmund, 7, 20–21, 204
Burnham, James, 24, 25, 202
containment and, 23
Francis and, 63, 193
JBS and, 43
Bush, George H. W., 34
conservative movement and, 58, 61
Duke and, 54–55, 56
economic decline and, 59
foreign policy of, 58
Gulf War and, 58–59, 66
neoconservatives and, 60
racial sentiments of, 56
taxes and, 59, 282

opposition to, 46, 47, 231
Orthodox, 237
right-wing and, 291
traditional, 235
worldview of, 47
Chronicles, 49, 64, 179, 205, 238, 239
attack on, 192
Fleming and, 190–193
Kauffman and, 191
Churchill, Hitler, and the Unnecessary War
(Buchanan), 186
Churchill, Winston, 186
Chute, Carolyn, 98
Citizenism, 254
Citizens for a Sound Economy (CSE),
127
Citizenship, 196, 278
City Journal, 112
Civic life, 85, 87
Civilization, 64, 92, 103, 226
culture and, 214–215
decline of, 215
white, 250
Civil rights, 33, 136, 166, 180, 311n21
legislation, 31, 152, 171
Republican Party and, 51
Civil Rights Act (1964), 49, 51, 141, 151,
315n13
Civil rights movement, 27, 251, 321n88
opposition to, 269
victory of, 49
white racial attitudes and, 266
Civil society, rootedness of, 98
Clark, Ed, LP and, 173–174
Clinton, Bill, 34–35, 281
CSE and, 127
election of, 286
Project for a New American Century
and, 337n35
tax rates and, 282
Clinton, Hillary Rodham, 9
Closing of the American Mind, The
(Bloom), 29
Cochrane, Gregory, 253
Coggin, John, 143
Colbert Report, Will and, 110
Cold war, 1, 22, 47, 58, 103, 121, 148,
176, 179, 197, 198, 240, 279, 280
Collective (group), 46, 161

Collectivism, 9, 10, 91, 157, 166, 197
economic, 15
involuntary, 296n10
mysticism and, 45
College Republicans, 140
Color of Change, Buchanan and, 190
Commentary, 49, 51, 59, 190
Commission on an All-Volunteer Armed
Force, 125
Communism, 44, 78, 130, 132, 148, 157,
176, 184, 226, 229, 236, 325n52
conservatism and, 24
containing, 121
hostility for, 1, 22, 23–24, 26, 103,
147
Soviet, 209, 236
Communist Party, 40, 41
Communitarianism, 74, 85–89, 95
Community, 12, 91, 98
decline of, 82, 83, 100
local economy and, 82
multiple coherent, 81
political, 83
rediscovery of, 82
self-ruling, 175
small-scale, 74, 101
true, 81
voluntary, 296n10
Confederate States of America, white
supremacy and, 262
"Confessions of a Right-Wing Liberal"
(Rothbard), 161
Conscience of a Conservative, The
(Goldwater and Bozell), 31
Conservatism, 116, 184, 185, 192, 268,
289, 297n23
advocating, 14
American, 19–27, 35, 72, 207, 242,
267, 269
anachronistic brand of, 290
antiwar, 99, 171
challenges for, 36, 270–288
contemporary, 13, 72
criticism of, 3, 72
crunchy, 95–97
cultural, 138
defining, 10–11, 220
demise of, 3, 288
economic, 58, 146